Introducing Microsoft Access Using Macro Programming Techniques

An Introduction to Desktop Database Development by Example

Flavio Morgado

Apress®

Introducing Microsoft Access Using Macro Programming Techniques: An Introduction to Desktop Database Development by Example

Flavio Morgado
Teresopolis, Rio de Janeiro, Brazil

ISBN-13 (pbk): 978-1-4842-6554-3
https://doi.org/10.1007/978-1-4842-6555-0

ISBN-13 (electronic): 978-1-4842-6555-0

Managing Director, Apress Media LLC: Welmoed Spahr
Acquisitions Editor: Joan Murray
Development Editor: Laura Berendson
Coordinating Editor: Jill Balzano

Cover image designed by Freepik (www.freepik.com)

Distributed to the book trade worldwide by Springer Science+Business Media LLC, 1 New York Plaza, Suite 4600, New York, NY 10004. Phone 1-800-SPRINGER, fax (201) 348-4505, e-mail orders-ny@springer-sbm.com, or visit www.springeronline.com. Apress Media, LLC is a California LLC and the sole member (owner) is Springer Science + Business Media Finance Inc (SSBM Finance Inc). SSBM Finance Inc is a **Delaware** corporation.

For information on translations, please e-mail booktranslations@springernature.com; for reprint, paperback, or audio rights, please e-mail bookpermissions@springernature.com.

Apress titles may be purchased in bulk for academic, corporate, or promotional use. eBook versions and licenses are also available for most titles. For more information, reference our Print and eBook Bulk Sales web page at www.apress.com/bulk-sales.

Any source code or other supplementary material referenced by the author in this book is available to readers on GitHub via the book's product page, located at www.apress.com/9781484265543. For more detailed information, please visit www.apress.com/source-code.

Printed on acid-free paper

For you, Bia,
My love,
For all those special moments
When the two of us are together
We share the best of our lives

Table of Contents

About the Author

Flavio Morgado is a food engineer with an MSc. degree in food science and technology, a VBA professional developer, and a professor of epidemiology, statistics, and medical Informatics at UNIFESO, a health sciences university in Rio de Janeiro, Brazil. Flavio has written more than 30 books, including *Programming Excel with VBA* (Apress) and *Microsoft Word Secrets* (Apress), and has translated many technical books. He also loves animals and the exquisite nature of the surrounding rainforest, and when he is not teaching, writing, or developing, he can be found running or riding his mountain bike through the Teresopolis Mountains, followed by his eight dogs, or spending time on the stunningly beautiful beaches of Cabo Frio in Rio de Janeiro.

About the Technical Reviewer

Douglas J. Steele has been working with computers, both mainframe and PC, for more than 45 years. (Why, yes, he did use punch cards in the beginning!) He worked for a large international oil company for more than 31 years before retiring in 2012. Databases and data modeling were his focus for most of that time, although he finished his career by developing the SCCM task sequence to roll Windows 7 out to more than 100,000 computers worldwide.

Recognized by Microsoft as an MVP for more than 17 years, Doug has authored numerous articles on Access, was coauthor of *Access Solutions: Tips, Tricks, and Secrets from Microsoft Access MVPs* (Wiley, 2010), and has been technical editor for a number of books.

Doug holds a master's degree in systems design engineering from the University of Waterloo (Ontario, Canada), where his research centered on designing user interfaces for nontraditional computer users. (Of course, this was in the late 1970s, so few people were traditional computer users at the time!) This research stemmed from his background in music (he holds an associateship in piano performance from the Royal Conservatory of Music, Toronto). He is also obsessed with beer and is a graduate of the Brewmaster and Brewery Operations Management program at Niagara College (Niagara-on-the-Lake, Ontario).

Doug is married, the father of two daughters, and the grandfather of three granddaughters and a grandson. He lives with his lovely wife of more than 38 years in St. Catharines, Ontario.

Acknowledgments

This book is the result of collaborative work carried out with the special team of professionals at Apress. It could not have been done without the involvement, help, and support of this entire team of specialists in the production of technical books.

First, I would like to thank my publisher Joan Murray, a Microsoft developer and Apress senior editor, for always believing in me and for inviting me to write again for Apress. That was how I ended up meeting Jill Balzano, my coordinating editor, who was always in touch, pushing me to finish this book on time and with the proper quality. I would also like to give a special thanks to Doug Steele, the technical reviewer who greatly improved the book, researching carefully and pointing out the mistakes I had made not only in the technical part but also in various approaches to the text (though we never met—our contact was completely electronic through the Internet).

I'd also like to say a special thanks to the USDA-ARS team (the Agricultural Research Services of the United States Department of Agriculture): the ones responsible for creating and sustaining the `sr28.accdb` Microsoft Access nutritional database,[1] which made it possible to create all the real examples in this book.

Finally, I want to thank the Microsoft Access development team, which is always looking to give us a better product that so many people around the world use to create desktop database solutions for their businesses and possibly to sustain their lives, and Microsoft for its Support website, from where one can find answers to most questions about Microsoft Access features.

For the record, this book was written entirely between March 2020 and September 2020—hard months when the COVID-19 pandemic claimed so many lives on the planet.

---

[1] US Department of Agriculture, Agricultural Research Service. 2016. Nutrient Data Laboratory. USDA National Nutrient Database for Standard Reference, Release 28 (Slightly revised). Version Current: May 2016. `www.ars.usda.gov/nea/bhnrc/mafcl`

Introduction

The book that you have in your hands was written with the intention of teaching you how to use Microsoft Access to create desktop databases.

Every effort has been made to provide an upward learning curve in each of its chapters, starting with the definition of what a relational database is and ending with advanced knowledge about how to use most of its objects and features.

There is no intention here to cover all features or usages of Microsoft Access—a special software that has fascinated multitudes of users around the world since its appearance in the 1990s. Instead, the book takes the path of introducing each of the main Access objects (tables, queries, forms, macros, and reports) and teaches you how to use the best of them so that you can understand how any database works and how to implement solutions from its data.

To provide a better experience when using such a powerful and capable software application, this book uses the `sr28.accdb` database in Microsoft Access, made available by the ARS-USDA website. ARS-USDA provides the best nutritional database of information in the world, in addition to being a rich source of resources for testing in Microsoft Access.

What's in the Book

This book is divided into six chapters whose complexity increases chapter after chapter. To get a picture of what you will find inside it, here is a summary of each chapter:

- Chapter 1, "A Primer on Databases," discusses what a database file is and how a database table is distinguished from an Excel worksheet table. It explains what a relational database is, explains the basic Access objects (tables, queries, forms, reports, macros, and modules), and briefly explains how the Microsoft Access interface works.

- Chapter 2, "Creating and Using Database Tables," begins by telling you how you can use some of the many database templates to gain knowledge of how a database is structured and works. It then explains how you can create some Access tables that will allow you to implement a simple nutritional database, using relational integrity between them.

- Chapter 3, "Using Queries," is where this book begins to use the `sr28.accdb` nutritional database to explain how a database is created and how to use a Query object to extract data from it. In this chapter, you will learn by example how to create many different types of queries. You will also learn how to use properties so you can get the best out of any Microsoft Access database.

- Chapter 4, "Using Forms," teaches how you can use the Form object to create an interface to the database records. You will be presented with the different form views and how to use many of the form controls to create a better user experience when presenting database record information, including the usage of subforms and charts.

- Chapter 5, "Using Macros," was created to introduce Microsoft Access macro programming: a high-level programming interface from where you can select actions that are performed in sequence to automate your database solutions. In this chapter, you will be presented with form events and how to correctly use them with simple macro code. You'll see different development scenarios where one, two, or more forms work together, perfectly synchronizing the database's records.

- Chapter 6, "Using Reports," is the last chapter in the book, where you will learn how to use the Report object to create nice, perfect printouts. You will be introduced to the report structure and its sections and grouping options. You'll also learn how to automate some of its tasks using simple macro code. You will also be presented with how you can print labels and use some report properties to achieve special results.

This Book's Special Features

Introducing Microsoft Access Using Macro Programming Techniques was designed to give you the information you need to understand Microsoft Access, from its most basic features to ones that may be considered somewhat advanced.

To make your life easier while reading this book, various features and conventions were used to help you get the most from the information presented.

- *Steps:* Throughout the book, each procedure is enumerated in a step-by-step list.

- *Commands:* I used the following style when talking about Access commands: "click the Controls list on the Form Design tab of the Ribbon." This means you must click the Controls list (the list filled with different control types) that appears on the Form Design tab of the Ribbon.

- *Menus:* To indicate that you should click the File menu and then select Options, I will say "select File ➤ Options."

- *Functions:* Microsoft Access functions appear as capital letters followed by parenthesis: IF(). They also use a monospaced font to make them look different from the regular text. When I list the arguments you can use on a function, they appear in a bullet list of options, using the same order that they appear in the function arguments list.

- *Macro actions and temporary variables:* Microsoft Access actions are formatted in a monospaced font to make them look different from the regular text.

Note   This box provides asides from the topic under discussion.

Tip   This box provides clues that may extend the usage of a feature.

Caution   This box provides information that you must read carefully to avoid some unexpected behavior of a feature.

Website Extras

All the examples presented on this book are available as downloadable files through Apress.com. I'll post any additions and corrections and other related information for this book there, if necessary.

Your Feedback Is Important

Your opinion is important for me. Since I really don't know how many of you will write me to give any feedback, I expect to answer everyone and, whenever possible, try to solve any question or problems that may arise. Since I have many duties, it is possible that it may take a little time for me to respond, but I promise to do my best. Please feel free to write me at `flaviomorgado@gmail.com`.

CHAPTER 1

A Primer on Databases

If you are reading this chapter, chances are that you do not have an end-to-end understanding of the intrinsic value of databases and why they are so popular and necessary for every business. Many database technologies and platforms exist, but few have stood the test of time like Microsoft Access, perhaps the most important and extensive desktop database in the world. It has been evolving since it was first released in 1992, and it is included with Microsoft Office 2019 Personal and Home editions for free.

This chapter will introduce the types of files accessed by computers; you will also learn why databases are so critical and how they are created. In addition, you will learn about relational databases, the object types they can contain, and how Microsoft Access implements them. We will also discuss the differences between an Excel spreadsheet and an Access table. After reading this chapter, you will have a foundational understanding of the Microsoft Access interface and recognize the building blocks of any Access database file and implementation.

Types of File Access

Programmers distinguish between two types of computer file access.

- *Sequential file access*: This is when the data in files can be accessed in an ordered, sequential manner. Files that provide this type of access are created by the most commonly used programs and include image files (JEPG files from digital cameras), text documents (created with Notepad or Microsoft Word), vector files (created by design programs such as CorelDraw or Adobe Illustrator), worksheet files (created by Microsoft Excel), and so on.

© Flavio Morgado 2021
F. Morgado, *Introducing Microsoft Access Using Macro Programming Techniques*,
https://doi.org/10.1007/978-1-4842-6555-0_1

- *Direct or random file access*: This is when the data in files can be accessed in a random, nonsequential manner. Files that provide this type of access are created by database programs such as Microsoft Access. The files have a precise register structure—and length—that is capable of accessing any desired register at any time.

The basic difference between a sequential and a direct or random-access file is that whenever you open a sequential access file, you load all its content into memory (more or less), manipulate the content in memory, and then save the content to the file again. If something bad happens between the time you change the file and before you save it again—like a power failure, for example—all the changes made to the file will be lost.

However, when you open a direct or random-access file (a database file, like the ones created by Microsoft Access), you make an access point to one of its tables, access one or more of its records (or rows), and manipulate one record at a time. In other words, you do not need to load all its records into computer memory.

You also do not have to save a database file or any of its tables after they are created. In fact, database programs such as Access do not have a "Save as" menu command: you open a table, access a single record, change any record field, and save the record to the file (and just *that* record!).

Even if you take advantage of a computer's speed to manipulate thousands of records at a time, whenever you use a database file, you will always change and save registers one by one. If something happens between the time you change a record and before you save it, you will lose just that single change made to that last updated record.

Access Tables vs. Excel Spreadsheets Files

Figure 1-1 shows a Microsoft Access table and a Microsoft Excel spreadsheet; while they look similar, they are not.

	A	B	C	D	E	
1	NDB_No	Shrt_Desc	Water_(g)	Energ_Kcal	Protein_(g)	
2	01001	BUTTER,WITH SALT	15.87	717	0.85	
3	01002	BUTTER,WHIPPED,W/ SALT	16.72	718	0.49	
4	01003	BUTTER OIL,ANHYDROUS	0.24	876	0.28	
5	01004	CHEESE,BLUE	42.41	353	21.4	
6	01005	CHEESE,BRICK	41.11	371	23.24	
7	01006	CHEESE,BRIE	48.42	334	20.75	
8	01007	CHEESE,CAMEMBERT	51.8	300	19.8	
9	01008	CHEESE,CARAWAY	39.28	376	25.18	
10	01009	CHEESE,CHEDDAR	37.02	404	22.87	
11	01010	CHEESE,CHESHIRE	37.65	387	23.37	

Sheet1

ABBREV

NDB_No ▾	Shrt_Desc	▾	Water_(g) ▾	Energ_Kcal ▾	Protein_(g) ▾
⊞ 01001	BUTTER,WITH SALT		15.87	717	0.85
⊞ 01002	BUTTER,WHIPPED,W/ SALT		16.72	718	0.49
⊞ 01003	BUTTER OIL,ANHYDROUS		0.24	876	0.28
⊞ 01004	CHEESE,BLUE		42.41	353	21.4
⊞ 01005	CHEESE,BRICK		41.11	371	23.24
⊞ 01006	CHEESE,BRIE		48.42	334	20.75
⊞ 01007	CHEESE,CAMEMBERT		51.8	300	19.8
⊞ 01008	CHEESE,CARAWAY		39.28	376	25.18
⊞ 01009	CHEESE,CHEDDAR		37.02	404	22.87
⊞ 01010	CHEESE,CHESHIRE		37.65	387	23.37

Record: 1 of 8790   No Filter   Search

Figure 1-1. *The same data set stored as a Microsoft Access table (top) and a Microsoft Excel spreadsheet (bottom)*

When observing the table structure that both applications use to manipulate data, you may think that they seem to be the same. However, the Microsoft Access table doesn't have the row and column headers shown in the Microsoft Excel file, while a Microsoft Access table shows the table record count at it bottom ("Record 1 of 8790").

Most important, the data in these two tables is manipulated differently by its host application. The Excel spreadsheet operates on the entire file. Any change on any of its cells will be saved if you save the Excel workbook file. The changes will be disregarded if the file is not saved before the application closes. By contrast, the Microsoft Access table can operate on one record at a time and cannot be saved as a whole, meaning every change on any of its cells information will be automatically saved to disk every time another row is selected. Remember, a database table is operated on by a direct or random-access file that cannot be saved; just its records (or rows) can be.

3

How to Build a Database

To create a database, first you need to know what information should be stored in it. Database developers use a technique called *system analysis*, defined as collecting and interpreting facts, identifying problems, and decomposing a system into components with the aim of studying a system or its parts in order to identify its objectives."[1] Database developers use system analysis so they can create the database tables needed to store and process the information they are working with. To understand how system analysis works, you'll need to understand terms such as *primary table, related table, primary key, relationship,* and *referential integrity.*

Consider, for example, the problem of creating a database capable of controlling a person's daily food intake by storing some personal and other information related to each meal eaten in a single day.

You may be tempted to store all this information in an Excel spreadsheet, storing each row of the spreadsheet as a record and each column of the spreadsheet as a field record, where the desired information, such as person data (name, address, mobile phone), meal information (meal date, meal time, meal name), and food consumed (food name, food category, quantity consumed) will be entered.

Figure 1-2 shows how most people who do not know the advantages of a databases would solve such a problem: using a Microsoft Excel file and inserting each person's meal information, with up to five different food items per meal. This approach uses a spreadsheet row to type each daily meal eaten.

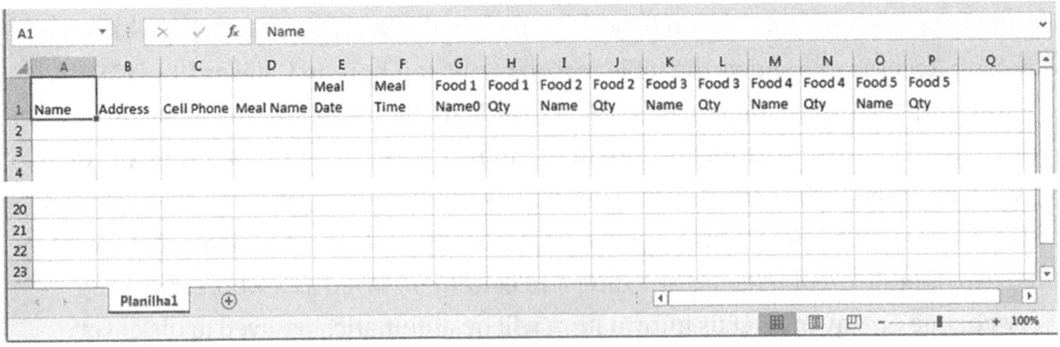

Figure 1-2. A Microsoft Excel spreadsheet with column names to store food information

---

[1]Extracted from TutorialsPoint.com: `https://www.tutorialspoint.com/system_analysis_and_design/system_analysis_and_design_overview.htm`

Let's see some of the problems that arise by using this popular approach.

- Each spreadsheet row is used to store a person's meal, with up to five food items.

- Any other meal eaten on the same day will need another spreadsheet row, which will duplicate information already used in previous rows, such as the name, address, cell phone, and meal date.

- Although Microsoft Excel is smart enough to repeat pre-inserted information in the same column, each time you insert repeated information (such as a person's name), this information is duplicated inside the file, which will force the file size to grow exponentially as new information is inserted.

- If any person needs to insert six or more food item on a single meal, the spreadsheet needs to be updated to accommodate this new design.

- There is no space to store a food item's nutritional data such as calories per food item. Although such column information can be inserted, it will be necessary to use one new spreadsheet column to type each food item's calories.

- You must scroll through the worksheet to insert each new record (spreadsheet row), which can be time-consuming.

- Most columns need to be wide or high enough to show the information typed on a single row (or record), which will force you to horizontally scroll the worksheet to insert data into the columns.

- The spreadsheet size will be restricted by your current system memory, and every time you store information in it, you will need to save it—or run the risk of losing the spreadsheet when you suffer a power or system failure!

It seems obvious that a single spreadsheet that stores data information on a row and column basis is not the right solution to solve this simple problem. You will need to use what is called a *relational database.*

Note   If you are interested in learning more about how to emulate a database on a Microsoft Excel spreadsheet using a macro-enabled workbook, take a look at Chapter 9 of *Programming Excel with VBA*, also published by Apress. That solution requires extensive knowledge of Visual Basic for Application (VBA) and has storage limitations since it requires continuous file access that needs to be loaded into memory and saved to disk.

Relational Databases

A relational database can automatically propagate one (or more) table field from one table record in the *primary table* into one (or more) field of another table record—known as the *related table*. This means that both tables are *related*, and just the primary table field value is necessary to associate all the records fields of these two tables.

To make these primary–related table structures correctly work, they must follow these simple rules:

- The primary table must have a field, called the *primary key*, that uniquely identifies each record.

- The related table must have a field, called *the foreign key*, of the same data type of the primary table's primary key field.

- The related table foreign key must not be the table's primary key (although in some database designs it can be)—allowing more than one related table record to have the same field value.

The database relationships imposed on the two tables require that the fields related be of the same data type, allowing three different relationship types.

- *One-to-one relationship*: For each record on the primary table, there can be only one record on the related table. Both primary and related tables fields are unique among all record values (they are both tables' primary keys).

- *One-to-many relationship*: For each record on the primary table, there can be many records on the related table. The primary table's field is the table's primary key, while the relational table field's foreign key is not unique, meaning that it is not the table's primary key, allowing its value to be repeated on many records from the related table.

- *Many-to-many relationship*: Each record in the primary and related tables can relate to any number of records (or no records). To accommodate such a relationship, the database requires a third table, known as the *associated* or *linking* table.

Referential Integrity

To guarantee that no records are lost on the related table (records not associated to a unique record on the primary table), the database engine can impose what is called *referential integrity*.

Referential integrity is "the property of a relational database that enforces valid relationships between tables, such that no foreign key can contain a value that does not match a primary key in the corresponding table," according to https://www.yourdictionary.com.

By using a database to impose referential integrity between two related tables, you can do the following:

- *Cascade updated related fields*: The database engine will automatically update changes on the related table records, based on any change on the primary table record (for example, if the primary key value changes to another unique value, all related fields will be automatically updated).

- *Cascade deleted related records*: By deleting a record from the primary table, all related records will be automatically deleted.

Whenever you try to impose referential integrity between any two database tables, the database engine will verify whether there are any inconsistent records on the many side of the relationship (meaning one or more record with no association with any record on the one side). If any are found, the database will not be capable of imposing such an integrity rule due to it breaking the golden rule of referential integrity that states: "...no foreign key can contain a value that does not match a primary key in the corresponding table."

Tips to Build a Database from Scratch

Before you begin to lay out a database (meaning, deciding which tables will be needed), it is important that you make a careful *system analysis* of the human tasks you want to automate. This analysis requires experience, practice, and inevitably significant interaction with the people who will manipulate the application and whose data is stored by the database.

These people need to show you how they are actually working with the data and may express what they expect the database to do. I suggest you follow these tips to achieve greater success on your approach to the proposed solution:

- Explain that it is necessary for you to understand what they are trying to achieve in the software application.

- Ask to see their data to figure out where the one-to-many table relationships are.

- Note all the information needed, such as the type of information (text, date, number) and the maximum size required for each of type. You need this information to create the fields of your database tables.

- Try to replicate a hard-copy layout in the software application.

- Verify whether there is any software solution already working, and if so, ask what the problem is with it.

- Ask for the complex jobs that need to be done with the click of a button—you will be surprised about how people want simple things done faster.

- Don't try to replicate the work as it was already done. Whenever you find is necessary, impose your personality to show that some tasks can be made simpler by a computer.

- Try to implement the solution one step at a time, giving yourself time to redo each step.

- Don't insert in your solution more than what is asked of you. You will be responsible for whatever you offer, even if they don't ask for it.

Creating a Database for Food Intake Control

Let's suppose that you were asked to build a database solution to control a person's food intake. In fact, the person who needs the database solution is a nutritionist who begins his explanation by showing you something on the spreadsheet shown in Figure 1-2. We will suppose that the nutritionist wants to do the following:

- Quickly insert and retrieve a person's data.

- Quickly insert any person's food intake behavior on a daily basis, using common daily meal names (breakfast, snack, lunch, dinner etc.) to identify each meal eaten on any given day.

- Insert the same meal more than once on a single day (some people eat the same food twice a day).

- Quickly select and insert food items on these meals.

- Quickly verify how any calories were ingested during each meal, on any day, or between any two dates, to take the appropriate nutritional actions.

After doing some system analysis on this problem, one can easily see that to correctly store all this information—some of it to be inserted only once—you need to store it in different tables, which is exactly what a database does.

Thinking as a database expert, you will need to create three different tables.

- *Persons*: A person's data will be stored only once (name, address, phone number, e-mail etc.)

- *Persons Meals*: Each person's meal data will be stored (meal name, meal date, meal time).

- *Persons Meals Foods*: Each meal's food information will be stored, including the food name, food quantity, and any other nutritional food information needed.

So, how will these tables relate to one another?

Relating the Tables

To relate these three tables, you need to create a primary key field on each table to uniquely identify each of its records and propagate this field value on the related table's foreign key field—which must be of the same data type.

The Persons table (the primary table) can have a primary key field called ID (a numeric type) that uniquely identifies each of its records, while the Persons Meals table (the related table) must have a field called Persons ID (with the same numeric type) that can receive each Persons table's ID value, relating both tables by a unique, common value.

Since the Persons table's ID field is the table's primary key (meaning it does not repeat within the records) and the Persons Meals table's Persons ID field is not (it can be repeated among records), those two fields can be used to create a one-to-many relationship between these two tables.

By imposing *referential integrity* between these two tables, you can guarantee that the Persons Meals table will never have any lost records, meaning that for each unique Person record (in the Persons primary table), there could be many Person Meals records related in the Persons Meals table (see Figure 1-3).

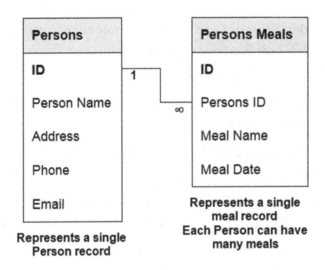

Figure 1-3. *A simple diagram identifying the relationship between two table records*

The 1 and ∞ characters identify which table is the primary table (the "one" side of the relationship) and which is the related table (the "many" side of the relationship). Note in Figure 1-3 that the ID field in the Persons table is presented in bold (meaning it's the table's primary key), while the Persons ID field in the Persons Meals table is not (meaning that it is not unique). Both tables are related with referential integrity imposed, and that is why the ID field has a 1 on its right (the "one" side of the relationship), below the relationship line, while Persons ID has a ∞ on its left (the "many" side of the relationship).

Also note that the Persons Meals table has an ID field (in bold), indicating that it is the table's primary key. Therefore, it also can be related to the Persons Meals Foods table, since this table has a Persons Meals ID of the same numeric type to associate its records. Figure 1-4 shows the final diagram of these three tables.

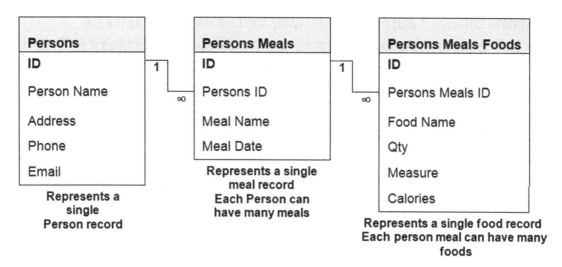

Figure 1-4. *A simple diagram identifying the relationship between three tables proposed to store data for a nutritional application*

By using such approach, each person's record (Person Name, Address, Phone, Email, etc.) can be recorded once and have as many Persons Meal records as necessary. Also, each person's meal can be recorded just once and have as many Persons Meals Foods records as necessary. Brilliant, isn't it?

The lesson is quite simple: you must create the database tables, relate them, and impose referential integrity before any record is inserted into your database!

Now let's see how Microsoft Access deals with its databases.

Microsoft Access Databases

Microsoft Access is a single-file interface program, meaning that each of its instances—windows opened—can deal with just one database at a time. If you want to open two Microsoft Access databases, you will need to open another Microsoft Access instance to achieve these tasks.

There are two kinds of Microsoft Access files.

- `*.MDB`: Produced by Microsoft Access 2003 or older files

- `*.ACCDB`: Produced by Microsoft Access 2007 or newer files

Note   Every file has a name and an extension. The name can have up to 256 characters (in Windows 10 it can be up to 32.767 characters), while the extension can have between 1 and 4 characters. While the filename identifies the file content for the user, the extension name sets the file type and identifies it for the Windows operating system. By default, file extensions are hidden so that you don't incidentally change them and make the file unassociated—or unable to be opened. To show file extensions on your system, select File ➤ Options to open the Folder Options dialog, go to the View tab, and uncheck the "Hide extensions for known file types" option.

There is a big difference between them: the older `*.MDB` format is faster on record access, while the `*.ACCDB` format that Microsoft Access 2007 uses offers new field types (such as Big Number and Attachment). The good news is that you can use any `*.MDB` file in Access 2007 or newer versions, which gives you a lot of flexibility.

Be advised that any Microsoft Access database can be considered a *folder*, in other words, a place where many files are stored. This means the database is easy to store and back up. And as a folder, the database uses sequential file access to store most of its objects and allows random file access to retrieve its records.

Any Microsoft Access database file can have many different types of files stored in it, such as tables, queries, forms, reports, macros, and modules. Since a database file can store and manage different kinds of file types in a single database, it can occasionally be corrupted, which is why you must do some backups and periodical maintenance.

Any Microsoft Access database has a size limitation of 2 gigabytes, which is quite high for data, not considering images and attachments. There is no limitation on the number of records in a table, allowing you to store millions of records in each table. Do a Google search for *Microsoft Access specifications* to get a big picture of its amazing capabilities.

Let's look at each of these objects in more detail to better understand the Microsoft Access database structure.

Note   I have used Microsoft Access files for more than two decades, and I've never had any corruption—although I have already witnessed some file corruption and a loss of information on huge tables (with more than a million records). Always make a backup of your database files to avoid such problems, which may be impossible to solve.

Tip   There is some third-party software that can recover a corrupted Microsoft Access file. Do a Google search for *Microsoft Access recovery* to find some of them.

Tables

Tables are the heart of any database, because this is where you will store the data that makes a database so special.

A Microsoft Access database can store all the tables you need, although a well-designed database will not need many of them and will have a limit on how many tables can be opened at a time (2,048 tables), with each one having up to 255 fields.

Fields

Each table you create needs to be defined in terms of fields—which is where the information is stored. Each field must have a defined type, which indicates the kind of information it contains.

Always use the smallest file type for a given field to guarantee that the table will occupy the least amount of space needed to store each of its records. By using such an approach, the table access to its records will be faster. Table 1-1 shows all the Microsoft Access data types.

Table 1-1. *Microsoft Access 2019 Supported Data Types (Using 8-Bit Bytes)*

Data Type	Usage	Size
AutoNumber	Unique numeric value generated by Access for each new record primary key.	4 bytes.
Number	Numeric data.	1, 2, 4, 8, or 16 bytes.
Currency	Monetary data, using up to four decimal places of precision.	8 bytes.
Large Number	Numeric data.	8 bytes.
Replication ID	Numeric data.	8 bytes.
Date/Time	Dates and times.	8 bytes.
Yes/No	Boolean 0 for false and -1 for true.	1 byte.
Short Text	Alphanumeric data (formerly known as Text).	Up to 255 characters.
Lookup	Used for Number or Short Text fields; shows a wizard that allows you to create a personalized list of items.	
Long Text	Large amounts of alphanumeric data (formerly known as Memo).	Up to about 1 gigabyte (GB), but form controls can show only the first 64,000 characters.
OLE Object	Pictures, graphs, or other ActiveX objects from another Windows-based application.	Up to about 2 GB.
Hyperlink	A link address to a document or file on the Internet, on an intranet, on a local area network (LAN), or on your local computer.	Up to 8,192 characters long (each part of a Hyperlink data type can contain up to 2048 characters).
Attachment	Files attached as pictures, documents, spreadsheets, or charts. This is not available in MDB file formats.	Up to about 2 GB.
Calculated	Formula used to show relations among record fields. This is not available in MDB file formats.	Short Text data: up to 243 characters long.Long Text, Number, Yes/No, and Date/Time should match their respective data types.

Write some notes about the field types and possible values whenever you create your table fields.

- *Numeric field*: Use the smallest possible number, remembering that they are considered 8-bit bytes (an 8-bit byte number can have a value up to $2^{8-1} = 255$). Any Numeric field can be an integer (Byte, Integer, and Long Integer) or real number (Single, Double, Replication ID, Decimal). Table 1-2 shows each possible Numeric field along with its scope.

Table 1-2. *Numeric Data Types Allowed on a Microsoft Access Table Field (Using 8-Bit Bytes)*

Numeric Type	Numeric Type	Bytes	Scope
Integer	Byte	1	0 to 255 (28 – 1).
	Integer	2	-32,768 to 32,767
	Long Integer	4	-2,147,483,648 to +2,147,483,647
	AutoNumber	4	-2,147,483,648 to +2,147,483,647
	Large Number	8	-9.223,372,036,854,775,808 to +9.223,372,036,854,775,807
Real numeric floating-point values	Currency (scaled Integer)	8	-922,337,203,685,477.5808 to +922,337,203,685,477.5807
	Single	4	-3.402823E38 to -1.401298E-45 +1.401298E-45 to +3.402823E38
	Double	4	-1.79769313486231E308 to -94065645841247E-324 +4.94065645841247E-324 to +1.79769313486232E308
	Decimal	12	+/-79,228,162,514,264,337,593,543,950,335 with no decimal point.+/-7.9228162514264337593543950335 with 28 places to the right of the decimalSmallest nonzero number is+/-0.0000000000000000000000000001
	Replication ID	16	Store a globally unique identifier required for replication (not supported by `*.accdb` files)

- *Yes/No*: Use this to store binary values that may have up to three different states: Null (not set), -1 = Yes or True, and 0 = No or False.

- *Text fields*: Use the smaller possible size needed for the field. (For example, for a person's name, the size recommended is about 80 characters).

Note   Some values such as SSID, phone number, IP address, etc., appear to be a number field, but they are not: they are numeric text and must be stored in a text field. The rule is, whenever a numeric value does not have any arithmetic operation on it, it must be considered as a text.

- *Memo fields*: Now called Long Text, this is a special field that allows you to insert a large amount of text. Use it for field types that do not have a size limit, like an Observation or History field.

- *Date fields*: Use this to store dates and times. The Date field is a real number, where its integer part stores the date and the decimal part stores the time (if any).

- *OLE Object*: Use this to store pictures of any kind.

- *Attachment*: Use this to store documents (Microsoft Word, Excel, or PowerPoint; Adobe Acrobat PDF files; etc.).

Field Properties

Besides defining the field type, each field can have many different properties that you can set. These properties relate to the field data type and will be mentioned throughout this book whenever be necessary.

The following are the most important field properties:

- *Name*: The field name, which identifies the value stored on it

- *Field | Size*: The field data type

- *Required*: The force field value insertion before saving the record

- *Indexed*: Indicates if the field has an index

Field Indexes

The Indexed property is one of the most important properties because it is the one responsible for creating the table's primary key and for accelerating the file access to the table records by creating an index for the field values.

The Indexed property can be set to the following:

- *No*: Removes any index on the field

- *Yes (No duplicates):* Creates a unique index on the field, creating the table primary key

- *Yes (Duplicates OK):* Creates a nonunique index on the field, meaning that the field value can be duplicate among table records

Whenever you set the Indexed property to Yes (No duplicates) or Yes (Duplicates OK), Microsoft Access will internally create a hidden file where each field value is stored. And it will use such a hidden file to impose the table's primary key.

As a rule of thumb, always create an index to a field in the following cases:

- If it is the table's primary key (Microsoft Access automatically defines this for you)

- If it is the table foreign key—set to Yes (Duplicates OK) on the foreign key field to allow a one-to-many relationship type

- For any field that you want to use as criteria for a search (or a query, as you will see later)

By creating an index on a field, the access to the table values will become faster—and your database application will be more efficient.

Multiple Fields Index

On the Query Design tab of Access, you click Indexes to open the Indexes window for the selected table. Besides showing all the indexes currently set for the desired table, this window allows you to create a multiple fields index, using up to ten fields (Figure 1-5).

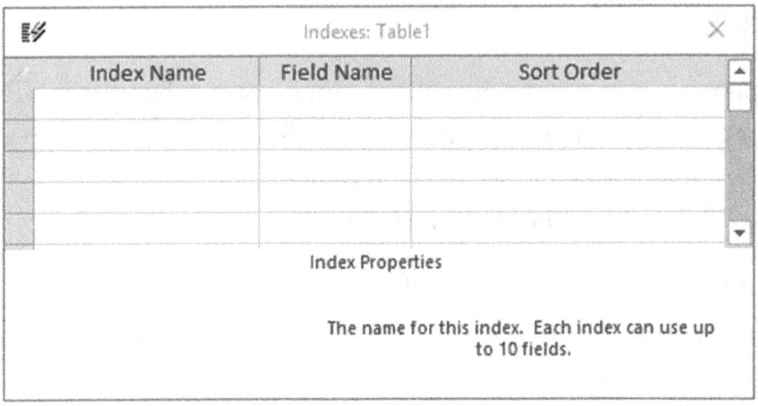

Figure 1-5. In the Indexes window you will see all indexes a table has and can also create a multiple fields index

---

Tip   Although you can create different multiple fields indexes for any table, Access allows you to use them in VBA code only, which is behind the scope of this book.

To create a multiple fields index, follow these steps:

1. On the Indexes Name column of the Indexes window, enter the name of the multiple field index.

2. On the Field Name column, select the desired table field.

3. On the Sort Order column, select the desired sort order for this field.

4. Select the empty row below the one that has the index name filled in, leave the Index Name cell empty, and select another field and sort order.

5. Repeat step 4 for every other field that you want to use on the multiple fields index.

Attention   It is advised that a multiple field index must be named using the names of the fields that are used to compose it, concatenated with no spaces.

Queries

A query is Structured Query Language (SQL) code that is defined in a graphical way and stored as an object in your database.

By creating a query, you will be able to select which table files you want to see, relate different tables, and recover special database information that is needed to build your database application interface.

Queries are important because they allow you to select specific record fields from different tables and present them in various ways. Using queries is a great way to learn about SQL, because you can design a query using a graphical interface and then view the SQL code created by Microsoft Access to execute the query.

Microsoft Access offers different types of queries. Each query has its own icon, and by default queries are grouped by type in the Database window. Table 1-3 shows the icon, name, and usage for the different query types, using the sequence shown in the Query Type area of the Query Design tab.

Table 1-3. *Query Types, Icons, and Usage*

Icon	Query Type	Usage
	Select	The most basic query, allowing you to access information stored in the database. This allows you to read data from and write data to tables.
	Make table	A select query that can be used to create another table based on the query results.
	Append	A select query that can be used to select records and append them on another table.
	Update	A select query that can be used to select records and change field values to a new value on a single operation.
	Crosstab	A totals query that can summarize data by grouping it and presenting a totals columns based on a certain field.
	Delete	A select query that can be used to select records and delete them from the desired table on a single operation.

(*continued*)

Table 1-3. (*continued*)

Icon	Query Type	Usage
⚭	Union	A SQL instruction that unites two or more queries on a single query result. This can't be represented in a graphical interface; it must be created manually, requiring some SQL knowledge.
⬤	Passthrough	A SQL instruction used to access tables from enterprise databases using other types of SQL (such as Transact-SQL from SQL Server).
☑	Data Definition	A query that uses the Data Definition Language (DDL), which allows you to change table and field properties.

Note   Right-click the All Access Objects area in the Database window and select View ➤ Icon to change the size of Access object icons.

All these types of queries can be turned into parameters or total queries by using the associated commands Totals and Append, found in the Show/Hide area of the Query Design tab:

- *Parameter query*: This is the same as a select query, but it allows you to define a parameter that will be prompt the user for field values, so it can dynamically define the query criteria. It can read and write values to tables.

- *Totals query*: This is a select query that can group and summarize data using different mathematical functions (such as sum, average, variance, standard deviation, etc.). It returns read-only values.

You will learn more about Microsoft Access queries in Chapter 3.

Forms and Reports

A form or report is a window where you can gather and present information from a database table or query using controls. A report can show information from one or more tables or from a query. By using subforms or subreports (a form or report inserted as a control inside another form or report), you can present one-to-many relationship information to the user.

Reports are a core part of building database applications, constituting the main object used to create your application interface.

Forms and reports have different structures and properties that control their behavior, and both depend on the control types you can insert on them to present information to the user. And of course, each control type has its own set of properties. We will talk more about them later in this book.

Macros

A macro is an automatic way to execute predefined steps that you select in a window. In other words, you can create macros to perform certain actions that automate your database solution.

Macros have a set of instructions that can mimic a formal programming language (like Visual Basic for Applications), but they don't require the user to type code and verify it. You just select the macro instructions from a list, putting them in a sequence to be executed one by one. This allows you to automate your database solutions and create applications with the least effort possible.

Modules

A module is a place where you can use VBA to program your database, which is beyond the scope of this book. Using modules, you can extend Microsoft Access and give your applications a professional touch.

Naming Conventions

Although Microsoft Access allows you to use names with spaces to identify its objects and field tables, I do not recommend doing that. Instead, I propose you follow a simple rule that states that if any object of a field needs more than one word to correctly identify it, these words must have no spaces but begin with a capital letter. For example, if a table needs to be called Persons Meals (with a space between words), it will be named as PersonsMeals (no spaces, with each word beginning with uppercase).

Note   If you name an object of a field with more than one word and spaces between the words, whenever you need to refer to these objects in a query, form report, or macro, you will need to enclose the name in brackets. For example, to refer to the Persons Meals table name, you will need to use [Persons Meals], or Microsoft Access will not be able to find it.

Since a Microsoft Access database can have different types of objects (or files stored in it), this book will use some conventions to easily distinguish them, based on international code conventions. The convention is to name each database object with a three-letter lowercase prefix that better identifies it, especially when you use macros and modules to automate your solution.

Specifically, Table 1-4 shows the naming conventions for database objects.

Table 1-4. *Rules for Database Objects Naming Convention*

Object Type	Name Prefix
Table	tbl
Query	qry
Form	frm
Report	rpt
Macro	mcr
Module	bas

By using such rules, any object must be named as objObjectName, where:

- obj: This is the three-letter prefix that identifies the object type.

- ObjectName: This is the name you want to give to the object.

This means that a table used to store person information should be named as tblPersons (the plural of each person record). But to keep things simple—and break the rules—this book will not prefix table names. Instead, any table will be named with the plural of the records it represents. For example, if a table records individual person data, it will be called Persons. If it stores food items, it will called Foods, and the tables cited in Figure 1-4 to store Persons Meals and Persons Meals Foods will be called PersonsMeals and PersonsMealsFoods, respectively.

Note   The international name rules also apply to table field types, which will not be used throughout this book.

Queries will be prefixed with the *qry* prefix. For example, if a query returns records from the PersonsMeals table, it will be named qryPersonsMeals, which will clearly differentiate it from another.

Note   Microsoft Access does not allow tables and queries to have duplicate names.

We'll do the same with forms and reports. A Persons by Phone Number form will be named frmPersonsByPhoneNumber, while the related report will be named rptPersonsByPhoneNumber.

A macro that is used to open a given form object, like frmPersonMeals, will be named mcrOpenfrmPersonsMeals.

Now you need to understand how Microsoft Access works so you can access all of these objects!

The Microsoft Access Interface

The best way to learn how Microsoft Access works is by observing an existing database structure. Since you are probably a novice with using this software interface, your best bet is to use one of its many templates to create a new database.

Whenever you open Microsoft Access 2019, it will show you its New window, offering you the chance to open a previous database that already exists on your computer, create a new one from scratch, or create a new database based on some of its many available templates (Figure 1-6).

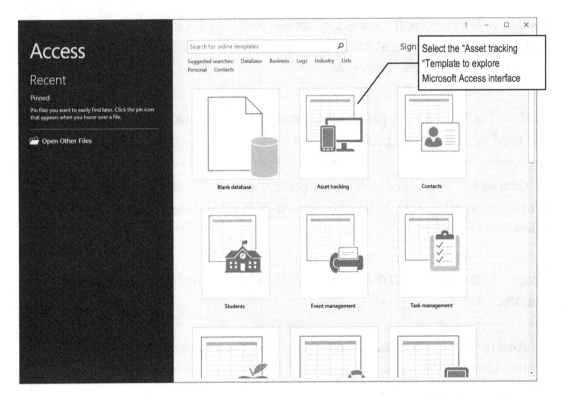

Figure 1-6. *The Microsoft Access 2019 New from Template window, from where you can select different types of templates to explore the many ways of using a database*

Note   I have no intention of commenting on the quality of the Microsoft Access templates. We'll use the "Asset tracking" template so you can better follow the explanations of this book.

Double-click the "Asset tracking" template and Microsoft Access will show you a presentation of the template interface. Then click Create to create a new `Microsoft Access.ACCBD` file (Figure 1-7).

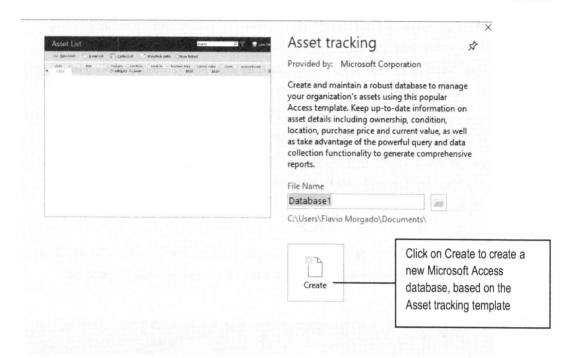

Figure 1-7. *Presentation window for the "Asset tracking" Microsoft Access database template*

When you click the Create button in any Microsoft Access presentation's Template window, Microsoft Access will show you a small window with a running progress bar while it creates a new database in your Documents folder.

Note   Some Microsoft Access templates ask you for the folder and filename that should be used to create the new database. This is not the case with the "Asset tracking" template, which will automatically create the `databasen.accdb` file in your Documents folder (where n refers to the next number in the series of database files whose name is prefixed by *database*). If you want to give the database a better filename (like the `Asset Tracking.accdb` file, you will need close Microsoft Access (or close the database) and edit the filename.

Most of the databases created by Microsoft Word templates show a default Form object waiting to receive its first record, along with a Welcome window offering assistance (the "Need help?" or "Like this or Want more?" links) and possibly a link to an Internet-stored video explaining how to use the template.

Note   It is strongly suggested that you watch the "Asset tracking" template presentation so you become acquainted with some important Microsoft Access concepts, such as adding and deleting records and laying out a form to deal with database records.

When you're done with the database's Welcome window, click the Get Started button at the bottom to access the Microsoft Access interface for this database (Figure 1-8).

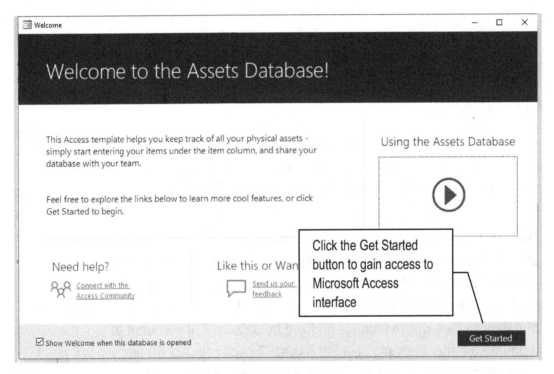

Figure 1-8. *This is the "Asset tracking" database's Welcome window, from where you get help, watch a small video about how this database works, or click the Get Started button to gain access to the Microsoft Access interface and the opened database objects*

Note   When you open the database, a macro called AutoExec launches the Asset List Form object in the Welcome screen. You can find this macro in the Database window's Macro area.

Any macro named AutoExec will automatically run when the database is opened. To avoid such behavior, hold down the Shift key when opening the database.

The Welcome window is also a Microsoft Access Form object, with specific controls that add help (like the links and the presentation) and a Command Button control (Get Started). It also has no border and floats above the Microsoft Access interface. The window is locked in place until it is closed—which is called a *modal form*. You will learn more about form types in later chapters.

The Database Window

The Database window is the docked list you see at the left of the Microsoft Access interface; it is used to manage all the databases objects (Figure 1-9).

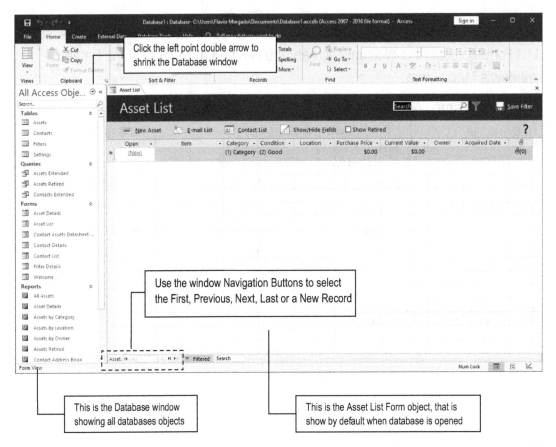

Figure 1-9. *This is the Microsoft Access database interface for the database1.accdb file created by the "Asset tracking" template and stored in the Documents folder (see the Microsoft Access title bar). It shows by default the Asset List Form object*

Note   The navigation buttons are the small buttons located on the bottom left of a table, query, form, or report that allow you to select the first, previous, next, or last record (or a page in a report). The rightmost button—the one with a yellow asterisk—allows you to select a new record and is enabled whenever the object allows you to insert a new record. The small text box between these buttons will show the record or page number, and you can click it and type a value to go straight to it.

Every Microsoft Access up to version 2003 presents the Database window as a floating window that can be sized, minimized, or maximized inside the program interface. Since Access 2007, it has become a docked window that loses part of its functionality, and you can't get rid of it. You can just shrink it to the application window's left border by clicking the right-pointing double arrow located in the Database window's top-right corner so that it doesn't occupy too much of the program interface.

Note in Figure 1-9 how the Database window for the "Asset tracking" template shows database objects grouped by type—under Tables, Queries, Forms, and Reports—each one with its own colored icon.

Note   The Database window can be collapsed or expanded by pressing the F11 key.

The Database window also allows you to configure how it will display its database objects by clicking the down-pointing arrow located in the top-right corner (Figure 1-10).

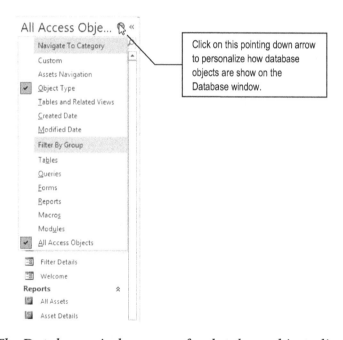

Figure 1-10. *The Database window menu for database objects display configuration*

The default view is Object Type with the Filter By Group option selected, which shows each object type inside its own group. As your database grows and new objects are needed to keep it running (especially new queries, forms, and reports), you may need to change the object order to Created Date so you can easily find recently created objects and interact with them.

Note   Microsoft Access specifications allow up to 32,768 objects inside a database. Most objects have no upper limit (although VBA allows just 100 Module objects, which is the interface limit to this object type). Do a Google search for *Access specifications* for more information about the limits.

The Relationship Window

Also shown in Figure 1-9, the "Asset tracking" database template creates a database that has four table objects: Asset, Contact, Filter, and Settings.

To understand how this database works, use the Relationships window, which can be evoked by click the Relationships button in the Relationships area on the Database Tools tab (Figure 1-11).

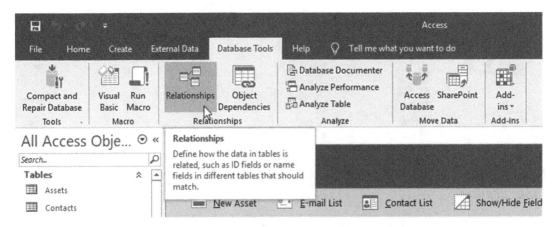

Figure 1-11. *Click the Relationships button to open the Relationships window*

When the Relationships window opens, it appears by default on the right of the Asset List, and it shows all the table relationships imposed by the person who created the database (Figure 1-12).

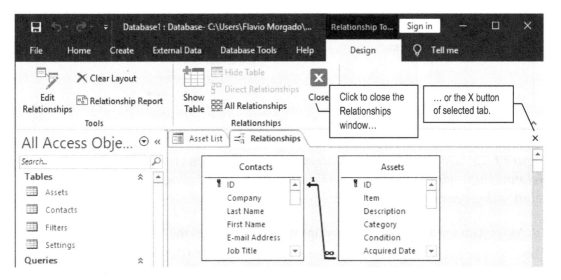

Figure 1-12. Microsoft Access Relationships window for the "Asset tracking" template database, showing a relation between the Contacts and Assets tables

Note in Figure 1-12 that both the Contacts and Asset tables have an ID field with a small key located on the right—meaning that this field is the corresponding table's primary key field—so its values are never repeated among the records.

Also note that there is a one-to-many relationship between the Contacts table (1) and the Assets table (∞). The related Assets table field is not shown by default; you must scroll down in the Assets table to show the related field name.

To verify which type of relationship was imposed between these two tables and fields, double-click the relationship line between them to show the Edit Relationships window (Figure 1-13).

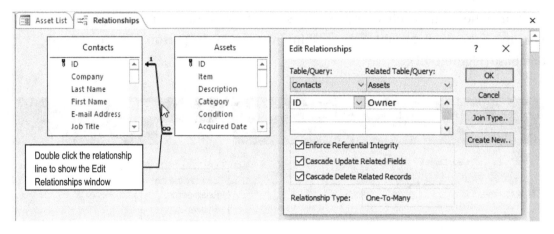

Figure 1-13. *Double-click the relationship line that joins two tables in the Relationships window to show the Edit Relationships dialog and verify the relationship type imposed*

As you can see, the Edit Relationships window indicates that the Contacts ID field (the table's primary key) is related to the Assets Owner field (the table's foreign key) and that it has enforced referential integrity between these two tables, using the Cascade Update Related Fields and Cascade Delete Related Records settings. This means that whenever the Contacts Record ID field changes, all the related records on the Assets table's Owner field will be automatically updated to reflect these changes. Also, if any contact record is deleted, every related record on the Assets table will be automatically deleted. In other words, there will never be an Assets record without a contact owner.

You are now becoming acquainted with database syntax!

Opening, Closing, and Displaying Database Objects

Look again to Figures 1-9, 1-12, and 1-13 and note that each opened window (Asset List and Relationships) has its own, docked tab in the Microsoft Access interface, and on the right of the tab list, there is a small close button (with an X) that allows you to close the selected tab.

Double-click any table (Assets, Contacts, Filters, or Settings) and they will appear on tabs in the order they were opened.

This type of interface is the default Microsoft Access way to show its opened objects, but it is also a property of this database called Show Tabbed Documents that is available in the Microsoft Access 2007 version.

You can change this interface to give your database applications a more Windows-like interface, where any opened window appears floating, one on top of another, as expected by many users around the word.

To change this database's default view set to Overlapping Windows, select File ➤ Options to show the Access Options dialog, select Current Database in the left pane, and choose Overlapping Windows in Document Windows Options (Figure 1-14).

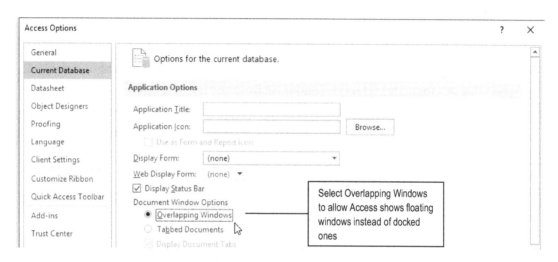

Figure 1-14. *To give a default Windows appearance to your applications, you can change any database appearance to Overlapping Windows, which will make Access dock any open windows on a tabbed interface*

Select Overlapping Windows to allow Access shows floating windows instead of docked ones

---

Note   Although there is no problem with the tabbed design proposed by Microsoft Access as the default interface to its databases, you will learn more about forms—and will produce better interfaces—if you change the default document window options to Overlapping Windows, as will be explained in the next chapters of this book.

Whenever you change the current database document window options to Overlapping Windows and close the Access Options dialog, Access will ask you to close and reopen the database so the changes can be implemented (Figure 1-15).

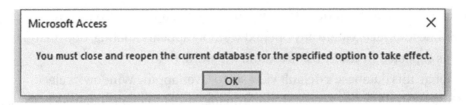

Figure 1-15. *Access needs to close and reopen the current database whenever you make a change to its default document window options in the Access Options dialog*

Click OK to close the message box. Select File ➤ Close to close the current database. Now select File ➤ Open and select the database from the list to reopen it in the new windowed way, where each object can float above one another, have its own close button in the top-left corner, and have its own set of maximize, restore, and minimize buttons located in the top-right corner (Figure 1-16).

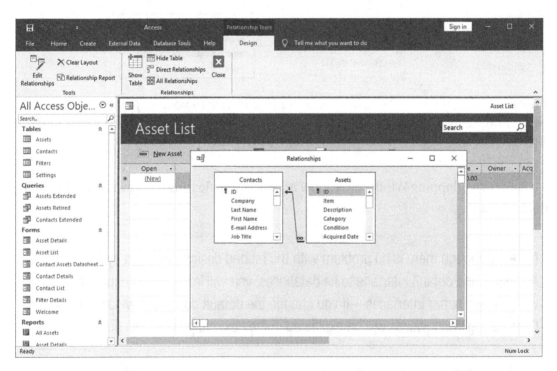

Figure 1-16. *This is how the "Asset tracking" database will look whenever you change your default document window options to Overlapping Windows, allowing each object to have its own window, with its own title bar and maximize, restore, and close buttons*

Summary

Microsoft Access is a relational database management system full of features that allow you to create data tables using different field types and relate them using referential integrity rules.

Access uses a single database file storage system that can contain different types of objects (tables, indexes, queries, forms, reports, macros, and modules), allowing you to explore the data stored in it in many different ways. You can use queries to relate its tables, forms to create a user interface, reports to create printouts, and use macros and modules to automate the interface.

In the next chapter, you will learn how you can create a database from scratch.

Summary

CHAPTER 2

Creating and Using Database Tables

In this chapter, you will learn how to create and use Access database tables. You'll define field types and properties, use the AutoNumber field type to create a primary key, and find out how a table behaves as records are inserted and deleted. You will also learn about record locks and how Microsoft Access manages them.

In this chapter, you'll do the following:

- Understand related tables and where information is stored.

- Learn the ins and outs of the many useful things in Microsoft Access such as the primary key, autonumbering, date/hour settings, and format, as well as best practices for using them.

- Create a table using Datasheet or Design view to view more properties in your database.

- Use the Short Text data type to insert text or numerical text codes (such as a phone number or Social Security number).

- Use the Input Mask Wizard to allow a precise type of value.

- Relate database tables to each other to allow Microsoft Access to impose referential integrity between two tables.

- Avoid accidental deletions.

All tables cited in this chapter can be obtained by extracting the `NutritionData.accdb` database from `CHAPTER02.zip`, which can be downloaded from Apress.com.

© Flavio Morgado 2021
F. Morgado, *Introducing Microsoft Access Using Macro Programming Techniques*,
https://doi.org/10.1007/978-1-4842-6555-0_2

The Nutritional Database Structure

Let's suppose you want to create a new Access database to track the nutritional value of food that people have eaten over the course of a day. Figure 2-1 shows a table diagram with the three related tables: Persons, PersonsMeals, and PersonsMealsFoods.

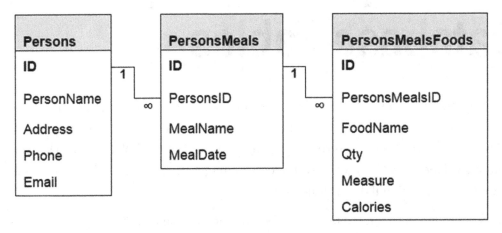

Figure 2-1. *The table relationships diagram for a nutritional food intake control database*

Take a minute to look at this table relationships diagram. We are already using the proposed naming conventions for this book, where every name has no spaces between words, and each new word is capitalized—both on table names (PersonMeals and PersonMealsFoods) and on table fields (PersonName, PersonsID, MealName, MealData, PersonsMealsID, and FoodName).

Also note that each table primary key field is called ID (there is an ID field for the Persons, PersonsMeals, and PersonsMealsFoods tables), while the related table foreign key field is named as <Primary Table Name>ID. The PersonsMeals foreign key is PersonsID, while the PersonsMealsFoods foreign key field is PersonsMealsID.

To define this database structure, you need to open Access, create a new database, create each table, and then relate them using the Relationships window. Let's see how to do this!

Creating the Nutritional Database

To create the nutritional database, open Access, and select Blank Database in the Blank Database window. This opens the floating "Blank database" windows, where Access will propose Database$n$ as the name in the File Name box for this new database (where n is an integer that adds 1 to the count of `*.ACCDB` files found in the current user's `Documents` folder) and offers the `Current user\Documents` folder as the default place to store the database.

Use the small folder button located to the right of the File Name box to select the folder where you want to create the new database, type a more significant name for the database (such as **NutritionData**), and click Create (Figure 2-2).

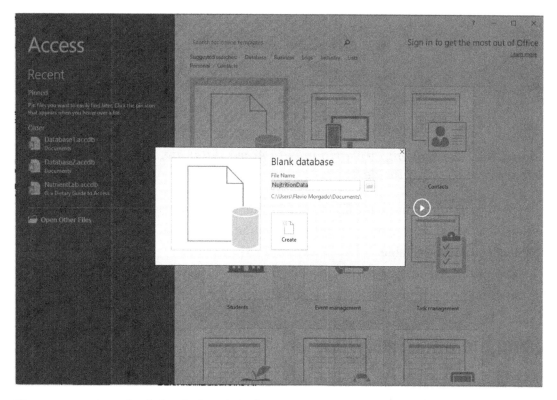

Figure 2-2. *Use the "Blank database" window to create a new, empty Access database at the desired folder*

Access will create a new, empty database called NutritionData in the default `Documents` folder and open. Access will propose a table called Table1 as the first object to be inserted inside the database (Figure 2-3).

Figure 2-3. *The new, empty NutritionData Access database, with Table1 as the first object to be stored inside it*

The Table1 object automatically created by the "Blank database" template is shown by default as a new docked object using the traditional Datasheet view. The ID field is already defined for the table.

You must now learn how to use the default Datasheet view so you can easily create the tables in the NutritionData database structure.

Using the Datasheet View

The Datasheet view shows that the new Table1 object has a datasheet with two columns (New and Click to Add), and the view has a Table Tools tool box that shows two tabs to define both Fields and Tableproperties (Figure 2-3).

Let's see how to use the Table Tools tab to define a new Table object.

Note   Although Table1 is presented as having just one field called ID, it really does not yet exist as a table, because you haven't saved it to the database. You need to define the fields it contains, indicating each field name and data type and, optionally, defining some of its properties.

As proof of this, close the proposed Table1 object by clicking the Table1 close button (the small "x" located to the right of the docked title bar) or right-click Table1 and choose Delete on the context menu that appears. Access will close the proposed Table1 object with no warning to save it.

Using the Table Tools Fields Tab

Note in Figure 2-3 that the newly created Table1 object has an ID field and that Access switches the Create tab to the Table Tools Fields tab. Here you can define the field behavior using the Properties, Formatting, and Field Validation areas.

Click the ID field and note that the Fields tab tools change to show the ID field properties. You can see in the Formatting area that Data Type is set to AutoNumber (Figure 2-4), enabling even more field properties that can be changed.

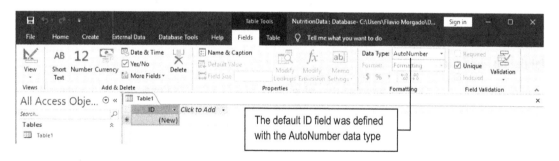

Figure 2-4. *The Fields tab of the Table Tools tollbar allows you to change some field properties according to the field type selected*

The Fields tab of the Table Tools toolbar offers other field properties that may become enabled/disabled according to the data type defined for the selected field, as shown in Table 2-1.

Table 2-1. *Field Properties That Can Be Defined Using the Fields Tab of the Table Fields Options*

Properties Area	
Name & Caption	Defines the field name and a tooltip that appears whenever you point the mouse to it
Default Value	Defines a default value for every new record
Field Size	Defines the field length for the Short Text data type, and defines the number scope for Number fields
Modify Lookups	Defines a list of values for some field types
Modify Expression	Defines the expression that will appear on a calculated field
Memo Settings	Used only by Memo fields, the ones that can receive a large amount of text
Formatting Area	
Data Type	Defines the base field type
Format	Indicates how the stored value will show up on the Datasheet view, queries, forms, and reports
Buttons formatting options	Allows you to select default formatting options, such as percent, currency, and decimals
Validation Field Area	
Required	Defines whether the value must be granted by the user; the record will not be saved if the value is empty
Unique	Defines whether the field cannot be replicated among table records (used for the table primary key)
Indexed	Defines whether the field is indexed, allowing fast searches on the table
Validation	Defines whether the field has an appropriate value before being defined

As you can see, there are different properties that can be defined for any single field. Note that the ID field was defined using the AutoNumber data type (a long integer value, automatically defined by the database engine) that allows only the Unique option to be enabled. Also, it is selected by default, meaning that the ID field will have a unique value for every table record.

Adding Fields with the Datasheet View

Using the Datasheet view, you can easily create other table fields in two ways.

- By using the tools located in the Add & Delete area of the Fields tab of the Table Tools toolbar

- By clicking the Click to Add option located at the right of the ID field and selecting the field type for the new field

Let's use both options to create new Table1 fields so you can decide which one is best suited for you.

Adding a Field Using the Fields Tab

Use the Add & Delete area of the Fields tab to add a new table field of a specific data type using a single mouse click.

For example, click the Short Text button to automatically add Field 1 using the Short Text data type. Look to the Fields tab's Properties area and note that Field1 has a Field Size setting of 255 characters and is set to the Short Text data type. You can also set it to the Required, Exclusive, and Indexed Validation Field options (Figure 2-5).

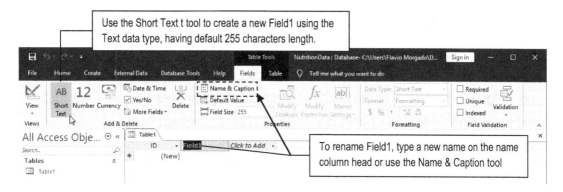

Figure 2-5. *Use the tools in the Fields tab's Add & Delete area to easily create new fields of a specific data type with a single mouse click*

Supposing that you are creating the Persons table as defined on Figure 2-1, this field must be named PersonName. Note in Figure 2-5 that the Field1 name is selected and has a blinking text cursor on it. To rename it to PersonName, use one of these methods:

- Click the column head, type the new name, and press Enter to define it before setting the other field properties.

- Use the Name & Caption tool, which will open the associated window where you can type a new name for the selected field (Figure 2-6).

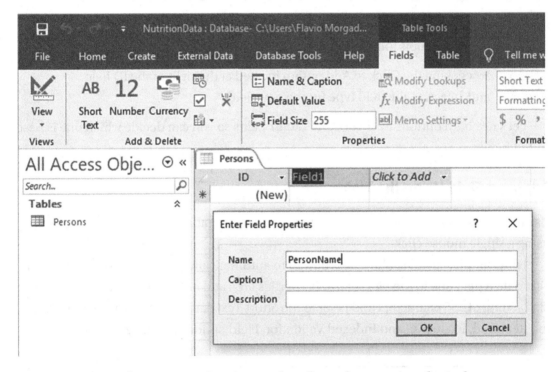

Figure 2-6. *Use the Name & Caption tool to show the associated window*

Note   Access has an odd behavior whenever you begin to edit any field name and, before updating the name, try to set some of its properties: it may leave the field name and select the ID field. You need to change the field name, press Enter to update it, and then change the other field properties.

The PersonName field must have enough space to store most real people's names. Let's say from your previous interviews about the database needs, you know it is supposed to use up to 80 characters. So, click the Field Size option and type **80** (for a maximum of 80 characters for this field).

It is also reasonable to suppose that no Persons table record should be inserted (saved to the disk) with the PersonName field blank. So, select the Required property to guarantee that any Persons record has a person name typed on it.

Note   It is not easy to guarantee that the PersonName field will receive a person's name. By checking the Required property for this field, you will assure that the database user must type something in the PersonName field to save the record, even if the user just types a number or any other keyboard symbol.

The nutritional application will also need to offer fast searches by people's names, so the PersonName field must be indexed. So, click the Indexed option located on the Field Validation area of the Fields tab, which will force Access to create an index for this field (Figure 2-7).

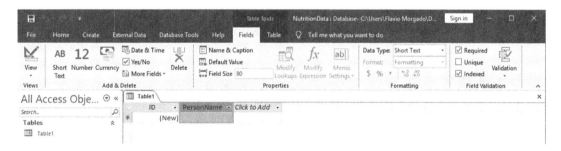

Figure 2-7. *Define the new Field1 text data type. Change its name to PersonName, set its Field Size to 80 characters long, and enable the Required and Indexed properties to guarantee that something will be typed in it and to allow for faster searches by people's names*

Adding a Field Using the Click to Add Option

You can also add more fields to Table1 using the Click to Add option located at the right of the last field defined on the Datasheet grid. Clicking this option will open a list of data types; you can select the one that must be associated to this new field type.

For this example, click the Click to Add option to open the data type list options and select the Short Text data type to create another Field1 field to the right of the PersonName field (Figure 2-8).

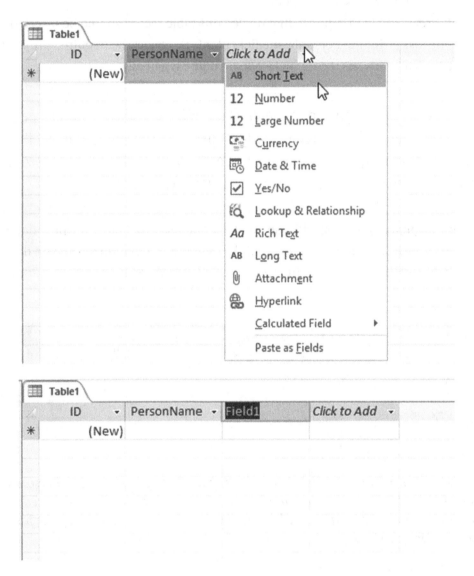

Figure 2-8. *You can use the Datasheet view to create new table fields, by using the Click to Add option to select the new field's data type and renaming it*

According to Figure 2-1, this new Field1 must be named Address, and from your previous interviews, you know that it may have up to 100 characters. Since you probably don't want to make searches on the Address field, you don't need to index it. Figure 2-9 shows Table1 in Datasheet view and the Fields tab as defined for the new Address field.

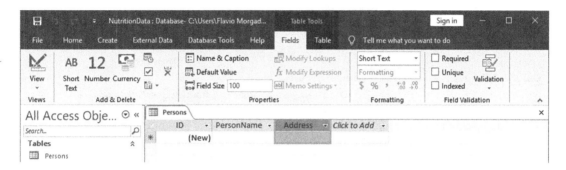

Figure 2-9. *This is the Table1 that has received a second Address field, defined as the Short Text data type, using up to 100 characters long*

Using Design View

At the moment, Table1 has three fields defined: ID (AutoNumber), PersonName (Short Text, 80 characters, Required, and Indexed), and Address (Short Text, 100 characters).

To add two more fields (Phone and Email) to create all the Persons table fields as defined by Figure 2-1, you can use Design view. This is the default way that every Access version uses to create a new table.

Look to the Table Tools tool's Fields tab shown in Figure 2-9 and note that the Fields tab offers the View tool as its first tool (the one with a triangle, pencil, and rule icon) in the Views area. Use it to switch any table object between Datasheet and Design view.

Since Table1 is on Datasheet view, click the View button to change Table1 to Design view. Access will immediately prompt you for a name to save this table in the database (Figure 2-10).

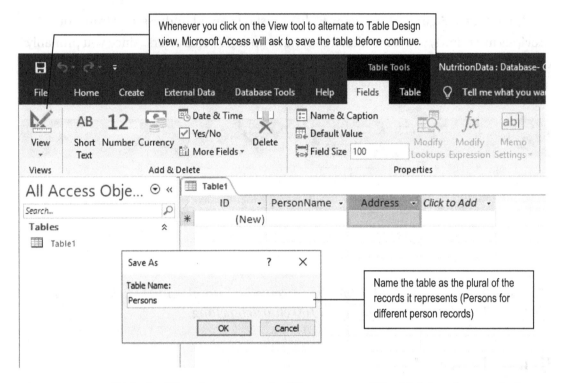

Figure 2-10. *Click the View button in the Views area of the Fields tab to switch Table1 to Design view. Since the table was not saved on the database, Access will ask you for the table name.*

Note   Whenever you make changes to table or field properties and switch from Design to Datasheet view, Access will ask to save the table. Note that it offers a Save As dialog box, meaning that you can create another table.

Tip   You can also alternate to Design view by right-clicking the Table1 tab name and selecting Design View in the context menu.

Type **Persons** (the plural of each person record) and click OK to save the table in the database and switch it to Design view, forcing Access to show the Design tab of the Table Tools toolbar (Figure 2-11).

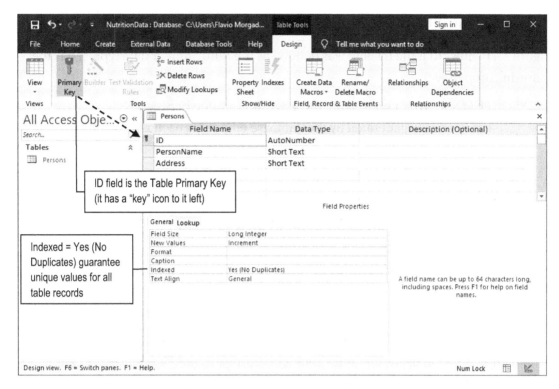

Figure 2-11. *This is the now the saved Persons table in Design view, having the fields ID, PersonName, and Address already defined in Datasheet view. Access automatically defines the ID field as the the table's primary key*

Note in Figure 2-11 that the Persons table appears in the Access Database window and that Design view shows a datasheet grid on top with three columns (Field Name, Data Type, and Description) and a second datasheet grid on it bottom that has two tabs.

- *General tab*: This shows all properties for the selected field on the top data grid, according to the data type of the selected field.

- *Lookup tab*: This can be used to define that this field must be filled using a List Box or Combo Box control.

Note   Adding clear descriptions for each field stored in the table is good programming practice. Use Design view's Description column to add some explanation to what is stored in each field. This may be necessary whenever the field name has no clear association to its content.

The AutoNumber Data Type

Figure 2-11 shows that the ID field was defined as the AutoNumber data type. It has the following properties:

- *Field Size*: When set to Long Integer, this is a value between $\pm 2^{31}$ automatically generated by the database engine for each new record (you can't change the Field Size property for a AutoNumber field).

- *New Values*: When set to Increment, this is the way that the AutoNumber field must be generated, meaning consecutive numbers beginning at 1. The alternative is Random, meaning that a unique number between $\pm 2^{31}$ will be automatically generated.

- *Format*: This indicates how the number should appear on the datasheet grid.

Note   As with Microsoft Excel, Access has a rich way to format field values, making them appear for the user differently from what is really stored in the field. Do an Internet search for *Access Format Property* for a complete list of available options.

- *Caption*: Use this to alias the field name. In this case, the Caption text will appear as the field name on the table's Datasheet view, although you still need to refer to this field using its default Name property when used by queries, forms, reports, macros, and VBA code.

Note   Although not explicitly specified, Access doesn't work well for some field names that you can avoid. The word *Name* is a reserved word that can't be used to name a field (that is why the field was named PersonName). Do an Internet search for *Access Reserved Words* for a complete list of names you must avoid.

- *Indexed*: When set to Yes (No Duplicates), this indicates that Access must keep an index file for this field, not allowing any value to be duplicated inside the table.

- *Text Align*: When set to General, this indicates how the ID field values will appear on the datasheet grid.

Note   Align = General means text values are left aligned, and numeric values are right aligned by default.

Also note that whenever you select the ID field on top of the datasheet grid, the Primary Key icon located in the Tools area of the Design view's Table Tools toolbar is selected (and that a small "key" icon is located at the left of the ID field name, indicating that it is the table's primary key).

Note   Any table can have more than one field defined as the table's primary key. To do this, select the desired field on the top datasheet grid and click the Primary Key icon. This will make Access set the field Indexed property to Yes (No Duplicates) and will put a key icon at the left of its name, meaning that each field value must be unique among all table records.

If more than one table field is defined as the table's primary key, both values should be unique on a single record among all other table records.

The Short Text Data Type

Click the PersonName field on top of the datasheet grid of Design view and note that Access will show even more options for a Short Text data type (Figure 2-12).

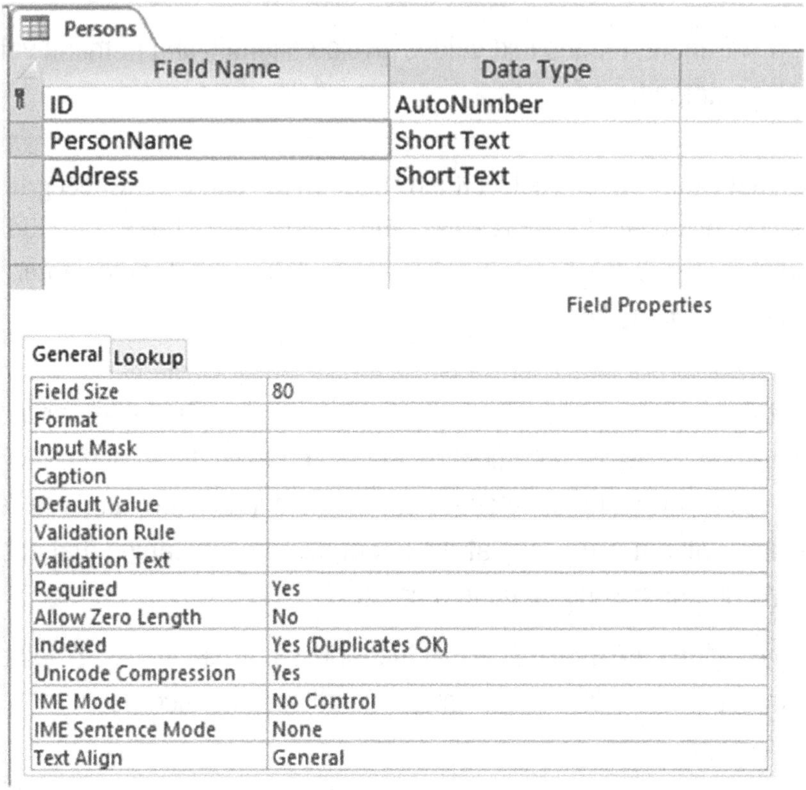

Persons		
Field Name	**Data Type**	
ID	AutoNumber	
PersonName	Short Text	
Address	Short Text	

Field Properties

General Lookup

Field Size	80
Format	
Input Mask	
Caption	
Default Value	
Validation Rule	
Validation Text	
Required	Yes
Allow Zero Length	No
Indexed	Yes (Duplicates OK)
Unicode Compression	Yes
IME Mode	No Control
IME Sentence Mode	None
Text Align	General

Figure 2-12. *The Short Text data type offers more properties to define using Design view*

As Figure 2-12 shows, the Short Text data type offers new properties.

- *Field Size*: This sets the number of characters that can be typed on the field (1 to 255 characters for Short Text field).

Note   It is a good programming practice to set the field sizes to the maximum space they can use. If you use a field size larger than that, the extra space will occupy unnecessary space in the database.

- *Format*: This defines how field content will show up.

- *Input Mask*: This allows you to restrain what can be typed on the field.

- *Caption*: In the table's Datasheet view, change the column header; in form or reports, define the Label caption associated with the field.

- *Default Value*: This defines a default value for new records.

- *Validation Rule*: This allows you to define a expression that must be true to insert the value on the field.

- *Validation Text:* This is the text to be shown if the validation rule expression is false.

- *Required*: If set to Yes, this requires that a value be inserted on the field.

- *Allow Zero Length*: If set to No, this allows you to insert a empty string ("") on the field.

- *Indexed*: This creates an index for the field so it can be searched faster. The YES (Duplicates OK) option indicates that more than one record can have the same value.

- *Unicode Compression*: This compresses the text inserted on the field when less than 4,096 characters are stored (for Latin characters whose first byte is 0).

- *IME Mode*: This controls the conversion of characters in East Asian versions of Windows.

- *IME Sentence Mode*: This controls the conversion of sentences in East Asian versions of Windows.

- *Text Align*: This defines how text will be aligned by default in Datasheet view or inside a Text Box control.

Note   By defining the PersonName field as shown here, the PersonName field's Indexed property is set to Yes (Duplicates OK), meaning that two or more Persons records can be fulfilled using the same name. This means two or more people can have the same name on the database, but they can be differentiated by adding SSN, DateOfBirth, and Address fields.

Since the Address field had no other property besides the Field Size set, it means that the database will allow you to insert a person record without typing its address. By setting the Address field's Allow Zero Length property to Yes, any Address value can be defined with an empty text value ("") or two consecutive double quotes—a zero length text.

Adding Fields with Design View

To add a new field to a Table object in Design view, click the next empty row on the top data grid, type its name, and select a data type at the right. Then look at its properties and set the ones you are interested in.

Figure 2-13 shows that the phone number was typed in the table's Design view; it was set to the Short Text data type with the Field Size property set to 15 characters (two characters for the country code plus two or three characters for the local area code plus nine or ten characters for the phone code).

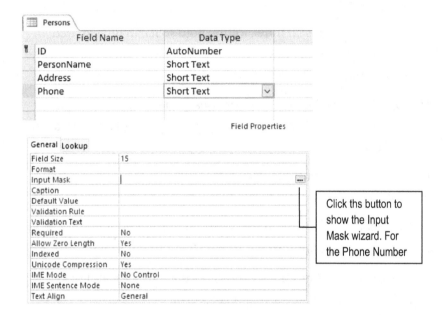

Figure 2-13. *Using Design view to insert the Phone field as a Short Text data type, with up to 15 characters length*

Note   Although Phone is a numeric value, it should not be defined using the Number data type, because you will never apply math to it (like square a phone number, sum two or more phones, etc.). It is considered numeric text and must be set to the Short Text data type.

Using an Input Mask for a Phone Number

Some Short Text fields may require a specific input mask so the user is forced to input specific characters (like letters or number) at specific field positions. The person's phone number may be such field, although it may vary a lot from region to region and from country to country.

Access allows you to define an input mask for any Short Text field by offering the Input Mask Wizard, which can be called whenever you click the small ellipsis button located to the right of the Input Mask property (it may ask you to save the table before showing the Input Mask Wizard).

The Input Mask Wizard will open and offer an option list for different types of text fields that may need an input mask. Figure 2-14 shows the Phone option selected, after clicking the Try It text box, which offers a way to test how the input mask will behave for this field.

Figure 2-14. *This is the Input Mask Wizard showing the Phone option selected in the list, after clicking the Try It text box to verify how the input mask will behave*

If the phone input mask does not fit your needs, offering too many characters perhaps, click the Edit List button to show the Customize Input Mask Wizard window, where you can change the options (Figure 2-15).

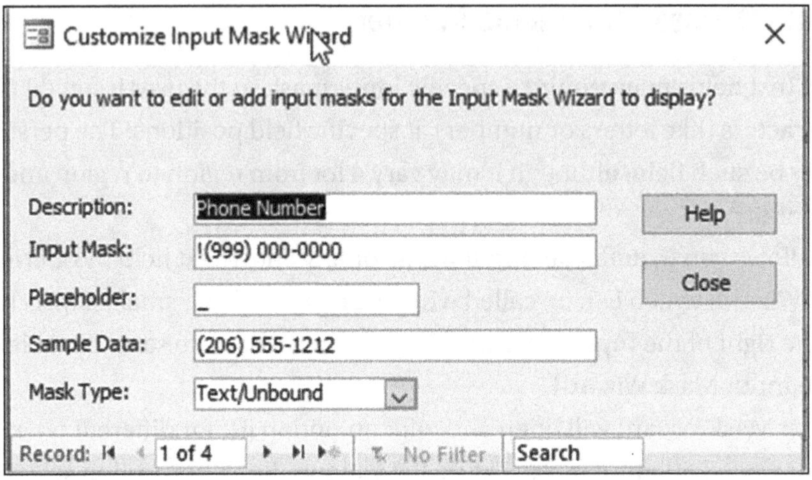

Figure 2-15. *The Customize Input Mask Wizard window, specifying how the Phone input mask is defined*

Note   The Customize Input Mask Wizard is indeed an Access form, showing five records by default. By changing the Phone Input Mask option by adding or removing characters to it, you will change this input mask on your Access copy. If you want to create a new Phone International input mask, click the New button and fill in all the proposed fields.

By closing the Customize Input Mask Wizard and clicking the Next button to continue the input mask creation process, the wizard will show you a new page, asking if you want to change the phone input mask or use the placeholder character reserved options, that is, the underscore (_) character by default (Figure 2-16).

Input Mask Wizard

Do you want to change the input mask?

Input Mask Name: Phone Number

Input Mask: !(999) 000-0000

What placeholder character do you want the field to display?

Placeholders are replaced as you enter data into the field.

Placeholder character: _

Try It:

Cancel   < Back   Next >   Finish

Figure 2-16. *The second Input Mask Wizard page asks if you want to change the input mask and the reserved space character*

By clicking the Next button, the wizard will show the last page, asking if you want to store the value with or without the input mask symbols (parentheses, hyphens, dots, etc.). The default value is to store just the values (no symbols), as shown in Figure 2-17.

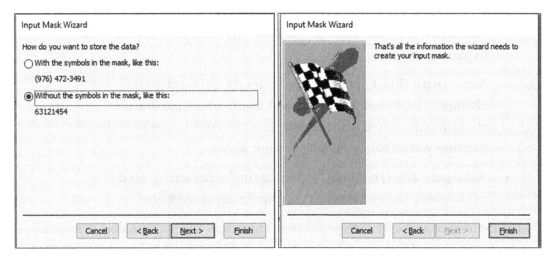

Input Mask Wizard

How do you want to store the data?

○ With the symbols in the mask, like this:

(976) 472-3491

◉ Without the symbols in the mask, like this:

63121454

Cancel   < Back   Next >   Finish

Input Mask Wizard

That's all the information the wizard needs to create your input mask.

Cancel   < Back   Next >   Finish

Figure 2-17. *The next Input Mask Wizard page asks if you want to store the input mask symbols or just typed characters (default value)*

Click Next to show the last Input Mask Wizard page, and click Finish to store the desired input mask on the Input Mask property of the Phone field (Figure 2-18).

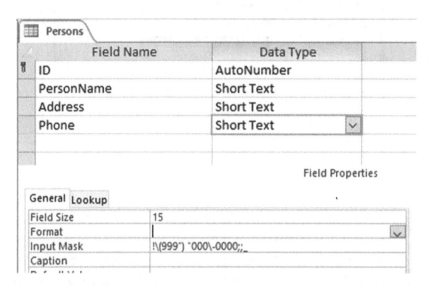

Figure 2-18. *This is how Access defines the Input Mask property with the aid of the Input Mask Wizard*

Understanding Input Mask Syntax

The input mask created by the wizard has three parts, separated by semicolons:

- *First part*: This is mandatory, including all necessary mask characters, placeholders, and literal data (parentheses, periods, and hyphens).

- *Second part*: This is optional; it indicates if embedded mask characters are stored within the field. Use 0 to indicate that the characters are stored with the data; leave it empty or use 1 to indicate that they will be displayed only and not stored.

- *Third part*: This is optional; a space or single character is used as a placeholder. The underscore (_) is the default placeholder.

The Input Mask property can use different characters and placeholders to indicate how a value will be fulfilled on a Text Box control. Table 2-2 lists the characters you can use and how they behave when inserted on an input mask for a Short Text field.

Table 2-2. *Characters and Placeholders That Can Be Used to Define an Input Mask*

Character	Usage
0	The user must enter a digit (0 to 9).
9	The user can enter a digit (0 to 9) or leave it blank.
#	The user can enter a digit, space, plus sign, or minus sign. If skipped, Access enters a blank space.
L	The user must enter a letter.
?	The user can enter a letter or leave it blank.
A	The user must enter a letter or a digit.
a	The user can enter a letter or a digit or leave it blank.
&	The user must enter either a character or a space.
C	The user can enter characters or spaces or leave it blank.
. , : ; - /	Decimal and thousands placeholders; date and time separators (according to your Microsoft Windows regional settings).
>	This converts all characters that follow to uppercase.
<	This converts all characters that follow to lowercase.
!	This causes the input mask to fill from left to right instead of from right to left.
\	The characters immediately following will be displayed literally.
" "	The characters enclosed in double quotation marks will be displayed literally.

Now, pay attention in Figure 2-18 to how the Input Mask Wizard composes the Input Mask property for the Phone field:

`!\(999") "000\-0000;;_`

The Input Mask code for the Phone field used two semicolons to separate each of the three input mask parts. Reading from left to right, they are as follows:

- *First part*: The mask code itself begins with a ! indicating that the field will be filled from left to right. The \ character indicates that the next character to its right (opening parenthesis) is a placeholder. The 999 characters used for the code area indicates that a number can be typed or left blank (no code area). Values inside double quotes are also placeholders (closing parenthesis and a space). The 0 character indicates that is mandatory to type seven digits for the phone number.

- *Second part*: Two consecutive semicolons (;;) were used to define the second part as empty, indicating that placeholders will not be stored within the Phone field value (this same as typing 1 after the first semicolon).

- *Third part*: The underscore (_) is the placeholder character to indicate that a value must be typed in this position.

Creating the Email Field

To finish this exercise, we need to create the Email field, as proposed in Figure 2-1 for the Persons table, using the Design view grid.

Click the next empty field name on the top table's Design View data grid and type **Email**, defining it as 100 characters long since it is quite unlikely that an email has more than 100 characters. Do not set any other properties (Figure 2-19).

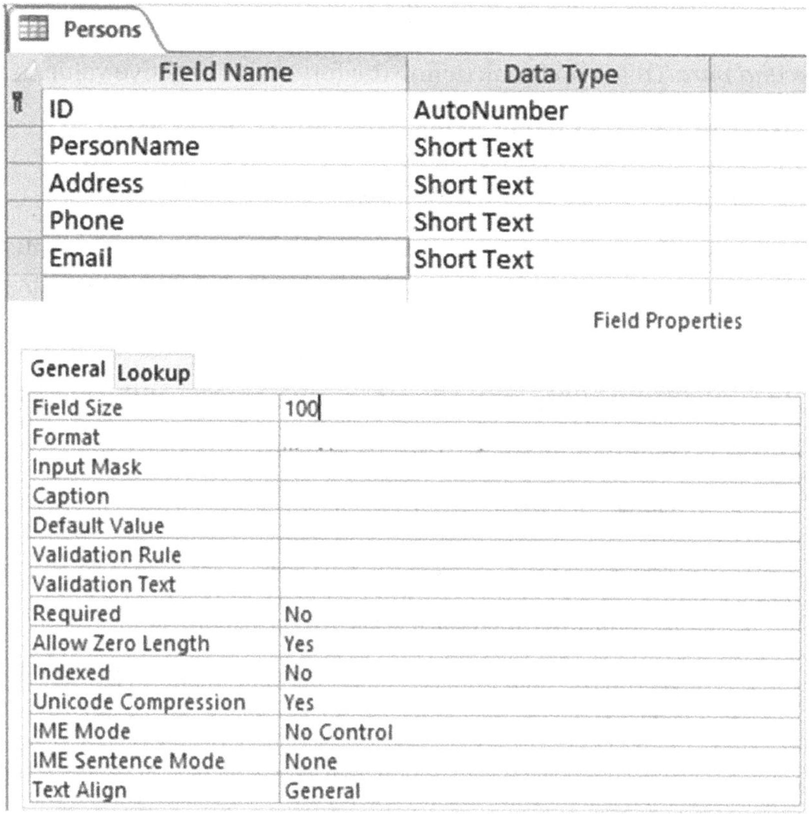

Figure 2-19. *Use the Persons table's Design view to add the Email field, setting it to a length of 100 characters long*

Note   Since there are many different field properties according to the data type selected, do an Internet search using the words *Access field properties* and view "Introduction to data types and field properties" at `support.office.com` for more details about its usage. As you proceed in this book, you will be presented with the more important ones.

Defining the Format Property for a Short Text Field

The Access Format property for the Number and Short Text data type fields works quite like the Microsoft Excel Format property for cells. It is composed by a text string that has up to four different parts, separated by semicolons, where each part relates to a specific value.

- *First part*: This is optional; define the format for positive values.

- *Second part*: This is optional; define the format for negative values.

- *Third part*: This is optional; define the format for zero values.

- *Fourth part*: This is optional; define the format for null values.

To create a custom format string to format any of these four areas, you must use specific format characters as placeholders or separators, as specified by Table 2-3.

Table 2-3. *Placeholders or Separators You Can Use on Any of the Four Format Areas (For Positive, Negative, Zero, or Null Values)*

Character	Usage
#	Displays a digit or blank space if no value is inserted in its position.
0 (zero)	Displays a zero if no value is inserted in its position.
. (dot)	Shows a decimal separator (it can vary according to Windows regional settings).
, (comma))	Show a thousand separator (it can vary according to Windows regional settings).
blank spaces, + - $ ()	Inserts blank spaces, math characters (+ -), and financial symbols (¥ £ $) anywhere in the format string. Common math symbols (such slash \ or /, and the asterisk *) must be surrounded with double quotation marks.
\	Forces Access to display the character that immediately follows (the same as surrounding something with double quotation marks).
!	Forces left alignment of all values for text characters placeholders (does not allow the use of # and 0 digit placeholders).
*	Forces the character immediately following the asterisk to become a fill character in the substitution of blank spaces left in the field. For example, Access right-aligns numbers and fills any area to the left of the value with blank spaces. By using a fill character anywhere in the format string, the blank spaces will be filled with what follows the asterisk.

(continued)

Table 2-3. (*continued*)

Character	Usage
%	Multiplies the value by 100 and displays the result with a trailing percent sign (must be the last character in a format string).
E+, E- or e+, e-	Displays values in scientific (exponential) notation.
"Text"	Inserts a "Text" prefix or suffix to the value.
[color]	Applies a color to any of the four format sections. You must enclose the color name in brackets. Use the next [color] strings: black, blue, cyan, green, magenta, red, yellow, or white.

Using Format on a Short Text Field

The concept of "Null" is quite interesting: it refers to a field where no value is inserted. The Short Text data type has two properties that control this behavior: Default Value, which is blank by default indicating that the field will be Null if no value be inserted, and Allow Zero Length = Yes, indicating that for every new record it will receive by default an empty string (""). The Number data type also has a default value that can be set to 0 (zero), since Null and Zero are different values.

Note   Null is considered as the ASCII code 0 (zero), and this value is stored inside the null fields. Access offers the ISNULL() function if any field is still empty (or in other words, if it received no data inside it).

Every new record that has no value inserted on its field may be considered as Null for all Short Text and Number data types whose Default Value property was not set. But as soon as you try to create a new record, the Short Text field will receive an empty string, which by definition is different from Null.

That said, you can use the fourth part of the Format property to show for every new record simple directions about what must be typed on Short Text fields. You can confirm the following by inserting this code on the Format property for the Email field:

```
;;;"Type Email with up to 100 characters"
```

This Format code has four parts separated by semicolons. The first three parts are empty (for positive, negative, and zero values), while the last part (null values) has instructions for the user about the email value (Figure 2-20).

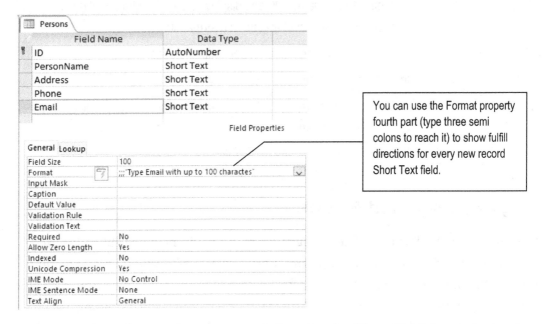

Figure 2-20. *Use the Format property Null option for Short Field data types to give the user a clue about how to type a value in any text field. You must switch to a table's Design view to see how it works*

Saving the Persons Table

Now that you have created all the Persons table fields, while the table is still in Design view, you must save it to the NutritonalData database so it will be ready to receive its data records. This can be done in different ways.

- By pressing the Ctrl+S shortcut.

- By clicking the small disk icon located on the Quick Access toolbar (located in the top-left window corner of the Access window).

- By switching the table's Design view to the table's Datasheet view and clicking the View button, located in the Views area of the Design tab. Access will prompt you to save the table first.

By using the first two methods, Access will save the Persons table, and you will need to click the View button to switch to Datasheet view, where you can see all the new fields defined for this table, ready to receive records (Figure 2-21).

Note   To widen or narrow any column in Datasheet view, double-click the column header right border (or just click and drag it to the desired width).

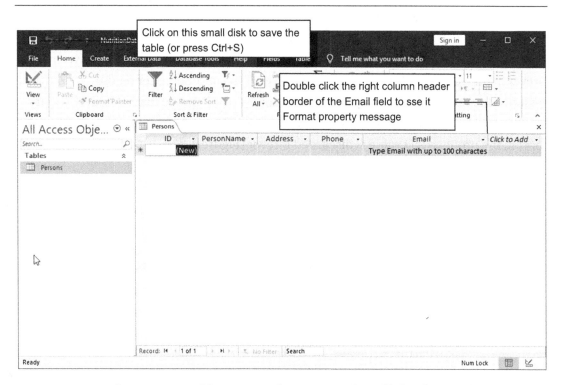

Figure 2-21. *The Persons table in Datasheet view after all the desired fields are defined*

Inserting Persons Records

With the Persons table opens in the Access interface, try to insert a new record by typing a single letter on the PersonName field. Then note these two things:

- The current record opens to Edit mode, receiving ID = 1 and a pencil icon on its row header.

- A new record is inserted below it (although the navigation buttons at the bottom of Datasheet view still show "Record 1 of 1").

Note that whenever you type a letter on the PersonName field, the Email field also loses its tip ("Type email with up to 50 characters"). This happened because the Email field's Allow Zero Length property was set to Yes. As soon as the record enters Edit mode, this field receives an empty string, which is not considered a Null value!

Now press Esc to abort the new record insertion and note that the record that you begin to type goes away (and the pencil icon returns to the default new record icon—the asterisk).

Type another letter on the PersonName field and note that this time the current record enters Edit mode, but now it receives ID = 2 (with a pencil icon on its row header).

The AutoNumber field for the Persons table now uses ID=2 (ID=1 goes away, forever...and will not be used again on this table). Type another letter on the PersonName field and press Esc successively, and you will notice that whenever you try to insert another record, its ID field will receive the new possible value, and when you abort it, the proposed ID value is discarded forever (Figure 2-22).

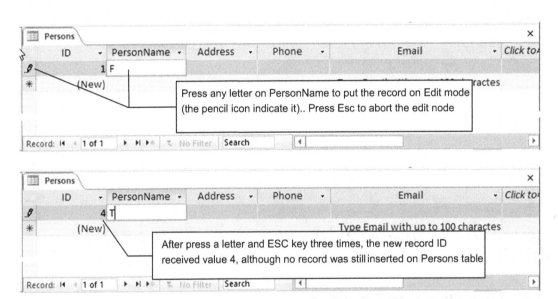

Figure 2-22. *Whenever you begin type anthing on a new record, Access will give the next ID based for the AutoNumber data type. By pressing Esc to abort the operation and typing anything to create another record, the next ID will be granted. The not-used ones are lost forever*

For most people, this behavior is odd, and they don't accept the fact that the AutoNumber field is just the table primary key, whose value is not important: just the fact that it unique among all records is.

So, the first lesson about the AutoNumber data type is that you can't control what value each record will receive, but you don't need to worry about it!

Note   By changing the ID field's New Values property from Increment to Random, each new value will be an incredible, enormous number that makes it unimportant to pay attention to.

Continue to type the first record and note how PersonName, Address, and Phone (with its input mask) behave. Note that the Edit icon is still present on the record. To save the new record, you can do one of the following:

- Keep pressing Tab until the next record is selected.

- Click another record.

- Close the Table window.

The edited record will be instantly saved to disk (Figure 2-23).

Note   There is no such thing like a Save Table command on databases. Whenever you click another table record, the one that was in Edit mode is immediately saved to the disk.

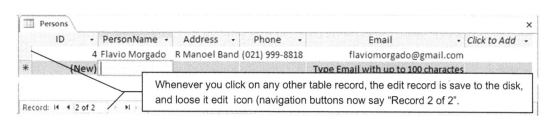

Figure 2-23. *To save any edited record, click any other record (or just close the table), and the edited record will be instantly saved or updated to the disk*

Creating the PersonsMeals Table

Now that you know how to create a table object, use the table's Datasheet or Design view to create the PersonsMeals table, which, according to Figure 2-1, must have the fields, data types, and properties set as specified in Table 2-4.

Table 2-4. *Fields, Data Types, and Properties Set for the PersonsMeals Table*

Field Name	Data Type	Properties to Set
ID	AutoNumber	
PersonsID	Number	Field Size = Long Integer Indexed = Yes (Duplicates OK)
MealName	Short Text	Field Size = 9 Required = Yes
MealDate	Date/Time	Format: Short Date Indexed = Yes (Duplicates OK)

Figure 2-24 shows the PersonsMeals table using Design view, so you can easily note all the proposed field names and data types. Note that the PersonsMeals table uses the Description (Optional) column to give a clue about what is stored in each table field.

Note   It is considered good programming practice to use the Description column to add a small comment to what is stored inside each database field. By proceeding this way, it will be easier for other people to understand the information stored inside each table field.

Some programmers use coded field names to avoid having unauthorized people use the database data. Personally, I dislike this approach.

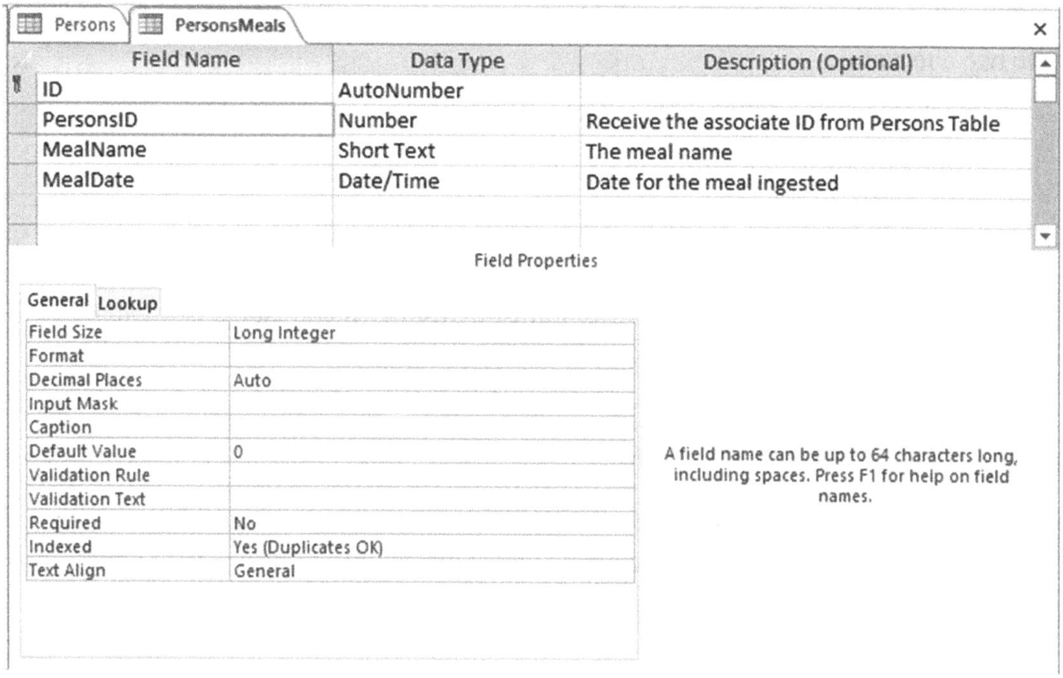

Field Name	Data Type	Description (Optional)
ID	AutoNumber	
PersonsID	Number	Receive the associate ID from Persons Table
MealName	Short Text	The meal name
MealDate	Date/Time	Date for the meal ingested

Field Properties

General Lookup

Field Size	Long Integer
Format	
Decimal Places	Auto
Input Mask	
Caption	
Default Value	0
Validation Rule	
Validation Text	
Required	No
Indexed	Yes (Duplicates OK)
Text Align	General

A field name can be up to 64 characters long, including spaces. Press F1 for help on field names.

Figure 2-24. *The PersonsMeals table in Design mode with the PersonID field selected. Since it is the foreign key to the Persons table (must be related to the Persons ID field, AutoNumber data type), it received the Number, Long Integer data type (same as AutoNumber)*

Using a Lookup List for the MealName Field

The MealName field has Field Size set to nine characters to allow you to insert the longest possible meal name: Breakfast (nine characters), Soup (four characters), Lunch (five characters), Snack (four characters), Dinner (six characters), and Supper (six characters).

To help or restrain what the user can insert on this field, you can make this field appear in Datasheet view using a Combo Box or List Box control, because both show a drop-down list of options.

- *List Box*: This restrains what the user can type to the elements of the list.

- *Combo Box*: This offers a list from where the user can choose an item, while allowing the user to type something out of the list.

To make a Number or Short Text field appear as a Combo Box or List Box control, you have two alternatives.

- Change the field's Data Type to Lookup.

- Use the Lookup tab found in the bottom grid of Design view for this field.

To see how both options works, let's begin using the Lookup data type, because it fires up the Lookup Wizard, which will simplify the things for you, because it will fill in the Lookup tab properties, allowing you to learn by example.

Using the Lookup Data Type

To make the MealName field receive a list filled with meal names from which the user can choose one option, click the MealName Data type column and choose Lookup Wizard (the last data type option, as shown in Figure 2-25).

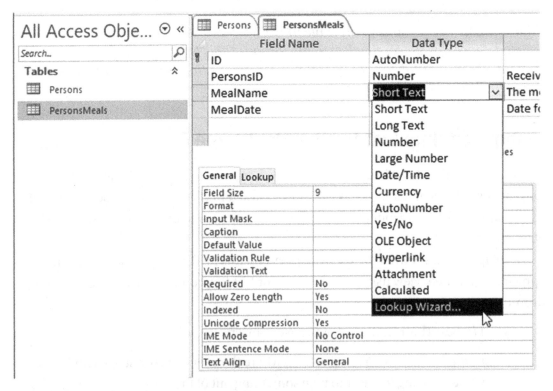

Figure 2-25. *To start the Lookup Wizard for any Number or Short Textf field, change the field Data Type to Lookup Wizard*

Note   The Microsoft Windows rules for good programming practice state that every menu option that opens another window must be followed by ellipsis, as you can see for the Lookup Wizard option.

Access will start the Lookup Wizard, which will ask if the list values will come from a table/query or from a list of typed options. See Figure 2-26.

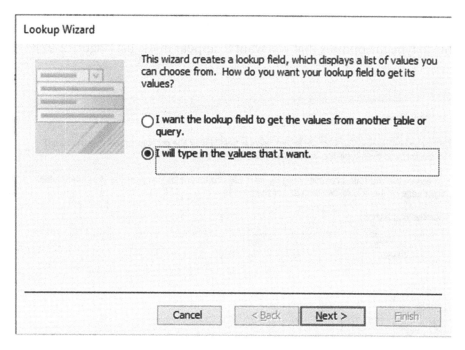

Figure 2-26.   *The Lookup Wizard asks if the list values will come from a table/query or from a list of typed options*

Depending on what you selected on the first Lookup Wizard option, the wizard will change the options you must provide on it in the next pages. By selecting the first option, "I want the lookup field to get the values from another table or query," you can use values stored on a table to define the field options.

Note   Whenever you use the Lookup Wizard on a table field that is the many side of a relationship and select a table or query that represents the one side of the relationship, and this relationship propagates a code value, Access can store the primary value in this field while showing another primary table field value in this table field, which can be somewhat confusing for the novice. You will see many examples of how this works in Chapter 4.

By selecting the "I will type in the values that I want" option and clicking Next, you will be able to type the options that you want to appear in the list (Figure 2-27).

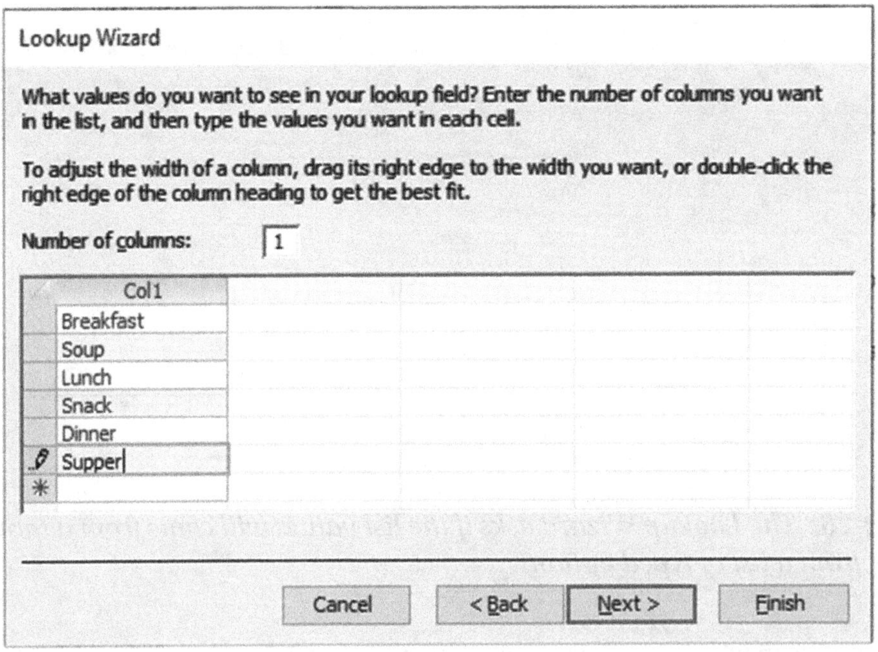

Figure 2-27. By selecting the "I will type in the values that I want" option on the first Lookup Wizard page, the second page will ask you to type all the values that you want, row by row.

Keep "Number of columns" set to 1, click the first empty option of the data grid, and type each meal name in the order you want it to appear on the list (press the down arrow to go to the next grid row). You must type Breakfast, Soup, Lunch, Snack, Dinner, and Supper.

Click Next, and the Lookup Wizard will show its third page, where you can decide the caption used to identify the list and select either Limit to List and Allow Multiple Values (Figure 2-28).

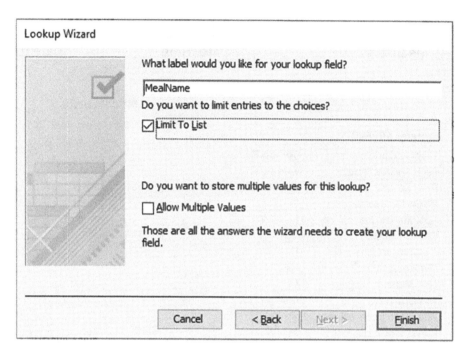

Figure 2-28. *The third Lookup Wizard page for typed list options, asking for a caption for the field and offering two new properties*

The Caption property will show the field name by default, but you can change it to another name, which will make the Lookup Wizard change the Field Caption property accordingly. The other two options are as follows:

- *Limit to List*: Check this option to not allow the user to add a new option to the list, in case they type anything different from the options you provide.

- *Allow Multiple Values*: This creates a multiselect list that will allow the user to select more than one list option for the field.

For the MealsName field, select the Limit to List option (to avoid having the user insert anything different from the meals on the list) and leave the Allow Multiselect Values option unchecked. Click Finish, and the Lookup Wizard will set the MealsName Field data type to Short Text, fulfilling the appropriate options on the Lookup tab for this field (Figure 2-29).

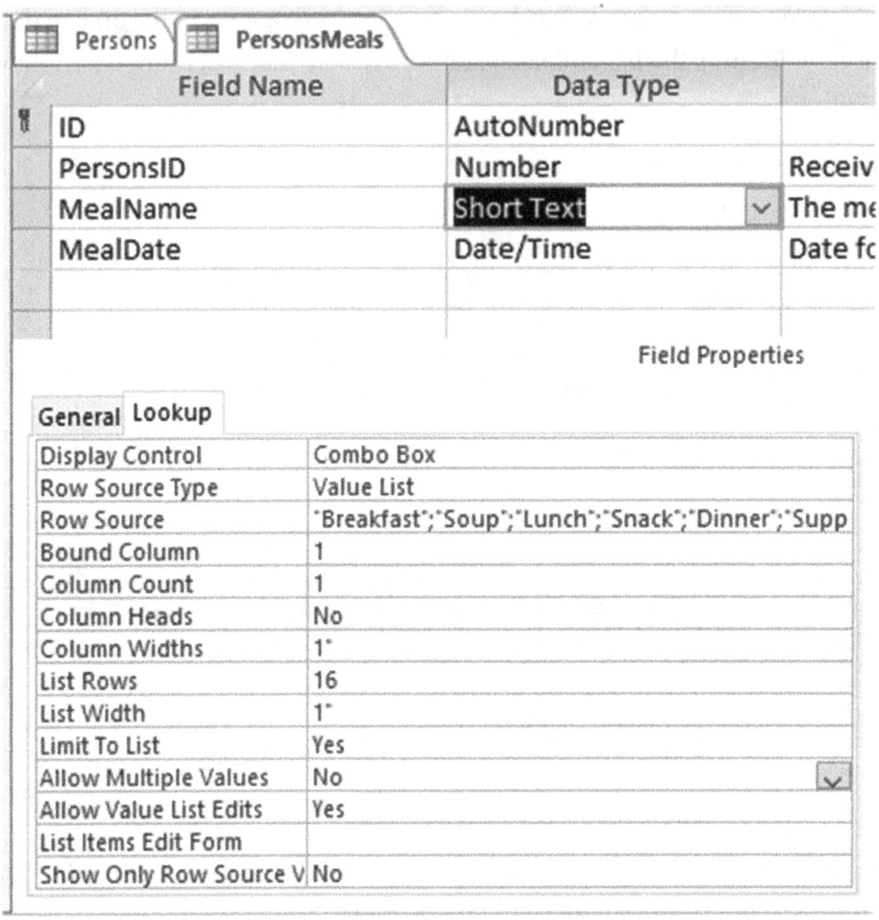

Persons	PersonsMeals	
Field Name	**Data Type**	
ID	AutoNumber	
PersonsID	Number	Receiv
MealName	Short Text ∨	The me
MealDate	Date/Time	Date fc

Field Properties

General **Lookup**

Display Control	Combo Box
Row Source Type	Value List
Row Source	"Breakfast";"Soup";"Lunch";"Snack";"Dinner";"Supp
Bound Column	1
Column Count	1
Column Heads	No
Column Widths	1"
List Rows	16
List Width	1"
Limit To List	Yes
Allow Multiple Values	No
Allow Value List Edits	Yes
List Items Edit Form	
Show Only Row Source V	No

Figure 2-29. *When you close the Lookup Wizard, it will fill the MealName field Lookup tab with the appropriate options, so the list will appear as you expected*

Note   Whenever you select the Allow Multiple Values option, Microsoft Access will check the Limit to List option and disable it. When the wizard finishes, it will also show a warning message asking you to save the table (Figure 2-30). The Allow Multiple Values option will automatically set these properties:

Display Control = List Box
Limit to List = Yes
Allow Multiple Values = Yes

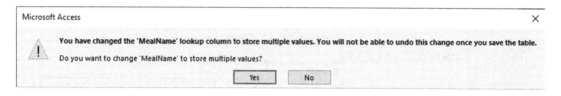

Figure 2-30. *This is the waning message given by the Lookup Wizard whenever you select the Allow Multiple Values option*

Whenever you set the Allow Multiple Values property for a field, each selected value cannot be greater than the specified Field Size property (or it will be truncated to the maximum field size), although all values selected can surpass this individual limit.

Access allows you to store up to 100 list values on a multiselected field (the one that has Property Allow Multiple Values = Yes).

Using the Lookup Tab

As you can see in Figure 2-29, the Lookup Wizard changes several properties on the Lookup tab for the MealsName controls.

- Display Control = Combo Box (type of control used to show the list options).

- Row Source Type = Value List (from where the list options come)

- Row Source = "Breakfast";"Soup";Lunch";"Snack";"Dinner";"Supper"

- (the list options, separated by semicolons, in order of appearance)

- Limit to List = Yes (allow just the list option values)

- Bound Column = 1

- Column Count = 1

- Allow Multiple Values = No

Switch the PersonsMeals table to Datasheet view, click the MealsName field, and note how Access limits the field entries to just the values offered by the drop-down list (Figure 2-31).

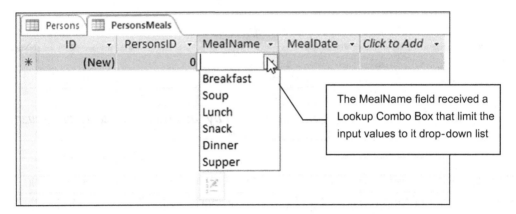

Figure 2-31. *This is the PersonsMeals table in Datasheet view after defining the MealsName Field Lookup properties to show a limited list of values, using the Lookup Wizard*

There are many other Lookup tab properties that you can set, which can vary according to what is selected on the Display Control property (Combo Box or List Box). Table 2-5 describes the available properties.

Table 2-5. *Field Lookup Properties (on the Lookup Tab)*

List Property	Meaning
Display Control	Combo Box lists all the available properties and may allow the user to type values not in the list. List Box lists all available properties except List Rows, List Width, and Limit to List. It allows just the list values. Text Box displays no properties and converts the Lookup properties to read-only.
Row Source Type	Specifies whether the list values will come from a table/query or from typed options.
Row Source	Defines the table/query name or the type's list options (separated by semicolons).
Bound Column	Works with the Column Count property. If the Row Source property offers more than one column, specify which column holds the field value (default is 1). This value can range from 1 to the number of columns in the row source. The column that supplies the value to store does not have to be the same column as the display column.

(*continued*)

Table 2-5. (*continued*)

List Property	Meaning
Column Count	Works with the Column Width property to define how many columns the list will show.
Column Heads	Specifies whether to display the first row values as column headings (or the field names whenever Row Source Type is set to a table/query).
Column Widths	Indicates each column width separated by semicolons (use 0 to hide a column). This works with the List Width property (that must be at least the sum of each individual column width).
List Rows	Defines the number of rows that appear in the drop-down list.
List Width	Defines the width of the drop-down list (which can be greater than the field width in the table's Datasheet view).
Limit To List	Defines whether the user can type a value that is not on the list.
Allow Multiple Values	Indicates whether the lookup field allows multiple values to be selected. You cannot change the value of this property from Yes to No.
Allow Value List Edits	Defines whether list items can be edited. By setting this property to Yes, right-click the Lookup field and select the Edit List Items menu option. This works only if the Column Count property is 1.
List Items Edit Form	Form name to use to edit the list item's if Row Source Type is set to Table/Query.
Show Only Row Source Values	Shows only values that match the current row source when Allow Multiples Values is set to Yes.

Note   You will see more about how to use Combo Box and List Box control properties in Chapter 4.

Using the Date/Time Data Type

The MealDate field of the Date/Time data type has another set of properties, including the Show Data Picker, which is set by default to "For dates." This setting means that Access will automatically associate it with a Calendar icon (on its right border). Clicking it allows you to select a date using a Calendar control (Figure 2-32).

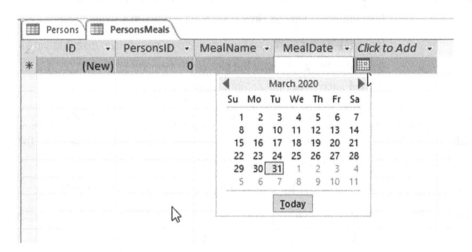

Figure 2-32. *Access sets the property Show Data Picker to "For dates" to any field associated to the Date/Time data type, like the MealDate field of the PersonsMeals table*

By changing the PersonsMeals table to Design view and selecting the MealDate field, you will note that Access offers another set of properties. Three of them can help you to insert a date value: Format, Input Mask, and Default Value (Figure 2-33).

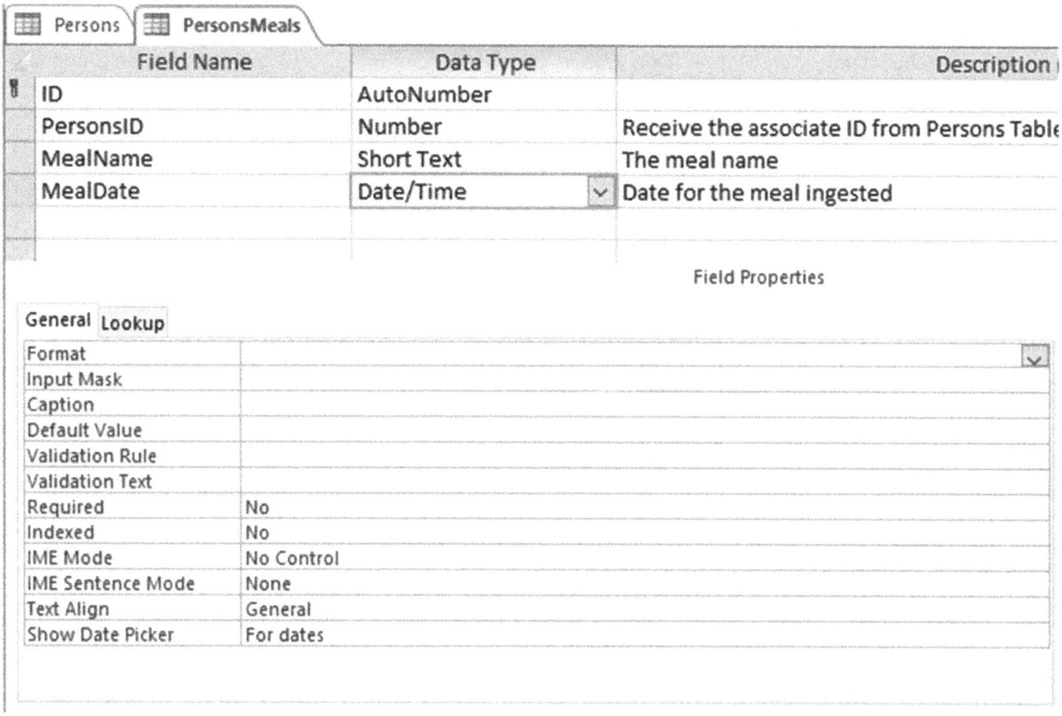

	Field Name	Data Type	Description
	ID	AutoNumber	
	PersonsID	Number	Receive the associate ID from Persons Table
	MealName	Short Text	The meal name
	MealDate	Date/Time	Date for the meal ingested

Field Properties

General Lookup

Format	
Input Mask	
Caption	
Default Value	
Validation Rule	
Validation Text	
Required	No
Indexed	No
IME Mode	No Control
IME Sentence Mode	None
Text Align	General
Show Date Picker	For dates

Figure 2-33. *The MealDate field, associated to a Date/Time data type, can use the Format, Input Mask, and Defaut Value properties to allow you to insert a date, an hour, or both*

Defining a Default Date/Time Value

Use the functions DATE(), TIME(), or NOW() on the Default Value property of a Date/Time field to automatically define the date, time, or both, respectively, for a new record according to the system clock (the opening and closing parentheses are mandatory for Access to identify them as functions).

Figure 2-34 shows the MealDate field in Design view, with its Default Value property set to the NOW() function. The figure shows what happens when you switch to Datasheet view: the new record is automatically filled with the current date and hour of the system clock, which, of course, can be changed by the user.

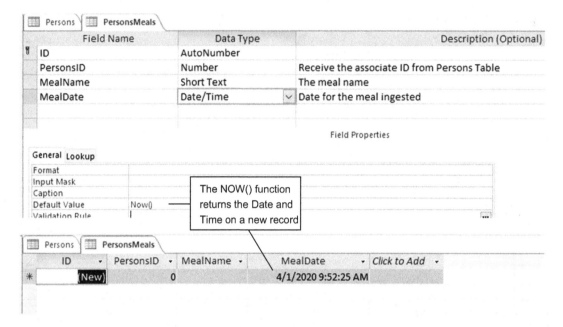

Figure 2-34. *Use the functions DATE(), TIME(), or NOW() to return the current date, time, or both as the Default Value property of any Date/Time field, according to the system clock*

Defining the Format Property for a Date/Time Field

Most operating systems, such as Microsoft Windows, treat dates and hour values as numbers. In fact, whenever you set a field to the Date/Time data type, you are indeed associating it to the Number, Double data type (an 8-byte floating-point data type that can store at least 15 significant digits). The integer part stores date values, while the decimal part stores hour values, using up to 15 milliseconds of precision.

In fact, dates are stored as a Long integer, where 0 (zero) represents 12/30/1899. Positive values count days since that date (1 = 1/1/1900). Negative integers represents days before 12/31/1899.

Hours are stored as a decimal value, meaning a fraction of a day. For example, 0.5 means 12 p.m.

Note   To insert a date and a time on a single field, type the date separating the month, day, and year by a slash or hyphen, add an space, and type an hour and minute separated by a colon (using mm/dd/yy hh:mm, or dd-mm-yy hh:mm). Note that you just need to type the two last digits for the year and that you do not need to type seconds, but if you want type it, separate it by another colon: hh:mm:ss).

The way that Access shows the return value of the NOW() function inserted on the Default Value property of the MealDate field (separating date and hour by an space, with the hour in 12-hour mode, followed by AM or PM, is in fact created by a predefined Format property). By using the Format property on a Date/Time field, you can choose among a set of predefined date/time formats, which can be automatically selected by expanding the Format list box for the Date/Time field. The list also shows examples of how they behave (see Figure 2-35).

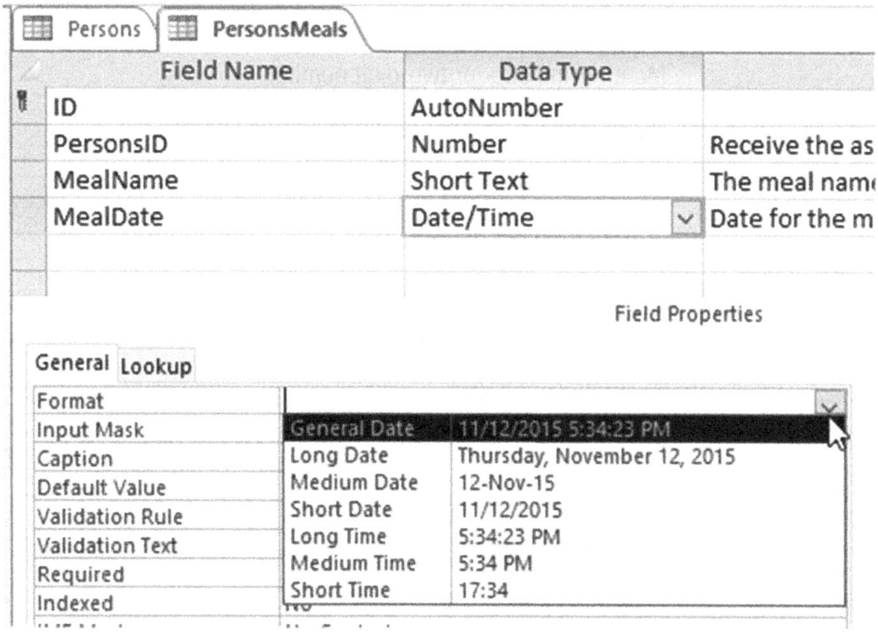

Figure 2-35. *Use the Format property list on any Date/Time field to choose one of the many predefined date/time formats available*

The default format is General Date, used to show the return of the NOW() function, which returns both the date and the time from the system clock. Each of these predefined formats uses specific format characters for placeholders and separators, as specified on Table 2-6.

Table 2-6. *Placeholders or Separators You Can Use on Any of the Four Format Areas (for Positive, Negative, Zero, or Null Values)*

Character	Description
Date separator	/ or – (the separator defined in the Windows regional settings)
Time separator	: (the separator defined in the Windows regional settings)
c	Displays the general date format
d or dd	Day of the month as one or two digits
ddd	Day of the week abbreviated to three letters
dddd	Day of the week spells out
ddddd	Short Date format
dddddd	Long Date format
w	Day of the week (1 to 7)
ww	Week of the year (1 to 53)
m or mm	Month using one- or two-digit number
mmm	Name of the month abbreviated to three letters
mmmm	Name of the month spelled out
q	Current calendar quarter (1–4)
y	Day of the year (1–366)
yy	Last two digits of the year
yyyy	Year with four digits
h or hh	Hour with one or two digits
n or nn	Minutes as one or two digits
s or ss	Seconds with one or two digits
tttt	Long Time format
AM/PM ; am/pm A/P; a/p	Twelve-hour clock with uppercase or lowercase letters (AM/PM, am/pm; A/P, a/p)

Now you know that the Format property employs different characters to return the year, month, day, day of week, day of year, week, hour, minutes, seconds, etc. Access implements Long Date format using a format string as follows:

dddd mmmm dd", "yyyy

> where

> > dddd = Day of week spelled out

> > mmmm = Month spelled out

> > ", " = Insert a dot and an space

> > yyyy = Year with four digits

Using an Input Mask for a Date/Time Field

If you want to make it easier or mandatory for the user to insert a specific value on a Date/Time field (like just the hour), you can use the Input Mask Wizard for this field, which will show only predefined input masks for dates or times, offering a nice way to learn how each one can be created.

Figure 2-36 shows the Input Mask Wizard after it was opened by clicking the ellipsis button to the right of the MealName Input Mask property, using the Long Time Input Mask selected as an example.

Note that to allow the insertion of a long time (12:00:00 PM, which includes hours, minutes, seconds, and AM/PM), it uses an Input Mask value of 99:00:00 >LL.

Note   See Table 2-2 for a list of character placeholders used to compose an input mask.

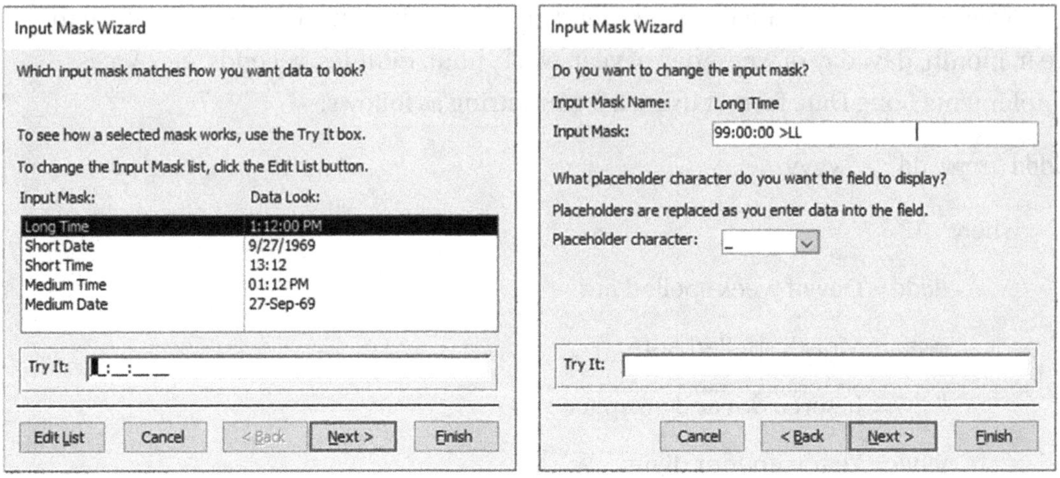

Figure 2-36. *Use the Input Mask Wizard on any Date/Time field to learn how you can create an input mask to force the user to insert a date or an hour using specific formats*

You may note that the Input Mask Wizard does not offer a predefined input mask to allow the user to insert a date and time simultaneously on a Date/Time field, which can be created using this input mask code:

`00/00/0000\ 00:00;0;_`

This input mask uses the 0 (zero) character placeholder to require that the user type the entire date and hour in 24-hour format. It also has three parts separated by two semicolons.

- the input mask;
- 0= on second part to save values and placeholders
- The _ character as Input Mask placeholder

Figure 2-37 shows that you can use an input mask to get the user input for the date and time on a single field and use a Format value to show a different value (day or week and month name fully spelled out).

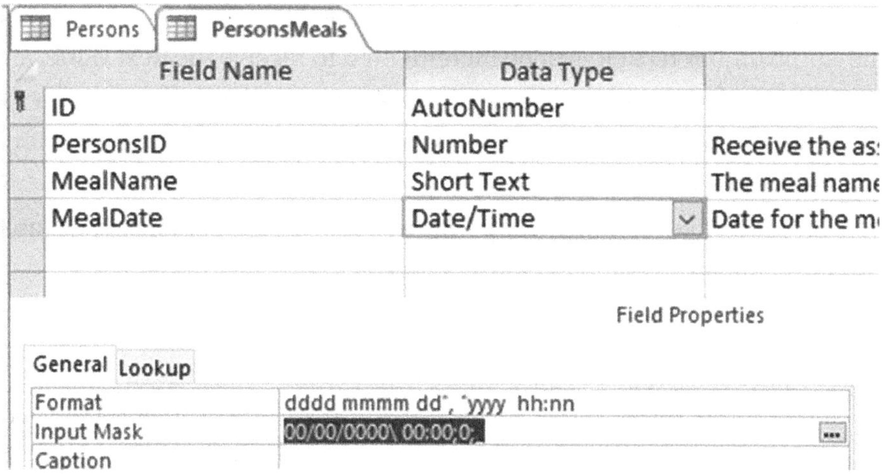

Field Name	Data Type	
ID	AutoNumber	
PersonsID	Number	Receive the as
MealName	Short Text	The meal name
MealDate	Date/Time	Date for the m

Field Properties

General Lookup

Format	dddd mmmm dd", `yyyy hh:nn
Input Mask	00/00/0000\ 00:00;0;
Caption	

Figure 2-37. *You can capture user input for a Date/Time field using an input mask to ask the user to type a date and an hour and show what is typed using a different format, which will include the day of week and month names spelled out*

Inserting PersonsMeals Records

After you've defined all the proposed fields for the PersonsMeals table, switch it to Datasheet view and try to insert a new record by selecting any MealName value in the list.

You will note that Access will instantly define ID as 1 for your first attempt (since ID is an AutoNumber field and the table's primary key).

Also try to type a meal date and hour and note how the input mask and the format proposed in Figure 2-37 works. You can type a numeric date while showing it using a literal expression.

Whenever you click the new record again, the PersonsMeals record will be saved to disk, the AutoNumber ID field will be incremented to receive the next value, and the PersonsMeals table will be waiting to receive another record. Also note that the MealName is only required on the PersonsMeals table. You can easily insert another record by just selecting again a MealName in the list of a new record.

Figure 2-38 shows five records successively inserted on the PersonsMeals table, each having a different MealName and PersonID set to 0.

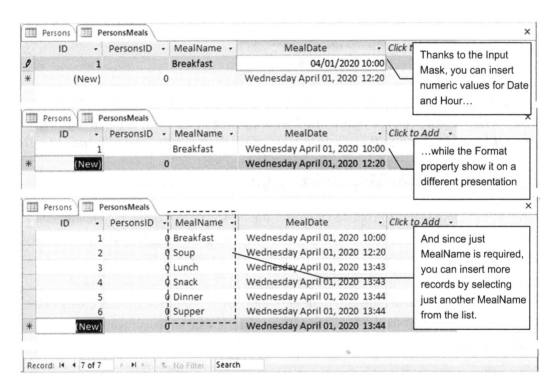

Figure 2-38. *Select a MealName using the list defined for this field, type a date and a time on the MealDate field, and click the new record below to insert the record on the PersonsMeals table. Note that you can insert numeric dates and times and show them in a different way using the Input Mask and Format properties*

Do you know what is really wrong with the records inserted on the PersonsMeals table typed in Figure 2-38?

It received six meal records that represent meals taken on a given date and time associated to nobody! No Persons table records were associated to the PersonsMeals records, which in terms of the database integrity makes no sense.

To avoid such discrepancies in the database records, you need to relate the Persons and PersonsMeals tables, enforcing referential integrity between them.

Relating the Persons and PersonsMeals Tables

To establish a relationship between the tables Persons and PersonsMeals, where Persons is the primary table and PersonsMeals is the related table with a one-to-many relationship (each Persons record can have many related PersonsMeals records), you must first delete all the records from the related table (PersonsMeals). This is because Access will search for such discrepancies when it tries to enforce referential integrity between them (PersonsMeals records with no association with a Persons record).

Deleting All the Table Records

To delete all the records from any table, apply the same approach used by Excel to clean up any spreadsheet, shown here:

1. Open the desired table by double-clicking it in the Database window to show its records.

2. Click the small gray button located on its data grid in the top-left corner (the one above the first row header and to the left of the first column header) to select all the table records.

3. Press the Delete key.

Access will show a warning message about how many records will be deleted from the table. Take care with such an operation, because differently from Excel, such mass deletions can't be undone on a database.

Figure 2-39 shows how you can use this approach to select and delete all PersonsMeals records at once.

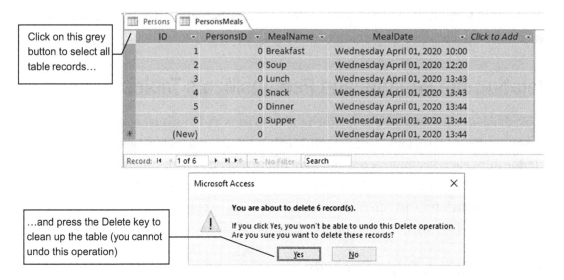

Figure 2-39. *To delete all table records at once, click the small gray button located in the table Datasheet view's top-left corner and press the Delete key. Access will ask for a confirmation before continue with the deletion. This operation can't be undone*

Now you must close both tables (Persons and PersonsMeals) so Access can enforce a relationship between them.

Referential Integrity Between Persons and PersonsMeals

Supposing that the related table (the one on the many side of a one-to-may relationship) has no record and that both the primary and related tables are closed, you are able to define a relationship between the primary table (one side) and the related table (the many side).

This operation is conducted by Access using the Relationships window that can be shown using two different strategies.

- By selecting the Relationships command located in the Relationships area of the Database Tools tab of the Ribbon

- By selecting the Relationships command located in the Relationships area on the Table tab of the Table Tools tab that appears whenever a table is opened on Access interface

Adding Tables to the Relationships Window

Whenever you show the Relationships window for a database where no relationships have been defined, Access will automatically show the Show Table windows, offering a list of all existing table objects for the current database.

Double-click the Persons table and then the PersonsMeals table to insert them into the Relationships windows and close the Show Table window to insert a table representation of both tables, showing its first field names, side by side (Figure 2-40).

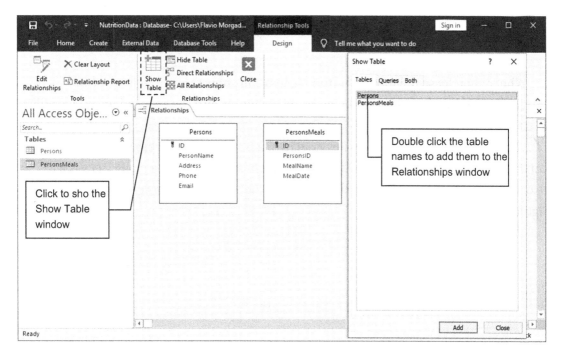

Figure 2-40. *Use the Show Table window to double-click the desired tables and add table representations to the Relationships window*

Note   If the Relationships window has been saved once, the Show Table window will not be automatically shown. You will need to click the Show Table command in the Relationships area of the Database Tools tab to show it again.

Tip   If needed, you can drag the table's representation on the Relationships window to a new position.

Close the Show Tables window to implement a relationship between the tables added to the Relationships windows.

Creating a Table Relationship

Follow the next steps to create a relationship between the two tables inserted in the Relationships window:

1. Click the field on the primary key field of the primary table to select it.

2. Drag the primary key field to the foreign key field of the related table.

When you release the mouse button, Access will show the Edit Relationships window, using a grid to indicate the name of each table and the selected fields that will be used on the new relationship.

If you have dragged a primary key field over a possible foreign key field (one that is not the primary key on the related table and that has the same data type), Access will also show the relationship type at the bottom of the window (in this case, one-to-many, Figure 2-41).

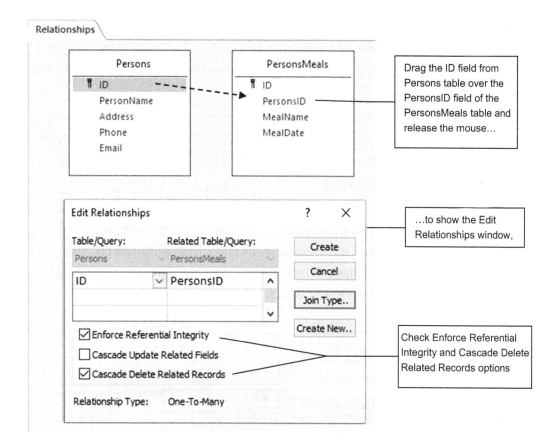

Figure 2-41. *Whenever you drag the primary key field from the primary table over the possible foreign key field of the future related table and release the mouse button, Access will show the Edit Relationships window, where you can set the relationship properties*

The Edit Relationships window offers three options at the bottom.

- *Enforce referential integrity:* This will force Access to look up if there is any record on the right table (related table) that violates the proposed one-to-many relationship.

- *Cascade Update Related Fields:* This will automatically propagate changes on all related table records, whenever the value of the primary key record of the primary table changes.

- *Cascade Delete Related Records:* This will automatically delete records on the related table whenever a record is deleted on the primary table.

91

Check Enforce Referential Integrity and Cascade Delete Related Records for this relationship between the ID field of the Persons table and the PersonsID field of the PersonsMeals table and click OK to close the Edit Relationships window and create the proposed relationship.

Note   Since the ID field of the Persons table received the AutoNumber data type (that cannot be changed), there is no need to check Cascade Updated Related Fields for the proposed relationship.

Access will check whether both tables are closed and whether there are any unassociated records inserted on the PersonsMeals table. If everything is OK, the relationship between the two tables will be established, using a line to indicate the relationship type (the one and the many sides, as shown in Figure 2-42).

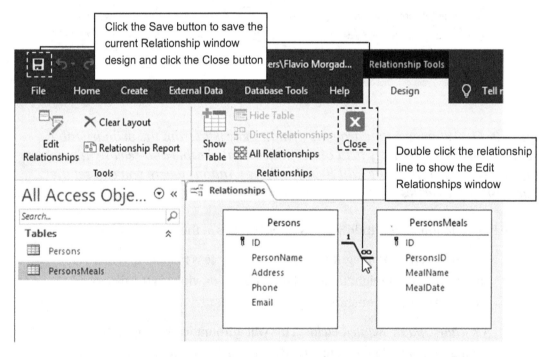

Figure 2-42. *By closing the Edit Relationhip window, Access will enforce the relationship between the Persons and PersonsMeals tables, using a join line to indicate the related fields and relationship type (1 to ∞)*

Note   To verify the relationship type enforced between any two tables, double-click the relationship line that joins them to show the Edit Relationships window.

Before closing the Relationships window, click the Save button on the Quick Access toolbar to save the current design. Access will always warn you before close the window whenever you have made any changes in it.

Note   Whenever you save the Relationships window, you are saving the tables' position inside the window, not the relationships created between the database tables.

Inserting Related Records

Now that the Persons and PersonsMeals tables are related with referential integrity enforced between them, open the PersonsMeals table and try to insert a new record by selecting any item in the MealName field list and then selecting another record.

The Access database engine will issue a warning message indicating that now you can't insert a PersonsMeals table record without associating it to an existing Persons table record (by typing an existing Persons table ID value on the PersonsMeals table's PersonsID field, as shown in Figure 2-43).

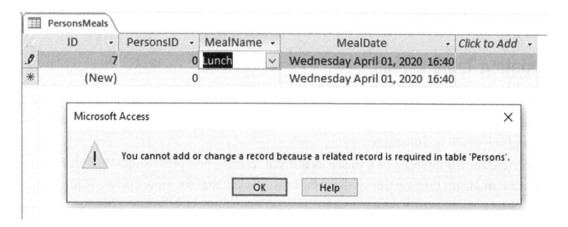

Figure 2-43.   *Because referential integrity was enforced between the Persons and PersonsMeals tables, you cannot add a PersonsMeals record without typing a valid PersonsID value (any existing Persons table ID value)*

The good news is that you can easily do this using the Persons table, the one side of the relationship, that now will show a small + character to the left of the ID field (primary key and related field). Click it to expand it, and note that Access will show all PersonsMeals fields below the selected record, ready to receive new records.

Select any list item on the MealName field to see that Access automatically propagates the ID field value of the current record on the Persons table to the PersonsID field of the PersonsMeals table (Figure 2-44).

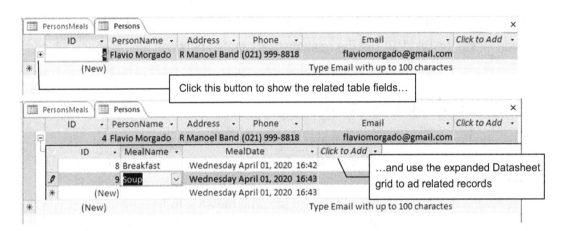

Figure 2-44. *Open the Persons table, click the + to the left of the ID field to expand it, and show all PersonsMeals field headers. Then click the MealName list to select different meals for each new record. Access will automatically fill in the PersonsID field (foreign key, related field, hidden by interface) with the Persons ID field*

Updating Table Values

The records you inserted on the PersonsMeals table were not automatically propagated to the PersonsMeals table if it is still open in the Access interface. Click the PersonsMeals tab and see that it is still empty.

To update any table, open it to see its current records, and press Shift+F9. Every insertion made on the one side of the relationship will instantly show up. See Figure 2-45.

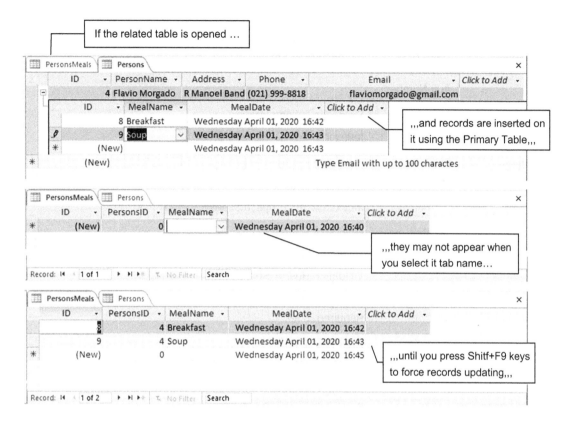

Figure 2-45. *Whenever you use the primary Persons table's Datasheet view to insert records on the related PersonsMeals table, if the PersonsMeals table is open, the records inserted may not appear instantly on it. Press Shift+F9 to force Access to update the table records*

Creating the PersonsMealsFoods Table

To finish the NutritionData database design, you must create the PersonsMealsFoods table. According to Figure 2-1, PersonsMealsFoods must receive the PersonsMealsID, FoodName, Qty, and Calories fields. See Table 2-7 for how to define the properties.

Table 2-7. *Fields, Data Types, and Properties Set for the Personsmealsfoods Table*

Field Name	Data Type	Properties to Set
ID	AutoNumber	
PersonsMealsID	Number	Field Size = Long Integer Indexed = Yes (Duplicates OK)
FoodName	Short Text	Field Size = 150 Required = Yes Indexed = Yes (Duplicates OK)
Qty	Number	Field Size = Single Default Value = 1 Validation Rule = >0 Validation Text = Quantity can't be zero or a negative value Required = Yes
Measure	Short Text	Field Size = 20 Required = Yes Lookup Properties: Display Control = Combo Box Row Source Type = Value list Row Source = oz; fl oz; g; ml; Tea spoon; Table spoon; Cup; Piece Limit To List = No
Calories	Number	Field Size = Integer

Click the Create tab, select the Table command, and use the Datasheet or Design view to define PersonsMealsFoods in the NutritionData database. Figure 2-47 shows this table in Design view, having all the Table 2-7 proposed fields and properties set (with a brief description of each field meaning).

Please note the following:

- *PersonsMealsID*: Set to Number. Set Field Size to Long Integer. This will be the table's foreign key. The foreign key field will store the associated PersonsMeals record's ID field.

- *FoodName*: Set to Short Text. Set Field Size to 150. This is used to store the name of any food or recipe name ingested during the meal.

- *Qty*: Set to Number. Set Field Size to Single to allow users to type decimal values, like 1,5 portions. This is used to store the amount of the food ingested during the meal.

Note   The Qty field has a default value of 1, Validation Rule is set to 0, and Validation Text indicates that zero or negative quantities are not allowed.

- *Measure*: Set to Short Text. Set Field Size to 20. This is used to store the type of measure expressed by Qty. It uses the Look Up tab to define a Combo Box that offers a list of common measures (oz; fl oz; g; ml; Tea spoon; Table spoon; Cup; Piece), with Limit To List set to No to allow insert a measure out of the list.

Figure 2-46 shows the PersonsMealsFoods table using two views, so you can see the Qty field set to a default value of 1, Validation Rule set to >0 (negative values are not allowed), Validation Text set to Quantity (which can't be a negative value), and Required set to Yes (a positive quantity must be typed).

Note   You can also set the validation rule and validation text properties on the table's Datasheet view by using the Validation tool in the FieldValidation area of the Fields tab (see Figure 2-4). Whenever you set a validation rule expression and this expression is evaluated as false, the Microsoft Access database engine will show a message box using the validation text to explain that the field validation rule was not set.

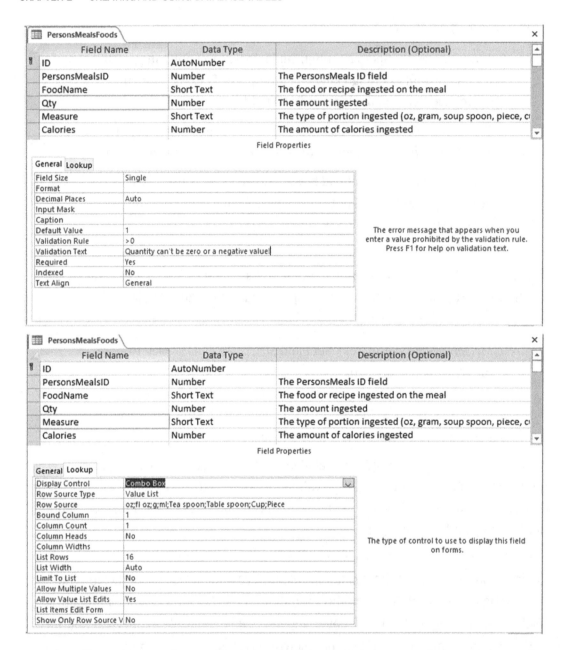

Figure 2-46. *The PersonsMealsFoods table in Design view, with all fields properties defined as shown in Table 2-7*

Having created and saved the PersonsMealsFoods table settings according to Table 2-7, view it in Datasheet view. Note that the Qty field already is set to 1, and the Measure field has a list showing some popular food measures (Figure 2-47).

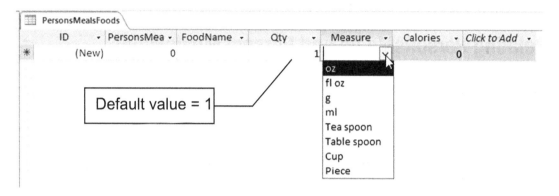

Figure 2-47. *The Qty field has a default value of 1 (and a validation rule that imposes it as a positive, nonzero value)*

If you type zero or a negative value on it (like -1) and press Enter to try to leave the field, Microsoft Access will show a message box with the Validation text defined for the field (Figure 2-48).

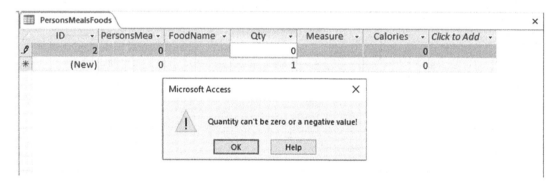

Figure 2-48. *Since Qty field has Validation Rule set to >0, if you type 0 or a negative value and try to leave the field, Microsoft Access will verify that the validation rule was broken and will issue a message box showing the Valitation Text property*

Since you already know that PersonsMealsFoods without a PersonsMealsID value means foods consumed not associated to a meal or person, if you added such records on the PersonsMealsFoods table, delete them all and close the PersonsMealsFoods table to impose referential integrity between it and the PersonsMeals table.

Relating PersonsMeals and PersonsMealsFoods

To relate PersonsMeals and PersonsMealsFoods on the NutritionData database, follow these steps:

1. Close all database tables.

2. Open the Relationships window (found in the Relationships area of the Database Tools tab).

3. Click the Show Table command to show the list of all database tables.

4. Double-click the PersonsMealsFoods table to add it to the Relationships window (Figure 2-49).

5. Close the Relationships window.

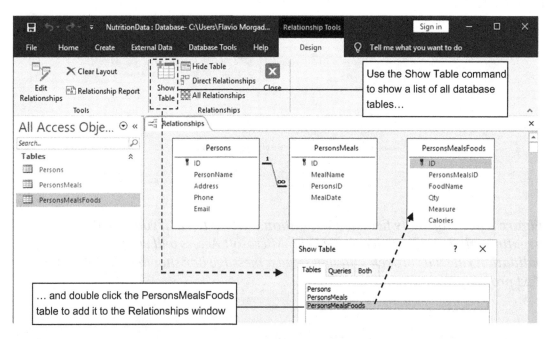

Figure 2-49. *Use the Show Table command to show the Show Tables windows and double-click the PersonsMealsFoods table to add it to the Relationships window*

After closing the Show Table window, click the PersonID field of the PersonsMeals table representation and drag it to the PersonsMealsID field of the PersonsMealsFoods table.

Microsoft Access will open the Edit Relationships window, which shows the related fields (PersonsMeals ID field related to PersonsMealsFoods PersonsMealsID) and at the bottom the relationship type (one to many, since the ID field is the PersonsMeals primary key and the PersonsMealsID field is a long integer—the same data type). Select the Enforce Referential Integrity and Cascade Delete Related Records options (Figure 2-50).

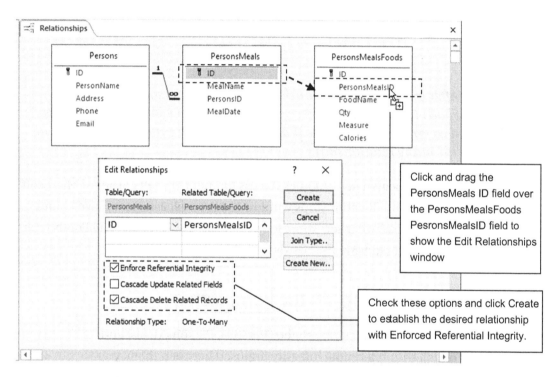

Figure 2-50. *After adding PersonsMealsFoods to the Relationships window, click the PersonsMeals table ID field and drag it over the PersonsMealsFoods table PersonsMealsID field. Release the mouse button to show the Edit Relationships window and check Enforce Referential Integrity and Cascade Delete Related Records*

Click the Create button of the Edit Relationships window to create the relationship and close the Edit Relationships window. Microsoft Access will show a new line joining both tables, indicating that they are now related (the 1 and ∞ symbols used on the join line indicates the relationship type, one to many, as shown in Figure 2-51).

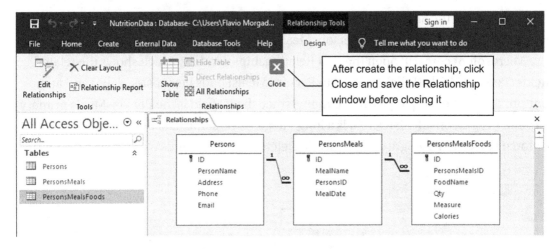

Figure 2-51. *After creating the relationship between the PersonsMeals and PersonsMealsFoods tables, Microsoft Access will show a line joining both tables using the 1 and ∞ symbols to indicate that it imposes referential integrity among them on a one-to-many relationship*

Click the small disk located on the Quick Access toolbar (top-left corner of Microsoft Access window) or close the Relationships window (Access will ask you to save before closing it). You are now ready to insert some food items on the PersonsMealsFoods table associated to any of the PersonsMeals records.

Inserting Related Records for Food Items

Now that all three proposed tables are related (Persons, PersonsMeals, and PersonsMealsFoods), with referential integrity imposed between them, you cannot insert a food item on the PersonsMealsFoods table unless you type a valid PersonsFoodsID value (any ID value existing on the PersonsMeals table).

The same way you inserted meal records on the PersonsMeals table using the Persons table in Datasheet view, now insert food items for any meal records.

1. Open the Persons table in Datasheet view.

2. Click any Persons ID field + icon to expand it and show the PersonsMeals table with its meal records.

3. Click any PersonsMeals ID field's + icon to also expand it and show the PersonsMeals table, ready to receive new food items for any inserted meal record.

Figure 2-52 shows how to insert a new food item for the first Persons table record, using its first PersonsMeals record, by clicking its ID field to expand Datasheet view to show the PersonsMealsFood table headers (according to the USDA, 1 cup (235g) of a whole milk yogurt has 149 calories).

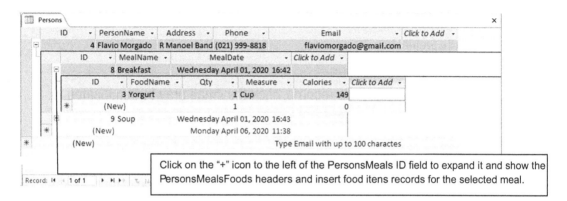

Figure 2-52. *Since all three tables of the NutritionData database are now related with referential integrity imposed between them, you can use the Persons table to insert PersonsMeals and PersonsMealsFoods records*

You can continue to insert as many food items on the PersonsMealsFoods table, automatically associating them to the selected PersonsMeals table record (and to the selected Persons table record).

Cascading Delete Records

Since all three tables (Persons, PersonsMeals, and PersonsMealsFoods) are related, with referential integrity imposed and the Cascade Delete Related Records option selected, you can easily delete related records by deleting any Persons table record.

For each deleted Persons table record, the database engine will delete every related PersonsMeals records, which will force cascading deletes on all PersonsMealsFoods records.

This means you can easily clear your database by clearing the Persons table.

To delete all Persons table records and consequently delete all PersonsMeals and PersonsMealsFoods related records, follow these steps:

1. Open the Persons table.

2. Click any desired row header record (the small gray square located to the left of the ID field).

3. Press the Delete key.

Note   To delete all Persons table records, click the small gray button located to the left of the table column headers.

Microsoft Access will show a message box stating that you are about to delete n records (according to the number of records selected). This operation can't be undone. Click Yes to proceed and clear all related tables. See Figure 2-53.

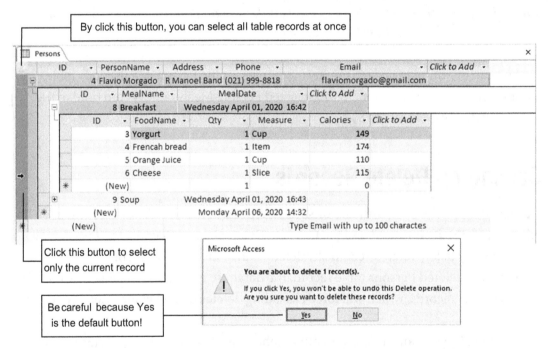

Figure 2-53. *Since Persons, PersonsMeals, and PersonsMealsFoods have referential integrity between them, the Cascade Delete Related Records option is selected. By deleting a record on the Persons table, all related records on the PersonsMeals and PersonsMealsFoods are also automatically deleted. By deleting all Persons records, you will clear the database*

Note Although the Cascade Delete Related Records option is quite efficient for deleting related records, it is also equally dangerous, since record deletion can't be undone on the database. By imposing this option on all related tables, you can easily destroy your database's source of information. To avoid such a problem, it is recommended that the last related table (in this case, PersonsMealsFoods) does not impose the Cascade Delete Related Records option. You will need to manually delete all its records before deleting any Persons record.

Summary

In this chapter, you learned about how Microsoft Access is a powerful database program that allows you to create a fully relational database by creating tables with different types of fields and properties that can be set to change the database behavior.

In the next chapter, you will learn about queries and their power to return database records and interact with the database tables.

CHAPTER 3

Creating Queries

If tables constitute the heart of any database, queries are the veins that keep the record information flowing at a high speed. In this chapter, you will learn about how to use queries to extract information from database tables. To achieve this, this chapter will use a professional database, full of tables and records, so you can better understand the power of queries.

You can download the files and database objects in this chapter by extracting the file CHAPTER03.zip from the following website:

https://github.com/Apress/intro-microsoft-access-using-macro-prog-techniques

The sr28.accdb Nutritional Database

The Nutrient Standard Reference file is from the Methods and Application of Food Composition Laboratory (MAFCL) of the Agricultural Research Services (ARS) of the United States Department of Agriculture (USDA), whose aim is to develop and maintain food composition databases for foods available in the United States. The file is named with *srxx*, where *xx* is a consecutive number that specifies the file version.

You can download this SR file for free from the MAFCL web page, which you can find by searching for *ARS SR database*. You'll find a ZIP file that offers two different file types.

- srxxASC.ZIP: This file contains TXT files, which use a comma-separated value (CSV) structure, that are ready to be imported into any database system. Each table is in a different file.

- srxxDB.ZIP: This file contains an Access database file, offering MDB versions up to sr26 and ACCDB versions for sr27 and sr28 files. This is the latest database version updated, published in 2015.

© Flavio Morgado 2021
F. Morgado, *Introducing Microsoft Access Using Macro Programming Techniques*,
https://doi.org/10.1007/978-1-4842-6555-0_3

Note   You can find a copy of the sr28DB.ZIP files in the Chapter01.ZIP file.

So, go ahead and download a copy of the sr28DB.ZIP file and extract it into any folder on your computer. You will find two files inside it.

- sr28.accdb: This is a Microsoft Access ACCDB file format, compatible with Access 2007 or later versions.

- sr28_doc.pdf: This is an Adobe Acrobat file that documents the database content and usage.

Note   The sr28.accdb file is the latest version of the ARS SR files published using a database format.

Once you have downloaded and extracted the contents of the sr28.accdb file, open the file inside Microsoft Access to show a list of its objects (tables, queries, and reports) in the Database window (Figure 3-1).

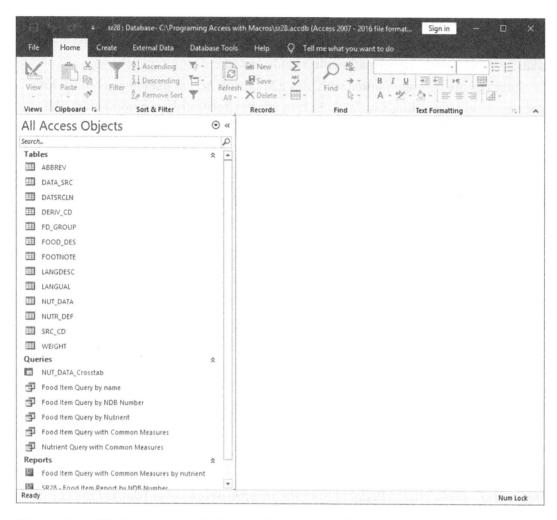

Figure 3-1. *The Database window of the sr28.accdb database, the latest SR file for nutritional information published by the ARS USDA website*

As you can see in Figure 3-1, the `sr28.accdb` database has lots of tables, but their names don't offer any significant meaning for usage. The database also has some native queries and report examples that you can use to see how to extract data from the database.

Note   The `sr28.accdb` native queries and reports will not be used in this book, but you can look at them to learn how they work. They will not be deleted from the book files in respect to the development team that built them and made them available to database users.

The ARS IT team offers us the `sr28_doc.pdf` file, which is a well-produced source of database documentation that indicates the table names and contents, their relationships, and what information their fields provide.

Since you are now acquainted with how a Microsoft Access database is built, your first step to understanding any database is to use the Relationships command on the Database Tools tab to show the Relationships window. Figure 3-2 shows how the 13 tables are related.

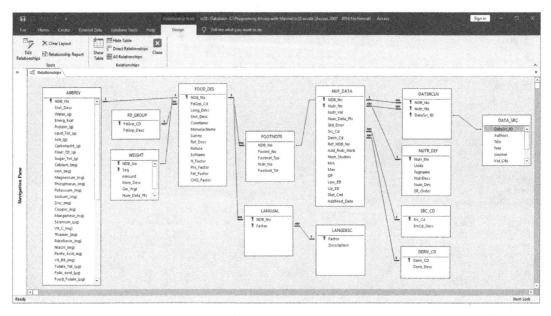

Figure 3-2. *The st28.accdb database's Relationships window. You can use the Relationships window to understand how the database works by observing the relationships of its 13 tables*

Did you say, "Wow..."?

Welcome to the world of professionally designed databases, which we are about to unveil! Table 3-1 lists all the `sr28.accdb` table names, descriptions, and number of records, according to the information grabbed from the `sr28_doc.pdf` file.

Table 3-1. *sr28.Accdb Database Tables*

	Table Name	Description	Records
Derived	ABBREV	Food item with nutritional information derived from the database	8,790
Principal tables	FOOD_DES	FOOD item DEScription	8,790
	NUT_DATA	NUTrient DATA (for each food item)	679,045
	WEIGHT	WEIGHT of most common measures for each food item	15,438
	FOOTNOTE	Additional information about how each food item nutrient value was determined	553
Support tables	FD_GROUP	FooD GROUP description	25
	LANGUAL	LANGUAL factor	38,301
	LANGDESC	LANGual factors DESCription	774
	NUTR_DEF	NUTRient DEFfinition	150
	SRC_CD	SouRCe CoDe	10
	DERIV_CD	Data DERIVation CoDe description	55
	DATSRCLN	SouRces of DATA LiNk	244,496
	DATA_SRC	SouRCes of DATA	681

Although the `sr28.accdb` database may appear scary at first, it is not! As shown in Table 3-1, the 13 tables are divided into two main groups: principal tables and support tables.

To make use of the nutritional information in the database, you can use the ABBREV derived table, the four principal tables, and the two support tables.

- *ABBREV*: This is not a principal database table but a derived table produced using the principal table records and a limited amount of nutrients (46). It has 8,790 records, which is the same as the FOOD_DES record count.

- *FOOD_DES*: This includes food item names (using a short or long description) with associated data (such as commercial and manufacturer names and a refuse, or waste, amount, if any). It has 8,790 food item records.

- *NUT_DATA*: This contains nutritional data expressed by 100g of each food item. Each record refers to nutrient information. This is the longest database table with 679,045 records.

- *WEIGHT*: This contains common measure amounts (in grams) for each food item. By using a direct rule, you can convert NUT_DATA information (expressed by 100g) to the common measure selected. It has 15,438 records (some food items have more than one common measure information available).

- *FD_GROUP*: This contains the name of food categories used to group food items. It has just 25 records.

- *NUTR_DEF*: This contains the name, unit of measure, and other information of the nutrient value described on the NUT_DATA table. It has 150 records, meaning 150 possible nutrient values for each food item.

Among these six tables, the only one whose records make sense on their own is the ABBREV table, which has 53 fields. These fields have up to 46 items of nutrient data information, including water, energy, and the two most common measures for their 8,790 food item records (although the NUT_DESC table offers up to 150 different nutrients). Figure 3-3 shows the ABBREV table opened in the Microsoft Access interface. (Note that the navigation buttons at the bottom of the table show "Record 1 of 8,790" and that Access uses the Short_Desc field from the FOOD_DES table to name each food item.)

NDB_No ▾	Shrt_Desc ▾	Water_(g) ▾	Energ_Kcal ▾	Protein_(g) ▾	Lipid_Tot_(g) ▾	Ash_(g) ▾	Carbohydrt_(g) ▾	Fib ▲
⊞ 01001	BUTTER,WITH SALT	15.87	717	0.85	81.11	2.11	0.06	
⊞ 01002	BUTTER,WHIPPED,W/ SALT	16.72	718	0.49	78.3	1.62	2.87	
⊞ 01003	BUTTER OIL,ANHYDROUS	0.24	876	0.28	99.48	0	0	
⊞ 01004	CHEESE,BLUE	42.41	353	21.4	28.74	5.11	2.34	
⊞ 01005	CHEESE,BRICK	41.11	371	23.24	29.68	3.18	2.79	
⊞ 01006	CHEESE,BRIE	48.42	334	20.75	27.68	2.7	0.45	
⊞ 01007	CHEESE,CAMEMBERT	51.8	300	19.8	24.26	3.68	0.46	
⊞ 01008	CHEESE,CARAWAY	39.28	376	25.18	29.2	3.28	3.06	
⊞ 01009	CHEESE,CHEDDAR	37.02	404	22.87	33.31	3.71	3.09	
⊞ 01010	CHEESE,CHESHIRE	37.65	387	23.37	30.6	3.6	4.78	
⊞ 01011	CHEESE,COLBY	38.2	394	23.76	32.11	3.36	2.57	
⊞ 01012	CHEESE,COTTAGE,CRMD,LRG OR SML CU	79.79	98	11.12	4.3	1.41	3.38	
⊞ 01013	CHEESE,COTTAGE,CRMD,W/FRUIT	79.64	97	10.69	3.85	1.2	4.61	
⊞ 01014	CHEESE,COTTAGE,NONFAT,UNCRMD,DF	81.01	72	10.34	0.29	1.71	6.66	
⊞ 01015	CHEESE,COTTAGE,LOWFAT,2% MILKFAT	81.24	81	10.45	2.27	1.27	4.76	
⊞ 01016	CHEESE,COTTAGE,LOWFAT,1% MILKFAT	82.48	72	12.39	1.02	1.39	2.72	
⊞ 01017	CHEESE,CREAM	52.62	350	6.15	34.44	1.27	5.52	
⊞ 01018	CHEESE,EDAM	41.56	357	24.99	27.8	4.22	1.43	
⊞ 01019	CHEESE,FETA	55.22	264	14.21	21.28	5.2	4.09	
⊞ 01020	CHEESE,FONTINA	37.92	389	25.6	31.14	3.79	1.55	
⊞ 01021	CHEESE,GJETOST	13.44	466	9.65	29.51	4.75	42.65	
⊞ 01022	CHEESE,GOUDA	41.46	356	24.94	27.44	3.94	2.22	

Record: I◄ ◄ 1 of 8790 ► ►I ►* ⊤ No Filter   Search

Figure 3-3. *This is the ABBREV table, the only sr28.accdb table that makes sense by itself. It has 8,789 records (rows) and 53 fields (columns). There is one column for the food item code (NDB_No), one for the food item description (Shrt_Desc), and 51 other columns to describe nutrient values for 100g of each food item*

The information stored by the other four tables described by Table 3-1 does not make sense by itself, because those tables were built using the concept of primary key propagation between the tables.

Open the NUT_DATA table, and note that it offers 679,045 records of useless information, because the records are related to the NDB_No and Nutr_No fields, which belong to other table records (Figure 3-4).

NDB_No ▾	Nutr_No ▾	Nutr_Val ▾	Num_Data_Pts ▾	Std_Error ▾	Src_Cd ▾	Deriv_Cd ▾	Ref_NDB_No ▾	Add_Nutr_Mark ▾	Num_St ▲
⊞ 01001	203	0.85	16	0.074	1				
⊞ 01001	204	81.11	580	0.065	1				
⊞ 01001	205	0.06	0		4	NC			
⊞ 01001	207	2.11	35	0.054	1				
⊞ 01001	208	717	0		4	NC			
⊞ 01001	221	0	0		7				
⊞ 01001	255	15.87	522	0.061	1				
⊞ 01001	262	0	0		7	Z			
⊞ 01001	263	0	0		7	Z			
⊞ 01001	268	2999	0		4	NC			
⊞ 01001	269	0.06	0		4	NR			
⊞ 01001	291	0	0		4				
⊞ 01001	301	24	17	0.789	1	A			
⊞ 01001	303	0.02	18	0.011	1	A			
⊞ 01001	304	2	18	0.047	1	A			
⊞ 01001	305	24	17	0.463	1	A			
⊞ 01001	306	24	18	0.622	1	A			
⊞ 01001	307	643	0		4	NR			
⊞ 01001	309	0.09	18	0.011	1	A			
⊞ 01001	312	0	18	0	1	A			
⊞ 01001	313	2.8	19	0.674	1	A			
⊞ 01001	315	0	18	0	1	A			

Record: I◄ ◄ 1 of 679238 ► ►I ►✱ No Filter Search

Figure 3-4. *This is the NUT_DATA table offering 679,045 records of useless information, unless you can relate the NDB_No and Nutr_No fields to something more significant than the numbers they contain*

As you can see, the only way to make sense of these tables records is to use the Relationships window to find a way to relate them and use information from more than one table at once, which is the main function of a query!

The Relationships Window: A Source for Data Flow

The Relationships window is a way to understand how you can obtain any information from the database tables, by following the joining lines used to indicate how two tables are related. Think about them as the pathway that indicates how to connect unrelated tables to show any set of related field values that may come from different database tables.

Let's take, for example, the LanguaL concept, which according to the LanguaL website (http://langual.org) stands for "Langua aLimentaria" or "language of food." It is "an automated method for describing, capturing and retrieving data about food... that can be systematically described by a combination of characteristics...which can be categorized into viewpoints and coded for computer processing...that can be used to retrieve data about the food from external databases."

By looking at the Relationships window, we can note that there is a pathway that joins the FOOD_DES (8,790 records), LANGUAL (38,301 records), and LANGDESC (774 records) tables. Specifically, each food item in the FOOD_DES table can have a different amount of information in the LANGUAL table, whose meaning is stored in the LANGDESC table. If there is a need to list each food item along with all the LANGUAL descriptors, you will need to use all three tables, but take information from just two of them (FOOD_DES and LANGDESC, because they are related by the LANGUAL table), as shown in Figure 3-5.

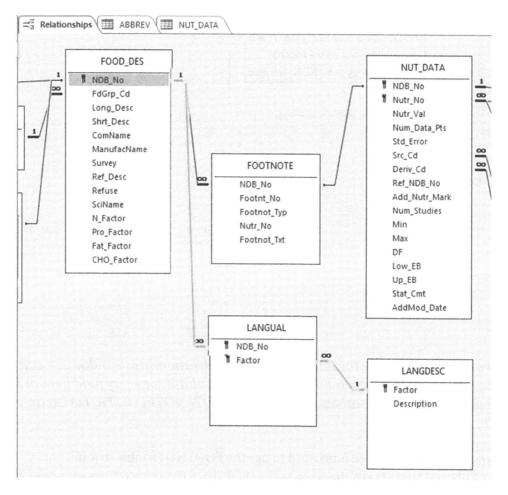

Figure 3-5. *Use the Relationships window to discover how to obtain information from database tables by following the join lines that relate them*

Note   The LANGUAL table is the joining table that provides a many-to-many relationship between the FOOD_DES and LANGDESC tables.

Note that not every possible relationship was imposed by the database administrators between its tables. For example, if you want to retrieve all nutrient information available on the NUTR_DEF table (150 nutrients, or records) for each food item of the FOOD_DES table, the Relationships window indicates that you will need to use the tables FOOD_DES, FOOT_NOTE, NUTR_DATA, and NUTR_DES (Figure 3-6).

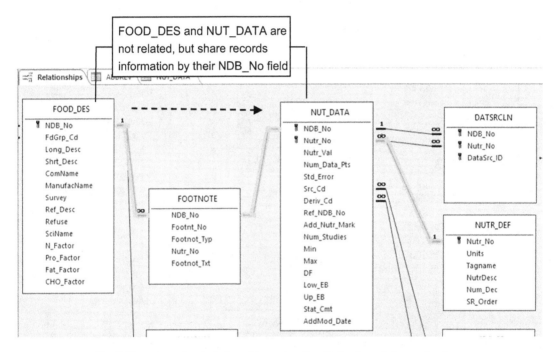

Figure 3-6. *By following the joining lines in the Relationships window, we can see that to retrieve all the nutritional information available for every food item in the database, we will use the tables FOOD_DES, FOOT_NOTE, NUTR_DATA, and NUTR_DES*

But this is not true: there is no need to use the FOOTNOTE table to join FOOD_DES and NUT_DATA, because both tables share the same information from the NDB_No field (used to compose the primary key of both tables), which is not related in the Relationships window. You will just need to use FOOD_DES (for the food item description), NUT_DATA (for nutrition information), and NUTR_DEF (to describe the nutrition information of each NUT_DATA record), which can be confirmed by reading the database documentation in the sr28_doc.pdf file.

So, the lessons are as follows:

- Always take a good look at the Relationships window to see how database tables are related.

- Check the database documentation for the meaning of each table field.

- Use the Relationships window's joining lines to find a path to the desired information, stored in different unrelated tables.

The tool that you will use to obtain information that comes from different database tables, whether they are directly related or not, is called a Select query.

Note You can find all the queries cited in the following sections (including the native ones cited at the beginning of this chapter) in the sr28_Queries.accdb database, which you can also extract from the Chapter03.zip file.

Select Queries

A Select query, as its name implies, is one that allows you to select field values from the desired records of one or more tables, related or not.

You can create a Select query, also called a *simple query*, by using the Query Wizard or Query Design commands found in the Queries area of the Create tab.

As a novice user of Microsoft Access, you will be tempted to use the Query Wizard, but as time goes on, you will not need it anymore. You will use the Query Design window to achieve the same results but faster. So, let's use both methods to create a query that returns some fields from the ABBREV table, which has enough records for you experiment.

Note All queries built in this chapter are available in the file sr28_Queries. accdb file that you can extract from CHAPTER03.ZIP.

Creating Queries with the Query Wizard

Let's suppose you want to extract the following information from the ABBREV table: NDB_No (the food ID), Short_Desc (food name), Water_(g), Energ_Kcal, Protein_(g), Lipid_Tot_(g), and CarboHydrt_(g). And say you want to do this for every one of its 8,790 records. You will create a subtable, or, in database jargon, a *recordset*.

To do this with the aid of a wizard, first close all opened tables and the Relationships window, and then click the Query Wizard option in the Queries area of the Create tab (Figure 3-7).

Tip   You do not need to open or close any database object to build or run a query using the Query Wizard or Query Design commands. It is suggested here so you can achieve the same results you see in this section's figures.

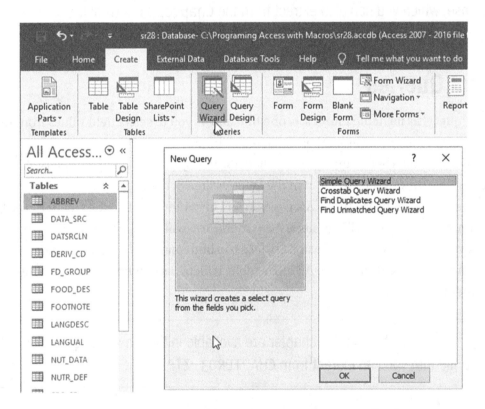

Figure 3-7.   *Click the Query Wizard button to start the wizard, where you can select what type of query you want to create. Select Simple Query Wizard to create a Select query*

Choose the first option, Simple Query Wizard, and click OK to start the wizard. In the wizard, you can select which type of query you want to create: "Detail (shows every field of every record" creates a Select query, and Summary creates a Total query (Figure 3-8).

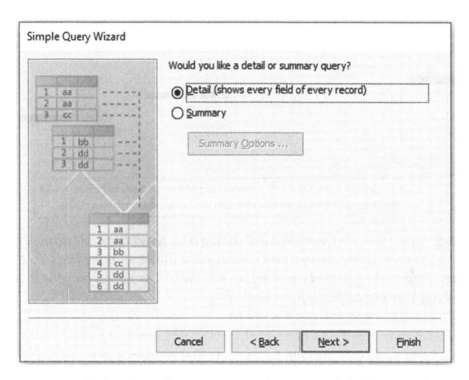

Figure 3-8. *Use the first Simple Query Wizard page to select the type of query that must be created*

Select the first option ("Detail (shows every field of every record)") and click Next to show the second page of the Simple Query Wizard, where you can select an existing table (or query) as the source of fields for the query you want to create. For this first query, select the ABBREV table and double-click the desired items of the Available Fields list to transfer them to the Selected Fields list (you can add items to the Selected Fields list from different tables and/or queries, as shown in Figure 3-9).

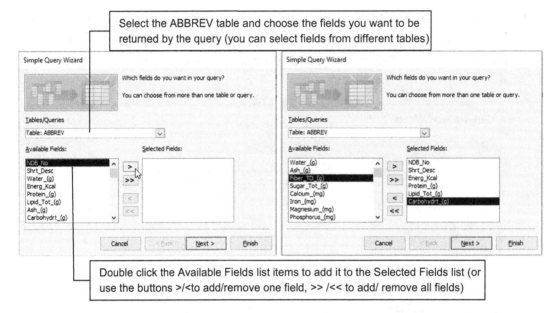

Figure 3-9. *In the Simple Query Wizard dialog box, select the table name (you can also select an existing query), and double-click the Available Fields list to add the desired field to the Selected Field list (or use the >/< or >>/<< buttons to add/remove the selected or all fields from each list)*

Caution   Any query accepts both tables and other existing queries as a data source for its records. This means you can create a query from a query, up until a point that the Microsoft Access database engine issues the message "Query Too Complex."

Tip   To make a query run faster, always select the least possible number of fields.

After all the desired fields are selected, click the Next button and type a name for the query (Microsoft Access will propose <Table> Query as the default name), using the rules stated in Table 1-3 (prefix every query name with "qry" to easily distinguish queries from table names). For this example, name it **qryFoodItems**. Keep the option "Open the query to view information" selected and click Finish to show the query records (Figure 3-10).

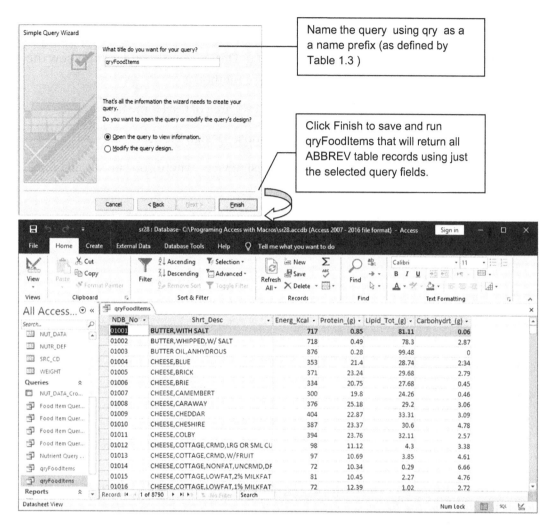

Figure 3-10. *Name the query qryFoodItems and click Finish to run the query and see its records (which will return just the selected fields)*

Note that qryFooditems returns all 8,790 records from the ABBREV table, because you didn't ask it to return just the desired records—something you can do by defining one or more query criteria using the Query Design view.

Using the Query Design View

Once a query has been created, you can switch it to Design view to understand how the job is done by the Query Wizard using one of these methods:

- Click the View button located in the Views area of the Home tab.

- Right-click the query tab name and choose Design View.

Microsoft Access will change the query to Design view, where you can see all tables and fields used by it (Figure 3-11).

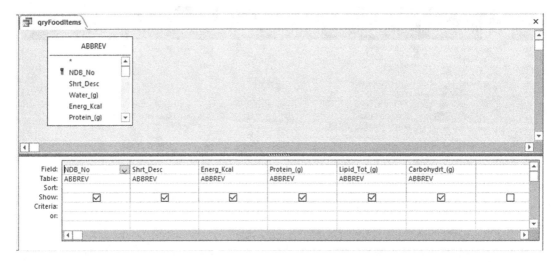

Figure 3-11. *This is qryFoodItems in Design view, indicating that it uses just the ABBREV table and the fields selected in the wizard (NDB_No, Short_Desc, Water_ (g), Energ_Kcal, Protein_(g), Lipid_Tot_(g), and CarboHydrt_(g))*

The Query Design view has two main areas.

- *Table's area*: This is the gray area located at the top that holds the table representations used by the query (along with their relationships, if any).

- *Grid area*: This is the grid located at the bottom, indicating the field names used by the query.

Tip   If necessary, you can drag the line that divides the top and bottom areas to give more space to showing the query tables.

The query grid located at the bottom of Design view has one column for each field used by the query and a set of rows that you can use to define query parameters.

- *Field*: This indicates the field name that will be returned by the query.

- *Table*: This indicates the table (or query) name that has the selected field.

- *Sort*: This allows you to select how the query will sort its records (Ascending or Descending). It allows multiple sorts that will be performed from left to right.

- *Show*: This indicates the fields returned by the query (it's useful to use a field as query criteria that you don't want to show on query results).

- *Criteria, Or rows*: This specifies each field criteria used to return query records. Criteria inserted for different fields on the same row indicate an AND operation. Both criteria must match; on different rows (Or row), indicating an OR operation, one or more criteria must match.

Field Name

Use the Field row column of each query field to give an alias to any field name or to create a column whose value is a constant or an expression based on arithmetic operators or functions, used alone or referring to any table field values.

To alias any field name, prefix it with the desired name followed by a colon (or show the property sheet for this field and change the field Caption property). For example, to make the Shrt_Desc Field appear as "Food name" on the query column, its column must become as Food Name: Shrt_Desc. Once you change a field name, click the View button of the Views tab to run the query and see the result (Figure 3-12).

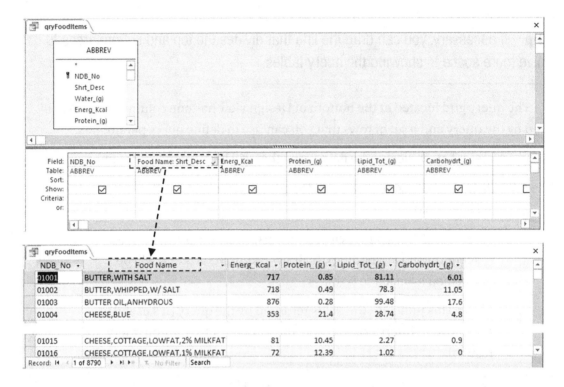

Figure 3-12. *You can alias any field name by prefixing it with the desired name followed by a colon*

Inserting a New Query Column

You can also insert another query column to create a *calculated* or constant field, by following these steps:

1. Select the column that must be on the right of the new column, pointing the mouse on the small gray area above the field head (the mouse pointer will turn into a pointing-down small black arrow).

2. Click to select the entire column.

3. Press the Insert key.

Access will insert the new column to the left of the selected column, ready to receive the field or expression that will be returned by the query (Figure 3-13).

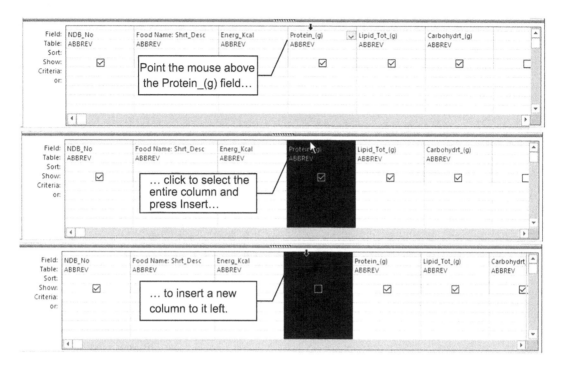

Figure 3-13. *To insert a new column on the query grid, point the mouse above the field that must be at the right of the new column, click to select the entire column, and press the Insert key*

Using the Expression Builder

To insert an expression or constant, first name the field and follow it by a colon. Then type the desired expression, or right-click the field and select Build from the context menu that appears (Figure 3-14).

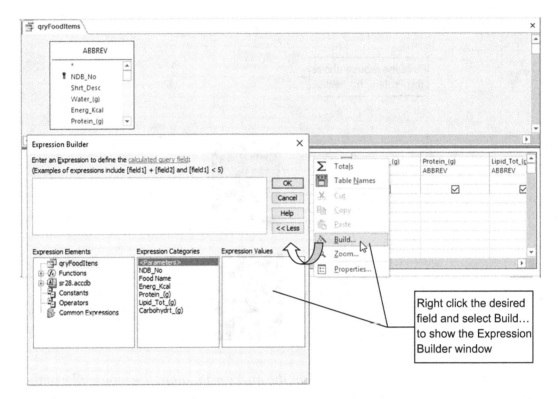

Figure 3-14. *To create a calculated query field, use the Expression Builder window, which can be opened by right-clicking the selected field and selecting Build in the context menu*

The Expression Builder helps you with the right syntax you must use to create an appropriate expression. It has an Expression text box at the top where you can type the expression, and it has three lists at the bottom where you can select the data you need for the expression.

- *Expression Elements:* This shows all the relevant objects for your expression, putting the query name on the top and selecting it by default.

- *Expression Categories:* This shows items that belong to whatever is selected in the Expression Elements list. By selecting the query name, you see the query field names. You can select Functions (which can be expanded), can select an appropriate function from a categorized list, and so on.

- *Expression Values:* This shows the values of what is selected in the Expression Categories list (if you selected a function category, it will show all the functions available in the selected category).

The Expression Builder is a powerful tool and will be cited as needed in this book. For now, let's suppose you want to calculate the Kcal value of each food by using the traditional calories formula, which multiples carbohydrates and proteins by 4 and lipids by 9 (calories per g). Since for each food value this information comes from the Protein_(g), Lipid_Tot_(g), and Carbohydrt_(g) fields, you can create the Kcal expression by using this formula:

```
Protein_(g) *4 + Lipid_Tot_(g) * 9 + Carbohydrt_(g) * 4
```

Caution   When building query field expressions, keep in mind that any expression is not evaluated from left to right. Instead, it is evaluated according to the operator order of precedence stated in Table 3-2.

Table 3-2. *Order of Precedence of Arithmetic, Comparison, and Logical Operators for Microsoft Access Query Expressions*

Precedence	Arithmetic			Comparison		Logical
1st	^	Exponentiation	=	Equality		Not
2nd	-	Negation	< >	Inequality		And
3rd	*, /	Multiplication and division	<	Less than		Or
4th	\	Integer division	>	Greater than		Xor
5th	Mod	Modulus	<=	Less than or equal to		Eqv
6th	+,-	Addition and subtraction	>=	Greater than or equal to		Imp
7th	&	String concatenation	Like, Is	Substring search		

Since the field names are a little different from their real name counterparts, use the "select qryFoodItems" item in the Expression Elements list, and double-click each field name in the Expression Categories list to insert it in the Expression text box. This box is where the expression is built (or click and drag it to the top of the Expression text box). Press the desired keyboard operator (like * or +) and select another field name, building the recommended expression for the Kcal field, as shown in Figure 3-15.

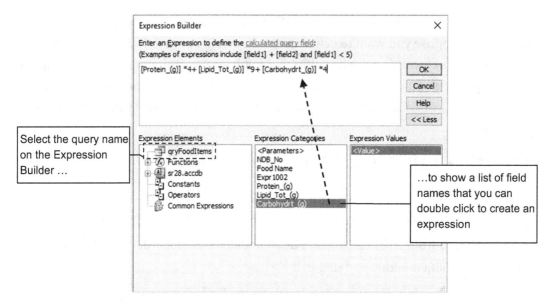

Figure 3-15. *To build an expression using the query field names in the Expression Builder window, select the query name in the Expression Elements list and double-click the field name in Expression Categories to add them to the Expression text box (don't forget to type the correct operators)*

Click OK when the expression is finished to insert it into the selected Field column of the query's Design view. Microsoft Access will automatically name it Expr1: Change it to "Kcal:" and click the View command of the Design tab to run the query and show its fields in Datasheet view (Figure 3-16).

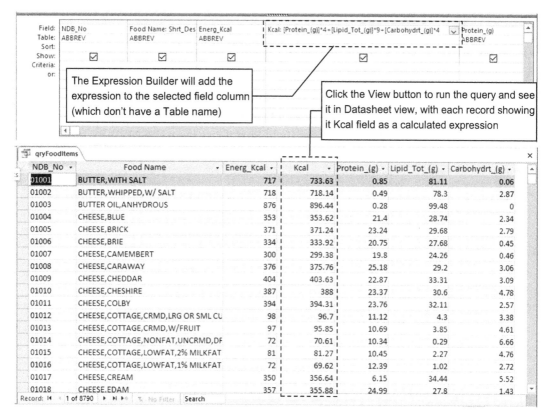

Figure 3-16. *When you close the Expression Builder, Access will add it to the selected query field, naming it Expr1. Rename it to Kcal: and click the View button of the Design tab to run the query and show the expression changes according to each record value*

Caution Did you notice that the Energ_Kcal field and Kcal calculated values differently for each food item? According to the `sr28_doc.pdf` documentation, this happens because the proposed calories formula is a generic way to calculate food gross energy (protein and carbohydrates have 4 calories/g, while lipids and alcohol have 9 calories/g), while each food has its own conversion factor for calories from protein, carbohydrate, and lipids, according to the energy value remaining after digestive and urinary losses are deducted from gross energy. These values can be found on the fields Pro_Factor, Fat_Factor, and CHO_Factor of the FOOD_DES table (not returned by the ABBREV table, but probably used for the calculation of the Energ_Kcal field).

Using Sort to Sort Records

To return records sorted by the desired fields, use the Sort row of the Query Design view to choose Ascending or Descending order for the desired field. Microsoft Access will apply the desired sort order from left to right (sort the first field, then the second field according to the first sorted field, and so on). Figure 3-17 shows how to sort all ABBREV table rows by aliased Food Name column (field Shrt_Desc from the ABBREV table).

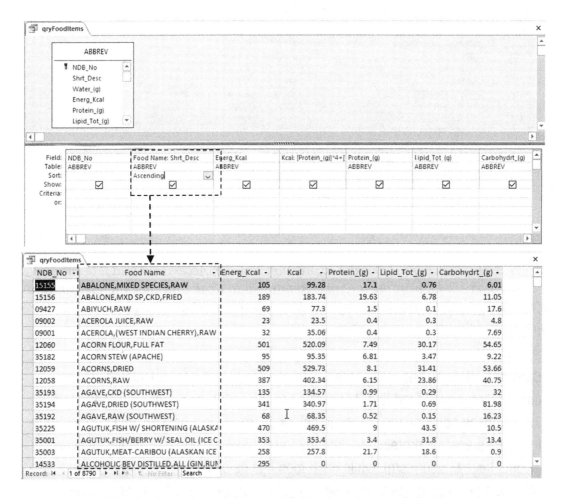

Figure 3-17. *Use the Sort row of the query's Design view to define how the query records must be sorted*

Note   This query was saved as qryFooodItemsAZ on the `sr28_Queries.accdb` database.

Tip   Set the Indexed property to Yes (Duplicates OK) for all table fields that you will apply a sort operation on. This is especially true for sorting on long tables, like ABBREV with more than 8,700 records.

To return records sorted by more than one field, keeping the same field sequence on Datasheet view, you can insert a new field on the query's Design view at the appropriate position, uncheck its Show option, and use it to sort the table. Figure 3-18 shows how you can sort the qryFoodItems records using two levels of sorting: first by the highest caloric food items (using a descending order of the Energy_Kcal field), and for each energy value found, sort them by Shrt_Desc field (Food Name) using ascending order.

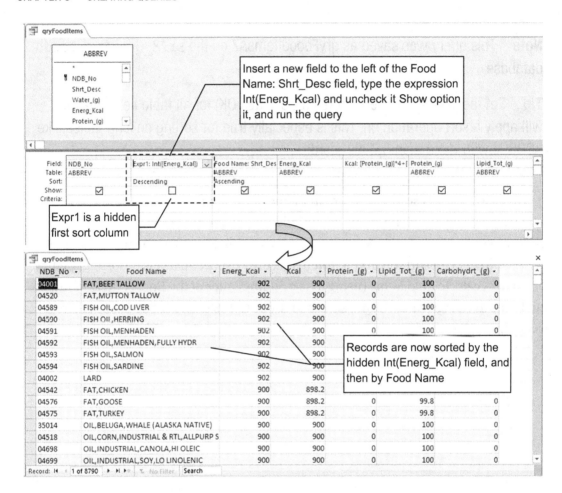

Figure 3-18. *To sort query records for more than one field, keeping the same field sequence on a query's Datasheet view, insert a new column into Design view, set its sort order, and uncheck the Show option*

Note   This query was saved as qryFooodItemsKcal on the sr28_Queries.accdb database. Access may change the presentation order of hidden fields in Query Design (hidden fields used for sort purposes are automatically sent to the end of query fields).

Tip   Use the Expression Builder to find bult-in function to create the desired expressions on the query Design view. The `INT()` function returns an Integer part of a value, and can be found by selecting Functions, Built-in Functions, on the Expression Elements list, and Math on the Expression Categories list (Figure 3-19).

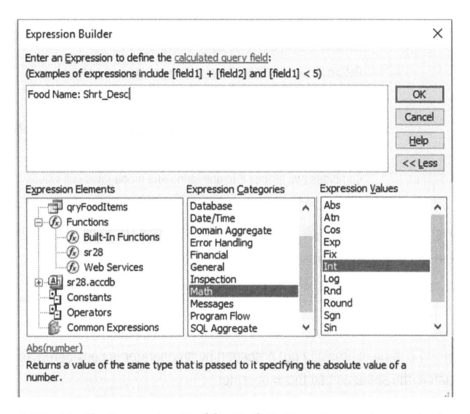

Figure 3-19. *Use the Expression Builder Built-In Function options to find useful functions by category, like the INT() function, found on the Math category*

Using Criteria to Filter Records

The query Design view Criteria rows is where thing really happens, because it allows the query to perform it main duty: produce the desired set of records.

Microsoft Access offers different operators that can be used on a query criteria field or expression to filter the records returned by the query. A record will be returned it the operator returns True. See Table 3-3.

Table 3-3. *Operators Used by Query Criteria Field to Filter Records. Only Records Whose Comparison Returns True Will Be Returned*

Operator	Purpose
<; <=; >; >=; =; <>	Mathematical operators that compare an expression and returns True or False
And	Returns True when Expr1 And Expr2 are true
Or	Returns True when either Expr1 Or Expr2 is true
Eqv	Returns True when both Expr1 and Expr2 are true or false
Not	Returns True when Expr is not true
Xor	Returns True when either Expr1 is true or Expr2 is true, but not both
&	Combines two strings to form one string
+	Combines two strings into one string and propagates null values
Is Null	Determines whether expression is Null or Not Null
Like "pattern"	Matches string values by using the wildcard operators *, ? and [ ]
Between val1 And val2	Determines numeric or date values within a range
In(val1,val2...)	Determines whether a value is found within a set of values

Caution   A criteria expression not preceded by an operator is considered as an exact match, the same as use the = operator.

Tip   Mathematical operators can be applied to number, dates (which is a number), and eventually to text values. When applied to text values, they will refer to the alphabetical order of compared expressions.

Caution   Null indicates an empty field that has no value that is different from a blank space (two successive quotes, "").

The FOOD_DES table uses the NDB_No field as the table primary key, associating to each food product a five length numeric text code that goes from "01001" to "93600" for the sr28.accdb database (verify by yourself by opening the FOOD_DES table, keep selecting it NDB_No field, press the Last Record button on Table Navigation Buttons (or press End+Down arrow to go to the last food item), since this table order by this field by default).

Any table primary key field is a good candidate for what is called an "exact match" search, because it is quite common on a database application to allow the user select a record by some different field (like the food name, on the Short_Des field) and return it using the food name primary key code (the NDB_No field value).

So, let's try a simple exact match criteria by using the Criteria field using an exact match to find the food items whose NDB_No = "10000", following these steps:

1. Open qryFoodItems on the Design view.

2. Type **10000** in the NDB_No criteria field (Access will note that this is a Short text field and will automatically enclose the values between double quotes).

3. Click the View button to run the query and return the desired record (Figure 3-20).

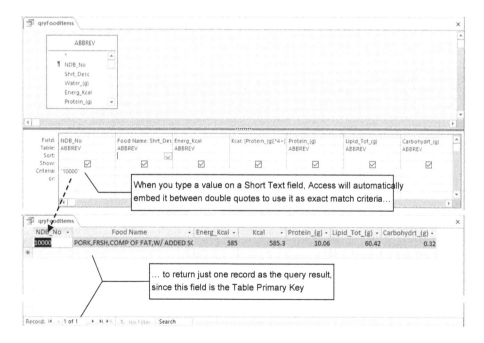

Figure 3-20. *By typing a value on the Criteria row of any field in query Design view, just records that has an exact match to this value will be returned*

This was easy and predictable, but you could not do it by the food name, because it is composed by a long string ("PORK,FRSH,COMP OF FAT,W/ ADDED..."), which is very unlikely to be typed on the query Criteria Shrt_Des field without make a mistake.

But sometimes you will need to return one or more selected records, using exact match criteria on the table primary key values. For this you can use one of the following strategies:

- Use the Criteria OR lines to type other primary key values.

- Use the OR operator on the same criteria value.

- Use the IN() clause on the criteria value.

So, to return three different food items whose NBD_No field are equal to "10000", "20001", and "31001" (existing NDB_No values found by running qryFoodItems using as criteria >"20000" and >"30000"), you can type these values for the NBD_No field Criteria, Or rows (Figure 3-21):

- Criteria row = 10000; first Or row = 20001; second Or row = 31001

- (Access will automatically enclose the values between double quotes).

- Criteria = "10000" Or "20001" Or "31001";

- Criteria = In("10000", "20001", "31001")

Caution   The last two criteria examples require that you enclose values between single or double quotes to avoid receive the message error "Data type mismatch in criteria expression."

Tip   Any Number field data type can use the IN() clause to return multiple exact match values. In this case, *do not* use double quotes on the criteria values. This is especially true when the table primary key has the AutoNumber data type (long integer).

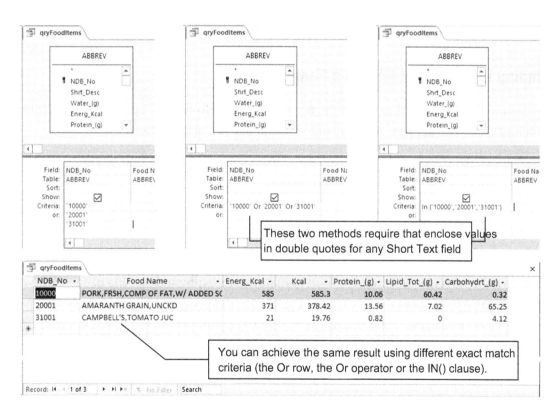

Figure 3-21. *To perform an exact match on any field (specially the Primary Key) to return different records, you can use the OR rows, the OR operator or the IN() clause*

Note   These queries were saved as qryFooodItemsCriteria1, qryFooodItemsCriteria2, and qryFooodItemsCriteria3 on the `sr28_Queries.accdb` database. However, criteria values typed for any query field using different Or rows is automatically is change by Access by a single expression using one Or Row. That is why qryFoodItemsCriteria1 and qryFoodItemsCriteria2 are the same when opened in Query Design view (try changing it to Criteria to use different rows, save and close the query, and reopen it to see by yourself). This happens because before saving the query, Access analyzes its Query Design view, creates the associate SQL instruction, and saves it. When it is opened again, the Query Design view is re-created using its SQL instruction.

Finding Records That Fit into a Range

Sometimes you may need to return the records that fit between two specified values (like different dates). To achieve such a result, you can use two approaches.

- *AND*: Use the AND operator with the =, >, >=, <=, or < mathematical operator to return the desired records.

- *BETWEEN*: Use the BETWEEN operator to return records that are >= Expr1 (greater than or equal to) or <= Expr2 (smaller than or equal to) values.

Since the ABBREV table returns food item nutrients expressed by 100g of each food item, to return food items that have between 30% or 50% protein in them (Protein field between 30g and 50g per 100g of food) sorted in descending order, you can use any of these two expressions on the Criteria row of the qryFoodItems query (Figure 3-22):

- >=30 And <=50

- Between 30 And 50

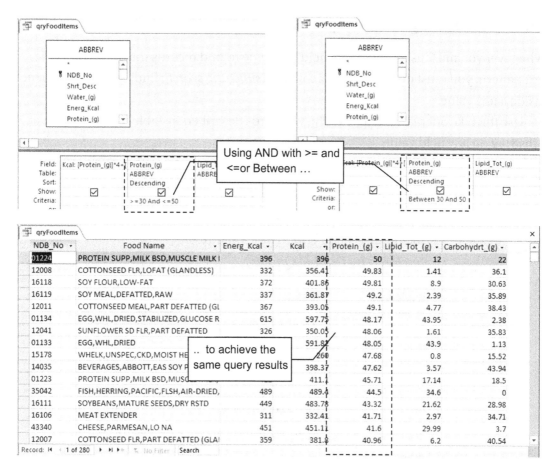

Figure 3-22. *To return records that fit within a range of field values, use AND with*
>= Expr1 or <= Expr2 mathematical operators, or use BETWEEN Expr1 and Expr2

Note   These queries were saved as qryFooodItemsAND and
qryFoodItemsBETWEEN in the sr28_Queries.accdb database.

Tip   Since the Protein_(g) field is set to a Number data type, there is no need to
enclose the search values between double quotes.

Caution   You can use both AND and BETWEEN operators with text values, as long
as you enclose Expr1 and Expr2 between double quotes. In this case, Access will
compare the alphabetical order of both string expressions.

Finding Records by Performing a Substring Search

Whenever you must use a Short Text field data type to find records that have a specific text pattern, you must perform what is called as *substring search*: finding a text fragment inside a text value.

Use the Like operator along with the wildcards described in Table 3-4 to perform a substring on any field value.

Table 3-4. *Wildcards Used by the Like Operator to Make a Substring Search Inside Any Text Field (They Must Be Enclosed by Double Quotes)*

Wildcards	Usage
*	Multiple characters
?	Single character
#	Number
[ ]	Range of characters
[a-z]	Range of characters
[0-9]	Range of digits
[!]	Outside a range
[!a-z]	Outside a range of characters
[!0-9]	Outside a range of digits
NOT	Negates the Like search

Tip   To search the wildcard characters *, ?, #, [, and - inside the field, enclose it in brackets [ ], like [*], [?], [#], [[ ], or [-]. Do not use brackets for the exclamation point (!) or closing brackets (]). Enclose them only inside the double quotes of the Like operator criteria (for example, Like "*!*" or Like "*]*").

To search for hyphens and other characters simultaneously, place them before or after all the other characters inside the brackets, like [-#*] or [#*-]. If you are using the exclamation point (!) after the opening bracket to negate the search, place the hyphen after the exclamation point: [!-].

Since Access interprets a single pair of brackets as a zero-length string, to search for a pair of opening and closing brackets ([]), also enclose them in a pair of brackets, like [[ ]].

Caution   To search for a single quotation mark inside a field, you need to type two successive quotations enclosed in another two quotations (four successive quotes), like """". Then mount an expression using the & concatenation character to include the quotation mark, for example, Like "*" & """" & "*".

The most used Like wildcard is the asterisk (*), which means *everything* or any amount of text. Table 3-5 show how to use the Like operator along with the * wildcard to find different records on the qryFoodItems query that have the word *orange* in different parts of the Shrt_Desc field (Figure 3-23).

Table 3-5. *Number of Records Found by Using the Like Operator on the Shrt_Des Field of the Qryfooditem Query*

Usage	Meaning	Records
Like "*"	The entire field	8,790
Like "orange*"	Any record that begins with the word *orange*	18
Like "*orange"	Any record that ends with the word *orange*	6
Like "*orange*"	Records that have the word *orange*	60

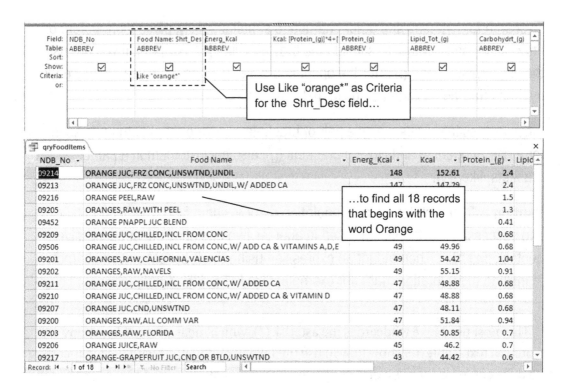

Figure 3-23. *Use the Like operator with the * wildcard to make a substring search inside any field. By using Like <word>* as the query criteria, Access will return all records that begin with <word> (int this case, orange in the Shrt_Des field)*

Note   This query was saved as qryFooodItemsLIKEorange in the sr28_Queries. accdb database.

Table 3-6 indicates how to use other Like operator wildcards, using examples that you must try on the qryFoodItems query for the Shrt_Desc field criteria.

Table 3-6. *Usage Examples of Like Operator Wildcards to Make Special Substring Searches for Food Item Names on the Shrt_Des Field of the Qryfooditem Query*

Usage	Food item names	Records
Like "*#*"	Has a number	1,568
Like "*#"	Ends with a number	19
Not Like "*#"	Does not end with a number	8,771
Like "[a-d]*"	Begins with the letters A, B, C, or D	3,776
Like "[!a-d]*"	Does not begin with the letters A, B, C, or D	5,014
Not Like "[a-d]*"	Does not begin with the letters A, B, C, or D	5,014
Like "*[']*"	Has a single quotation mark	590
Like "*" & """" & "*"	Has a quotation character (")	989

Using Dynamic Criteria

Microsoft Access also allows you to ask the user to type a criteria parameter before it executes the query and return the desired results. This can be done by enclosing a user question between braces on the field Criteria row to force the query to open the Enter Parameter Value dialog box, where the question must be answered by the user. Obviously, you will need to use the operators and wildcards cited in the previous section.

Figure 3-24 shows how you can make the qryFooditems query ask the user to type the minimum protein amount as a parameter before selecting the desired food items that match this criteria, using this dynamic criteria in the Protein_(g) field criteria:

```
>=[Minimum Protein amount (in g)?]
```

Caution   Since the ABBREV table returns nutrients per 100g of food, by typing an integer value as a parameter for the Protein_(g) field, you will indeed type the nutrient % for the food: 60g protein /100g of food = 60% protein.

Tip   Press Shift+F9 to rerun a dynamic query forcing it to show the Enter Parameter Value dialog box and type a new parameter value.

Caution   If a query has more than one dynamic criterion, they will be successively asked to the user, from left to right as they appear in the query design grid.

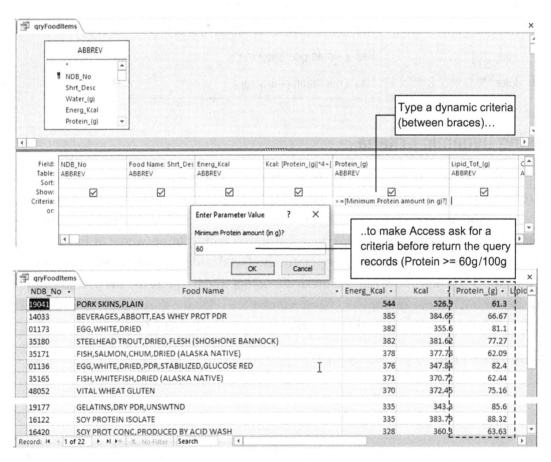

Figure 3-24. *To create a dynamic criterion, type a question between braces in the criteria field. Microsoft Access will ask for it and use it as a query parameter. You may use operators and wildcards to select the desired record*

Note   This query was saved as qryFoodItemsDynamic in the `sr28_Queries.accdb` database.

To create dynamic criteria to search for food item names using a substring search, you must use the & concatenation operator to concatenate the dynamic criteria parameter to the Like operator wildcard *, by typing something like this on the Shrt_Des field criteria (Figure 3-25):

```
Like "*" & [Type any part of the food item:] & "*"
```

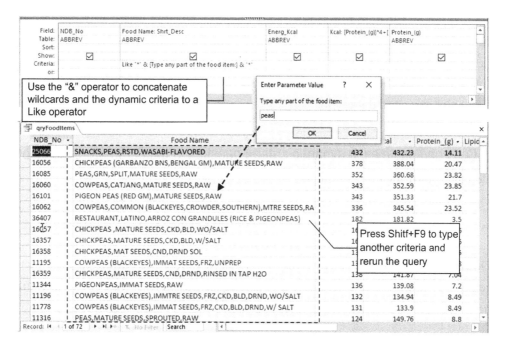

Figure 3-25. *You can use the & operator to concatenate the dynamic criteria and create complex arguments for the Criteria field*

Note   This query was saved as qryFooodItemsDynamicSubstring in the `sr28_Queries.accdb` database.

Figure 3-25 shows how to use such a technique on qryFoodItems, and if the user clicks OK without typing a value in the Enter Parameter Value dialog box, a Null value will be returned, and the Like operator will become as follows:

Like "*" & Null & "*" = Like "**"

The query will return all food items (verify by yourself)!

Set Dynamic Criteria Data Type

The Enter Parameter Value dialog box returns a string by default, which is nice for Short Text fields but can lead to undesired results on numeric, currency, or date/time fields (Access may eventually misinterpret the values you expected it to convert to numbers, money values, or dates).

On the other hand, you can also avoid having the user type the wrong type of data in a dynamic query: if the field requires a date value, the user can't type a string, and so on.

Use the Parameters command in the Show/Hide area of the Design tab in the query Design view to set each dynamic criterion. This will show the Parameters dialog box, where you must type the same dynamic criteria question used on each query field and define it as the expected data type.

Tip   Copy and paste each dynamic criteria question in the Parameters dialog box to guarantee that they are identical.

Figure 3-26 shows how you can use a qryFoodItems query to use two dynamic criteria and the Parameters dialog box to define their data types (Short Text for the Shrt_Des field and Single for the Protein_(g) field). Also note the Parameters dialog box changed the dynamic criteria order, by first asking for the Minimums Protein amount and then asking for a food name part (changing the order of the design grid).

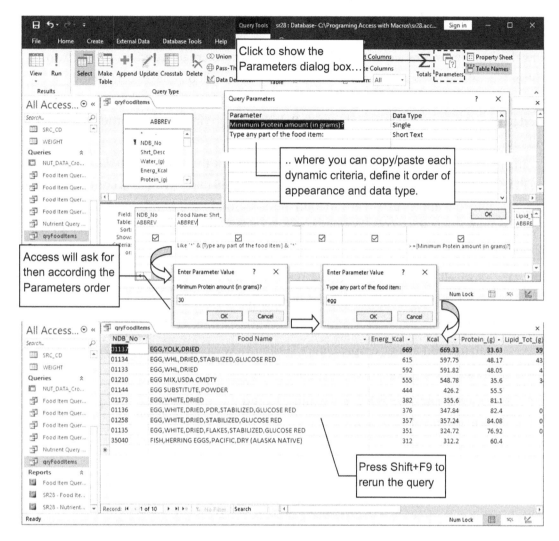

Figure 3-26. *Use the Parameters dialog box to set the dynamic criteria order and/ or its data types. By leaving the Data type column empty, the parameter will be considered a text value*

Note   This query was saved as qryFooodItemsCriteriaParameter in the `sr28_ Queries.accdb` database.

Caution   Be aware that Access will keep asking for the parameter question if you delete it from the query design grid but keep it in the Parameters dialog box. It must be deleted from both places for the query to get rid of it.

Creating Queries Using Design View

Now that you know how a query works, let's learn how to create queries on your own, without the aid of a wizard, because this is the way you will be able to extract the information you want from any database. To do this, just keep in mind that you may need to open and interpret the database's Relationships window to find the tables that will return the desired information.

In Figure 3-2, note that the Relationships window for the sr28.accdb database offers the FD_GROUP table (directly related to the FOOD_DES table), which is considered as a support table that allows use to group food items by food category. To create a new query that uses both the FOOD_DES and FD_GROUP tables without the need of a wizard, follow these steps:

1. Close all the opened windows in the Microsoft Access interface so its interfaces best resemble the figures of this chapter.

2. Click the Query Design button in the Queries area of the Create tab to open a new, empty Query Design view window and automatically show the Add Tables window.

3. Double-click the FD_GROUP table to add it to the query design grid (Figure 3-27).

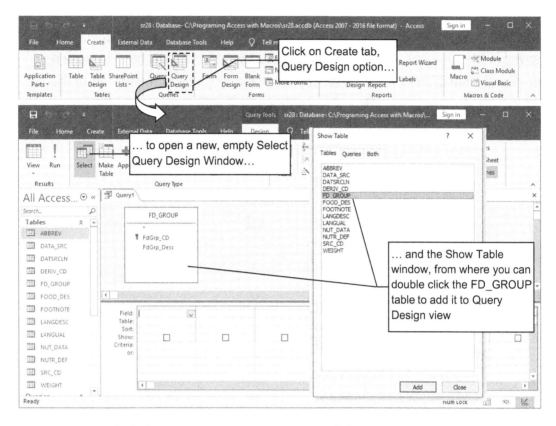

Figure 3-27. *Click the Query Design command of the Create button to open an empty Query Design view window and the Show Tables window*

4.   Close the Show Table window, and click and drag the asterisk located on top of the FD_GROUP representation table for the query design grid.

5.   Run the query to see it return all the fields from the FD_GROUP table for all its 25 records (Figure 3-28).

Caution   When you build a query using the Query Design view, that query is not saved in the database. Access will name it Query1, and you will need to close it or click the small disk on the Quick Access toolbar (located at the top left of the Access window) to save it. Do not forget to prefix it with *qry* to follow the query name rules stated in Table 1-3.

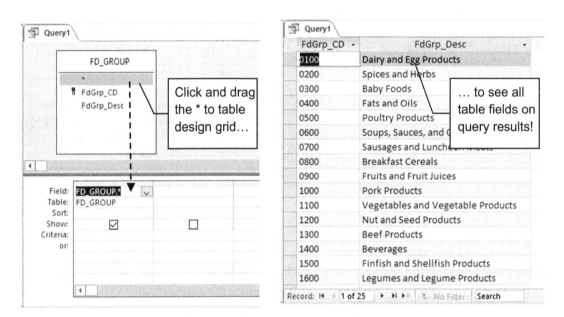

Figure 3-28.   *Click and drag the asterisk (*) from the FD_GROUP table to the query design grid and run the query to see all the table fields sorted on the query's Datasheet grid*

Note   This query was saved as qryCategories in the sr28_Queries.accdb database.

Using the Query SQL View

The Query Design view is indeed a graphic representation of the Structured Query Language (SQL), which creates an SQL statement with the necessary syntax to return the selected table, fields, field names, expressions, sort order, show fields, and criteria, if any.

So, whenever you create a query, you are indeed creating a SQL statement that can be viewed by clicking the arrow of the View command in the Views area of the Design tab and selecting SQL View (Figure 3-29).

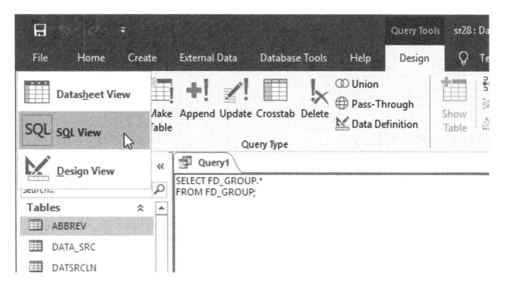

Figure 3-29. *Use the SQL view to see the SQL statement created by the Query Design view that generates the records returned by the query*

Figure 3-28 and Figure 3-29 show the simplest Select Query in Design view and its equivalent SQL statement: one that returns all possible table fields from a single query, which is quite the same as opening the table (the line break you see in Figure 3-25 is not part of the SQL statement).

```
SELECT FD_GROUP.* FROM FD_GROUP
```

Since the * represents all table fields, you cannot sort by it. So, to sort this query by the FdGrp_Desc field (category name), you need to add it to the right of the FD_GROUP.* field, set its sort order, uncheck its Show option, and run the query to show its records sorted (Figure 3-30).

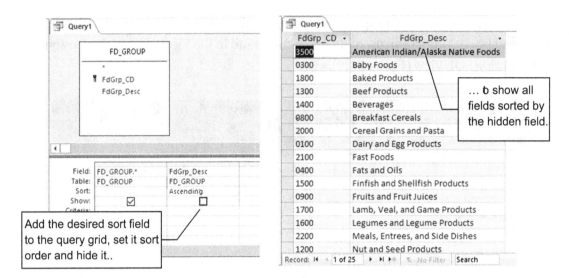

Figure 3-30. *To sort a query that uses the * to return all table fields, you must add the sorted field to the design grid, set its Sort order, and uncheck its Show option*

Note   This query was saved as qryCategoriesAZ in the sr28_Queries.accdb database.

Caution   Since the * will show all field names in the query results, by adding another copy of any table field to the query design grid, when the query runs, it will rename the duplicated field as Expr1—since no query can have two fields of the same name.

Now switch the query to SQL view, and note that its SQL statement changes to include the sort field by adding an ORDER BY clause.

```
SELECT FD_GROUP.* FROM FD_GROUP ORDER BY FD_GROUP.FdGrp_Desc;
```

Return to the query's Design view and add criteria to show only those categories where FdGrp_CD (group code) is greater than 2000; drag the FdGrp_CD field to the right of the hidden FdGrp_Desc field, uncheck its Show option, and type **>2000** for Criteria (Figure 3-31).

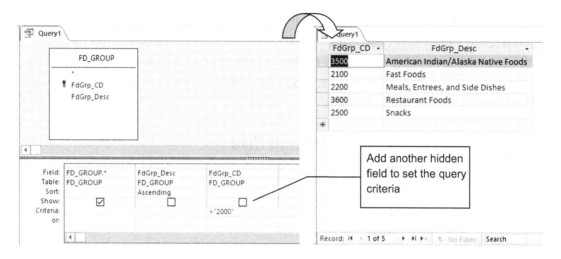

Figure 3-31. *To set the query criteria, add the desired field to the design grid, uncheck its Show option, and define the criteria*

Note   This query was saved as qryCategoriesAZcriteria in the sr28_Queries. accdb database.

Change the query to SQL view to see how the criteria changes the SQL statement to include the criteria.

```
SELECT FD_GROUP.* FROM FD_GROUP WHERE (((FD_GROUP.FdGrp_CD)>"2000")) ORDER
BY FD_GROUP.FdGrp_Desc;
```

Note that now the SQL statement includes a WHERE clause to define the query criteria.

Think of the Query Design view as a way to learn and/or obtain the SQL statement necessary to produce complex queries. To your knowledge, any SQL statement has four main clauses, which indicates the following:

- SELECT: The query fields (and alias). The asterisk means all fields.

- FROM: The query tables and relationships.

- WHERE: The query fields used as criteria to filter records.

- ORDER BY: The query fields used on sort and the sort order.

By using Microsoft Access—or any relational database—you really don't need to create a Query object to return the desired records. You can do this using just the SQL statement, which can be generated by code—as long as you understand how to create it.

From now on, as this book evolves, I will call your attention to both the query design grid and its associated SQL statement.

Adding Tables to the Query Design Grid

To add the FOOD_DES table to the query design grid, click the Show Tables command found on the Query Setup area of the Design tab, double-click the FOOD_DES table, and close the Show Table dialog box (Figure 3-32).

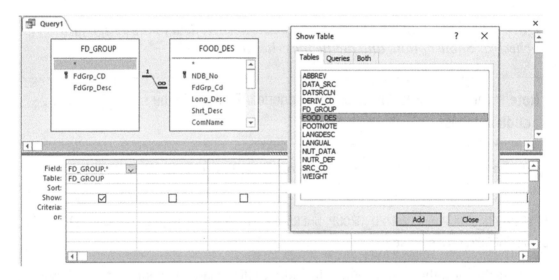

Figure 3-32. *Use the Show Table dialog box to add other tables to the query design grid. They will inherit any relationship defined in the Relationships window*

Note that FD_GROUP and FOOD_DES inherited the one-to-many relationship imposed between them, which has a practical meaning on the query records. Each of the 8,790 food items from FOOD_DES have only one food category record related on the FD_GROUP table. In other words, this query will not show more than 8,790 records.

Now you need to add the desired fields from the FOOD_DES table to the query design grid. As an exercise, click the FOOD_DES asterisk and drag it to the right of the FD_GROUP!* field; then click the View button to run the query (Figure 3-33).

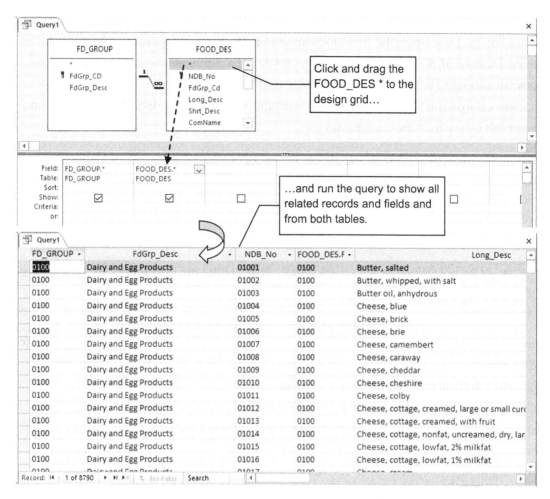

Figure 3-33. *Use the Show Tables dialog box to add the FOOD_DES table to the query design grid and then click and drag FOOD_DES "*" (all fields) to the right of the FD_GROUP.* field (indicating that the query must return all fields from both tables)*

Note   This query was saved as qryCategoriesFoodItems in the `sr28_Queries.accdb` database.

Caution   Queries that use more than one table to generate its recordset may allow you to add records on all tables simultaneously, being considered as read-write queries. In this case, the query will always show a new record row at its bottom and its New Record navigation button will be enabled (the one with a ▶ ✱ symbol).

Note that now every query record is associated to a given food category represented by the FdGrp_Desc field (the first food category is Dairy and Egg Products) and that the query returned all 8,790 records from the FOOD_DES table, because there is a one-to-many relationship between the FD_GROUP and FOOD_DES tables.

Now choose the View ➤ SQL View command and note that the SQL statement used to run this query becomes more complex:

```
SELECT FD_GROUP.*, FOOD_DES.* FROM FD_GROUP INNER JOIN FOOD_DES ON FD_
GROUP.FdGrp_CD = FOOD_DES.FdGrp_Cd;
```

Note the following about this SQL statement:

- The SELECT clause now uses FD_GROUP.*, FOOD_DES.*.

- The FROM clause now uses INNER JOIN to indicate how tables are related inside the query.

The lesson here is quite simple: you don't need to learn SQL to produce SQL statements that recover the fields and records you want. Whenever you need to generate a SQL statement, just do it in the query's Design view, show the SQL View command, and select and copy the statement to the clipboard.

You can delete the FD_GROUP.* and FOOD_DES.* fields from the query's Design view by dragging the mouse over each group and pressing the Delete key. Then you can drag just the desired field from both tables and use an alias to produce a more meaningful table. Figure 3-34 shows how you can use just the FdGrp_Desc field from FD_Group (named Category), Long_Desc (named Food Name), and Refuse from the FOOD_DES tables, sorting records first by Category and then by the Food Name field.

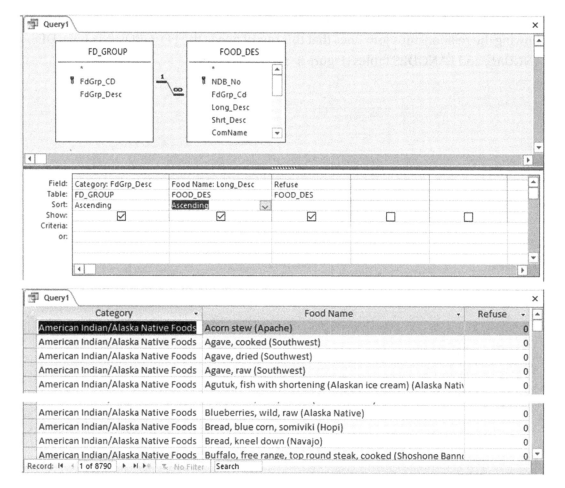

Figure 3-34. *Drag only the desired fields from the query tables, name them using meaningful descriptors, and sort the records to produce a more useful query*

Note   This query was saved as qryCategoriesFoodItemsAZ in the `sr28_Queries.accdb` database.

You can create more complex Select queries by using the Relationships window to verify which tables are needed to recover the desired information. Let's suppose that you want to create a nutritional table that returns all possible LANGUAL descriptors associated to each food item, classified first by food category, then by food name, and then by LANGUAL descriptor.

Looking at the Relationships window shown in Figure 3-2, you will realize by following the relationships join lines that this query needs the FD_GROUP, FOOD_DES, LANGUAL, and LANGDES tables (Figure 3-35).

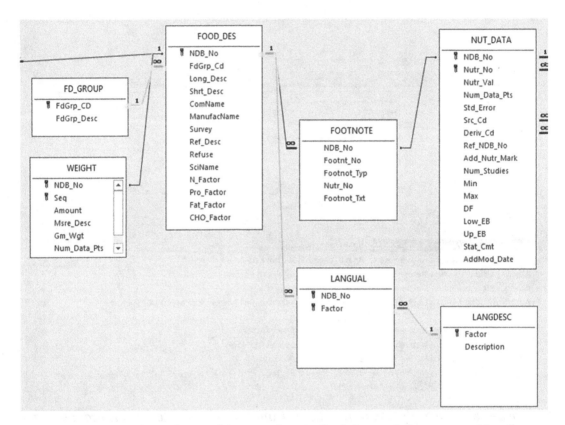

Figure 3-35. *Use the Relationships window to find the path between tables that allow you to recover the desired record information from the database*

Figure 3-36 shows the query's Design view that uses all four tables (you can create them by using the Query Design button and the Show Tables window). Note that the view has the FdGrp_Desc (from FD_GROUP), NDB_No, Long_Desc, and Refuse (from FOOD_DES), and Description (from LANGDESC) tables. The LANGUAL table is used just to produce the many-to-many relationship between the FOOD_DES and LANGDESC tables.

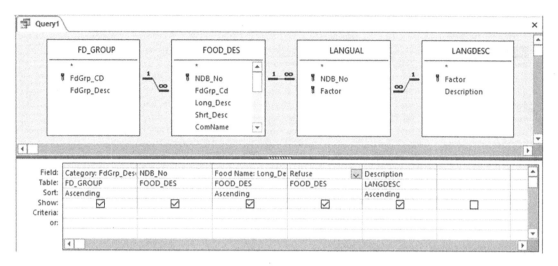

Figure 3-36. *To add the LANGUAL descriptors associated to each food item, you need to add the LANGUAL and LANGDESC tables to the query design grid*

Note   This query was saved as qryCategoriesFoodItemsAZLangual in the sr28_Queries.accdb database.

Tip   Use the SQL View command to see how complex the SQL statement is that is associated to this query design.

Since this is a multitable query that links four tables with referential integrity imposed between them and no criteria set, it will return a record count of its most populated table, LANGUAL, which has 38,301 records (Figure 3-37).

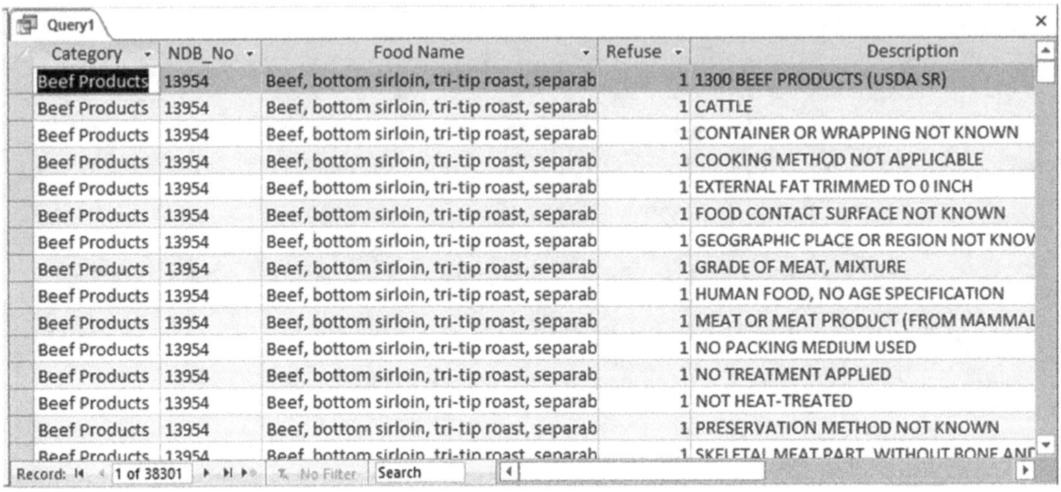

Query1

Category	NDB_No	Food Name	Refuse	Description
Beef Products	13954	Beef, bottom sirloin, tri-tip roast, separab	1	1300 BEEF PRODUCTS (USDA SR)
Beef Products	13954	Beef, bottom sirloin, tri-tip roast, separab	1	CATTLE
Beef Products	13954	Beef, bottom sirloin, tri-tip roast, separab	1	CONTAINER OR WRAPPING NOT KNOWN
Beef Products	13954	Beef, bottom sirloin, tri-tip roast, separab	1	COOKING METHOD NOT APPLICABLE
Beef Products	13954	Beef, bottom sirloin, tri-tip roast, separab	1	EXTERNAL FAT TRIMMED TO 0 INCH
Beef Products	13954	Beef, bottom sirloin, tri-tip roast, separab	1	FOOD CONTACT SURFACE NOT KNOWN
Beef Products	13954	Beef, bottom sirloin, tri-tip roast, separab	1	GEOGRAPHIC PLACE OR REGION NOT KNOV
Beef Products	13954	Beef, bottom sirloin, tri-tip roast, separab	1	GRADE OF MEAT, MIXTURE
Beef Products	13954	Beef, bottom sirloin, tri-tip roast, separab	1	HUMAN FOOD, NO AGE SPECIFICATION
Beef Products	13954	Beef, bottom sirloin, tri-tip roast, separab	1	MEAT OR MEAT PRODUCT (FROM MAMMAL
Beef Products	13954	Beef, bottom sirloin, tri-tip roast, separab	1	NO PACKING MEDIUM USED
Beef Products	13954	Beef, bottom sirloin, tri-tip roast, separab	1	NO TREATMENT APPLIED
Beef Products	13954	Beef, bottom sirloin, tri-tip roast, separab	1	NOT HEAT-TREATED
Beef Products	13954	Beef, bottom sirloin, tri-tip roast, separab	1	PRESERVATION METHOD NOT KNOWN
Beef Products	13954	Beef, bottom sirloin, tri-tip roast, separab	1	SKELETAL MEAT PART, WITHOUT BONE AND

Record: 1 of 38301 No Filter Search

Figure 3-37. *A multiple table query that joins all its tables with referential integrity imposed between them will produce a record set whose record count is related to the most populated table, which is, in this case, LANGUAL, with 38,301 records*

Returning All Possible Records from a Query

Did you notice the first category shown in Figure 3-37 is Beef Products, while Figure 3-34 shows all food items presented as the first category of American Indian/Alaska Native Foods?

Since both tables are first sorted by the Category column, the answer to this question is quite simple: there is no LANGUAL record associated to the American Indian/Alaska Native Foods category!

This happens because whenever we impose a one-to-many relationship between two tables, the one side may have records that do not have any related records on the many side.

In other words, there are FOOD_DES records (one side) that may not have any related record on the LANGUAL table.

Whenever you add two tables to a query design grid and they inherit a relationship, the join line between them will follow a default rule that forces the query to show only the related records of both tables.

To see the query rule imposed by two related query tables, double-click the line that joins them to show the Join Properties dialog box, where you can define which records must be returned by the query (Figure 3-38).

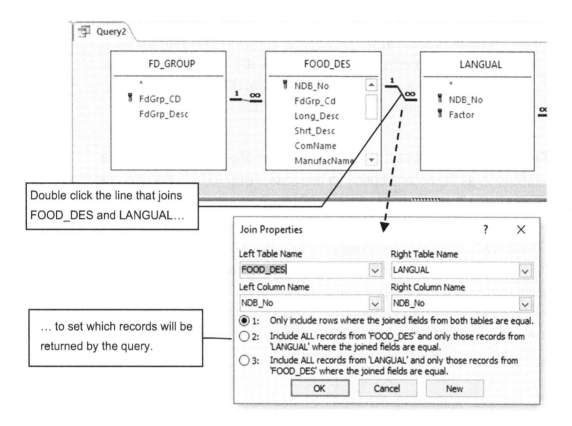

Figure 3-38. *Double-click the line that joins two query tables to show the Join Properties dialog box, where you can define which records must be returned by the query*

The Join Properties dialog box shows the tables and fields names related by the query and offers three types of relationships.

- *Only include rows where the joined fields from both tables are equal*: This is the default option, allowing only existing related records of both tables to be returned.

- *Include all records from FOOD_DES and only those records from LANGUAL where the joined fields are equal*: This option forces the query to return all FOOD_DES records and just LANGUAL records that relate to them (LANGUAL fields will appear as empty columns, using NULL values).

- *Include ALL records from "LANGUAL" and only those records from "FOOD_DES" where the joined fields are equal*: This option does the opposite, forcing the query to return all LANGUAL records and the FOOD_DES records that relate to them (FOOD_DES fields will appear as empty columns, using NULL values).

Tip   The Join Properties dialog box will always show the one side of the relationship as the second option (in this case, FOOD_DES is the one side). The third option will always be the table on the many side.

Set this join using the second option ("Include ALL records from "FOOD_DES...") to force the query to show all FOOD_DES records and just related LANGUAL records (records not related should appear with null values for every LANGUAL field). Close the Joint Properties dialog box and note that the query's Design view changes the join line between the FOOD_DES and LANGUAL tables to a right-pointing arrow to indicate what records the query will recover (Figure 3-39).

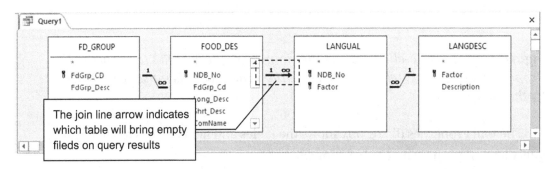

Figure 3-39. Whenever you change the join properties between query tables, an arrow indicates the table that will return empty fields records for no related records

But there is a tip here: you can't change just this join line, because the LANGUAL table also has a join line between it and the LANGDESC table. If you try to run the query, Access will answer with quite a disturbing warning, indicating that "...this Sql statement can't be executed because it contains ambiguous outer joins." This means it requires a complex procedure to solve the situation (Figure 3-40).

Figure 3-40. *Whenever you have a multiple tables query where the middle join line changes to return records, Access will complain that you are creating ambiguous references that can't be solved by the SQL engine*

Note   This defective query was saved as qryCategoriesFoodItemsAZLangualJoinDefective on the `sr28_Queries.accdb` database.

The solution to such a problem is quite easy. Whenever you change a query join line property to show all the records from one of the related tables, all other join lines for all other related tables on the same arrow direction must receive the same join property change.

You can see this in action by double-clicking the join line between the LANGUAL and LANGDESC tables and changing the join properties to also show all LANGUAL records (Figure 3-41).

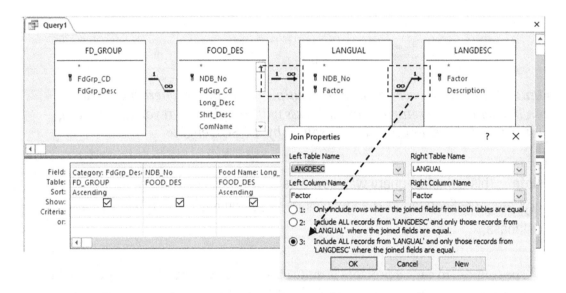

Figure 3-41. *To end the "... ambiguous outer joins" message that causes the SQL statement not to run, you must set the relationship join to all other tables on the arrow direction, which can be made by changing the join line property between LANGUAL and LANGDESC to show all LANGUAL records*

Note   This fixed query was saved as qryCategoriesFoodItemsAZLangualJoinFixed in the `sr28_Queries.accdb` database.

Caution   Since the LANGDESC table is on the one side of the relationship, the correct join option is the third: the one that returns all LANGUAL records (the many side of the relationship).

Now run the query and see that it can recover all FOOD_DES records. Look at the empty Description fields that returned Null values, and the record count is 44,429 records, as shown in Figure 3-42.

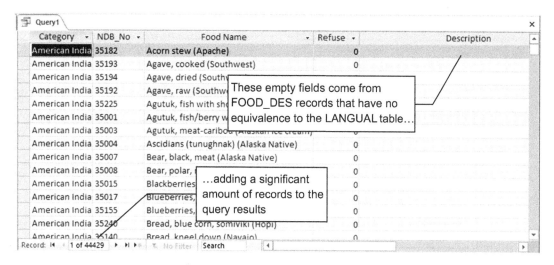

Figure 3-42. *When all query tables have a consistent relation between them in Design view, Access can run the SQL statement and return all the desired records (in this case, it includes all FOOD_DES records that have no LANGUAL table equivalence, returning empty LANGUAL.Description fields for such records)*

You may be wondering how all of these techniques are useful, but the time will come that you will need to search for fields not related on your database tables.

To make things more practical, the last query can easily return all FOOD_DES records that have no related records on the LANGUAL table by just setting the LANGUAL table's Description field to Is Null. Just records without a LANGUAL description will be returned (Figure 3-43).

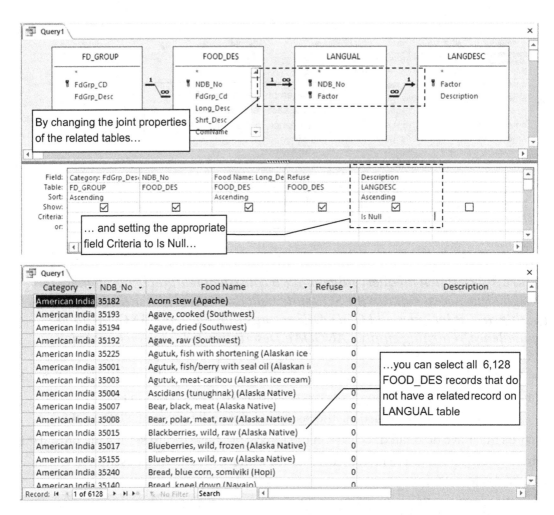

Figure 3-43. *Set the query field criteria that must return empty values to Is Null to force the query to recover all of the table records on the one side that do not have related records in the table on the many side*

Note   This query was saved as qryCategoriesFoodItemsAZNoLANGUAL in the sr28_Queries.accdb database.

Tip   As an exercise to do on your own, use the Find Unmatched Query Wizard with just the FOOD_DES and LANGUAL related tables. It will set Criteria to Null for the related field, as explained earlier, in the table's Join Properties dialog box (this can be found in the FOOD_DES Without Matching LANGUAL query in the sr28_Queries database).

Setting Query Properties

Besides the use of Field, Sort, Show, and Criteria to define how a query will return records, you can also set some query properties that select the records that must be returned.

There are many different query properties. Some are used by the old MDB database format only, and others are for external data sources (such as SQL Server and Oracle databases). To open the query property sheet, follow these steps:

1. Create a new, empty query using the Create tab's Query Design option.

2. Click the gray area between the query tables to unselect any field or table.

3. Click the Property Sheet command of the Show/Hide area of the Design tab.

This will make Microsoft Access show the Property Sheet window with all the possible query properties (which may change according to the query type). Table 3-7 defines the usefulness of each property.

Table 3-7. *Microsoft Access Query Properties*

Property	Usage
Description	Describes the query usage.
Default View	Defines how query records are shown.
Output All Fields	No: Shows only fields in the query grid with the Show option checked. Yes: Shows all available query table fields.
Top Values	Defines a specified number of a percentage of query records (like first 10, or first 10%).
Unique Values	No: All query records are returned.Yes: Records that duplicate data in all table fields are omitted.
Unique Records	No: All query records are returned.Yes: Returns only unique records based on all the displayed fields.
Run Permissions	Valid only for MDB files.

(*continued*)

Table 3-7. (*continued*)

Property	Usage
Source Database	Specifies the external database where query tables (or queries) reside.
Source Connect Str	Name of the application used to create an external database.
Record Locks	Determines what happens when two users try to edit the same record at the same time.
Recordset Type	Specifies the kind of recordset returned (Dynaset allows the edition). Snapshot is read-only.
ODBC Timeout	Number of seconds to wait before a timeout error occurs for a query that uses an Open Database Connectivity (ODBC) database.
Filter	Defines the subset of records to be displayed when a filter is applied.
Order By	Defines how records are sorted in a form, query, report, or table.
Max Records	Specifies the maximum number of records returned by an ODBC database to a Microsoft Access database (.mdb).
Orientation	Determines the orientation view (left to right or right to left).
Subdatasheet Name	Specifies the table or query bound to the subdatasheet.
Link Child Fields	Specifies a SubForm or SubReport or Chart control name linked to a query field used by a form (usually the many side of a relationship).
Link Master Fields	Specifies a Form or Report field (usually the one side of a relationship) that synchronizes with the Link Child Fields property of a subform or subreport or chart.
Subdatasheet Height	Determines the display height of a subdatasheet when expanded.
Subdatasheet Expanded	Specifies the saved state of all subdatasheets within a table or query.
Filter On Load	Defines a filter that is imposed over a query SQL instruction (it is automatically added whenever you filter query records and save the query).
Order By On Load	Defines a sort order imposed over a query SQL instruction (it is automatically added whenever you sort query records and save the query).

Three of these options will be used to control the records returned by the query: Top Values, Unique Values, and Unique Records.

- *Top Values*: Returns the *top* records, according to the query sort order

- *Unique Records*: Discards replicated records regarding all table fields used by the query, used or not on the query design grid

- *Unique Values*: Discards replicated records regarding just the fields with the Show option checked

Let's see this in action when creating queries using a data source other than an existing query.

Selecting Top Values

Let's use the query qryCategoriesFoodItemsAZLangual shown in Figure 3-35, which returns 38.301 records, to return the ten first food items that have higher Refuse amounts. Follow these steps:

1. Create a new query using the Query Design tool on the Create tab.

2. Select the Queries tab in the Show Tables dialog box, double-click qryCategoriesFoodITemsAZLangual to add it to the Query Design view, and close the Show Tables form.

3. Press and hold the Ctrl key while clicking the fields Category, Food Name, and Refuse and dragging them to the query design grid.

4. Set the Refuse field's Sort option to Descending.

5. Click the gray area to select the query.

6. Click the Property Sheet command on the Design tab to show the query's Property Sheet window.

7. For the Top Values property, type **10**.

8. Run the query to return the first ten records according to the greatest refuse part (Figure 3-44).

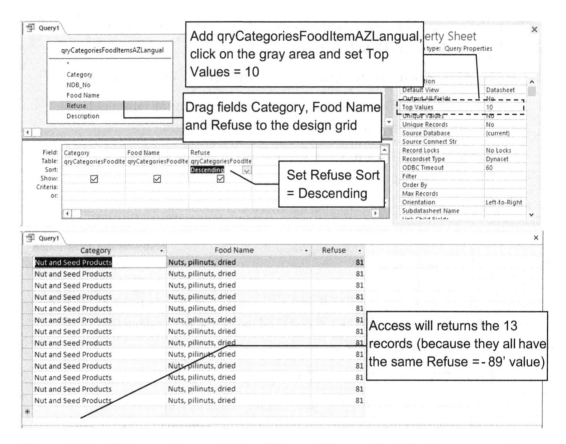

Figure 3-44. *Using qryCategoriesFoodITemsAZLangual as the data source, drag the Category, Food Name, and Refuse fields to the data grid; set Refuse Sort to Descending; and in the Property Sheet window, set Top Values to 10*

Use the query's SQL View option and note that this query SQL instruction now receives the TOP 10 SQL instruction after the SELECT statement:

```
SELECT TOP 10 qryCategoriesFoodItemsAZLangual.
Category, qryCategoriesFoodItemsAZLangual.[Food Name],
qryCategoriesFoodItemsAZLangual.Refuse FROM qryCategoriesFoodItemsAZLangual
ORDER BY qryCategoriesFoodItemsAZLangual.Refuse DESC;
```

Selecting Unique Values

Note that the query returned 13 records instead of 10. This interesting behavior happened because all these records have the same refuse amount (81g per 100g, or 81%) and the record seems to be the same (they vary in the Description field, not selected to be shown by the query).

To return only unique records, follow these steps:

1. Click the View button to show the query's Design view.

2. Show the Query Property Sheet window.

3. Set Unique Values to Yes.

4. Run the query again.

Figure 3-45 shows the result for which records must be returned from qryCategoriesFoodITemsAZLangual when you set Top Values to 10 and Unique Values to Yes.

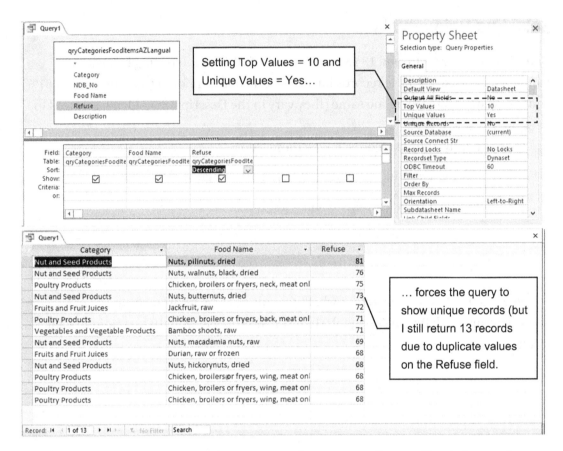

Figure 3-45. *By setting Top Values to 10 and Unique Values to Yes, it forces the query to show different records, although it returns the first 13 records whose Refuse amounts are higher due to duplicate values on the Refuse field and different values at the end of some Food Name column records (which is too lengthy to be shown here)*

Note   This query was saved as qryCategoriesFoodlTemsAZLangual_TopValues_ UniqueValues in the `sr28_Queries.accdb` database.

Caution   The query behavior regarding Top Values may be unexpected, but it is correct. Let's suppose you were seeking the first 10 notes in a classroom of 100 students. If 15 of them take the highest note, you should expect that a query with Top Values set to 10 could return all of them, right?

Use the SQL View option, and note that the Unique Records property was translated to the SQL DISTINCT instruction (which still uses the TOP 10 instruction).

```
SELECT DISTINCT TOP 10 qryCategoriesFoodItemsAZLangual.
Category, qryCategoriesFoodItemsAZLangual.[Food Name],
qryCategoriesFoodItemsAZLangual.Refuse FROM qryCategoriesFoodItemsAZLangual
ORDER BY qryCategoriesFoodItemsAZLangual.Refuse DESC;
```

If you want to use qryCategoriesFoodITemsAZLangual to return just the category names of the food values that have a Langual description, drag only the Category field to the query grid and set Unique Values to Yes. The query will run through all 38,301 records and fast return just the unique Categories field (Figure 3-46).

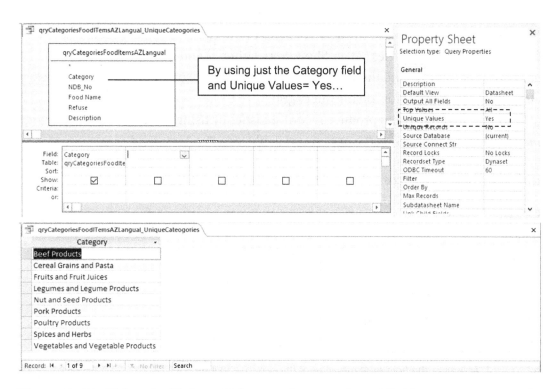

Figure 3-46. *Using the Unique Values and some selected fields, you can return the desired information from a table or a query. In this case, using the Category field from qryCategoriesFoodITemsAZLangual and setting Unique Values to Yes forces the query to return the 9 categories that appear on all 38,301 query records*

> **Note**   This query was saved as qryCategoriesFoodItemsAZLangual_
> UniqueCategories in the `sr28_Queries.accdb` database.

Use the SQL View option and note that the query uses the SQL `DISTINCT` instruction after the `SELECT` statement.

```
SELECT DISTINCT qryCategoriesFoodItemsAZLangual.Category
FROM qryCategoriesFoodItemsAZLangual;
```

Total Queries

A Total query is a Select query that groups records according to a desired value. To create a Total query, you need to add the desired tables or queries to the query design grid, set all the desired field properties (Alias, Show, Sort, Criteria) and query properties (Top Values, Unique Values), and then click the Totals button (the one with the sigma Greek letter) to show the Totals row on the query grid.

Total queries are great to produce record statistics by using what are called *aggregate functions*. Table 3-8 shows all the options available for a Total row field.

Table 3-8. *Microsoft Access Total Row Options for Total Queries*

Aggregate Function	Usage
Group By	Groups records according to the field value
Count	Counts grouped records
First, Last	Finds the first or last grouped record
Min, Max	Finds the Max or Min values of the grouped records
Avg	Averages the field or expression of the grouped values
StDev	Calculates the sample standard deviation for any field or expression of the grouped values
Sum	Sums the field or expression of the grouped values
Var	Calculates the sample Variance for any field or expression of the grouped values
Expression	Allows type an expression to group values
Where	Used whenever a Total Query column must be used as criteria

---

Note   Although not cited in Table 3-8, StDevP and VarP, which calculate the standard deviation and variance for a population, can also be used on a Total query using the Expression option.

The aggregate functions Group By, Count, First, Last, Min, and Max can be applied to fields of any data type, while Sum, Avg, StDev, Sum, and Var can be applied just to the Number data type or any expression that returns a numeric value.

Let's see some practical examples of Total queries using some of the previous queries created in this chapter.

Grouping Records

A Total query that uses just the Group By clause for all fields dragged to the query design grid returns one distinct record for each field, no matter the state of its Show property.

If you drag all fields from the available query data sources (tables or queries), the query will return a result similar to setting the property Unique Values to Yes. If the original field values does not repeat on each query record, the recordset obtained will be the same.

Figure 3-47 shows that the records count for a Total query based on all qryCategoriesFoodItemsAZ fields (shown in Figure 3-34) when setting Total to Group By for all fields is the same. Both queries will return 8,790 records, because they are all distinct records (the same result will be obtained by unchecking the Total command and setting the query property Unique Values to Yes), and there is nothing to aggregate.

Caution   A Total query always returns a read-only recordset, meaning that you cannot change any record value or insert it a new record. It does not have a new record row, and its New Record (► ★) navigation button will be disabled.

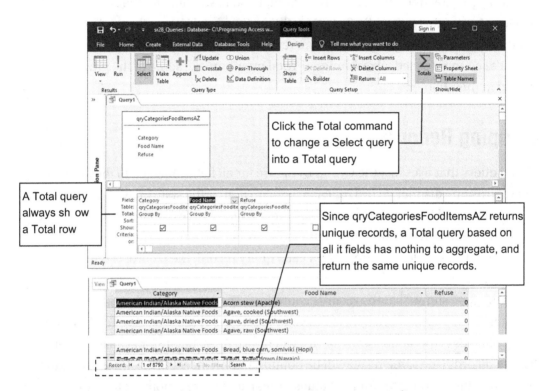

Figure 3-47. *If a query record source returns unique records (lime qryCategoriesFoodItemsAZ), any Total query where all its fields use just Group By as an aggregate function will return the same unique records*

Note   This query was saved as qryCategoryFoodItemsAZGroupBy in the sr28_Queries.accdb database.

The result will be the same if you uncheck the Show property of the Food Name field and run the query, because a Total query uses all fields on the design grid to produce the aggregated recordset, whether or not it is shown a recordset field.

But if you remove the Food Name field from the query design grid (by clicking its header and pressing the Delete key) and run the query again, the Total query will group records by the Refuse amount value (Figure 3-48).

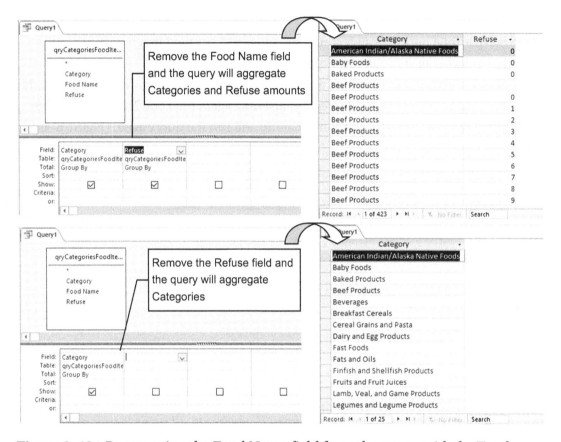

Figure 3-48. *By removing the Food Name field from the query grid, the Total query will begin to aggregate records by the Refuse amount (returning 423 records of varying Category and Refuse amounts). By removing the Refuse field, it will aggregate records by category (returning 25 categories)*

Note   This query was saved as qryCategories_RefuseGroupBy in the sr28_Queries.accdb database.

If you change the query to SQL view, you will notice that it received the GROUP BY instruction after the FROM statement.

```
SELECT qryCategoriesFoodItemsAZ.Category FROM qryCategoriesFoodItemsAZ
GROUP BY qryCategoriesFoodItemsAZ.Category;Counting records
```

To make a Total query count records, you must add any field that has values to the query grid and change its Total row from Group By to Count.

Let's suppose you want to extend the second query shown in Figure 3-48 to count the food items that exist on each food category. Just drag again the Food Name field to the query grid, change its Total row option to Count, and run the query again (Figure 3-49).

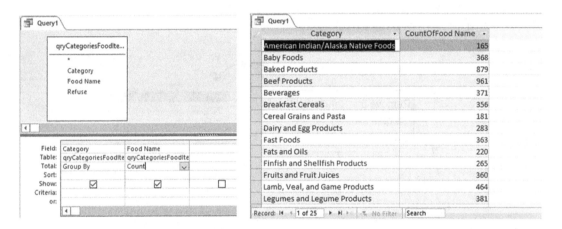

Figure 3-49. *To count aggregate records, add the desired field to the query grid and change its Total row to Count. Access will aggregate all records according to the fields to its left and then will count the records inside the aggregation*

Note   This query was saved as qryCategories_FoodCount in the `sr28_Queries.accdb` database.

Caution   Whenever you use a Total query aggregate function different from Group By, Access will change the aggregated field name to <FunctionOf><FieldName>. That is why the aggregated Food Name field name was changed to CountOfFood Name. You alias it to return a more legible result.

To see more practical values, let's consider that the sr28_doc.pdf documentation file shows on page 16 its Table 1 (called Number of Foods in the Database (n = 8,789) Containing a Value for the Specified Nutrient). Figure 3-50 shows part of this table, which was published in a two-column format.

Table 1.—Number of Foods in the Database (*n* = 8,789) Containing a Value for the Specified Nutrient

Nutr. No	Nutrient	Count	Nutr. No	Nutrient	Count
255	Water *†	8788	317	Selenium, Se *†	7089
208	Energy *†	8789	313	Fluoride, F	554
268	Energy	8756	401	Vitamin C, total ascorbic acid *†	7971
203	Protein *†	8789	404	Thiamin *†	8155
257	Adjusted Protein	4	405	Riboflavin *†	8173
204	Total lipid (fat) *†	8789	406	Niacin *†	8152
207	Ash *†	8464	410	Pantothenic acid	6544
205	Carbohydrate, by difference *†	8789	415	Vitamin B$_6$ *†	7884
291	Fiber, total dietary *†	8195	417	Folate, total *†	7528
269	Sugars, total *†	6957	431	Folic acid *†	6750
210	Sucrose	1743	432	Folate, food *†	7021

Figure 3-50. *Partial view of Table 1, located on page 16 of the sr28_doc.pdf file, that counts the number of food items that contain a value for each specified nutrient*

This is clearly the result of a Total query that, according to Figure 3-2, which shows the sr28.accdb Relationships window, uses three sr28.accdb tables: NUTR_DEF (to get the nutrient name), NUT_DATA (to get the nutrient value), and FOOD_DES (to count the food items).

Caution   Note in Figure 3-2 that the database designer did not create a direct relationship between FOOD__DES and NUT_DATA (there is the FOOTNOTE table to relate them). Since both FOOD_DES and NUT_DATA have the NDB_No field (which according to the sr28_doc.pdf file have the same meaning), there is no need to use the FOOTNOTE table.

To create this Total query, follow these steps:

1. Click the Query Design button located on the Create tab to create a new, empty query and show the Show Tables window.

2. In the Show Tables window, double-click the FOOD_DES, NUT_ DATA, and NUTR_DEF tables (in this order so your query will look like this example). Close the Show Tables window.

3. Since FOOD_DES is not related to any of the two other tables, click the FOOD_DES NDB_No field and drag it over the NUT_DATA NDB_No field to relate both tables on the query design.

Attention   Tables added to the query's Design view and not related to other tables will force the query to return the number of records that is proportional to the multiplication of all its records and the records returned by the other tables.

Tip   If you want, use the Relationships window to create a relationship between the tables FOOD_DES and NUT_DATA by their NDB_No fields (there is no need to impose referential integrity on this relation). By doing so, the next time you add the tables FOOD_DES and NUT_DATA to any query design grid, they will inherit the relationship.

Drag the following fields (on this other):

a. *From NUTR_DEF table*: Nut_No and NutrDesc fields (alias NutrDesc as Nutrient)

b. *From FOOD_DES table*: NDB_No (Alias NDB_No as Count)

4. Click the Totals button in the Show/Hide area of the query's Design tab to show the query Total row.

5. On Field NDB_No, set the following:

a. Total = Count

b. Sort = Descending

Run the query and note that it will take a while to return its results (showing a "Running" progress bar on its status bar), because we are using two of the biggest database tables: NUT_DATA (679,238 records) and FOOD_DES (8,790 records). The query will return records for each nutrient that has a food item with a value, sorted by food count in descending order (Figure 3-51).

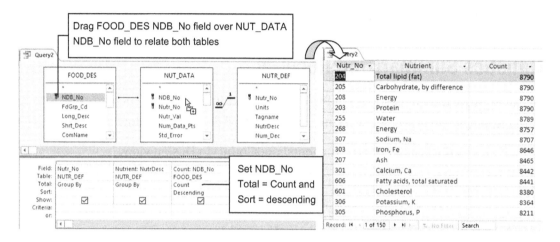

Figure 3-51. *To count how many food items each nutrient has, create a Total query with FOOD_DES, NUT_DATA, and NUTR_DEF tables, relating FOOD_DES and NUT_DATA by their NDB_No fields, and drag the NUTR_DEF Nutr_No and NutrDesc, and FOOD_DES NDB_No fields to the query grid. Alias each field and set NDB_No Total to Count and Sort to Descending*

Note   This query was saved as qryNutrientsFoodCount in the sr28_Queries. accdb database.

Caution   There is a difference on the food items count between the Access table and the sr28_doc.pdf table (Access counts one more food item for each nutrient). I bet that Access is not wrong.

Here is the query SQL view adding the COUNT() aggregate function as a field on its SELECT statement:

```
SELECT NUTR_DEF.Nutr_No, NUTR_DEF.NutrDesc AS Nutrient, Count(FOOD_DES.NDB_No)
AS [Count] FROM FOOD_DES INNER JOIN (NUTR_DEF INNER JOIN NUT_DATA ON NUTR_DEF.
Nutr_No = NUT_DATA.Nutr_No) ON FOOD_DES.NDB_No = NUT_DATA.NDB_No GROUP BY
NUTR_DEF.Nutr_No, NUTR_DEF.NutrDesc ORDER BY Count(FOOD_DES.NDB_No) DESC;
```

Statistics Summarizing Records

We can improve the query shown in Figure 3-52 by adding a full statistical resume for each nutrient, such as average, variance, and standard deviation. Follow these steps:

1. Show the last query (qryNutrientsFoodCount) in Design view.

2. To calculate the average for each nutrient, drag the Nutr_Val field from the NUT_DATA table to the design grid (alias it as Average).

3. Set the average by setting the Nutr_Val field Total to Avg.

4. To calculate the standard deviation for each nutrient, drag the Nutr_Val field again from the NUT_DATA table to the design grid (alias it as StDev).

5. Set StDev by setting Nutr_Val field Total to StDev.

Run the query and note that Access will take the same time to calculate the count, average, and standard variation values for each nutrient (Figure 3-52).

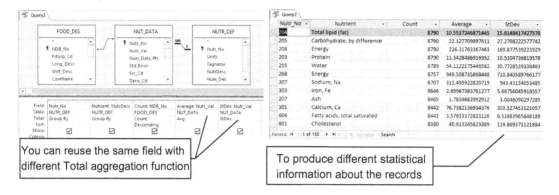

Figure 3-52. *To create a statistical resume of data, use the same value field, changing its Total function. Note that Access will return results with 12-decimal precision)*

Note   This query was saved as qryNutrientsStatistcs in the `sr28_Queries.accdb` database, containing Average, StDev, Min and Max values for each nutrient, rounded to two decimal places.

Caution   If you try to also calculate the Min and Max values of each nutrient, the query may seem to replicate records, but it does not. The reason for this behavior is the 12-decimal precision calculated value, which may differ on the 12th decimal place. To avoid this problem, click each aggregated field head to select it, show the Property Sheet window, set the field Format to Fixed and Decimal Places to 2 (or other desired precision), and run the query.

Crosstab Queries

A Crosstab query is a type of Total query where you can take unique field values and turn them into field columns. Thinking about the query recordset result as a matrix, having rows and columns, a Crosstab query can be considered as a transpose of that matrix, with the difference being that unique field values will be turned into field names.

The Crosstab query is always read-only: its recordset records values can't be changed or used to add a new record.

To create a Crosstab query, you need to create a new query and click the Crosstab command in the Query Type area of the query's Design tab to make Access add a Total row and a Crosstab row to the query design grid.

The Crosstab row will offer four options for each field.

- *Not Show:* Hide the field while still using it to group records using the specifications of the Total row.

- *Row heading:* Define how many query fields you want to appear as a query's grouped field.

- *Column heading:* Define just one query field whose unique values will be turned into query column fields.

- *Value:* Define just one query field to return the aggregate results for the Row Headings and Column Heading fields according to the field's Total aggregate option (you can't use Group By on this field Total row).

Caution Since Access limits any table or query to have up to 255 fields, any Crosstab query field count can't surpass this value when considering all of its "Row heading show" fields plus the fields returned by the unique values of the selected Column heading field, or you will receive Error = 776, "Too many crosstab column headers."

A good example of a Crosstab query is the ABBREV table found on the sr28.accdb database and also used to create (by exporting to Excel) the associated ABBREV.XLSX Excel spreadsheet that you can also download from the USDA ARS MAFCL website. It uses records from FOOD_DES as row headers, specific nutrients from NUTR_DEF as column headers, and NUT_DATA Nutr_Val as the values (Figure 3-53).

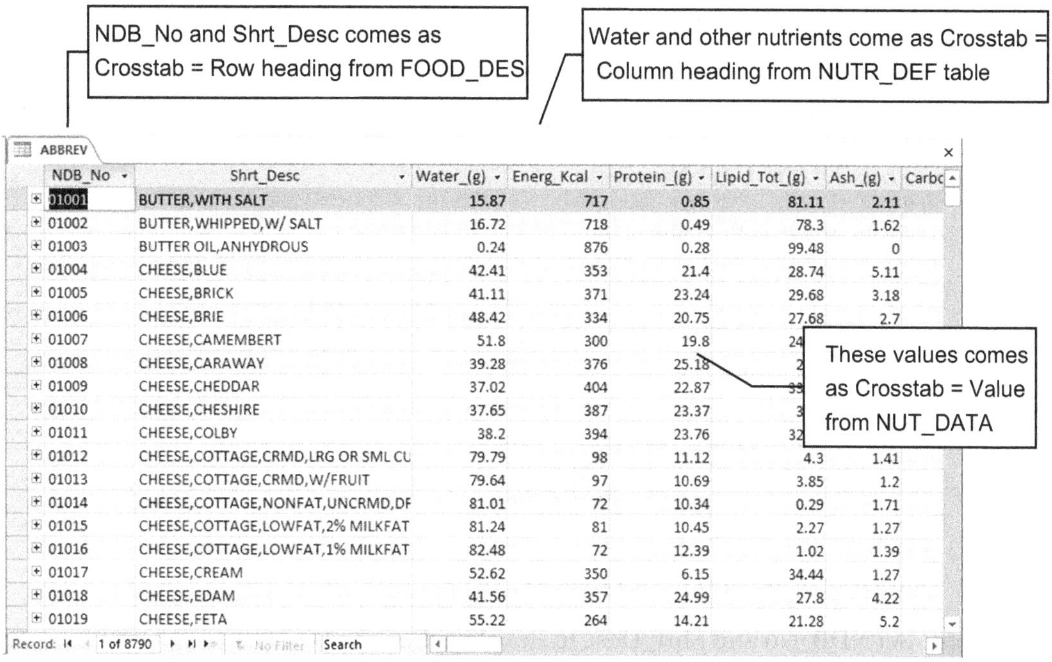

NDB_No and Shrt_Desc comes as
Crosstab = Row heading from FOOD_DES

Water and other nutrients come as Crosstab =
Column heading from NUTR_DEF table

NDB_No	Shrt_Desc	Water_(g)	Energ_Kcal	Protein_(g)	Lipid_Tot_(g)	Ash_(g)	Carbc
01001	BUTTER,WITH SALT	15.87	717	0.85	81.11	2.11	
01002	BUTTER,WHIPPED,W/ SALT	16.72	718	0.49	78.3	1.62	
01003	BUTTER OIL,ANHYDROUS	0.24	876	0.28	99.48	0	
01004	CHEESE,BLUE	42.41	353	21.4	28.74	5.11	
01005	CHEESE,BRICK	41.11	371	23.24	29.68	3.18	
01006	CHEESE,BRIE	48.42	334	20.75	27.68	2.7	
01007	CHEESE,CAMEMBERT	51.8	300	19.8	24		
01008	CHEESE,CARAWAY	39.28	376	25.18	2		
01009	CHEESE,CHEDDAR	37.02	404	22.87	33		
01010	CHEESE,CHESHIRE	37.65	387	23.37	3		
01011	CHEESE,COLBY	38.2	394	23.76	32		
01012	CHEESE,COTTAGE,CRMD,LRG OR SML CU	79.79	98	11.12	4.3	1.41	
01013	CHEESE,COTTAGE,CRMD,W/FRUIT	79.64	97	10.69	3.85	1.2	
01014	CHEESE,COTTAGE,NONFAT,UNCRMD,DF	81.01	72	10.34	0.29	1.71	
01015	CHEESE,COTTAGE,LOWFAT,2% MILKFAT	81.24	81	10.45	2.27	1.27	
01016	CHEESE,COTTAGE,LOWFAT,1% MILKFAT	82.48	72	12.39	1.02	1.39	
01017	CHEESE,CREAM	52.62	350	6.15	34.44	1.27	
01018	CHEESE,EDAM	41.56	357	24.99	27.8	4.22	
01019	CHEESE,FETA	55.22	264	14.21	21.28	5.2	

Record: 14   1 of 8790   ► ►I ►   No Filter   Search

These values comes
as Crosstab = Value
from NUT_DATA

Figure 3-53. The sr28.accdb database ABBREV table was created by using a Crosstab query to turn the nutrient descriptions into table column headers

By inspecting Figure 3-2, which shows the database Relationships window, one can realize that to create such a query result, it will need the FOOD_DES, NUT_DATA, and NUTR_DEF tables. So, let's create a Crosstab query that will return a more precise food item nutrient table that returns all 8,790 food items but uses *all 155 nutrients* available on the NUTR_DEF table. Follow these steps:

1. Click the Query Design command of the Create tab to create a new query and show the Show Tables window.

2. In the Show Tables window, double-click the FOOD_DES, NUT_ DATA, and NUTR_DEF tables (in this order so your query will be identical to this book's figures) to add them to the query Design view and close the Show Tables window.

3. Since FOOD_DES and NUT_DATA were not related by default in the Relationships window, click the FOOD_DES NDB_No field to select it and drag it over the NUT_DATA NDB_No field to relate them in the query's Design view.

4. Double-click the next table fields to add them to the query grid (in this order):

   a. *From FOOD_DES*: NDB_No and Shrt_Desc.

   b. *From NUTR_DEF*: NutrDesc.

   c. *From NUT_DATA*: Nutr_Val.

5. Click the Crosstab command found in the Query Type area of the query's Design tab to show the Total and Crosstab rows in the query design grid.

6. Since there is only one nutrient value for each food item (represented by its NDB_No field), set the Nutr_Val field Total to First.

7. Set this Crosstab options for the query fields:

   a. Set NDB_No and Shrt_Desc to Row Heading.

   b. Set NutrDesc to Column Heading.

   c. Set Nutr_Val to Value.

Run the query and see its results (Figure 3-54).

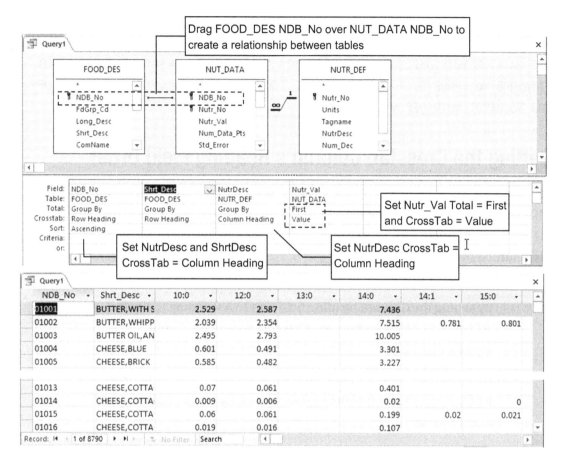

Figure 3-54. *To create a complete nutrient table using all food items and nutrients available, make a Crosstab query that uses FOOD_DES NDB_No and set Shrt_ Desc as Crosstab to Row Heading (sorted Ascending by NDB_No), NUT_DEF NutrDesc as Crosstab to Column Heading, and NUT_DATA Nutr_Val as Total to First and Crosstab to Value.qry*

Note   This query was saved as qryFoodItemsNutrientsAZ in the sr28_Queries. accdb database, containing Average, StDev, Min, and Max values for each nutrient, rounded to two decimal places.

Change the query to SQL view, and note that its SQL instruction uses the TRANSFORM FIRST statements to create the Crosstab query (note that it is becoming too complex to be created manually).

```
TRANSFORM First(NUT_DATA.Nutr_Val) AS FirstOfNutr_Val SELECT FOOD_DES.
NDB_No, FOOD_DES.Shrt_Desc FROM FOOD_DES INNER JOIN (NUTR_DEF INNER JOIN
NUT_DATA ON NUTR_DEF.Nutr_No = NUT_DATA.Nutr_No) ON FOOD_DES.NDB_No = NUT_
DATA.NDB_No GROUP BY FOOD_DES.NDB_No, FOOD_DES.Shrt_Desc ORDER BY FOOD_DES.
NDB_No PIVOT NUTR_DEF.NutrDesc;
```

Setting the Crosstab Column's Heading Field Order

You may have noted that the nutrients order returned by the NUTR_DEF NutrDesc field (that was defined as the Crosstab Column Heading field) is alphabetical (beginning from the Fatty Acids names such as 10:0, 12:0, and so on) and that there are nutrient values not returned by the ABBREV table.

You can change the unique Crosstab Column Heading field order in one of two ways.

- By setting the Column heading field Sort to Ascending (default sort order) or Descending, which will make Access define it in alphabetical order

- By setting the query Column Headings property to the field order you want so that the unique field values appear on the recordset of the query records

Figure 3-55 shows how the query fields appear when you change the NutrDesc Crosstab setting's Column Heading field's Sort order to Descending.

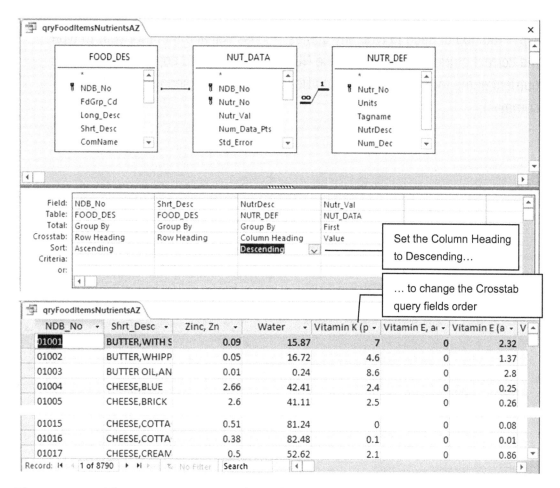

Figure 3-55. *The easiest way to make a change on the field order of a Crosstab query Column Heading field is to change its sort order to Descending*

The other way is to define the query's Column Headings property by typing all Column Headings fields separated by a comma (the default Microsoft Windows list separator) in the order you want to appear on the query recordset. But be advised that the field names must match exactly the records returned by the Column heading field and that just the names type will appear on the query recordset.

Figure 3-56 shows what happens when you type the next nutrient's NutrDesc field values on the query Column Heading properties separated by commas (default Windows list separator): Water, Protein, Energy, Ash.

Tip   You do not need to type any quotes. Access will add them for you. To type the correct nutrient names, open the NUTR_DEF table and copy and paste each nutrient name to the query's Column Headings property (separating them with commas).

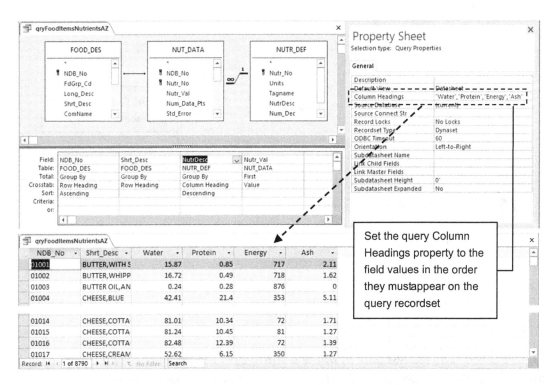

Figure 3-56. *Use the query Property Sheet window to define the query Column Headings property with the exact field values, separated by a comma, in the order that you want them to appear on the query recordset (just the typed values will be shown)*

Note   This query was saved as qryFoodItemsNutrientsSelected in the sr28_ Queries.accdb database.

Change the query to SQL view and note that the Crosstab query's SQL instruction uses the PIVOT statement to define its Column Headings property (and that it is also too complex to be written by hand).

190

TRANSFORM First(NUT_DATA.Nutr_Val) AS FirstOfNutr_Val SELECT FOOD_DES. NDB_No, FOOD_DES.Shrt_Desc FROM FOOD_DES INNER JOIN (NUTR_DEF INNER JOIN NUT_DATA ON NUTR_DEF.Nutr_No = NUT_DATA.Nutr_No) ON FOOD_DES.NDB_No = NUT_ DATA.NDB_No GROUP BY FOOD_DES.NDB_No, FOOD_DES.Shrt_Desc ORDER BY FOOD_DES. NDB_No, NUTR_DEF.NutrDesc DESC **PIVOT NUTR_DEF.NutrDesc In ("Water","Protein ","Energy","Ash");**

Creating a Column Headings List

There is more than one way to define a query's Column Headings property to reflect a long list of field names in the desired order, and all of them are based on a query that returns the same unique records that will be used by a Crosstab query's Column Heading field.

- By manually copying each record value from the base query and paste it into the Column Heading property, separating each with a comma

- By writing a VBA function that uses this base query to generate a long string that concatenates this unique record values, separating them with a comma

- By exporting the base query to an Excel spreadsheet, doing some operations on them, and copying and pasting them into Notepad, from where you will generate the list of concatenated values

The first option is prone to copy/paste errors. The second option uses VBA, and although it is the best technique, it requires knowledge that is far beyond the scope of this book.

So, let's use the third technique, exporting a query result. Take a look again at the query shown in Figure 3-56 and its associated SQL instruction.

Note that its SQL code has a PIVOT instruction that encloses all desired field names between parentheses, each one enclosed with its own quotes, separated by commas. We will generate a long list of field names and copy and paste it inside the SQL PIVOT parentheses. Follow these steps:

1. Open the query qryNutrients in Design view, and note that it uses the NutDesc field to generate a recordset of nutrient names ordered by the Nut_No fields (which will be the Crosstab field order). Run the query.

Caution   The qryNutrients uses as criteria <>268 to discard this item because table NUTR_DEF has two different Energy records: "NDB_No = 208, Energy in Kcal" and "NBD_No = 268, Energy in KJ").

---

2. Click the Excel command in the Export area of the External data tab to export these query results to Excel.

3. Click OK in the Export – Excel Spreadsheet window, note where the spreadsheet will be saved (your Documents folder with the same query name), click the OK button to go to the next page wizard, and click Close to finish the exportation (Figure 3-57).

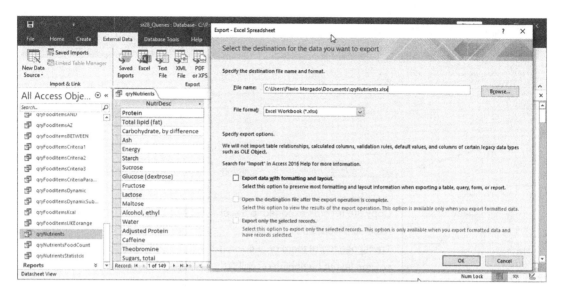

Figure 3-57. *Open qryNutrients, click the External Data ➤ Excel command to show the Export – Excel Spreadsheet window, click OK, and close it to export its results to the qryNutrients.xlsx Excel workbook (located in your Documents folder)*

4. Open the `qryNutrients.xlsx` file on your Excel copy. Note that cell A1 holds the field name (NutDesc).

5. Click cell A2 (Protein) and press the Ctrl+Shift+Down arrow to select all nutrient names (cells A2:A150).

6. Press Copy (Ctrl+C) to copy the selection to the Clipboard.

7. Press Ctrl+Home to go to cell A1, click cell D1, and use the Paste ➤ Transpose command to change the row-by-row layout into a column-by-column layout.

8. Press Copy (Ctrl+C) to copy the transposed values (you don't need the spreadsheet anymore; see Figure 3-58).

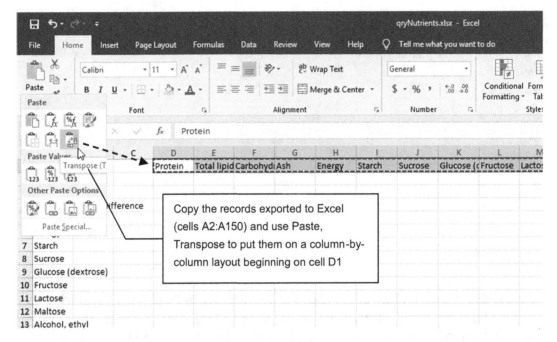

Figure 3-58. *Open the exported query results into Excel, select all nutrient names (cells A2.A150), click cell D1, and select Paste ➤ Transpose. Then copy the transposed results to the Clipboard*

9. Open Notepad and paste the transposed results. They will be pasted as a single row of nutrient names, separated by a Tab character.

10. Note that no nutrient name is enclosed in quotes or separated by a comma. We will do this by using Notepad Edit ➤ Replace command.

   a. Select the wide blank space that separates two nutrient names (the one that separates "Protein" from "Lipid", or "...(fat)" from "Carbohydrate").

   b. Select the Edit ➤ Replace command (the Tab character will be automatically inserted in the "Find what" text box).

   c. For the "Replace with" option, type a quote, a comma, and another quote (,).

   d. Click Replace All to change every Tab character to this sequence.

e. Every nutrient name but the first and last is now enclosed is quotes and separated by a comma. Press Ctrl+Home to select the beginning of the file and type a comma to enclose "Protein."

f. Press Ctrl+End to select the end of file and type a quote to enclose the last nutrient, "...n-7.

g. Select the entire file (Ctrl+A) and copy to the Clipboard the desired sequence of field names, separated by commas (Figure 3-59).

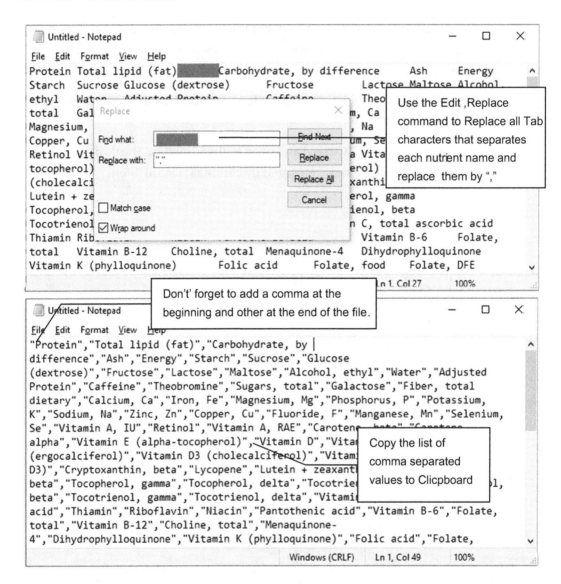

Figure 3-59. *Paste the transposed values into Notepad, select the Tab character that produces a wide blank space between field names, and apply the Edit ➤ Replace command to replace each Tab character with a comma. Don't forget to add a quote at the beginning and end of the file. Press Ctrl+A to select the entire file and Ctrl+C to copy the nutrient names to the Clipboard*

11. Open qryFoodItemsNutrientsSelected in SQL view, select all the food items inside the PIVOT parentheses, and paste the list of field names.

12. Run the query. If everything is correct, Access will execute the Crosstab query and return the records with the field names in the desired sort order (Figure 3-60).

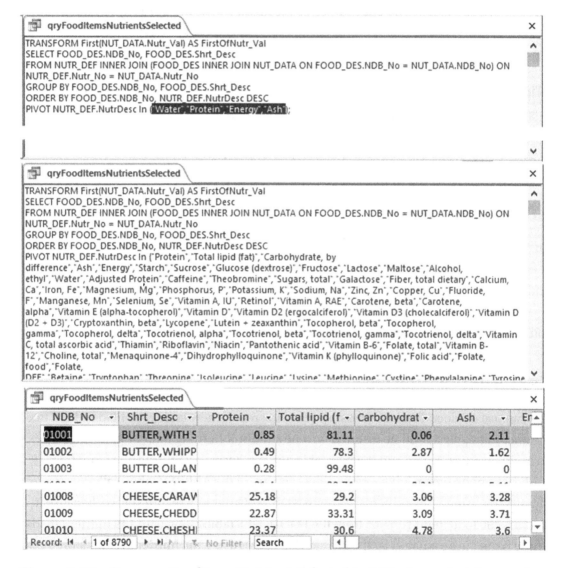

Figure 3-60. *Open qryFoodItemsNutrientsSelected in SQL view, select the nutrient names inside the PIVOT instruction parentheses, and paste the desired list of nutrients copied from Notepad*

Note   This query was saved as qryFoodItemsNutrientsNDB_NoOrder in the `sr28_Queries.accdb` database.

Caution   Although the query works as expected, the query's Column Headings property cannot hold this long comma-separated field names list. Due to this limitation, every time you open qryFoodItemsNutrientsNDB_NoOrder query in Design mode, Access will show an error message ("The expression you enter exceeds the 1,024-character limit for the query design grid"), but the PIVOT instruction will still be there when you change the query to SQL view.

Tip   The easiest way to change the query field order is by running the query and using the Datasheet view to drag fields to a new position. Save the query to store the desired field presentation order.

Action Queries

An Action query is one that is based on a Select, Total, or Crosstab query and is capable of acting on the database by creating a new table (with or without records) or by adding, updating, or deleting records on any table.

Let's see each possible action query so you can understand how you will use them on your database applications.

Create Table Queries

You can use a Select, Total, or Crosstab query to create a new table. The fields added to the query design grid will be inserted on a new table, inheriting their original data type. To avoid inserting records on the new table, use a criteria that returns no records.

Let's suppose you want to create a new version of the ABBREV table, called MyABBREV using qryFoodItemsNutrientsNDB_NoOrder as a record source, because it has all 8,790 food items records from the FOOD_DES table along with 149 nutrient fields whose names are available on the NUTR_DEF table (using the nutrient values stored on NUT_DATA table).

To create the MyABBREV table, follow these steps:

1. Use the Create ➤ Query Design command to create a new query and show the Show Tables window.

2. In the Show Tables window, select the Query tab, double-click qryFoodItemsNutrientsNDB_NoOrder to add it to the query design, and close the Show Table window.

3. Drag the * from qryFoodItemsNutrientsNDB_NoOrder to the query design grid, indicating that all query fields will be inserted as fields of the new MyABBREV table.

4. Click the Make Table command in the Query Type area of the query's Design tab, Access will show the Make Table window, where you can select whether the table will be created on this or on an external database.

5. Type MyABBREV on the Table Name text box and click OK to close the Make Table window.

Tip   Click the Make Table command to show the Make Table window again.

---

6. To have some control about which food items will be inserted on the new table, turn the query into a dynamic criteria query by dragging the field Shrt_Desc to the query grid, unchecking its Show option, and inserting this expression on its Criteria row:

```
Like "*" & [Type any part of the food name] & "*"
```

7. Save the query with a significant name, like qryCreateMyABBREVTable.

8. Since this is an Action query, you can do the following:

   a. Click the View button to type anything and verify which records will be returned. The MyABBREV table will not be created.

   b. Click the Run button to execute the query, filter its records, and create the MyABBREV table (Figure 3-61).

Tip   The Run button does the same action to Select, Total, and Crosstab queries. But for Action queries, it is used to execute the query. It has the same effect as double-clicking the query name on the Database window.

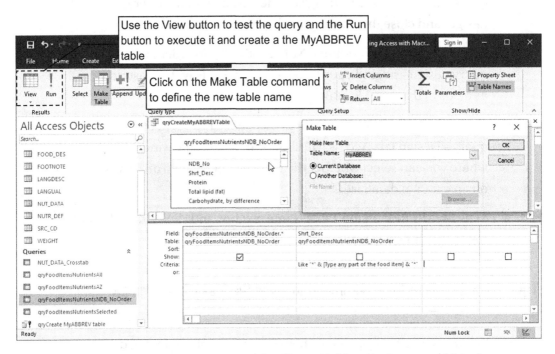

Figure 3-61.   *Create a new query, use the Show Table window to add it the qryFoodItemsNutrientsNDB_NoOrder query, drag the query * to design grid, and make it a dynamic criteria by adding the Like expression for the hidden Shrt_Desc field. Click Make Table command to turn into a Make Table query and type the name of the new table (MyABBREV)*

Note   This query was saved as qryCreateMyABBREVTable in the sr28_ Queries.accdb database. For your information, it runs about 30 percent faster on the old MDB Access file format and runs about 60 percent faster on Access 2003.

Now that you created the Make Table query, any time you execute it (by clicking Run or by double-clicking it in the Database window), the table will be re-created. Access will warn you that the existing table will be deleted before the new one can be created. Since this is a dynamic criteria query, you can create different MyABBREV tables by typing different options in the Enter Parameter Value window.

- Type an improbable food name part (like XYZ, for example) to create an empty MyABBREV table.

- Type nothing to add all food items to the MyABBREV table.

- Type an existing food name part (like **apple**) to add just food items that have this in their names to the MyABBREV table.

Whatever you type as criteria for the Make Table query, Microsoft Access will run the query first and will tell you how many records will be inserted on the new MyABBREV table (Figure 3-62).

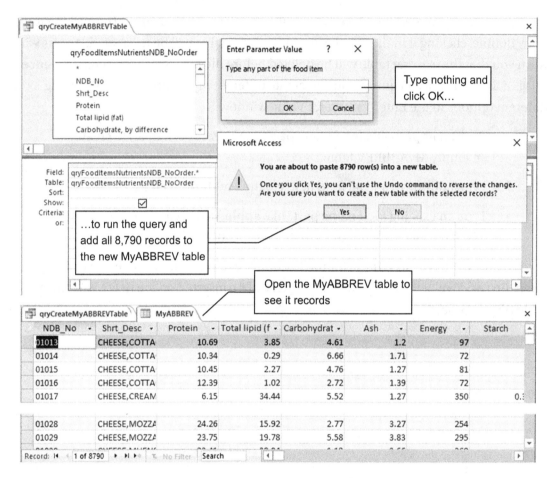

Figure 3-62. *Run qryCreateMyABBREVTable to create the MyABBREV table. By typing nothing into the dynamic criteria input box, all 8,790 food item records will be inserted on the new MyABBREV table. After running the query, double-click the Database window to open it and show its records and field structure*

Caution   A Create Table query does not create indexes or the table's primary key. After creating a table this way, consider showing it in Design view to set its primary key and create the desired indexes on its fields.

Change the query to SQL view and note that the Create Table query SQL instruction uses the INTO statement to define the affected table.

```
SELECT qryFoodItemsNutrientsNDB_NoOrder.* INTO MyABBREV FROM
qryFoodItemsNutrientsNDB_NoOrder WHERE (((qryFoodItemsNutrientsNDB_NoOrder.
Shrt_Desc) Like "*" & [Type any part of the food item] & "*"));
```

Delete Queries

A Delete query is a Select query that may use criteria to select table records and delete records from a table.

Note that a Delete query may act on a large scope of records, considering that if the table affected is on the one side of the relationship, with referential integrity imposed with the Cascade Delete Related Records property checked, records from the many side will also be automatically deleted. Since this action can't be undone, you may consider backing up your database before running it.

Use a Delete query whenever you need to quickly clean a table or the entire database without disrupting the relationship between its tables.

Considering the MyABBREV table created in the previous section, follow these steps to easily delete its records using a Delete query:

1. Use the Create ➤ Query Design command to create a new query and show the Show Tables window.

2. In the Show Tables window, double-click the MyABBREV table to add it to the query design and close the Show Tables window.

3. Click the Delete command in the Query Type area of the query's Design tab. Access will show a Delete row on the query design grid.

4. Drag Shrt_Desc from the MyABBREV table to the query: it will automatically receive the Delete = Where option.

5. Turn it into a dynamic criteria query by typing this expression on the Shrt_Desc field's Criteria row:

   ```
   Like "*" & [Type any part of the food name] & "*"
   ```

6. Save the query with a significant name, like
   qryDeleteMyABBREVRecords.

7. Click the Run button to execute the query, filter its records
   according to what you type on the dynamic criteria Input Box,
   and delete the selected records from the MyABBREV table (type
   nothing to delete all the table records, as shown in Figure 3-63).

Caution   Microsoft Access will issue two warnings before deleting the records.
The first will warn you that you are about to delete records and that it can't be
undone; the second will tell you how many records will be deleted.

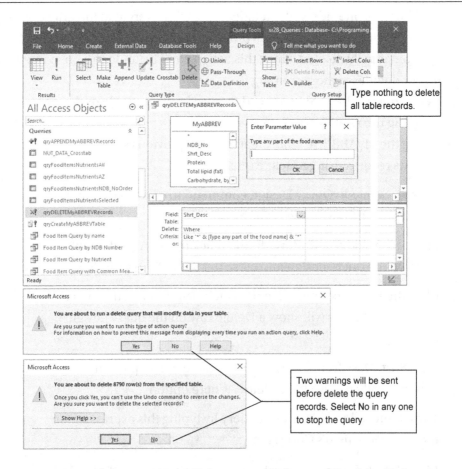

Figure 3-63. *Use a Delete query to delete records from any table. To have some
control over which records will be deleted, turn it into a dynamic criteria query
using the Like operator*

> **Tip**   You must use qryCreateMyABBREVTable first to create the MyABBREV table before running the qryDeleteMyABBREVRecords Delete query, which can also be found in the `sr28_Queries.accdb` database.

Change the query to SQL view, and note that the Delete query SQL instruction uses the DELETE statement to define the affected table.

```
DELETE MyABBREV.Shrt_Desc FROM MyABBREV WHERE (((MyABBREV.Shrt_Desc) Like
"*" & [Type any part of the food name] & "*"));
```

Append Queries

Use an Append query whenever you want to add records to a table. It is usually used along with a Delete query on temporary tables that may be used to resume data to generate special reports.

Be aware that the records you want to insert must comply with the table primary key (they may not conflict with already existing records). Consider the MyABBREV table created in the previous section that has no primary key or index on its NDB_No and Shrt_Desc fields. By using an Append query, you can easily duplicate table records.

Since the MyABBREV table was created by a Create Table query based on the qryFoodItemsNutrientsNDB_NoOrder query, we will use this table to create an Append query to add the desired records to the MyABBREV table. Follow these steps:

1. Use the Create ➤ Query Design command to create a new query and show the Show Tables window.

2. In the Show Tables window, double-click the qryFoodItemsNutrientsNDB_NoOrder table to add it to the query design and close the Show Table window.

3. Click the Append command in the Query Type area of the query's Design tab. Access will show the Append window, where you can select from the list the table that will receive the new data, located in this or in an external database.

4. Close the Append table, and note that Access added an Append To row to the query design grid.

5. Drag the * from the qryFoodItemsNutrientsNDB_NoOrder table to the query design grid. Access will automatically set MyABBREV.* on its Append row.

6. To have some control over which records will be deleted, turn it into a dynamic query. Drag Shrt_Desc from the qryFoodItemsNutrientsNDB_NoOrder table to the query's design grid. It will automatically receive Shrt_Desc on its Append row.

7. Delete the field name Shrt_Desc from the Append To row, since it's already included as part of the MyABBREV.* option.

Caution When using an Append query, whenever you drag a field to the query design grid, Access will automatically search for this field name on the destination table, and if it is found, the same name will be added to the Append to row of this field. Since you dragged the * from the qryFoodItemsNutrientsNDB_NoOrder table, the query will have two fields to add a value to the Shrt_Desc field, which will generate a query error "Duplicate output destination Shrt_Desc." For this reason, you must clear the Append option for the Shrt_Desc criteria field.

---

8. Turn it to a dynamic criteria query by typing this expression on the Shrt_Desc field Criteria row:

```
Like "*" & [Type any part of the food name] & "*"
```

9. Save the query with a significant name, such as qryAppendMyABBREVRecords.

10. Click the Run button to execute the query, filter its records according to what you type in the Enter Parameter Value box, and append the selected records to the MyABBREV table (type nothing to append all the records, as shown in Figure 3-64).

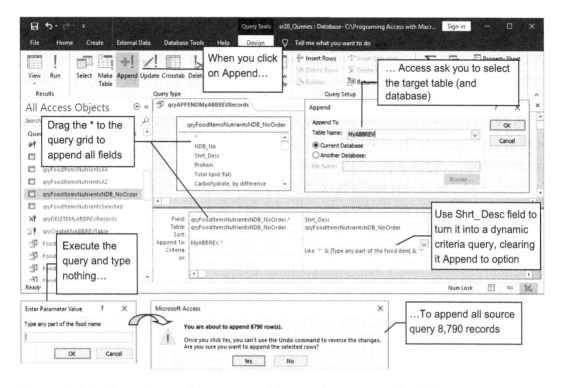

Figure 3-64. *Use a Append query to add records to any table. To have some control about which records will be deleted, turn it into a dynamic criteria query using the Like operator. Don't forget to clear the Append To option of the criteria field whenever you drag the source query * field to the query grid*

Change the query to SQL view and note that the Append query SQL instruction uses the INSERT INTO statement to define the affected table and the SELECT statement to define its record source.

```
INSERT INTO MyABBREV SELECT qryFoodItemsNutrientsNDB_NoOrder.* FROM
qryFoodItemsNutrientsNDB_NoOrder WHERE (((qryFoodItemsNutrientsNDB_NoOrder.
Shrt_Desc) Like "*" & [Type any part of the food item] & "*"));
```

Update Queries

Use an Update query to change the field values of any table records according to a specified criteria. It is useful to change a huge amount of records at a time to make them easier to maintain.

Be aware that you cannot change any AutoNumber field value, and possibly the table primary key whenever it has a defined a relationship with other table, using referential integrity between them. Also note that some fields may have property Required set to Yes, property Allow Zero Length set to No, or a defined validation rule that may act on the changes you are trying to make using the Update query.

As an exercise, let's suppose that you want to add a Kcal field on the MyABBREV table Number that uses the Single data type and whose value must be defined according to the food item amounts of carbohydrate, protein, and lipid (as previously described in the section "Using the Expression Builder" for a calculate field, as shown in Figure 3-65).

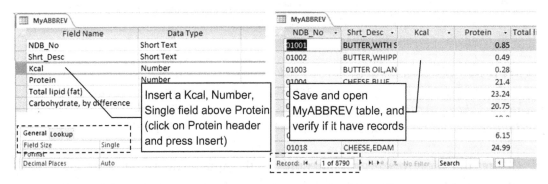

Figure 3-65. *Open the MyABBREV table in Design view, click the file's Protein header, and press the Insert key to insert a row above it. Add the Kcal field as a Number, Single data type. Save the table and open it in Datasheet view to see the new, empty Kcal field*

Supposing that the MyABBREV table has records, you can easily update all its records' Kcal field using an Update query. Follow these steps:

1. Use the Create ➤ Query Design command to create a new query and show the Show Tables window.

2. In the Show Tables window, double-click the MyABBREV table to add it to the query design and close the Show Tables window.

3. Click the Update command in the Query Type area of the query Design tab. Access will show the "Update to" row for the query design grid.

4. Drag the field Kcal from the MyABBREV table to the query design grid.

5. Right-click the Update option of the Kcal field and choose Build to show the Expression Builder window.

6. In the Expression Elements list, select the sr28_Queries.accdb, Tables, MyABBREV item, and double-click each field name in the Expression Categories list to create the "Update to" expression using this formula:

    ```
    ([MyABBREV]![Protein] + [MyABBREV]![Carbohydrate, by
    difference] )*4 + [MyABBREV]![Total lipid (fat)] *9
    ```

7. Save the query with a significant name, such as qryUpdateMyABBREVKcal.

8. Close the Expression Builder and click Run to execute the Update query on all MyABBREV records (Figure 3-66).

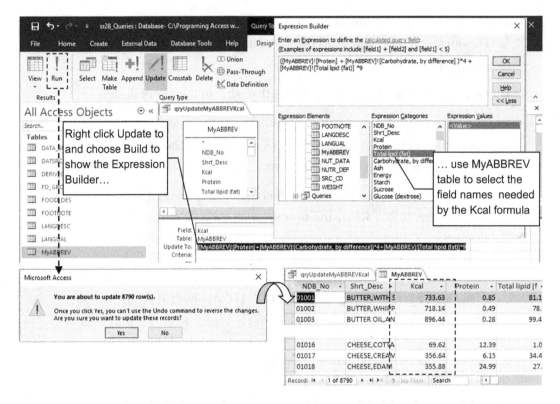

Figure 3-66. *Right-click the Update option of the Kcal field, select Build to show the Expression Builder, click the MyABBREV table, and double-click the field names needed to build the Kcal expression formula. Run the query to update all the table records*

Caution   This approach will just work for the existing table records. If MyABBREV receives new records, their Kcal field will not be automatically updated.

Special Queries

Besides the already cited queries that have a graphic interface to create the SQL instruction for you, Microsoft Access has also other types of queries that use some special technique or offer just the SQL Design view, meaning that you must know the SQL language to create them. I will call them *special queries*.

You can find them in the Query Wizard or in the Query Type area of the Query tab:

- *Union*: Allows the results of two different queries to be joined into a single recordset

- *Pass-Through*: Allows you to send special SQL statements to an external client-server database (like SQL Server and Oracle)

- *Data Definition*: Allows you to manipulate the database structure, creating, changing, and deleting tables, relationships, fields, and indexes

Special Queries from the Query Wizard

Open a Query Wizard and note that besides the Simple Query and Crosstab Query Wizards, it offers two other options (see Figure 3-7).

- Find Duplicates Query Wizard

- Find Unmatched Query Wizard

The first runs through a table's records and returns all records that duplicate information in one or more of its fields. The second finds records from the table on the one side that have no existing records in the table on the many side of the relationship.

Find Duplicate Records

This is useful whenever you need to find duplicate records on a table. They can be inserted for many reasons, and the most important is because the database interface does not offer a precise way of searching for a record existence before inserting an identical new one.

Supposing that you want to investigate table FOOD_DES to search for duplicate food names regarding the Shrt_Desc field, follow these steps:

1. Click the Query Wizard command on the Create tab to open the Query Wizard window (see Figure 3-7).

2. Choose the third option, Find Duplicates Query Wizard, and click OK to show the Find Duplicates Query Wizard window.

3. Select the table you want to find duplicate records (FOOD_DES) and click Next.

4. Select the table fields you want to search for duplicate information (Shrt_Desc) and click Next.

Caution   If you select more than one field, the wizard will create an AND query: one that will find records where all selected fields are duplicated.

---

5. Select all the other table fields you want to appear on the query results and click Next (Figure 3-67).

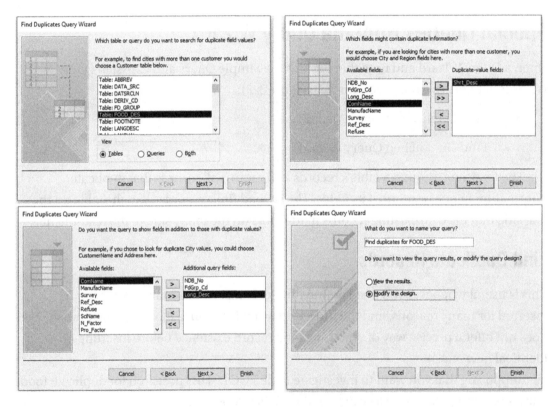

Figure 3-67. *Use the Find Duplicates Query Wizard to create a query that will return all records with duplicate information on a given field*

6. For didactical reasons, on the last wizard screen, select Modify the Design to realize how the wizard created the query and click Finish to show it in Design view (the query will be saved as "Find Duplicates on <Table>").

The wizard will create a query that uses an IN() instruction that receives a Total query as an argument (note the SQL instruction used in its Criteria row, as shown in Figure 3-68). It found six different food items with the same Shrt_Desc field but different NDB_No primary keys.

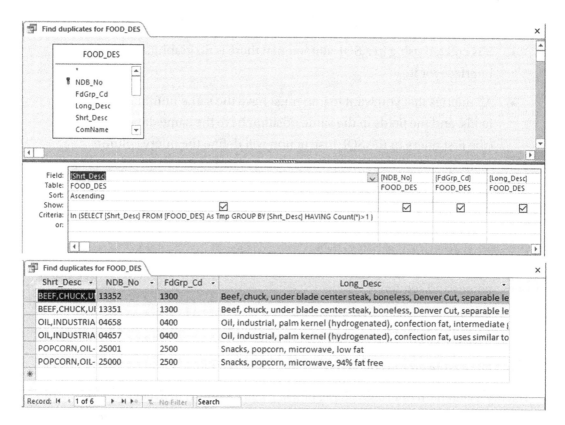

Figure 3-68. *You can also use Select statements on Field or Criteria rows of a query. To return duplicated records, the wizard uses a SQL statement to return the records that will be used by an IN() criteria instruction*

Note   This query was saved as Find duplicates for FOOD_DES in the sr28_Queries.accdb database.

213

Union Queries

A Union query is one that takes two or more queries records and returns all of them as a single query. There will be times that you will need to generate two or more Select, Total, or Crosstab queries and use all their records as a single record source.

Any Union query has two main requirements.

- It is created using just SQL statements; there is no graphical interface for it.

- All queries that you want to join must have the same number of fields, and the fields in the same position have the same data type (the first query in the SQL instruction will define the query column names).

The best strategy to create a Union query is to first create each query using the query Design view and use its SQL view to copy its SQL instruction. To join two different queries, you must use three different query windows.

- *One to create the Base query*: One that will offer all the desired field names and sequence.

- *Another to create the Union query*: This is identical in structure to the base query but returns different records.

- *Once more for the Union query*: This uses only the SQL view.

Having tested both queries, you need to show each one in SQL view and select and copy its SQL instructions to the Union query, using the word UNION between each SQL instruction.

As an example, suppose you want to use a single query to return the first ten records of the FOOD_DES table united with the first ten records of the LANGDESC table (although they have nothing in common). To achieve this target using a Union query, follow these steps:

1. First, create the base query that returns the first ten FOOD_DES records.

   a. Click the New Query command on the Create tab to show the query Design view and the Show table window Select the FOOD_DES table (it is supposed to be Query1).

b. Close the Show Table window and drag fields NDB_No and Shrt_Desc to the query's Design view.

c. Click the Property Sheet command found on the Design tab and set Top Values to 10.

d. Run the Base query; note that it returns the first ten FOOD_DES records.

2. Now create the united query that returns the first ten LANGDESC records using the same field names of the base query (it is supposed to be Query2).

a. Click the New Query command on the Create tab to show the query's Design view and in the Show table window select the LANGDESC table.

b. Drag the fields Factor and Description to the query's Design view.

c. Since a Union query requires that all queries have the same field names and order, rename the field Factor to NDB_No and the field Description to Shrt_Desc.

d. Click the Property Sheet command on the Design tab and set Top Values to 10.

e. Run the query and note that it returns the first ten LANGDESC records (but with altered field names, as shown in Figure 3-69).

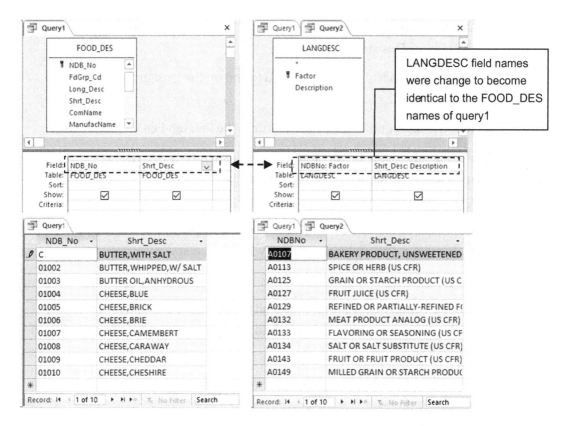

Figure 3-69. *Create each query using Design view assuring that both return the same fields and in the same order. Both queries were set to return their first 10 records*

3. Now create the Union query.

    a. Use the Query Design tool of the Create tab to create a new query, close the Show Table window without selecting any table, and click the Union command. Access will show an empty query using its SQL view (it is supposed to be Query3).

    b. Click the base query (Query1), show it in SQL view, and select and copy all its SQL instruction.

    c. Click again on the Union query window (Query3, in SQL View) and paste the base query (Query1) SQL instruction.

    d. Press Backspace to remove the semicolon (last SQL character), press Enter to insert a new row, type UNION, and press Enter to insert a new row.

e. Click the second query (Query2), show it in SQL view, and select and copy all its SQL instruction.

f. Click again in the Union query window (Query3) and paste the second query's SQL instruction right below the Union word.

g. Run the query to see all that it returns all records from both tables (with no sense between them, as shown in Figure 3-70).

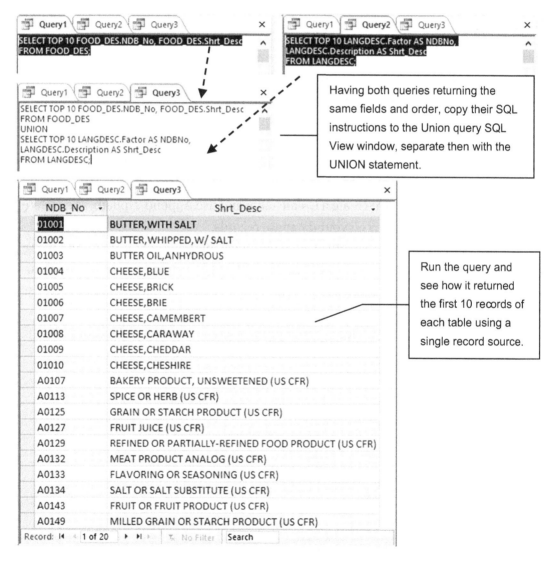

Figure 3-70. *Use each query SQL view to copy each query's SQL instruction and paste them into the SQL view of the Union query, separating them by the word UNION*

Note   This query was saved as qryUnionFOODDES_LANGDESC in the `sr28_Queries.accdb` database.

Tip   To sort a Union query, manually add the ORDER BY <field> at the end of the SQL instruction (before its final semicolon).

Summary

You will use Microsoft Access queries to gather any desired information from a database. To create a query, you can get help from a Query Wizard or create it on your own, using the Query Design view, which is my preferred way of making them.

You can create a Select, Total, or Crosstab query to generate the desired information, keeping in mind that just a Select query can generate a read-write recordset; all other queries are read-only. To recognize a read-write recordset, verify whether it offers a new record. If it doesn't, it is read-only.

By using a query, you can create a Create table and use Append, Update, and Delete queries to make bulk changes on your database records.

The query Design view is a sophisticated graphical interface to SQL code, and using the SQL view of any query, you can learn how to write SQL instructions or just use then as a field or criteria of other queries or to build Union queries to return a single recordset from different queries.

In the next chapter, you will learn about forms to create a user interface for your database records.

CHAPTER 4

Using Forms

Now that you know that tables store data as records and queries show the records in a variety of ways, you should know that your database applications will not show tables or queries to users. All database applications use *forms* to create your database user interface.

In this chapter, you will learn how to use Microsoft forms (and controls) to create efficient interfaces to present your database records to your users. You can obtain all the files cited in this chapter by extracting the file `CHAPTER04.zip` from the following website:

`https://github.com/Apress/intro-microsoft-access-using-macro-prog-techniques`

Creating a Form

Microsoft Access allows you to create a Form object on your database via different methods using the tools in the Forms section of the Create tab (Figure 4-1).

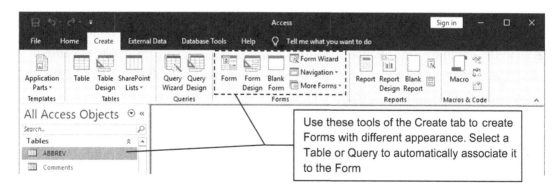

Figure 4-1. *Use the tools in the Forms area of the Create tab to create a Form object. To automatically associate the object to a table or query, first select the desired data source in the Database window*

© Flavio Morgado 2021
F. Morgado, *Introducing Microsoft Access Using Macro Programming Techniques*,
https://doi.org/10.1007/978-1-4842-6555-0_4

Each of these buttons will create a form with a different layout:

- *Form tool*: Enable this tool by first selecting a table or query in the Database window. The form will be created and shown using a Form view, and its appearance may vary according to the table relationships.

- *Form Design*: Create a blank form and show it in Design view.

- *Blank Form*: Create a blank form and show it in Layout view.

- *Form Wizard*: Create forms using different types of presentation with the aid of a wizard.

- *Navigation*: Create a form that uses a Navigation control to create a dashboard where you can show other database objects.

- *More Forms*: Create forms with different types of presentations without using a wizard.

Since there are many ways to create a form, let's begin by using the Form Wizard so you can better understand some layout differences among the different methods.

Using the Form Wizard to Create Forms

As with queries, you can create a form using the Form Wizard to help you learn the different ways to show record information to the users of your database application.

Since a form can show information from the records returned by any table or query saved in the database, this chapter uses the `sr28_Forms.accdb` nutrition file, because it has all the `sr28.accdb` tables plus all the queries created on `sr28_Queries` in Chapter 3.

By using the Form Wizard, you can create two types of forms.

- *Simple forms*: These forms show records from a single table or query.

- *Forms with subforms*: These forms show records from the "one" and "many" sides of any table relationship.

Attention   If you are already familiar with the Visual Basic for Application (VBA) interface and the UserForm object that it offers, it is important to notice that it is quite different from the Microsoft Access Form object. The Form object has an extensive set of properties and different behavior based on a number of events not available in the UserForm object.

Creating Simple Forms with the Form Wizard

To help you understand the different types of forms the Form Wizard can automatically create for you, this chapter will use the FOOTNOTE table because it has just five fields, allowing you compare them more easily with this chapter's figures.

Follow these steps:

1. Click the FOOTNOTE table in the Database window and then click the Form Wizard command in the Forms area of the Create tab to open the Form Wizard window (Figure 4-2).

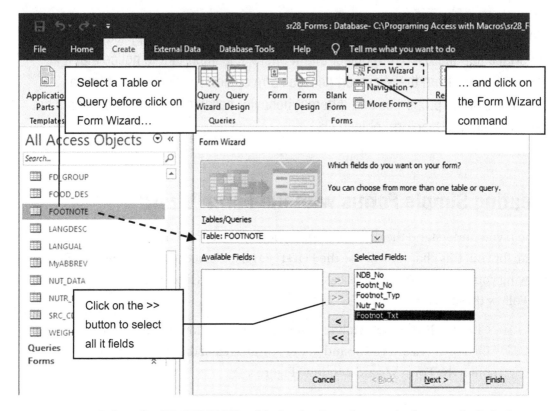

Figure 4-2. Select the FOOTNOTE table in the Database window and click the Form Wizard command on the Create tab to show the Form Wizard window

2. In the Form Wizard window, click the >> button to add all the Available Fields list items to the Selected Fields list and click Next.

3. The Form Wizard will ask to select the form type you want to create: Columnar, Tabular, DataSheet, or Justified. Choose the desired form, and click Next.

Note   These different types of forms will be discussed in this chapter. They differ in the way that they present record information (using a single or multiple records at a time) and how the controls are disposed of in the Form Detail section.

---

4. The Form Wizard will show its last window with the default form
    name, the table, or the query name you selected in its first step.

Tip   To follow this book's naming convention rules, as defined in Chapter 1,
always name forms with the "frm" prefix to easily distinguish them from tables or
queries and other database objects.

---

5. Define the form name and select whether the new form must be
    shown using Form or Design view (Figure 4-3).

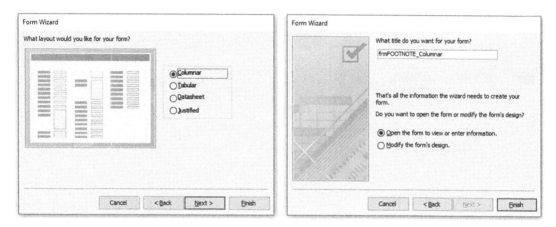

Figure 4-3.   *In the second Form Wizard's step, select the form type, and in its last
step, accept or define the form name, choose to open the form on Form or Design
view, and click Finish*

Microsoft Access will create a new Form object, using the defined name and type,
and will show it in the Database window. Figure 4-4 shows all four types of forms you can
create using the Form Wizard for the FOOTNOTE table.

Note   All four types of forms created by the Form Wizard can be found in the sr28_Formst Database window named as FOOTNOTE_<FormType>, where <FormType> is Columnar, Tabular, Datasheet, or Justified.

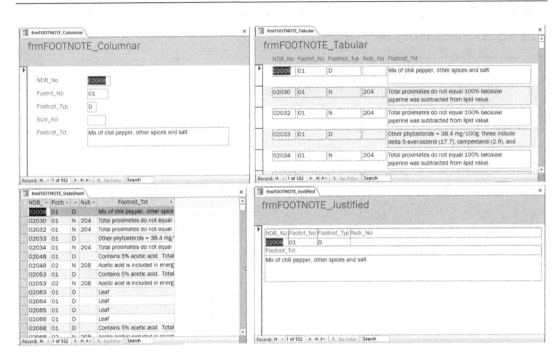

Figure 4-4.   *The four types of form you can create for the FOOTNOTE table using the Form Wizard*

Note   You can find all these forms created by the Form Wizard for the FOOTNOTE table in the sr28_Forms.accdb file that you can extract from Chapter04.zip.

The difference? Besides cosmetic changes on the field presentation and layout, two of them show one record at a time (frmFOOTNOTE_Columnar and frmFOOTNOTE_Justified), and the other two show many records at once—like tables and queries do (frmFOOTNOTE_Tabular and frmFOOTNOTE_Datasheet).

As you might suppose, they change a Form property to show one or many records at a time (the form's Default View property).

Creating Simple Forms with the More Forms Command

Besides using the Form Wizard, you can create simple forms using the More Forms command in the Forms area of the Create tab.

This command does not offer a wizard where you can select which fields you want to appear on the form. It just creates the form in a single step.

Its options are as follows:

- *Multiple Items*: This is similar to the Tabular Form Wizard type (the difference is that it uses fields with the same height).

- *Datasheet*: This is similar to the Datasheet Form Wizard type (the difference is that it shows columns with a better defined width).

- *Split Form*: This is a form that is split in half by two parts: the top area shows a single record similar to the Columnar Form Wizard type, while the bottom part shows many records using the Datasheet view. Click a record on the bottom area to select it in the top area.

- *Modal Dialog*: This allows you to create a floating, modal form that can be used to grab user attention. It does not show by default any record information: just OK and Cancel buttons.

Tip   A modal form is one that will keep the focus until it is closed (or hidden). It stops the workflow of the application, not allowing the user to do anything in the Access interface until it closes the form. A dialog form is one that has no sizeable border; no minimize, restore, and maximize buttons; and no form selector or navigation buttons.

Figure 4-5 shows all the other types of forms you can create using the More Forms options. All but the modal dialog type will automatically show FOOTNOTE table records.

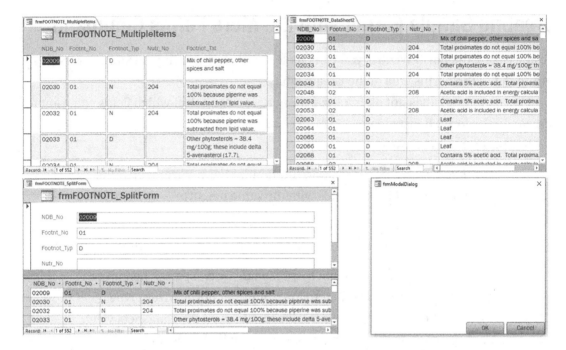

Figure 4-5. *Other types of simple forms you can create for the FOOTNOTE table using the More Forms option*

Note   You can find all the forms created by the More Forms command for the FOOTNOTE table in the `sr28_Forms.accdb` file that you can extract from `Chapter04.zip`.

Creating a Form/Subform with the Form Wizard

Up until now, you may be wondering if there are any differences between a simple form and a table or query Datasheet view besides the way the records are presented. The answer is yes, and you will see why later in this chapter.

But you can appreciate the real difference whenever you use the Form Wizard to create a form/subform that is capable of showing records from any two directed related tables that have referential integrity set between them using a one-to-many relationship.

Using the Form Wizard, you can create forms that automatically synchronize records of three cascading related tables—as long as they have referential integrity set on a one-to-many relationship.

Creating a Form with a One-Level Subform

Investigating the Relationships window shown in Figure 3-2, you will note that you can use the FOOD_DES and WEIGHT tables because they have a direct one-to-many relationship (each food item can have many different types of presentations according to the WEIGHT table records).

Follow these steps to create a form/subform using these two tables:

1. Select the table that represent the "one" side of the relationship in the Database window (FOOD_DES) and click the Form Wizard command on the Create tab.

2. On the Form Wizard's first page, double-click the fields NDB_No, Long_Desc, and Refuse to add them to the Selected Fields list.

3. Still on the first page, click the Table/Queries box to expand it, and select the WEIGHT table in the list.

4. Double-click the fields Amount, Msre_Desc, and Gm_Wgt to also add them to the Selected Fields list.

5. Click Next in the wizard to detect the direct relationship between these two tables and define how the form must group its records, using the "one" side (FOOD_DES) or the "many" side (WEIGHT).

6. Keeps FOOD_DES selected ("one" side) and note that the wizard allows us to show the data in two different ways: using "Form with subform(s)" (one single form) or "Linked Forms" (two independent windows forms that synchronize its records).

Caution   The Linked form proposed by the Form Wizard to show two different windows is not working well and will produce a "buggy" form. Later in this book, you will learn how to synchronize two forms using a simple macro.

---

7. Keep the "Form with subform(s)" option selected and click Next. The wizard will show to present the data: using a Tabular or Datasheet view. Select Datasheet view to get a better subform view and click Next.

8. The wizard will show the name of the two forms it will create: one for the "one" side (FOOD_DES) and another for the "many" side of the relationship (the WEIGHT subform, as shown in Figure 4-6).

Note   Following the rules proposed in Chapter 1, prefix both form names with the "frm" tag.

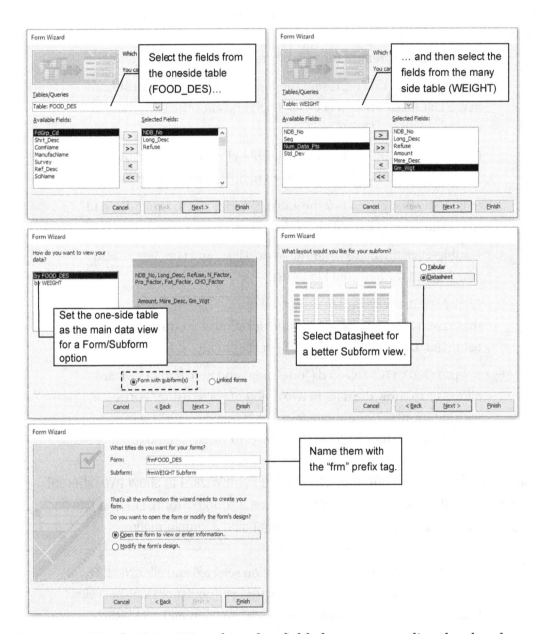

Figure 4-6. *Use the Form Wizard to select fields from any two directly related tables that have a one-to-many relationship with referential integrity imposed to automatically create a form/subform structure*

9. Keep "Open the form to view or enter information" selected and click Finish.

The Form Wizard will create both forms (frmFOOD_DES and the frmWEIGHT subform). Open frmFOOD_DES and show the first FOOD_DES record (Butter Salted) and all four of its WEIGHT measures for portions. Each form has its own navigation buttons, which you can use to select another food item or food measure. Use the main form (frmFOOD_DES) navigation buttons to change the food item and note how it synchronizes the WEIGHT records of its subform (Figure 4-7).

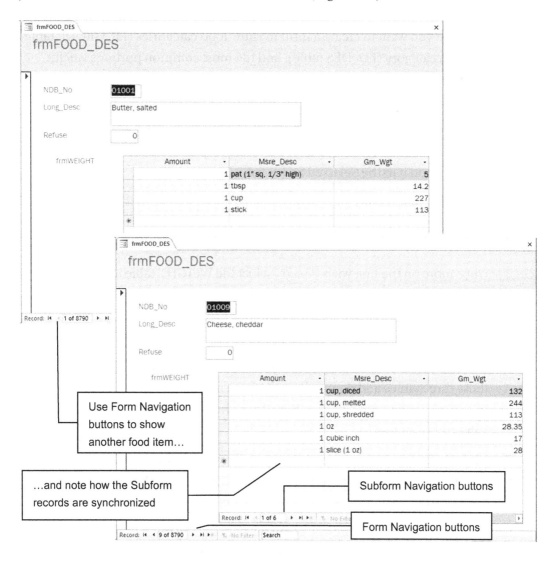

Figure 4-7.   *Using a form/subform strategy, you can show records from a one-to-many relationship using a single window*

Note   As Figure 4-7 shows, you will find frmFOOD_DES and the frmWEIGHT subform in the `sr28_Forms.accdb` file that you can extract from `Chapter04.zip`.

Creating a Form with a Two-Level Subform

Microsoft Access allows you to create up to two levels of subforms, which means that any subform can have its own subform to synchronize up to three tables at once using a single interface.

Supposing that you want to create a form to show food categories (FR_GROUP table), food items of each category (FD_DES table), and the most common portions weight (WEIGHT table), you can use the Form Wizard to create such a form with two subforms. Follow these steps:

1. Open the Form Wizard, and on its first page select the FD_GROUP table in the Table/Queries box. Select its Fd_GrpDesc field and click > to add it to the Selected Fields list.

2. Still on the first wizard page, select the FOOD_DES table in the Table/Queries list, select the desired fields (NDB_No, Shrt_Desc and Refuse), and click > to add it to the Selected Fields list.

3. Once more on the first wizard page, select the WEIGHT table in the Table/Queries box, select the desired fields (Amount, Msre_Desc, and Gm_Wgt), and click > to add it to the Selected Fields list (see Figure 4-8).

4. Click Next. The wizard detects the direct relationship between these three tables and defines how the form must group its records (keep selected FD_GROUP and the "Form with subform(s)" option).

5. Click Next and note that the wizard now offer two options to show the two subforms (one form for FD_DES and another for WEIGHT tables). Select Datasheet view on both options.

6. Click Next, and the wizard will show the name of the three main forms it will create: one for FD_GROUP, one for FOOD_DES), and another for WEIGHT.

7. Rename the forms by prefixing them with the "frm" tag (and eventually add a suffix to the ones the wizard warns it will overwrite, like the frmWEIGHT subform, created in the previous section; see Figure 4-6).

8. Click Finish to make the Form Wizard create the form with its two subforms, each one having its own navigation buttons. Use the main form navigation buttons to show different food categories, and note how the food items of these categories are automatically synchronized and how the common measures of the selected food item are automatically shown in the second-level subform (Figure 4-9).

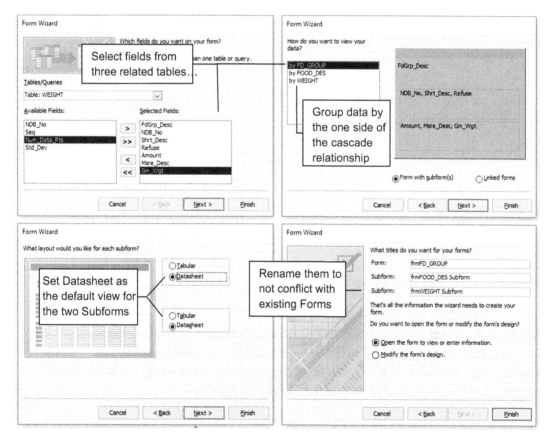

Figure 4-8. *Using the Form Wizard, you can select fields from up to three related tables (with referential integrity imposing a cascading one-to-many relationship between them) to create a two subform-level main forms (always view the data by the table that has the "one" side of the cascade relationship)*

Note   As Figure 4-8 shows, you will find frmFD_GROUP, the frmFOOD_DES subform, and the frmWEIGHT subform inside the `sr28_Forms.accdb` file that you can extract from `Chapter04.zip`.

Attention   Although the Form Wizard created two subforms to represent the three tables' cascade relationships, it does not create a subform with another subform inside it (frmFOOD_DES does not have a subform inside it). But this approach is perfectly possible to build using the form's Design view.

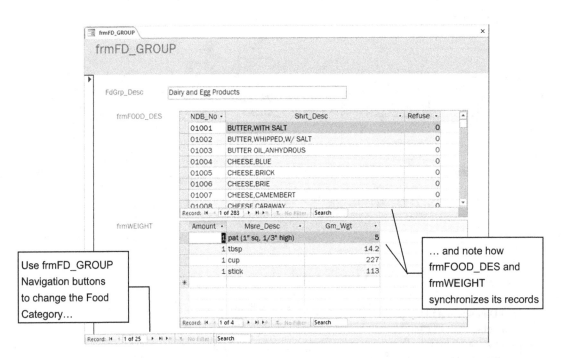

Figure 4-9. *Use the frmFD_GROUP form navigation buttons to change the food category, and note how the frmFOOD_DES subform automatically changes its records. Also note that the selected food item will automatically show its most popular common measures on the frmWEIGHT Subform2*

Form view Properties

Microsoft Access forms can be shown using four different types of views.

- *Form view*: This shows record values and is the way the users of your application will see them.

- *Design view*: This shows the form structures, where you can set form and control properties to build the user interface.

- *Layout view*: This shows record values while allowing you to change most of the form (and control) properties on the run. It is great to do some fine-tuning of the interface.

- *Datasheet view*: This shows record values using a datasheet like the one offered by a query to show its records.

To show any form using these different views, you must first select the form in the Database window and then do the following:

1. Double-click the form to open it in Form view.

2. Right-click the form and select Open ➤ Design View or Layout View button.

3. After a form is opened in Design view or Layout view, you can use the View command of the Form Design tab to select the desired view mode.

4. Right-click the form title bar and select the desired view.

The next section will show how to use Form Design view to set Form properties.

Using Form Design View

Microsoft Access offers a nice and fast way to create forms for any table or query based on predefined templates, which can save time and also helps you to learn how a form works.

But for my taste—and I want to make it clear that this is a matter of taste—the forms automatically produced by the Form Wizard or More Forms tool are simply a standardized, clumsy, amateur way to produce a database interface.

If you need to create professional interfaces, you need to use the form design and create your own forms so they best translate your personalized way of producing software.

Because of this way of looking at software development and the many form format properties available that simply don't work on anchored windows used by default on the Microsoft Access tabbed documents interface, from this point on this book will just use the alternative way of showing Microsoft Access objects, namely, using Overlapping Windows, as explained earlier in this book.

In the `Chapter04.zip` file, you will find the `sr28_Forms_Overlapping.accdb` database, which is a copy of the `sr28_Forms.accdb` database with the Overlapping Windows option set. This will be used from now on in this chapter.

Tip   To use this interface, select the Overlapping Windows option in the Current Database section of the File ➤ Options dialog box. Since this is a database preference, Microsoft Access will ask you to close and reopen the database before this option will take effect.

The Form Design Window

Whenever you create a form using the Form Design tool in the Forms area of the Create tab, Access will create a new, empty form window and show it along with the form's Property Sheet (Figure 4-10).

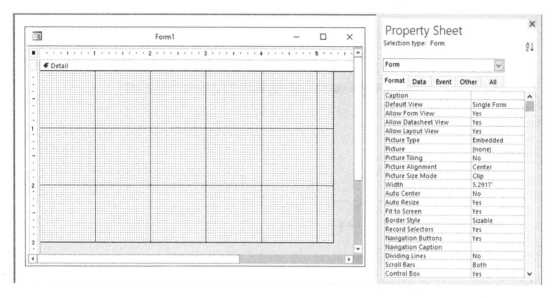

Figure 4-10. *This is a default form design window, floating in the Microsoft Access interface after setting the Current Database ➤ Overlapping Window option*

The first thing you'll note is that it has a horizontal and a vertical ruler, a Detail section filled with lots of clumsy dots and lines, and a Property Sheet that uses five tabs to organize and show the many properties available to control a Form object.

The dots you see are the grid: a granulated way to automatically snap and align controls in the Detail section. Since to my taste it seems to pollute the screen—and make it somewhat difficult to show some figure details that will be used in this chapter—I will hide the window by right-clicking the Detail section and unchecking the Grid option.

When you right-click the form's Detail section, you will notice that it has other hidden options: Show Page Header/Footer and Show Form Header/Footer. Check the second option to also show the Form Header and Footer sections (see Figure 4-11).

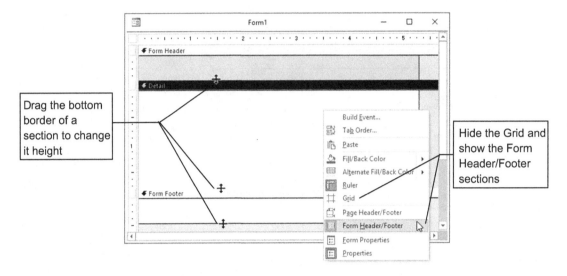

Figure 4-11. *A form in Design view, with the grid hidden and the Form Header and Footer sections*

The form's Detail section is used to put controls linked to the field records of the table or query used by the form, while the Form Header and Form Footer options are used to put unlinked controls (like command buttons). The Page Header and Page Footer are just used to put information that will be printed on a page whenever you print the Form Datasheet view—they are not shown on the screen (just in Print Preview).

You can change the height of the form sections by pointing the mouse to its bottom line and dragging it vertically.

Note   Everything except the Datasheet view and the dialog forms created by the Form Wizard or More Forms tools shown in previous figures have the Form Header section showing, using a Label control to show the form name (with the Form Footer section reduced to zero).

Selecting the Form and Its Sections

You can set properties for both the form and each of its sections. Form properties relate to the way the entire form window behaves, while section properties relate just to that specific portion of the form.

So, you will eventually need to select what part of the form you want to control and set the desired properties. To select the form or its section, you can select the desired object in the Property Sheet box. Or you can do the following:

- To select the form:

  - Click the small square positioned in the top-left corner of the form's Design view.

  - Click the gray area that surrounds the Form section in Design view.

- To select a section, click any section part not used by a control (the section background or its header).

Since the Form object and its sections have a lot of different properties, let's explore some of them, comparing with the forms created by the Form Wizard or More Forms options, whenever possible.

Setting the Form's Record Source

To define the records shown by a form and what a user can do with them, you need to select the Form object and use the Form Data tab's Property Sheet.

Basically, you just need to set the form's Record Source type to the name of a table, query, or SQL instruction to make it capable of showing its records. To define the form record source, you can do the following:

- Click the Record Source property arrow to expand its list and select the name of a table or query saved on the database (Figure 4-12).

- Click the ellipsis button located to the right of Record Source property to show the form's Query Builder window, where you can create a query, save it, or just store its SQL instruction on the form's Record Source property.

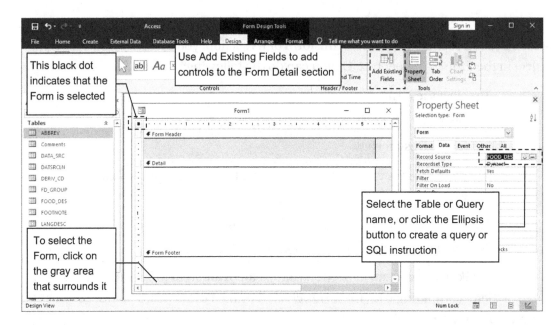

Figure 4-12. *Set the form's Record Source property to associate it to a table, query, or SQL instruction. Use the ellipsis button to show a query Design view window, where you can create a query or type a SQL instruction*

Adding Fields to the Form Detail Section

Once you set the form's Record Source property, click the Add Existing Fields command in the Tools area of the Form Design tab to show the Field List window with all its fields returned by the table, query, or SQL instruction.

Attention   If the form uses a Crosstab query for its Record Source property, be advised that you must set the query's Column Heads property to the field names returned by the query (for more details, see the "Setting Crosstab Column Heading Field Order" section of Chapter 3).

Now you need to add the desired fields to the form by selecting the desired fields in the Field List windows (Ctrl+click to select individual fields, Shift+click to select a field sequence) and dragging them from the Existing Fields section in the Form Details section. By default, all dragged fields will be associated to a Text Box control (Figure 4-13).

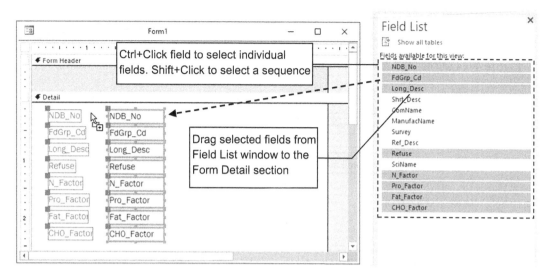

Figure 4-13. *Click the Add Existing Fields tool to show the Field List window, and select and drag the desired fields to the form's Detail section*

Note   This form is called Form1 in sr28_Forms_Overlapping.

Attention   The control used by a field can be changed according to the field data type. Yes/No fields will use a Check Box. Any field that has a Lookup property defined will use a Combo Box.

To see the form return its records, use the View command to select one of these possible form record views:

- *Form view*: This is the default form view as the user will see it, showing all visible form sections. You cannot make design changes using this view. By default, it will show one record at a time—but you can change its default view to show many records at once.

- *Layout view*: This is the same as the Form view, but you can make changes to the form structure (adding or removing fields and changing form/control properties as the form runs).

- *Datasheet view*: This is an alternative view, similar to the table's Design view. It shows many records at once.

Figure 4-14 shows the form from Figure 4-13 using Form and Datasheet views.

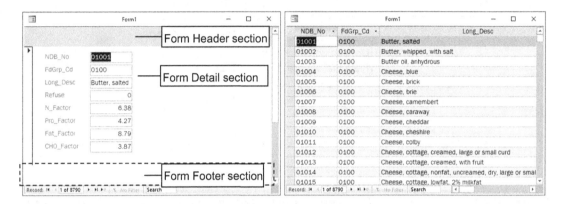

Figure 4-14. *By default, any form can be shown using the Form or Datasheet view—as long as this form property is not disabled by user action. The Form Header/Footer will be shown just on the Form view. The Form and Page Header/Footer will be shown just on the form's Datasheet view's print preview*

Note   Form controls' position and layout will be covered later in this chapter.

Using Layout View to Set Form Properties

The Form object has an extensive list of Data and Format properties that you can try more easily using Layout view, because it allows you to change form (and control) properties on the run.

Follow these steps to change a property using Layout view:

1. For the View command, select Layout View.

2. Right-click the form detail section and choose Form Properties.

3. On the form's Property Sheet, select the Data or Format tab, change the desired property, and observe how the form behaves.

Attention   Some properties require that you close the form or show it in Design view before it can take effect.

Setting Form Data Properties

Besides setting the form's Record Source property, you can customize how the records will be manipulated by the user by setting Form Data properties.

Table 4-1 show the Form Data properties and their usage.

Table 4-1. *Form Data Properties*

Form Data Property	Usage
Record Source	Name of a table, query, or SQL instruction.
Recordset Type	Type of recordset returned. Use Dynaset for read-write; use Snapshot for read-only records.
Fetch Default	Indicates if Access uses the default field values for new records.
Filter	Type of filter currently applied to form records (same as the SQL clause WHERE statement).
Filter On Load	Type of filter applied to form records when the form loads.
Order By	Defines the form record's classification (discarding the table or query order).
Order By On Load	Defines the form records' classification when the form loads.
Wait for Post Processing	Makes the form wait until macro processing on the form records is finished before processing the next form operation.
Data Entry	The form is just used to insert new records.
Allow Additions	Allows the form to insert new records.
Allow Deletions	Allows the form to delete records.
Allow Edits	Allows the form to edit record fields.
Allow Filter	Allows a filter to be applied to the form records.
Record Locks	Defines how the form will behave on a network whenever two users try to change the same record at the same time.

Most Form Data properties are defined by default to give the expected form behavior, but you can use some of them to change the way the records are manipulated by the user.

- *Recordset Type*: Set this to Snapshot to avoid any record change or, in other words, to make the form records read-only. The record fields cannot be changed, and a new record cannot be added.

- *Data Entry*: Use this on forms designated to insert new data; the user will not be able to see existing records. It requires the property Allow Additions to be set to Yes. The user will be able to see the new records added to the form. When Data Entry is set to Yes, the form will jump to a new record, and its navigation buttons will show "Record 1 of 1."

- *Allow Additions*: Set this to No to avoid record insertions. When Allow Additions is set to No, the New Record button is disabled on the form navigation buttons.

- *Allow Deletions*: Set this to No to avoid record deletions.

- *Allow Edits*: Set this to No to avoid editing existing records. If Allow Additions is set to True, new records can be edited until they are saved in the table.

Figure 4-15 shows how Form1 from Figure 4-13 will appear in Layout view with Data Entry set to Yes (it shows a new record, while its navigation buttons indicate "Record 1 of 1").

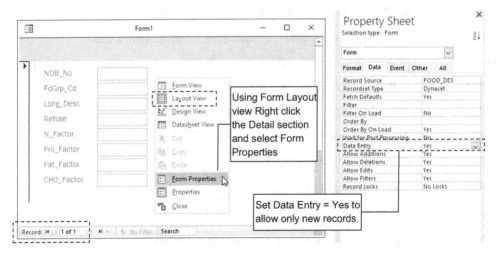

Figure 4-15. *Using Layout view, you can set form properties while the form runs and watch the results. When Data Entry is set to Yes, the form allows new records*

Setting Form Format Properties

All forms have an extensible list of Format properties that allow control over how the form window will behave. By correctly using the Format properties, you can improve the user experience with your database interface and create a different kind of form, which can be used both to show records and to produce the database interface.

Figure 4-16 shows Form1_FoodItems, created previously in this chapter, with some Format properties set so you can best understand their usage and meaning (it has Caption set to Food Item, Navigation Buttons set to Yes, Dividing Lines set to Yes, and Scroll Bars set to Both).

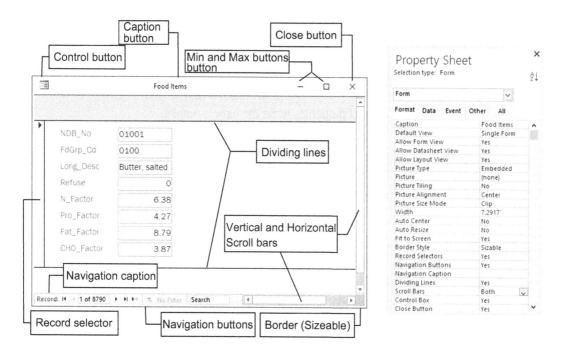

Figure 4-16. *Form elements that you can change by manipulating the Form Format properties*

Since there are too many form properties to be approached, Table 4-2 shows the ones that will be mentioned in this chapter grouped by the Property Sheet tab where they reside.

Table 4-2. *Main Form Properties Grouped by Property Sheet Tab*

Tab	Property Name	Usage
Format tab	Caption	Defines the text of the form's title bar (or tab). This will receive the form name until filled.
	Default View	Defines how records will be shown. Single Form is set to one record at a time; Continuous Form is set to scrolling records (many at a time). Datasheet is set to Datasheet view. Split splits the form into two showing both a single form and a Datasheet view.
	Allow Form view	Allows a form to be viewed using all its sections (Form Header, Form Detail, and Form Footer).
	Allow Datasheet View	Allows a form to be viewed like a table's Datasheet view.
	Allow Layout View	Similar to Form view, allowing changes to some form and control Format properties while the form is running.
	Width	Sets the form width (and all its sections).
	Auto Center	Auto-centers the form on the screen when it is open.
	Auto Resize	Auto-resizes the form to show all its sections (and to the width of the Detail section) when it is open.
	Border Style	Defines the form border style. None means the form has no border; Thin sets it so the user can't change the form size; Sizable sets it so the user can change the size; Dialog sets it so the form has a thin border and no Min and Max buttons.
	Record Selectors	Shows/hides the record selector, which is used to select the current record for deletion.
	Navigation Buttons	Shows/hides the navigation buttons at the window's bottom.
	Navigation Caption	Changes the navigation caption text.
	Dividing Lines	Shows or hides a dividing line that separates the Form Header, Detail, and Footer sections.

(continued)

Table 4-2. (*continued*)

Tab	Property Name	Usage
	Scroll Bars	Shows/hides horizontal and vertical scroll bars. This appears automatically whenever the form content is too high or wide to the current window size.
	Control Box	Shows/hides the icon located in the top-left window corner (used to close, move, minimize, or maximize the window).
	Close Button	Shows/hides the form's close button (the X located in the window's top-right corner).
	Min Max Buttons	Shows/hides the Minimized, Restore, and Maximize window buttons in the window's top-right corner.
	Split Properties	Works with Default View set to Split to divide the form into two areas. You can set Split Form Orientation to a split position, Split Form Splitter Bar to Show/Hide, Split Form Datasheet to Read only/Read-write, Split From Printing to Form only/Datasheet only.
Data tab	Record Source	Specifies an existing table or query name or sql instruction used to return form records.
Other tab	PopUp	Set to Yes to make the window float over the screen (outside the Microsoft Access interface).
	Modal	Set to Yes to make the form a modal window: one that stops all processing until it is closed.
	Cycle	Determines the behavior of the Tab keys on the Detail controls. All Records means that by pressing Tab on the last field, the form advances to the next record. Current Record means to cycle the controls without leaving the current record. Current Pagekeeps the focus on the current website page controls.

Looking at the forms created by the Form Wizard and More Form tools for the FOOTNOTE table, you will notice that frmFOOTNOTE_Tabular (Figure 4-4) and frmFOOTNOTE_MultipleItems (Figure 4-5) have the property Default View set to Continuous. Their Detail section repeats continuously, showing multiple records in a single form window, while frmFOOTNOTE_SplitForm shows the Detail section above using a single record view, with the form's Datasheet view at the bottom, because it has the property Default View set to Split Form and Split Form Orientation set to Datasheet on Bottom (Figure 4-17).

Tip   frmFOOTNOTE_SplitForm also allows you to vertically drag the splitter bar and edit records on the datasheet because it has the properties Split Form Splitter Bar set to Yes and Split Form Datasheet set to Allow Edits.

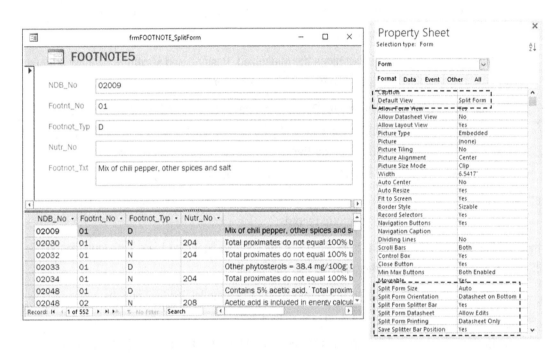

Figure 4-17. *The frmFOOTNOTE_SplitForm created by the Form Wizard with properties Default View set to Split Form and Split Form Orientation set to Datasheet on Bottom. Other Split properties allow you to drag the splitter bar and edit records on the split form datasheet*

Form frmModalDialog (Figure 4-5) is the one that differs in behavior, because it has no Record Source property, it has disabled access to Microsoft Access, and it does not allow the Layout View mode (property Modal set to Yes). Also, it has a thin border that cannot be resized (property Border Style set to Dialog) and can float outside the Microsoft Access interface over other opened Windows applications (property PopUp set to Yes, as shown in Figure 4-18).

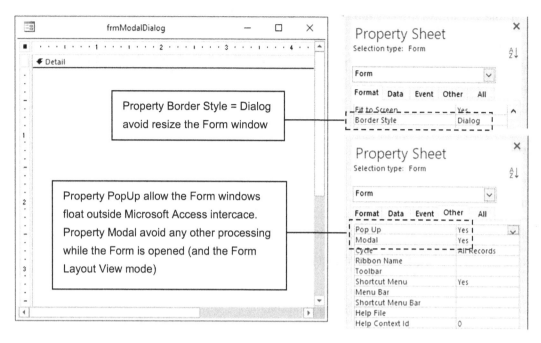

Figure 4-18. *frmModeDialog has a different behavior, not allowing the form to be resized, not allowing access to the Microsoft Access interface, and floating outside the Access window because it has the properties Border Style set to Dialog, Popup set to Yes, and Modal set to Yes*

The other properties shown in Table 4-2 will be commented on in this book whenever a form needs to use them. For now, it is enough that you understand that they exist and what each one does.

Setting Form Section Properties

Besides setting properties associated to the data or format of the form window, you can also set properties for each form section.

To show and change any visible form section's Format properties, follow these steps:

1. For the View command, select Layout View.

2. In the Property Sheet, select the Detail, FormFooter, or FormHeader sections in the list.

3. Use the section's Format tab to change the desired property and observe how the form behaves.

Table 4-3 shows the Format properties available for each form section.

Note   There are no Section Data properties—they are just associated to the form itself.

Table 4-3. *Form Section Format Properties*

Format Properties	Usage
Visible	Shows or hides a section
Height	Sets the section height (automatically set by dragging the section's bottom border)
Back Color	Sets the section background color
Alternate Back Color	Sets the alternate Detail section background color
Special Effect	Allows you to define the appearance of a section
Auto Height	Automatically adjusts the section height when the controls are resized
Can Grow	Automatically grows the section when a text box or subform control has the property Can Grow set to Yes
Can Shrink	Automatically shrinks the section when a text box or subform control has the property Can Shrink set to Yes
Display When	Allows you to define whether the section will show on the screen or when printing
Keep Together	Forces Access to try to print a form section together on a single page
Force New Page	Forces Access to begin the section printing on a new page
New Row or Col	When printing forms, specifies if a new row or column must be inserted before, after, or before and after the section

As with the Format properties, we will discuss Section properties later in the book. For now, just pay attention that the forms created by the Form Wizard, More Forms, and Form Design tools (Figures 4-5, 4-6, 4-7, and 4-12) show the Form Header section with a light blue background color because their property Back Color is set to Text2, Lighter 80%, while frmFOOTNOTE_Tabular and frmFOOTNOTE_Datasheet, as shown in Figure 4-4, and all but frmModeDialog in Figure 4-5 alternates the Detail section background color between white and light gray because they have the properties Background set to Background 1 and Alternate Back Color set to Background 1, Darker 5% (Figure 4-19).

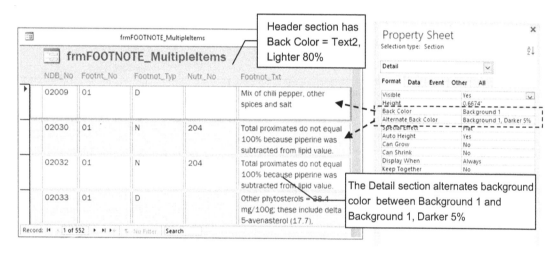

Figure 4-19. *Use Section properties to change the section background colors and create a more distintive record presentation when Form Default View is set to Continuous or Datasheet*

Note   Since both fmrFOOTNOTE_Tabular and frmFOOTNOTE_MultipleItems have Default View set to Continuous to allow multiple records to display, they differ in the way they lay out the controls: frmFOOTNOTE_Tabular uses a loose design where controls can be dragged inside a detail section, while fmrFOOTNOTE_MultipleItems uses a table design that stitches controls to an invisible table grid, which can be manipulated using the Arrange group of the Form Design Tools tab on the Ribbon.

In the next sections, you will learn how to use form controls to give your database applications a more attractive layout.

Using Form Controls

Microsoft Access offers an impressive number of native controls that you can use to improve the user experience using your database applications, available in the controls list in the Controls area of the Form Design tab.

Although some of these controls seem to be the same as the ones in VBA, they may work quite differently, showing a more extensive interface (properties and events) that facilitates the creation of a graphic interface. Figure 4-20 describes each of the controls available in the Microsoft Access 2019 interface.

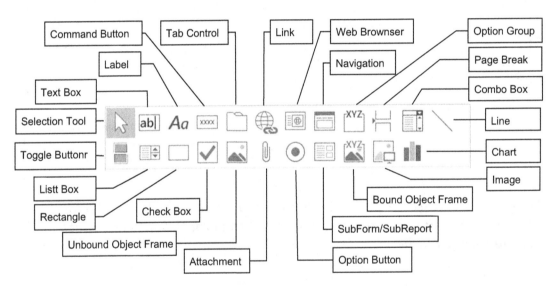

Figure 4-20. *Microsoft Access 2019 native control types available to use on forms and reports*

They vary so much to allow a user to be able to insert or select a variety of controls on the form interface.

Bound Controls

Some controls are considered to be "bound controls" because they have a Control Source property that ties a control to a field returned by the form's Record Source property. Table 4-5 describes these controls.

Table 4-5. *Microsoft Access Bound Controls Used on Forms and Reports*

Tool	Control Name	Usage
abl	Text Box	Allows any kind of information (text, number, dates, etc.) to be typed
	Combo Box	Allows you to select an option from a drop-down multicolumn list
	List Box	Allows you to select an option from a multicolumn list
	Option Group	Holds a set of Option Buttons, Check Boxes, or Toggle Buttons that return the control value
	Toggle Button	Inside an Option Group control, alternates between pressed and not pressed (used to select different options)
✓	Check Box	Used alone to represent a binary option (check/uncheck) or inside an Option Group control to represent binary options
⊙	Option Button	Used inside an Option Group control, allows you to select an option from many
	Attachment	Allows you to insert an external file to a field of the Attachment data type
	Bound Object Frame	Shows an image or other object stored on a table field of the OLE object data type
	SubForm/ SubReport	Allows you to insert a form as a subform (or a report as a subreport) to represent a one-to-many relationship between tables in a single interface
	Chart	Shows a dynamic chart on a form or report

Follow these steps to associate any field returned by the form's Record Source property:

1. Select the desired control on the Control list in the Controls area of the Form Design tab.

2. Click the Add Existing Fields tool to show the Field List window with all the available fields.

3. Select the field on the Field list that you want to bind to the control.

4. Click the desired form section to add the control or drag the mouse to define the control size.

The control will be inserted, and its Control Source property will be set to the selected field (Figure 4-21).

Tip   To unbind any control from a field, select the control in the form's Design view, show the Property Sheet window's Data tab, and delete the Control Source property value.

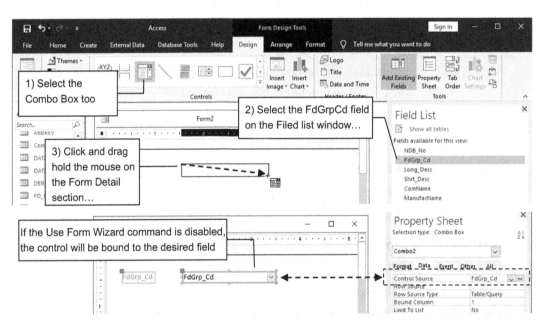

Figure 4-21. *To insert a control bound to any the form's Record Source field, show the Field List window, select the desired field, click the desired bound control, and drag the mouse to the form's Detail section to define the control size*

Attention   By clicking the Controls List arrow of the form's Design tab, you will notice that it has the Use Control Wizard option selected by default. Some controls (such as Option Group, Combo Box, List Box, etc.) will automatically open the Form Wizard unless you deselect this option.

Unbound Controls

All other controls are considered to be unbound controls because they cannot be associated to a field from the form's Record Source property (although most controls that have a Control Source property can be used unbound—not linked to a form's Record Source field). They are used to create the form's graphical interface, and some of them will be mentioned throughout this book as necessary. Table 4-6 describes these controls and their usage.

Table 4-6. *Microsoft Access Unbound Controls Used on Forms or Reports*

Tool	Control Name	Usage
Aa	Label	Inserts static text on a form to inform the field name or content of a control bound to a form field
▭	Command Button	Executes an action (macro or VBA procedure)
▢	Tab Control	Allows you to create tabbed interfaces inside a form, with different pages, each one with its own set of controls
⊕	Link	Inserts a link to an external file or website on a form
▣	Web Browser	Shows an Internet website inside a form or report
▭	Navigation	Creates a dashboard from where you can open forms, queries, or reports
⊢	Page Break	Inserts a page break on a section when it is printed
╲	Line	Draws a line on a form section
▢	Rectangle	Draws a rectangle on a form section
▦	Unbound Object Frame	Inserts an image or an object that is drawn at design time

Follow these steps to draw a bound or unbound control to a Form or Report section without binding it to any field from the form's Record Source property:

1. Select the desired control from the Control list in the Controls area of the Form Design tab.

2. Click the desired form section to insert the control or drag the mouse to define the control size (Figure 4-22).

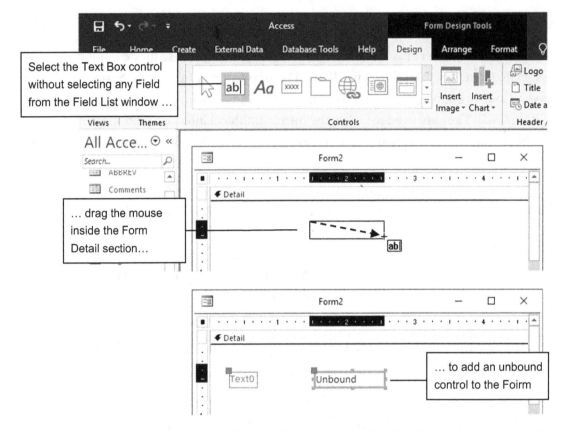

Figure 4-22. *To add an unbound control to a form, select the desired control in the controls list, make sure that no field is selected in the Field List window, and click and drag the mouse to the form's Detail section*

Many previous figures showed that whenever a control is added to a form section, it also receive an associated label to identify its content. The next section explores how to use this association, how to break it, and how to rebuild it.

The Label-Control Association

Whenever a Text Box (or any other bound control) is inserted on a form section, it automatically receives the companion of a Label control, positioned at its left side. This association is desired because the user can also select the control by clicking its Label control.

Both controls receive a default name, which is composed by the control class (Label, Text) and a form controls zero-based counter (the first control is zero). The first Text

Box receives the name Text0, while the first Label control receives Label1. To set this association, the Text Box control's Label Name property receives the Label control Name property, while the Label control Caption property receives the Text Box control's Name property.

Each control has specific handles (squares on its borders) to manipulate its size and position. The bigger handle located on the control's top-left corner is called the *control handle* and is used to reposition the control. The seven small squares handles located on other control corners (and on its top and bottom horizontal center) allow you to size it (Figure 4-23).

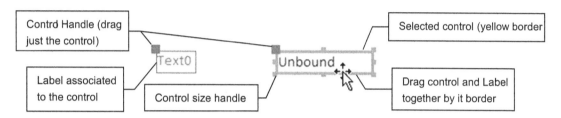

Figure 4-23. *Each control inserted on a form section using Design or Layout view automatically receives a bound Label control, both having their own handles to position and size them on the form*

To manipulate the size and position of a control and its label, follow these steps:

1. Point the mouse to the control (or Label) border and drag it to a new position to reposition both of them on the form section.

2. Use the control (or Label) handle (top-left corner) to drag it and reposition it alone, without disturbing the position of the associated control.

3. Use the small size handles located on the corners to size the control.

Tip   You can use the Label or Text Box control handle to reposition the controls near one another to make a better use of the form design.

Break and Rebuild a Label-Control Association

It is quite simple to break and rebuild any label-control association.

- To break the association between a control and its label, click the label and delete it or cut it to the Clipboard. If you paste it again onto the form, the label will no longer be associated to its previous control.

- To rebuild any label-control association, you can do one of the following:

  - Set the Text Box control's Label Name property on the Other tab to the name of an existing Label control.

  - Cut and paste the Label control over an existing control.

    a. Drag a new Label control to the Form section.

    b. With the Label control selected, cut it to the Clipboard (Ctrl+X).

    c. Select the control that must be associated to the label.

    d. Paste the control in the Form section (Ctrl+V).

Since there are a lot of control types not counting the default label-control association, it is a good programming practice that you also use a naming convention rule to better identify the controls inserted on a form.

Naming Conventions Rules for Microsoft Access Controls

To follow "best programming practices," keep following the Redick name convention rules proposed for naming Microsoft Access objects.

As stated earlier, these rules suppose that any control used on a form or report must follow these rules:

- Begin with a three-letter small caps prefix that identifies the control type.

- Use a name that identifies its content, beginning with a capital letter and with all other letters in small caps.

- If it needs more than one word, the words must be concatenated with no space in between them, each one beginning with a capital letter.

Table 4-4 shows the prefixes used by this book's naming convention rules.

Table 4-4. *Control Naming Conventions*

	Control Type	Prefix		Control Type	Prefix
Bound controls	Text Box	txt	Unbound controls	Label	lbl
	Combo Box	cbo		Command Button	cmd
	List Box	lst		Tab Control	tab
	Option Group	grp		Link	lnk
	Toggle Button	tgl		Web Browser	web
	Check Box	chk		Navigation	nav
	Option Button	opt		Page Break	brk
	Attachment	att		Line	lin
	Bound Object Frame	bof		Rectangle	ret
	SubForm/SubReport	subFrm or subRpt		Unbound Object Frame	uof
	Chart	cht			

Now let's see some properties available to most control types.

As with forms and sections, controls also have their own set of properties, many of them shared by most controls.

Considering that the Property Sheet is hidden, to show any control's Property Sheet using the form's Design view or Layout view, you can do one of the following:

- Double-click the control border.

- Select the control and click the Property Sheet command of the form's Design View tab.

The Property Sheet window will be shown with its combo box already indicating the selected control.

There are a set of common properties available to any control type, while each control can have specific properties to change its appearance and behavior. The next section will cover the common control properties, while the specific properties will be cited in each specific control section.

Common Control Properties

Table 4-7 describes the common properties available to all Microsoft Access controls, indicating the Property Sheet tab where they reside.

Table 4-7. *Microsoft Access Control Properties*

Tab	Property	Usage
Data Tab	Control Source	Name of the field to which the control is bound
	Default Value	Default value for new records
	Validation Rule	Expression that specifies the values accepted by the control
	Validation Text	Message text shown when Validation Rule is False
	Enabled	Enables control to receive data
	Locked	Blocks control from changing data, but allows the user to select its content
Format Tab	Visible	Makes control visible or invisible
	Special Effect	Determines the control appearance by changing its border options from among Flat, Etched, Raised, Sunken, Shadowed, and Chiseled
	Width	Control width
	Height	Control height
	Top	Position of control's top-left corner
	Left	Position of control's left side
Other Tab	Name	Defines control name
	Label Name	Name of the label associated to the control
	Datasheet caption	Name used on the form's Datasheet view column
	ControlTip Text	Text on a floating tip that appears when you point the mouse to the control
	Tab Index	1 based; indicates the selection order of the controls on the form
	Tab stop	Indicates whether the control receives the focus when the Tab key is pressed
	StatusBar Text	Text that appears on the status bar when the control is selected
	AutoTab	Selects the next control in the tab order whenever the current control is fulfilled

In the next sections, you will learn about these properties (along with specific control properties) for the most used controls, beginning with the most popular of them: the Text Box.

Text Box Control

The Text Box is the most versatile control because it can receive any kind of information (text, number, date, logical, etc.). It is also the default control used to represent record data whenever a field name is dragged from the Field List window to a form section in Design or Layout view (see Figure 4-13).

Since it has lots of properties, let's begin by studying some of them so you can understand how they can affect the appearance and functionality of a form.

Enabled and Locked Properties

All controls have the properties enabled (with the default value set to Yes) and locked (with the default value set to No), already cited in Table 4-7. By using both properties, you can create different types of formatting regarding the control change and its selection.

Figure 4-24 shows the unbound frmTextBox_EnabledLocked (that you can extract from Chapter04.zip) both in Design and Form views. It has four unbound Text Box controls that use both properties so you can better appreciate the control interface behavior.

Note that all Label controls were dragged by its handle to the top of the associated Text Box to make better use of the form's Detail section space. Also, note that the first two Text Boxes (the ones with Enabled set to Yes) have the Control Tip property set (point the mouse to it and wait a second to see the floating tip).

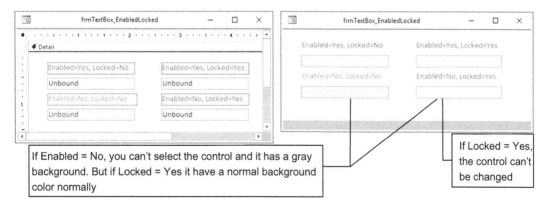

Figure 4-24. *frmTextBox_EnableLocked uses four unbound Text Box bound controls that explore the usage of the control properties Enabled and Locked*

259

Tip   Since the Enabled and Locked properties are common to all control types, any control will show the same behavior regarding its values.

The Text Box default behavior happens when Enabled is set to Yes and Locked is set to No, meaning that you can select and change it contents. When Enabled is set to No and Locked is set to No, the control becomes disabled and uses a light gray background color—you can't select it or change its contents. When Enabled is set to Yes and Locked is set to Yes, the control can be selected, but its content can't be changed. When Enabled is set to No and Locked is set to Yes, the control can't be selected or changed, but it appears with the normal background color.

There are some characteristics of form frmTextBox_EnabledLocked that deserve to be mentioned.

- It opens centered in the Microsoft Access window (property Auto Center set to Yes).

- It automatically fits the Detail section's height and width (Auto Resize set to Yes).

- It has a sizeable border (Border Style set to Sizable).

- It shows a gray bar.

Note   The gray bar that may appear on the bottom of a form window is probably due to a bug that appears when the property Scroll Bars is set to Both and the form window has enough horizontal and vertical space to show its Detail section.

- It has a specific Tab order. Press the Tab key to cycle between the form's Text Boxes (just the top two Text Box controls will react to the Tab key due to the bottom two having their property Enabled set to No).

Since it has both Scroll Bars (vertical and horizontal), whenever you shrink the form size by dragging its border, they will automatically allow scrolling for the Detail section (and the gray border will disappear, as shown in Figure 4-25).

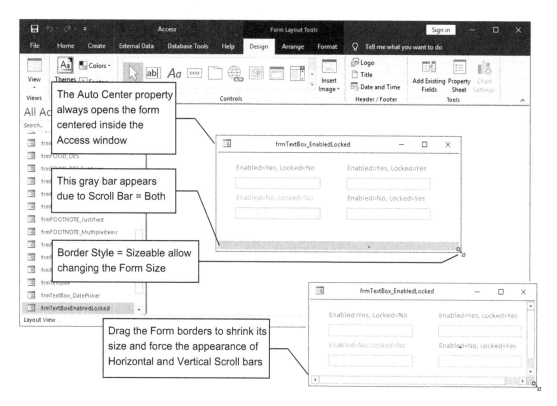

Figure 4-25. *frmTextBox_EnabledLocked uses the properties Auto Center set to Yes, Border Size set to Sizeable, and Scroll Bars set to Both. They make it appear centralized on the Access interface, and it can be redimensioned by dragging its borders*

The control's Tab orders are set by using the Tab Order command in the Tools area of the Form Design tab. It will show the Tab Order window, from where you can select each form section and drag its controls to the desired tab order—the form will change its Tab Index properties automatically. See Figure 4-26.

Attention   The Tab Index property will work only for controls whose property Tab Stop is set to Yes.

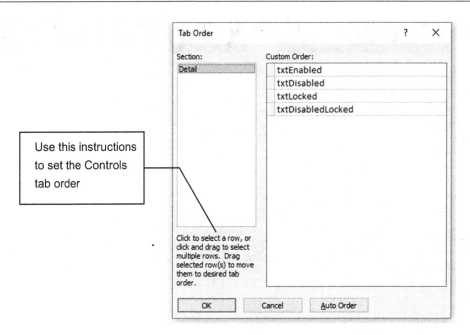

Figure 4-26. Use the Tab Order window to define the control's Tab sequence by dragging them to the desired position. It will change its control's Tab Index property

Now let's explore other specific Text Box properties.

Specific Text Box Properties

The Text Box control has specific properties that allow a better control about what you can type on it (some of these properties are also available to other control types). Table 4-8 describes them.

Table 4-8. *Microsoft Access Text Box Control Properties*

Tab	Property	Usage
Format tab Tab	Format	Defines the format of the control content
	Decimal Places	Rounds number values to desired precision
	Show Date Picker	Shows a calendar to select dates when Format is set to Date (or Control Source is set to a Date/Hour field data type)
	Scroll Bars	Shows or hide a vertical and/or horizontal scroll bar
	Line Spacing	Sets text line spacing
	Can Grow	Allows the text box grow to show more content when the form is printed
	Can Shrink	Allows the text box to shrink and hide its content when it has no text
Data /Other tab	Text Format	Offers two choices of text: Plain Text and Rich Text (allows formatting)
	Input Mask	Defines an input mask to better control what can be typed
	Enter Key Behavior	Changes the Enter key behavior to move to the next field or insert a line break (the Enter character, ASCII code 13) on the Text Box content

Use the Property Sheet's Format tab to set how the value typed on the Text Box must appear whenever you press Enter. To get better control over what can be typed, use the Input Mask property in the Property Sheet's Data tab.

Attention   The Format and Input Mask properties were already covered in the sections "Using an Input Mask for a Phone Number" and "Defining the Format Property for a Short Text field" of Chapter 2.

Show Date Picker and Input Mask Properties

The Text Box control can be optimized to receive valid dates using the Input Mask property or a Date Picker control to select it from a calendar—not both.

The Date Picker control is automatically shown in the Text Box control when:

- The property Show Date Picker is set to For Dates.

- It is bound to a Date/Time field data type.

- It is an unbound control with the property Format set to one of the default available date formats (General, Medium, Long, or Short Date formats).

- It has no input mask.

Whenever these rules are followed, Microsoft Access will show a small calendar located at the control's right corner, where the user can select the desired date.

By setting the Format property, the user can type (or select) a date using a short format (like mm-dd-yy) and show it in another way; Format set to Long Date spells both the weekday and month names for the selected date.

Using the Validation Rule and Validation Text properties, the control can also check whether the date selected is valid for the application (like a date equal or greater than system date). But be advised that whenever the Text Box control uses the property Validation Rule (and Validation Text) along with the properties Input Mask or Show Date Picker, in the case the user selects a date, it will no longer be able to delete it from the control. The Text Box will stuck firing the validation rule requiring a date selection.

Figure 4-27 shows the unbound form frmTextBox_DatePicker, which has four Text Box controls that use the properties Input Mask, Default Date Picker, and eventually Validation Rule and Validation Text to allow you to check its behavior.

All four Text Box controls have the properties Format set to Long Date and Show Date Picker set to For Dates, but just the two Text Boxes at the bottom automatically show the Date Picker calendar when selected, because they have no input mask.

The Text Box controls at the left have no validation rule, allowing you to type and delete its content by pressing the Delete key.

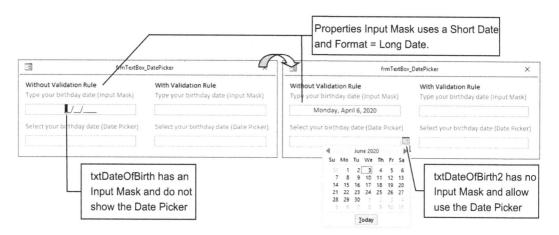

Figure 4-27. *When a Text Box control has Property Show Date Picker set to For Dates and no input mask, it automatically shows the Date Picker calendar to select a date. And if it has no validation rule, the Text Box content can be deleted*

But whenever you use the Validation Rule property (and Validation Text), the Text Box will no longer be able to allow you to delete its content, because by doing this it will break the validation rule.

For example, txtDateOfBirth3 (with Input Mask) and txtDateOfBirth4 (with Data Picker) use a validation rule to require that the year of the birthday date selected be greater than 1900 (the person must be born at least in the 20th century), by setting these properties:

- Validation Rule = Year([txtDateOfBirth3]) > 1900

- Validation Text = Year must be > 1900

Tip   The validation rule encloses the Text Box name in squared brackets to find its value on the form. Use the Expression Builder to help you create such an expression. It was already explained in section "Use the Expression Builder" of Chapter 3.

Whenever you type a birthday date using year 1900 or earlier, the validation rule will be broken, and the validation text will fire. But if you type a valid date (year > 1900) and then try to delete it, the empty control will also break the validation rule, because it will have no date—and no year to test. The Text Box control will be stuck asking for a date with "Year must be > 1900" (Figure 4-28).

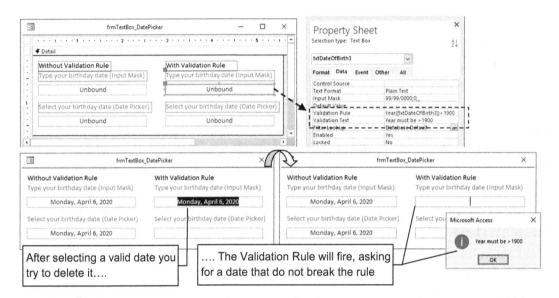

Figure 4-28. *Whenever you use a validation rule, chances are that the control will ask for a value because an empty value breaks the rule*

Note   You may be tempted to create complex expressions using the logical OR operator to verify whether the control is not null (like setting Isnull([txtDateOfBirth3]) OR Year([txtDateOfBirth3]) > 1900). This will not work because Microsoft Access will evaluate both expressions before using the logical OR operator—and the second expression will always fail when the control is null). Try to use just a single expression (like Year([txtDateOfBirth3]) > 1900 that will work).

Pay attention to these properties of frmTextBox_DatePicker:

- It is not centered on the screen (Auto Center set to No); it stores the screen position (the form's Top and Left properties) from where it was last saved in the form's Design view.

- It automatically fits the Detail section's height and width (Auto Resize set to Yes).

- It has no sizeable border or maximize or minimize buttons (Border Style set to Dialog).

- It has no dark gray bottom bar (Scroll Bars set to None).

- It has Min Max buttons set to None.

- It sets the tab order to first select the controls on the left and then on the right (from top bottom). See Figure 4-29.

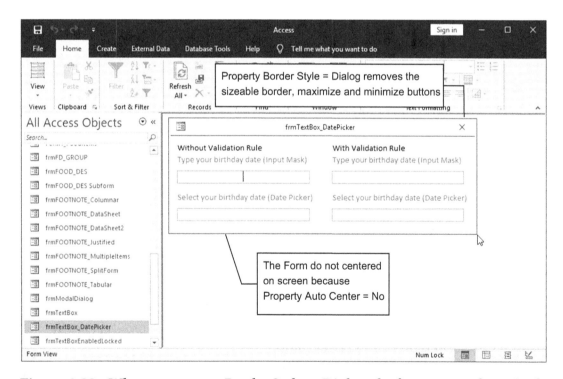

Figure 4-29. *Whenever you set Border Style to Dialog, the form cannot be resized or show its minimize and maximize buttons. By setting Auto Center to No, it will use its Top and Left properties to open where it was last saved on the form's Design view*

Can Grow and Can Shrink Properties

Use the properties Can Grow and Can Shrink to allow a Text Box control to change its size to adjust its content whenever it is printed. They do not work on Form view or Layout view—just in Print Preview.

The property Can Grow makes the Text Box grow vertically to show more text lines, while the property Can Shrink makes it shrink up to the height defined on the form's Design view.

Open frmTextBox_CanGrow in design mode to verify how the property works. It is linked to the query qryFoodItemsAZ, which shows food item names stored on table FOOD_DES ordered by the Food Name field (alias for the FOOD_DES Shrt_Desc field).

The Food Name text box (automatically named by dragging the controls from the Field List window) has its Can Grow property set to Yes, which will make it grow to show more lines whenever you print preview the form, while Can Shrink set to Yes could make Food Name Text Box disappear for any item without a food name inserted (Figure 4-30).

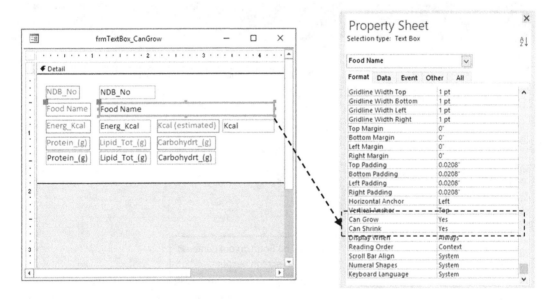

Figure 4-30. *Use the property Can Grow to allow a Text Box to grow vertically whenever the form is on Print Preview mode*

Note these characteristics of the form's frmTextBox_CanGrow Design view:

- It was set to show continuous records (Default View set to Continuous Form).

- It does not automatically fit the Detail section's height and width. Instead, it has a Design view size defined to allow you to view two records at a time (two times the Detail section's height, set by try-and-error alternating between Form and Design views), using the last Form Height and Width properties (Auto Resize set to No).

- It is not centered on the screen (Auto Center set to No).

- It shows just the vertical scroll bar (Scroll Bars set to Vertical Only).

- The controls were manually aligned to give a better form layout (some Labels at the left, and others go at the top of their associated controls).

- Its Detail Section property's Alternate Background Color is set to Background 1, Darker 5% (which will allow alternate each record background color).

Change it to Form view mode. It shows two records at a time due to it being a continuous form, alternating its Detail section background color among records. Change its records and note that the Food Name Text Box does not grow in Form view mode. Switch to Print Preview (File ➤ Print ➤ Print Preview), go to page 3, and note that the Food Name Text Box grew for some records to show the entire contents (Figure 4-31).

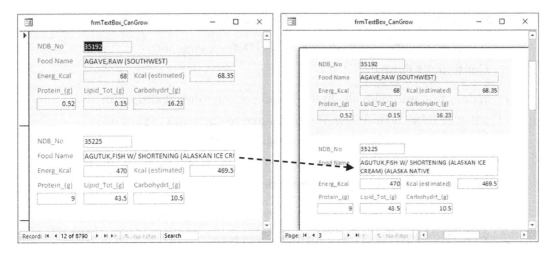

Figure 4-31. *Use property Can Grow to allow the Text Box to change its height on Print Preview, whenever it needs more vertical space to show it content. The Food Name shown at the left in Form view mode grew in Print Preview mode (at right). Also, set the Detail Section property Keep Together to Yes so that information isn't split between printed pages*

Text Format and Enter Key Behavior Properties

Two Text Box properties allow you to change a Text Box to a small text processor: Text Format (Data tab) and Enter Key Behavior (Other tab).

When Text Format is set to Rich Text, the Text Box allows text formatting: you can set bold, underline, text color, paragraph formatting, etc. By setting Enter Key Behavior to New Line in Field, when pressing Enter on a Text Box, you do not move to the next control in the form's Tab order. Instead, it inserts an Enter character (ASCII code 13) on the text, breaking it to a new paragraph.

Attention   But be advised that both properties insert hidden characters on the text that cannot be inserted on a Short Field data type. You will need a Long Text field data type to store these hidden characters and show the formatted text.

Open the unbound frmTextBox_TextFormat in Design mode, click its txtRitchText Text Box, and note that it has the properties Scroll Bars set to Vertical, Can Grow set to Yes, and Can Shrink set to Yes on the Format tab; Text Format set to Rich Text on the Data tab; Enter Key Behavior set to New Line in Field on the Other tab (Figure 4-32).

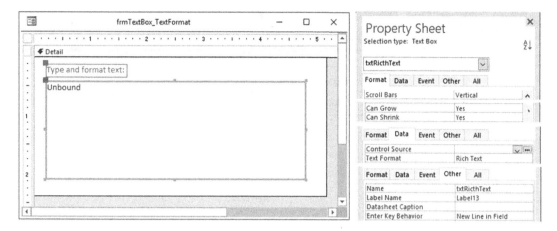

Figure 4-32. *Whenever you set the properties Text Format to Rich Text and Enter Key Behavior to New Line in Fields, you can turn a single Text Box into a small text processor*

Change it to Form view, insert some text, and use the Home tab's Text Formatting area tools to format it the way you want. Then show the form in Print Preview and note how the Can Grow and Can Shrink properties act on the Text Box (Figure 4-33).

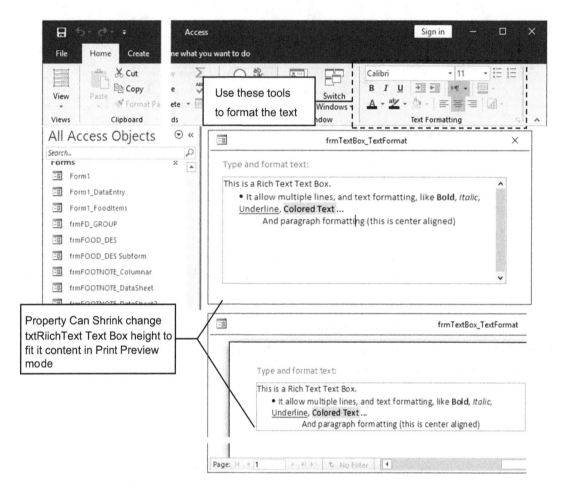

Figure 4-33. *Show Form frmTextBox_TextFormat in Form Mode view and use the tools in the Text Formatting area of the Home tab to format the Text Box text. Use Print Preview mode to check how the Can Grow and Can Shrink properties act on the Text Box control*

You will note on form frmTextBox_TextFormat that it has the following characteristics:

- Not centered in the Microsoft Access window (Auto Center set to No).

- No sizeable border or minimize or maximize buttons (Border Style set to Dialog).

- Since it has no record source, it also has no navigation buttons or record selector because its properties' navigation buttons and record selector was set to No).

- It automatically resizes the Detail section's height and width (Auto Resize set to Yes).

Input Mask Property for Password

Using the Input Mask property, you can turn the Text Box into a password collector, where everything that is type appears with an asterisk.

Such an approach is commonly used on a form employed to capture the username and password on most database applications. (I personally dislike applications that use this approach, unless it deals with very sensitive data—or the client who bought it asks for it.)

Open the unbound form frmTextBox_Password in Design view, and you will note that it has only two text boxes: one for the username and other for the password (Figure 4-34).

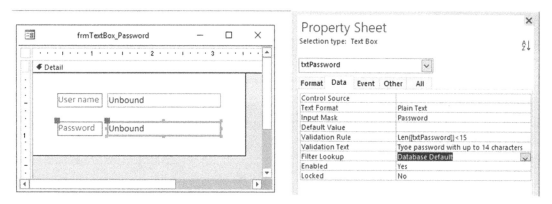

Figure 4-34. *Show frmTextBox_Password in Design view and note that it has two Text Box controls (txtUserName and txtPassword). Both have Validation Rule and Validation Text properties to restrict the length of text that can be typed, and txtPassword has Input Mask set to Password (created by the Input Mask Wizard)*

The LEN() Function

The LEN() function allows you to check the number of characters that was typed on any string value, like a control value or property.

The LEN( ) function has this syntax:

LEN(String)

where:

- String is a string expression between quotes or an expression that returns a string (like a variable name or property value). If the String argument contains Null, then Null will be returned.

Show frmTextBox_Password in Form view and type a username. If it is greater than 25 characters, the validation rule (Len([txtUserName]) < 26) will be broken, and the validation text will be shown in a dialog box. The same is true for txtPassword, which allows just 14 characters with its validation rule (Len([txtPassword]) < 14, as shown in Figure 4-35.

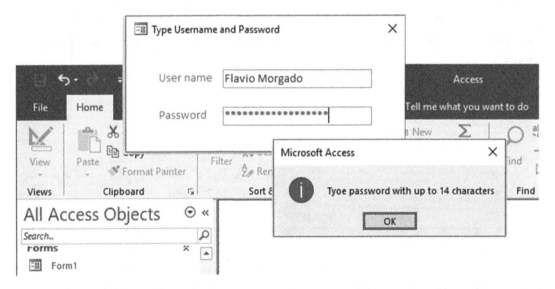

Figure 4-35. frmTextBox_Password uses a validation rule on both controls to restrict the length of the username and/or password. The txtPassword Text Box uses Input Mask set to Password to show asterisks to hide the password typed

Attention   Since both Text Boxes use the LEN( ) function (with the Control Name property between squared brackets as an argument) to limit the text amount, whenever you type and clear the text, when you try to leave the empty control, the validation rule will be broke, because the LEN( ) function can't operate over a null Text Box.

Note the following characteristics of frmTextBox_txtPassword:

- It is horizontally centered in the Microsoft Access window, although the property Auto Center is set to Yes, because its Property PopUp is set to Yes.

- No sizeable border, although its Border Style is set to Sizeable because its property Modal is set to Yes.

- No minimize or maximize buttons (Min Max Buttons set to None)

- Since it has no Record Source property, it also has no navigation buttons or record selector because its navigation buttons and record selector were set to No).

- It automatically resize to the Detail section's height and width (Auto Resize set to Yes).

- It is modal to the Microsoft Access interface—you can't use Access until it is closed (Modal set to Yes).

- It can float outside the borders of the Microsoft Access interface (Pop Up set to Yes).

Control Source for Expressions and Aggregate Functions

The property Row Source of the Text Box control can also be used to calculate expressions that use a single field record value and to calculate the entire recordset used by the form, which is especially useful when Default View is set to Continuous Form.

If the expression is used in the Detail section, it will refer to the current record; but by putting it on the Form Footer section and using any of the aggregate functions (other than Group By, mentioned in Table 3-7 of Chapter 3), you can create a subtotal expression or statistic for all form records.

To show how it works, this section uses the WEIGHT table records to calculate the individual weight of each element of a food item's common measure, by dividing Gm_ Wgt by Amount and using the expressions inserted into the Text Box controls of the Form Detail and Footer sections.

Open frmWEIGHT_SubTotalsExample in Design view, and note that it has some Text Box controls whose Control Source properties are expressions, so like an Excel formula, they begin with a = sign and relate to other form controls with or without an aggregate function (Figure 4-36).

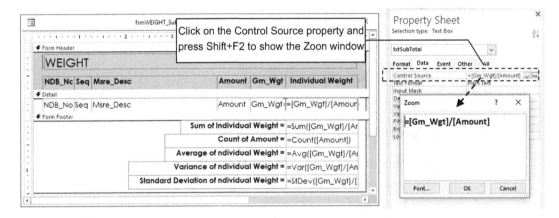

Figure 4-36. *Use the Text Box's Control Source property to build expressions that begin with an = character and relate to form controls. An expression inserted in the Detail section refers only to the current record. By putting it on the Form Footer section and using an aggregate function, it will relate to all currently viewed form records (by applying a filter to the form, it will recalculate all aggregate functions)*

As Figure 4-36 shows, whenever the Control Source property is selected and you press Shift+F2, Access shows the Zoom window that will help you to build the desired expression.

Note that the txtSubTotal Text Box inserted on the Detail section calculates a record subtotal using an expression on its Control Source property that refers to control names between squared brackets, bound to fields of the Weight table:

```
=[Gm_Wgt]/[Amount]
```

All Text Box controls inserted in the Form Footer section have an aggregate function to calculate values that refer to all form records.

To calculate statistics such as Sum, Average, Variance, and Standard Deviation for all txtSubTotal Text Box values on the Form Detail section, the Text Box controls inserted in the Form Footer section use the same expression as the argument to their aggregate function. For example, to calculate the sum of all txtSubTotal values, the txtSum Text Box uses the same txtSubTotal expression as an argument to the SUM() aggregate function.

`=Sum([Gm_Wgt]/[Amount])`

Attention   Access doesn't accept the use of a Text Box control name that uses an expression as an argument to an aggregate function inserted on another Text Box control. For example, if txtSubTotal is inserted in the Detail section, use an expression such as =(`[Gm_Wgt]/[Amount]`), you can't use it as an argument to an aggregate function such as =Sum(`txtSubTotal`) inserted on the Form Footer. Instead, use =Sum(([Gm_Wgt]/[Amount]).

To count the number of records returned by the form's Record Source property, the frmWEIGHT_SubTotalsExample form uses the txtCount Text Box on the Form Footer section using the COUNT() aggregate function, which receives as an argument just the Amount field, because it is guaranteed that it is fulfilled on all table records.

`=Count([Amount])`

Note   The COUNT() aggregate function will discard all empty records—the ones that return a Null value.

Since frmWEIGHT_SubTotalsExample's Record Source property has a SQL instruction that uses the dynamic criteria =Like [NDB_No] & "*", whenever the form is opened (or requeried after opened by pressing Shift+F9), it will ask for NDB_No or any numeric expression that begins a series of NDB_No records (press Enter without typing a value to return all WEIGHT table records). Figure 4-37 shows the result of typing 10 to show all 610 WEIGHT table records whose NBD_No fields begin with 10, calculating the desired subtotal records and aggregate functions almost instantly.

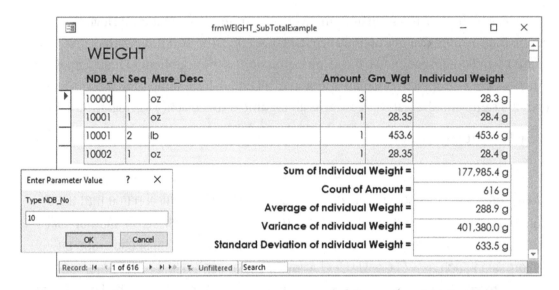

Figure 4-37. *Since frmWEIGHT_SubTotalExample is bound to a dynamic query that uses the LIKE operator, whenever it opens, the Enter Parameter Value will ask for an NDB_No or any numeric sequence that begins a series of them (no value or * will return all WEIGHT records). The aggregate function in the Form Footer section will return statistics for all form records*

Combo Box and List Box Controls

The Combo Box and List Box controls are used to limit what can be typed on a table field, although the Combo Box control can also be used as a superb search tool.

Both offer a multicolumn list, with the difference that the Combo Box is a Text Box with a drop-down list that allows you to type the information to be associated to the control value, while the List Box is a steady control that just allows clicking in one (or more) of its items to define its value.

The Combo Box is more economical regarding screen space, because it needs only one text row, while the List Box normally uses as many rows as you want, needing more vertical space in a Form Detail section.

Both controls have almost the same set of special properties that allow control over the list items and their appearance, as described on Table 4-9.

Table 4-9. *Microsoft Access Combo Box and List Box Controls' Properties*

Tab	Property	Usage
Format tab	Column Count	Indicates how many columns the control list will show.
	Column Widths	Sets each list column width in inches (separated by semicolons).
	Column Head	Defines if the list will show a column title as its first item.
	Separator Character	Indicates the separator character used for a value list.
	List Rows	Combo Box only; sets the default number of items on the drop-down list.
Data tab	Row Source	Indicates the source for the items on the list: name of a table, query, or typed items separated by commas.
	Row Source Type	Defines the type of row source: Table/Query, Values List (for typed values), or Field List (used when Row Source is set to Table or Query).
	Bound Column	Indicates which of the list columns will return the control value.
	Limit To List	Combo Box only; indicates if the user can type an item outside of the list.
	Allow Value List Edits	Allows you to right-click the list and choose Edit List Items in the shortcut menu to add, remove, or edit the items in the list.
	List Items Edit Form	Name of the form to be opened whenever Allow Value List Edits is set to Yes.
	Inherit List Values	When the control source is a lookup field, use its Control Source property to populate the list. This requires that Row Source Type is set to Value List.
	Show Only Row Source Values	Defines whether the list can display values that aren't specified by the Row Source property.

These special properties control how the Combo Box and List Box controls show a list of items where the application user can select a value, which can come from a constant list of values or a list of records returned by a table or query.

Since there are lots of properties that are quite difficult to understand at first glance, Microsoft Access uses a wizard to help you set them depending on what you want the control to do. It is available whenever the Use Control Wizards option is selected in the Controls List drop-down (see Figure 4-38).

Since the Combo Box Wizard performs different actions for these two types of lists, let's begin by exploring how to create a Combo Box (or List Box) filled with a list of values.

Using the Combo Box Wizard with a List of Values

Consider, for instance, that you need to offer a form where the user must define a person's civil status, which is supposed to be described with the words Single, Married, Divorced, and Widowed.

You will be surprised by how these words can vary on a database record whenever you offer a Text Box control to the user for this task: it is surely better to use a Combo Box or List Box from where the desired civil status can be selected.

Also, instead of creating a Civil Status field using a Short Text data type with eight characters (the length of the longest status, Divorced), you decide instead to represent the civil status in your database as a Number, using a Byte field (the smaller data type that uses just 8 bits), where 1 is set to Single, 2 is set to Married, 3 is set to Divorced, and 4 is set to Widowed.

For both strategies, a Combo Box or List Box must be the control of choice to guarantee that the correct civil status be set by the user. The first strategy (text insertion) will need a single-column list, while the second (number insertion using text selection) needs a two-column layout.

Creating a One-Column List of Values Combo Box

Follow these steps to create a Combo Box with a single list of values using the Combo Box Wizard:

1. Use the Form Design tool on the Create tab to create a new form in design mode.

2. Select the Combo Box tool in the controls list of the Form Design tab and click the Form Detail section.

3. Considering that the Use Control Wizards option is selected, the Combo Box Wizard will open, asking you to indicate from where the list options must come (Figure 4-38).

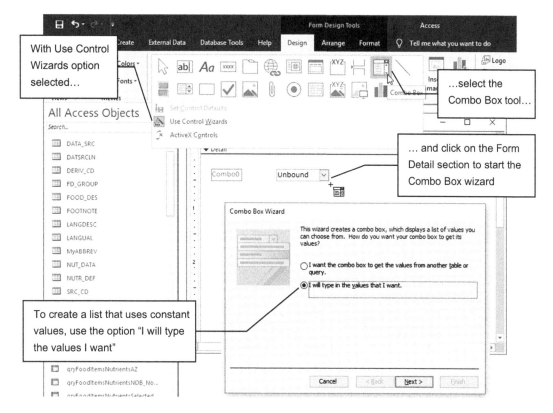

Figure 4-38. *Whenever the Use Control Wizards option is selected in the controls list of the Form Design tab, when you select the Combo Box (or List Box) tool and click the Form Detail section, the wizard opens, asking from where the list options comes*

Tip   If you click Cancel to close the wizard, the control will be placed with default values in the form section. The only way to start the wizard again is by deleting the control and inserting another one.

---

4. To create a Combo Box whose items come from a list of values, select the "I will type the values I want" option and click Next.

5. The Combo Box Wizard will ask for the number of columns in the list and give you a table grid to type the list values. To create a single column list, keep "Number of columns" set to 1 and type in different rows the four possible options: Single, Married, Divorced, and Widowed (Figure 4-39).

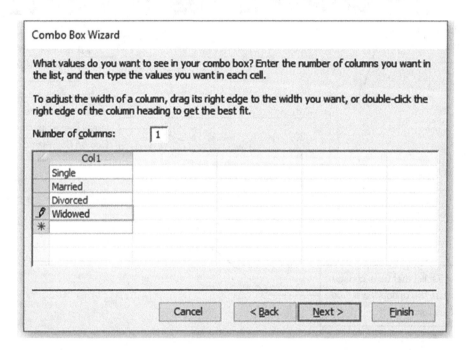

Figure 4-39. *For a Combo Box with a constant list of values, the second page of the wizard allows you to indicate the list's number of columns and offer a place to type the list values*

6. Click Next, and the Combo Box Wizard will ask for the text you want to use on the Label control associated to the Combo Box. For this exercise, type **Civil Status** (Figure 4-40).

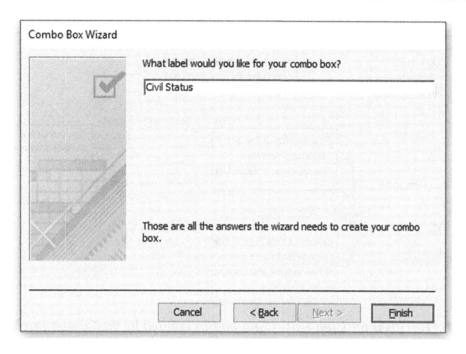

Figure 4-40. *The last Combo Box Wizard page asks for the text that must be used by the Label associated to the Combo Box control. Type Civil Status and click Finish to create the control (Figure 4-39)*

7. Click Finish to create the control in the form's Detail section and use the Property Sheet window to explore the control form and data properties.

The Combo Box Wizard will create the Civil Status Combo Box in the Form section. Alternate to Form view, and click the Civil Status Combo Box arrow to expand its drop-down list and see its values. Select one of its items to define the control value; then press F4 to expand the list and note it is selected in the list. Show the form in Design View or Layout View and explore the Combo Box properties (Figure 4-41).

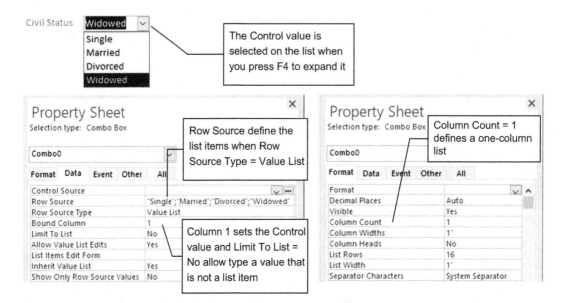

Figure 4-41. *This is the Civil Status Combo Box created by the Combo Box Wizard that uses a one-column list filled with a constant list of values*

To set up this one-column list, use the Combo Box Wizard to set these properties:

- Row Source = "Single"; "Married"; "Divorced"; "Widowed"

- Row Source Type = Value List

- Bound Column = 1

- Column Count = 1

- Limit To List = No

- Allow Value List Edits = Yes

- Column Widths = 1"

- List Width = 1"

The property Limit to List being set to No indicates that the Combo Box allows the user to type a civil status not in the list—which may be nonsense. Setting the properties Column Widths, List Width, and Width to 1 sets the width of the first column, list width, and control width.

Since this is a one-column list with the property Allow Value List Edits set to Yes, you can right-click the Combo Box control and select Edit List Items on the context menu to show the Edit List Items dialog box, where you edit, add, or delete the items in the list (Figure 4-42).

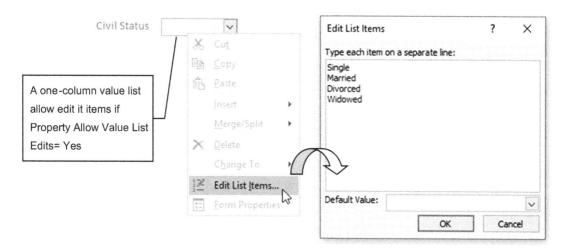

Figure 4-42. *Whenever a Combo Box has just one column and the property Allow Value List Edits is set to Yes, you can right-click it and select the Edit List Items option to show the Edit List Items dialog box, where you can add, delete, or update the items on the list*

Creating a Two-Column List of Values Combo Box

To continue this exercise, let's consider the alternative where the civil status is stored on the database as Number, where 1 is set to Single, 2 is set to Married, 3 is set to Divorced, and 4 is set to Widowed.

Follow these steps to create a Civil Status Combo Box that uses two columns (civil status code and civil status name):

1. Click the Combo Box tool to select it and click an empty space of the form's Detail section.

2. On the first Combo Box Wizard page, select "I will type the values I want" and click Next.

3. On the second Combo Box Wizard page, set "Number of columns" to 2, and on the table grid type into the Col1 column the civil status codes (the values 1, 2, 3 and 4, one per row) and in Col2 the CIVIL STATUS text (the values Single, Married, Divorced, and Widowed, as shown in Figure 4-43).

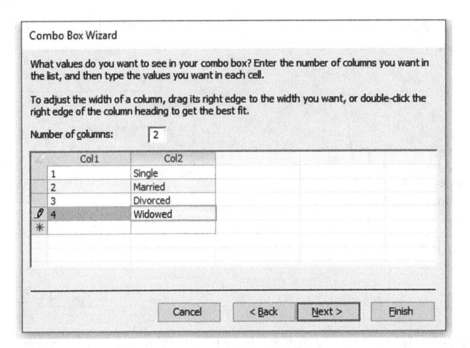

Figure 4-43. *To create a Combo Box with a two-column list, set "Number of columns" to 2 on the second wizard page, type the civil status code on Col1, and type the civil status name on Col2*

4. Click Next, and the Combo Box Wizard will ask you to select which list column will return the Combo Box value. Select Col1 (the Civil Status code, as shown in Figure 4-44).

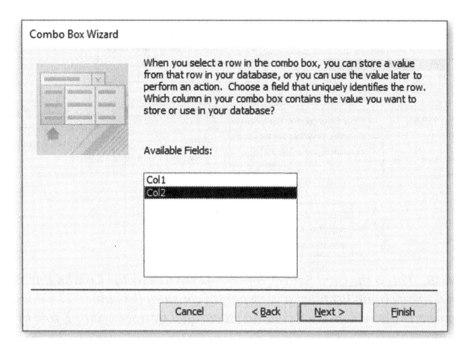

Figure 4-44. *Whenever you set a Combo Box list with more than one column, the wizard will ask you to select which column will return the Combo Box value. Since we want to allow the user to select a civil status name and return a civil status code, select Col1*

5. Click Next to show the last Combo Box Wizard page, type again **Civil Status** for the text of the Label associated to the Combo Box, and click Finish to create the control.

Once again, the Combo Box Wizard will create the Civil Status Combo Box in the Form section. Switch it to Form view, and press F4 or click the Civil Status Combo Box arrow to expand its drop-down list to see its two column values. Select any list item and note that the Combo Box value received the civil status code (Figure 4-45).

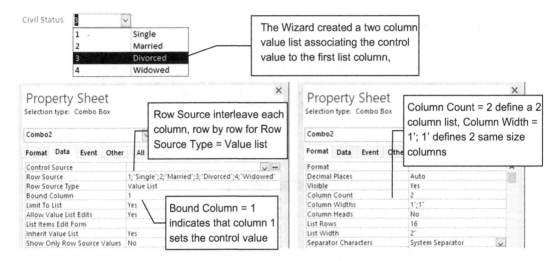

Figure 4-45. *This is the Civil Satus Combo Box created by the Combo Box Wizard that uses a two-column list filled with a pair of constant list values. The Row Source property intercalted each column (separated by a semicolon), row by row*

To set up this one column list, the Combo Box Wizard set these properties:

- Row Source = 1; "Single"; 2; "Married"; 3; "Divorced"; 4; "Widowed"

- Row Source Type = Value List

- Bound Column = 1

- Column Count = 2

- Limit To List = No

- Allow Value List Edits = Yes

- Column Widths = 1"; 1"

- List Width = 2"

Although Limit to List is set to No and Allow Value List Edits is set to Yes, the list can't be edited because it has two columns.

Column Widths is set to 1", 1", which defines two 1-inch columns, while List Width set to 2" sets the drop-down list width as the sum of each column width, which makes it double the control width (Width set to 1").

Note   The Combo Box Wizard that uses a two-column value list could do a better job. On the second page (where it asks for the column values), it could have a "Hide key column" option. On its third page (where it asks to select the column that returns the Combo Box value), it could have a "Hide key column" option, so the user can select a civil status expression while the control stores its code.

By repeating the previous two exercises using the List Box control, you will be able to compare how both controls work when using these two methods. Form frmComboBoxListBox_ValueList did it for you and also fixed the two-column Combo Box and List Box to allow both to select a civil status, while Hidden assigns a civil status code to the control value (Figure 4-46).

Figure 4-46. *Use frmComboBoxListBox_ValueList to check how the wizard created both a Combo Box and a List Box using one or two columns. The Combo Box and List Box at the right allow you to select a civil status while storing a code as the control value*

Combo Box or List Box with Hidden Bound Column

Change frmComboBoxListBox_ValueList to Design view, click cboCivilState3 (located at the right), and show its Property Sheet. Then inspect its Format and Data tabs (Figure 4-47).

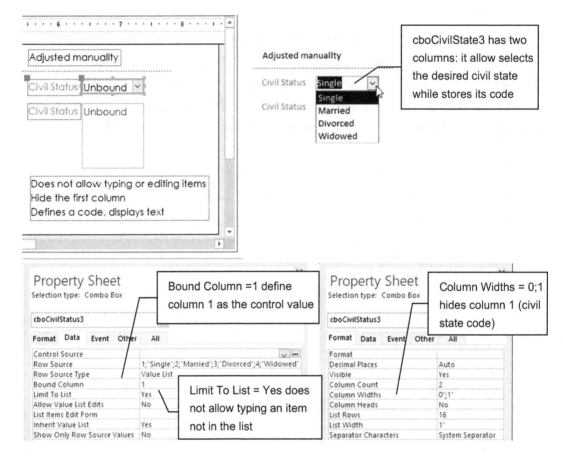

Figure 4-47. *To use a two-column Combo Box or List Box control, where the user selects a list item while the control receives a hidden code, use Property Bound Column to indicate the column control value, and use Column Widths to hide the bound column*

Using the Combo Box Wizard with a List of Records

The Combo Box and List Box Wizard changes the options on its first page to ask what the control must do according to the form section where you want to create it.

- By clicking the form's Detail section, the wizard will offer two options, one to allow you to create a control to select a value from a table or from query records and the other to allow you to select it from a constant list of values (see Figure 4-38).

- By clicking the Form Header section, besides the two basic options, the wizard will offer a third option that allows you use the control as a search tool.

Let's begin by creating a Combo Box that allows you to show records from a table or query on the Form Detail section.

Creating a Two-Column List of Records Combo Box

Use the Relationships window of the sr28_Forms_Overlapping database to verify that the table's FD_GROUP (food category records) and FOOD_DES (food item records) share a one-to-many relationship among their FdGrp_CD fields—each FOOD_DES record stores the FdGrp_CD primary key to set the food category association.

Since each FOOD_DES record is associated with a single FD_GROUP record, the FOOD_DES FdGrp_Cd is a good candidate to use a Combo Box to better show its value (Figure 4-48).

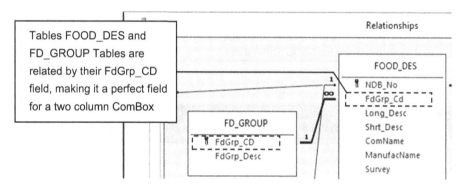

Figure 4-48. *Use the Relationships window to find the related fields that are good candidates to use a Combo Box to best express the field value on the "many" side of the relationship*

This one-to-many relationship is the classic case where a form can be used to create an interface where each FOOD_DES record uses a two-column Combo Box to represent the FdGrp_CD field showing the food category name, instead of its code.

Follow these steps to create a form associated to the FOOD_DES table and insert it in a Combo Box for the FdGrp_CD field to associate it with the FD_GROUP table:

1. Use the Form Design tool on the Create tab to create a new form in design mode.

2. Show the form's Property Sheet, and on the Data tab, set Form Record Source to FOOD_DES.

3. Click the Show Existing Fields tool of the Form Design tab to show the Field List window, press and hold the Ctrl key to click the NDB_No and Lng_Desc fields, and drag them to the Form Detail section.

4. Select the Combo Box tool in the controls list of the Form Design tab, and click and drag the FdGrp_Cd field from the Field List window to the Form Detail section to fire the Combo Box Wizard (Figure 4-49).

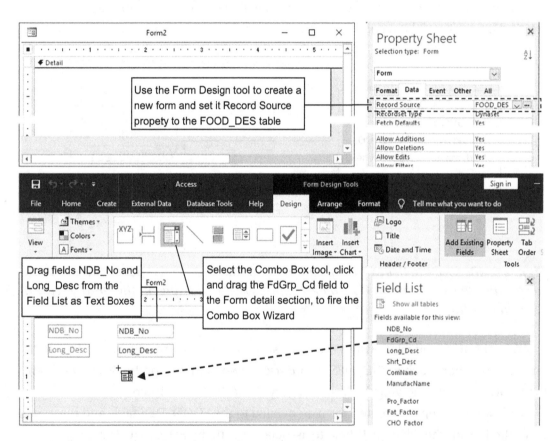

Figure 4-49. *Create a new form whose Record Source is set to FOOD_DES, drag fields NDB_No and Long_Desc as Text Boxes, select the Combo Box tool, and click and drag the FdGrp_CD field to the Form Detail section to fire the Combo Box Wizard*

5. On the first Combo Box Wizard page, select the option "I want the Combo box to get the values from another table or query" and click Next.

6. The wizard will ask you to select a table or query. Select the FD_GROUP table and click Next to show its fields (Figure 4-50).

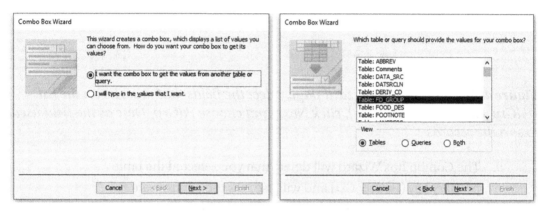

Figure 4-50. *To fill a Combo Box list with records, select its first option on the Combo Box Wizard's first page and then choose the table or query from where the records come. This figure shows how to select the FD_GROUP table as its row source*

7. Click the >> button to select both FD_GROUP Table fields (FdGrp_CD and FdGrp_Desc) and click Next.

8. The Combo Box Wizard will ask if you want to sort the list items by one of the selected fields. Select FdGrp_Desc for Ascending, and click Next (Figure 4-51).

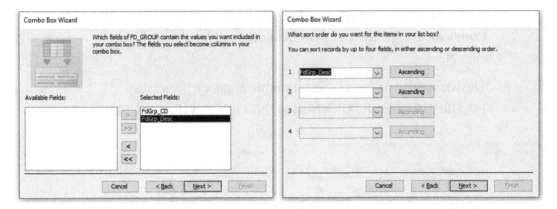

Figure 4-51. *On the third wizard page, select the fields that must be on the list (FdGrp_CD and FdGrp_Desc), click Next, and choose FdGrp_Desc as the field used to sort the records*

9. The Combo Box Wizard will detect that you selected the table primary key (FdGrp_CD) and will use it as the control value, automatically hiding it on the list (checking the "Hide key column (recommended)" option). Click Next (Figure 4-52).

10. The Combo Box Wizard will ask if the Combo Box value must be associated to a field, already selecting the FdGrp_Cd field (because it was preselected when the control was dragged). Click Next.

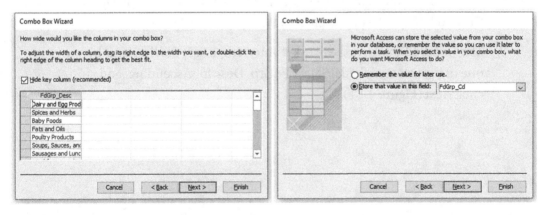

Figure 4-52. *Since you selected the table primary key field (FdGrp_CD), on the fifth wizard page, check the "Hide key column (recommended)" option to hide it on the Combo Box list, and on the sixth page, it will automatically select the field that you dragged from the Field List window (FdGrp_Cd from FOOD_DES table) as the Control Source property*

11. Use the last Combo Box Wizard page to associate the Combo Box
    Label to the words Food Category (the wizard will propose using
    the field name), and click Finish to create the control in the form's
    Detail section (Figure 4-53).

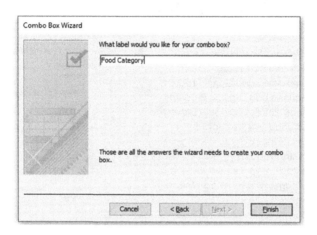

Figure 4-53. *On the last wizard page, type Food Category as the caption for the*
Combo Box's associated Label and click Finish to insert the control on the Form
section

Figure 4-54 shows frmComboBox_FOOD_DES that has the Food Category Combo
Box created by the Combo Box Wizard and that its list of items is composed by the
records from the FD_GROUP table, alphabetically sorted by its FdGrp_Desc field, with
all its relevant properties from the Data and Format tabs.

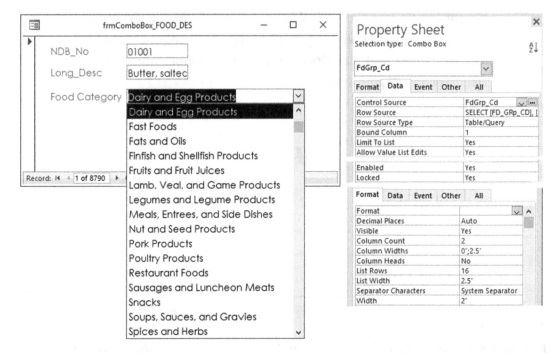

Figure 4-54. *The Food Category Combo Box from frmComboBox_FOOD_DES uses the FD_GROUP table records to fill its list of items. Since both tables are related by the FdGrp_CD field, which is hidden from the first list column, the control can show the food category name instead of its code*

To set up this two-column list associated to the FD_GROUP table, the Combo Box Wizard sets these properties on the control's Data and Format tabs on its Property Sheet:

- Control Source = FdGrp_Cd

- Row Source = `SELECT [FD_GROUP].[FdGrp_CD], [FD_GROUP].[FdGrp_Desc] FROM FD_GROUP ORDER BY [FdGrp_Desc]`

- Row Source Type = Table/Query

- Bound Column = 1

- Column Count = 2

- List Rows = 16

- Limit To List = Yes

The Combo Box Wizard always creates a 1-inch control with a 1-inch list of items that allow you to change its value. To improve the control functionality on the form, the next properties were also changed:

- Column Widths = 0; 2.5"

- List Width = 2.5"

- Width = 2"

- Locked = Yes

The Combo Box's second column width was changed to 2.5 inches, as was its List Width setting (to allow you to select an item without truncating its text), while the control's Width was set to 2 inches—which is enough to show the food category name.

It also has Locked set to Yes to allow the user to expand the list but not change its value so as not to ruin the Food Item and Food Category association.

To inspect how the wizard brings records to the Combo Box list, click the ellipsis button located to the right of the Row Source property to show the Query Builder with the graphic representation of the SQL instruction used by the control (Figure 4-55).

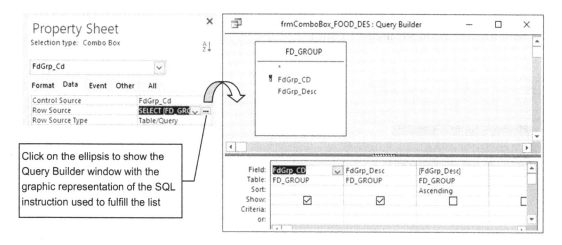

Figure 4-55. *Whenever Row Source Type is set to Table/Query, you can use the Row Source ellipsis to show the Query Builder window and see how the SQL instruction was created*

Attention   The Query Builder is a modal window, meaning you can't use the Access interface while it is opened.

Tip   Whenever Row Source Type is set to Table/Query, you can use the Row Source arrow to expand a list of database saved queries and select one to be used to fill the control list of items.

As a bonus, open frmComboBoxListBox_QueryRecords that has two columns of Combo Box and List Box controls produced by the wizard, all of them using the FD_ GROUP table to fill its lists.

The Combo Box and List Box of the right column have Column Heads set to Yes to show the field names on its first row, and both have the first column unhidden using Property Control Width set to 0,5", 1".

The List Box works the same, but a multicolumn Combo Box with two or more visible columns shows a fundamental concept: the first visible column will always appear as the selected list item, while the true control value can be returned by any other list column as defined by its Bound Column property (by setting Bound Column to 2, the true right Combo Box control value shown in Figure 4-56 is the food category name on the second list column, not the food category code).

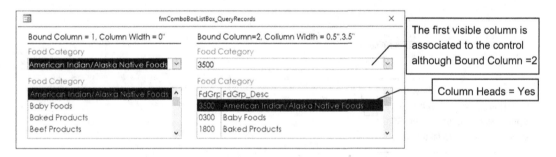

Figure 4-56. *Use frmComboBoxListBox_QueryRecords to see how a two-column list works on the Combo Box and List Box controls when its first column is hidden or shown*

The Check Box and Option Group Controls

The Check Box control is commonly used to set a Boolean option (True/False) in the user interface. It can be used alone in any form section to allow checking an interface option or, more rarely, inside an Option Group control to offer a multiple selection group of options. It can be used unbound or bound to any Yes/No or Number data type (although this will be a waste of bytes on database storage).

Be aware that the Check Box can be made a triple state control, as opposed to simply binary, by setting its Triple State property and allowing three different options: Null (no value, gray appearance), checked (True=-1), and unchecked (False set to 0).

It does not require a wizard to set it up: just select it in the controls list and click the Form section in the form's Design view to draw a new Check Box control. If you want to create a multiselection group, draw a rectangle around the check box and use a Label control on its top to simulate this group.

Form frmCheck Box shows how the Check Box behaves as you set the properties Default Value (Null, True of False), Triple State, Enabled, and Locked. It also shows how to simulate a group of selection items (Figure 4-57).

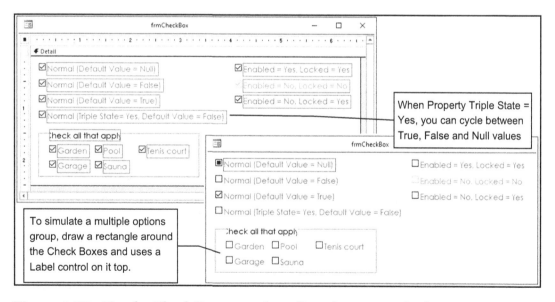

Figure 4-57. *Use the Check Box control to allow the user to check an option on the interface. Since it is a triple state control, it can return True, False, or Null values (if bound to a table field with Triple State set to Yes, the data field must allow null values)*

All form Check Box controls were named with the "chk" prefix (according to the control naming conventions stated earlier), and the tab order can be verified using the Tab Order command of the form's Design tab (the form first selects the first column, then the second column, and finally the items inside the multiple selection list, as shown in Figure 4-58).

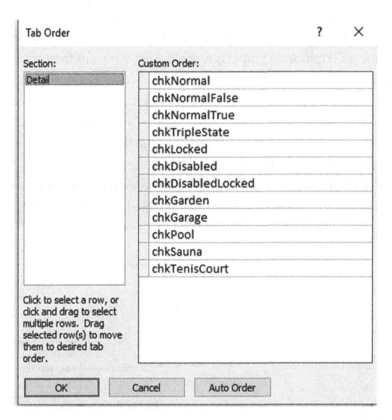

Figure 4-58. *Use the Tab Order window to verify or change the control tab order of each section. By using the control naming conventions to clearly identify each control, it will be easier to set the corret tab order*

Also note that the controls are perfectly aligned, which can be a nightmare using the mouse. To achieve this result, hold the Ctrl key to select the controls you want to align vertically or horizontally and then use the Sizing & Ordering tools of the Form Arrange tab to align and size them. By aligning the labels, their associated controls will be repositioned accordingly (Figure 4-59).

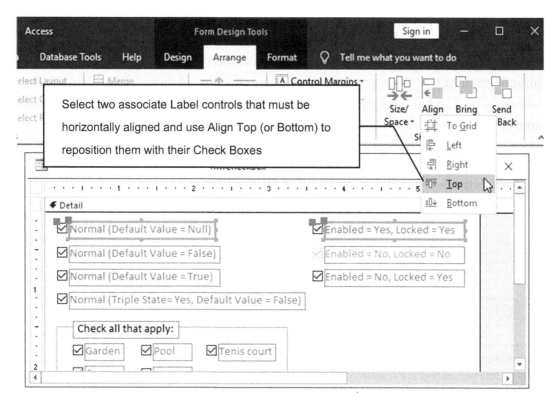

Figure 4-59. *Use the form Design view's Arrange tab commands to perfectly align, distribute, or size controls horizontally or vertically*

Tip   After select the controls to distribute, align, or size, you can also right-click one of them and select the desired command on the context menu that appears.

Note that the first Check Box (chkNormal) is Null by default (it has a dark gray square), because its Default Value property was not defined. But whenever you click it, it will begin to cycle between True/False and will never be Null again (unless you use a macro). Only chkTripleState has its property Triple State set to Yes, allowing you to cycle among the three possible options.

Also note that a Locked Check Box can be selected, but its value cannot be changed. A disabled Check Box cannot be selected and is grayed out on the interface, and a disabled and locked Check Box is not grayed and cannot be selected.

Needless to say, form frmCheckBox has interface characteristics defined by its Format properties: no record selector, navigation button, or sizeable borders.

Option Group, Toggle Button, and Option Button Controls

The Microsoft Access Option Button control works differently than VBA's UserForm Option Button control, because if you insert more than one of them on any form section, they will behave independently of each other, allowing you to select more than one at the same time (Figure 4-60).

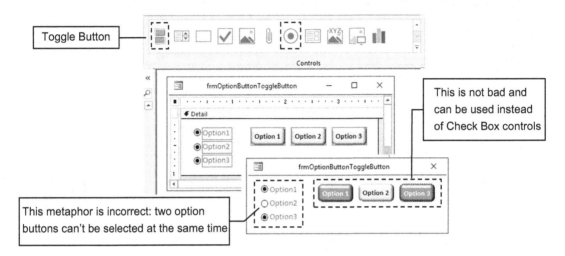

Figure 4-60. *Never use Option Button controls alone in a form section to indicate options that the user must select. Although it will work as expected, the correct control for such a user interface is the Check Box*

Whenever there is a need to create a mutually exclusive list of options, you must use the Option Group control because it manages the controls put inside it allowing just one to be selected at a time.

To create a mutually exclusive list of options with the aid of the wizard, follow these steps:

1. Select the Option Group tool in the controls list of the form's Design tab and click (or drag it) in the form's Detail section.

2. Supposing that the Use Control Wizards option is selected, the Option Group Wizard window will appear and ask on its first page for the name of the options you want to use. Click Next (this exercise uses the civil states as mutually exclusive options, as shown in Figure 4-61).

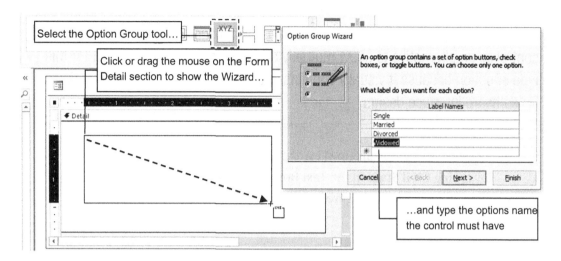

Figure 4-61. *To create a mutually exclusive list of options to select a person's civil state, select the Option Group tool, click the Form Detail section, and type the option names on the first Option Group Wizard page*

3. The second Option Group Wizard page will ask to select if the Option Group will have a default selected option, proposing the first of them as the default control value. Select the first option "Yes, the default option is "Single" and click Next.

4. The third Option Group Wizard page will ask to attribute a value to each option, proposing a numbering sequence to each one (Single=1, Married=2, Divorced=3, and Widowed=4). Accept the proposed values and click Next.

5. The fourth Option Group Wizard page will ask you which type of control you want to use to select the desired civil state option: Option Buttons (default), Check Boxes, or Toggle Buttons. It will also ask what appearance the control must have; click the option Etched (default), Flat, Raised, Shadowed, or Sunken to see how they will change the appearance of the Option Group control. Keep Option Buttons and Etched selected and click Next.

Attention   Although the Option Group Wizard proposes the use of the Check Box control as an alternative to show mutually exclusive options, never use it for this type of option because it visually conflicts with the standard interface guidelines for software interface design.

6.   On the last Option Group Wizard page, define the control name by typing **Civil State** in the Text Box, and click Finish to insert the control on the form (Figure 4-62).

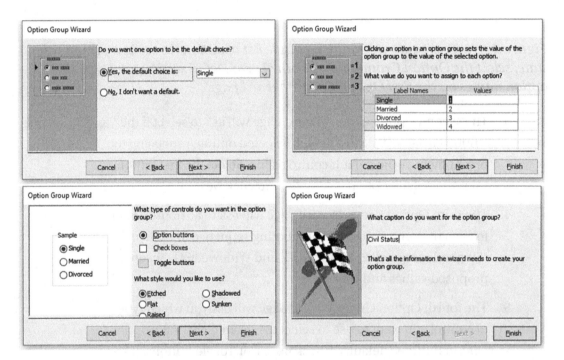

Figure 4-62.   *The Option Group Wizard asks you to create a mutually exclusive list of options. It asks for the option's name, its associated value, the type of control and appearance, and the text to be used on the Label associated to the control*

To make an Option Group work, the wizard changes these options:

- *Option Value*: This is changed on the first wizard page; define each control value, when selected, that in turn define the Option Group value.

- *Default Value*: This defines the default option selected if it is set to any control Option value (leave this option empty or set it to a value different from any control's Option value to make the Option Group appear unselected).

- *Style*: This determines the control appearance by changing its border options. You can select from Flat, Etched, Raised, Sunken, Shadowed, and Chiseled.

Open frmOptionsGroup to see the different appearances that an Option Group can have according to the type of control and appearance selected (Figure 4-63). Each Option Group has a different Default Value property, allowing each one to appear with a different civil state selected.

Microsoft Access 2019 uses by default a washed-out appearance with a white background selected for its Form Sections background. I have changed it to Background 2, Darker 5% (light gray) so you can better understand the difference between the control's Style property (Etched, Flat, Raised, Sunken, Shadowed, and Chiseled), which also helps you better appreciate how the Toggle Button appears when it is selected/unselected.

The form also uses the proposed Check Box control for a mutually exclusive option such as the person's civil state—which is considering an amateur approach to graphic interface design.

Note   The Toggle Button was created in the first Microsoft Access version and has been kept as an interface control since then. It has no equivalence in the VBA Form interface and needs a gray background so it can better show how it performs when selected. The same is true for the Style property, available to all Microsoft Access controls.

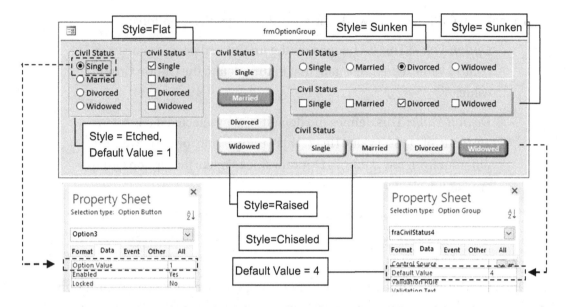

Figure 4-63. *Use frmOptionGroup to see how the wizard sets the control's Option value and to see how the Option Group Default Value and Style properties change their appearance (with variations on the type of control used by the group)*

Attention   The Civil Status Option Groups that use Check Box controls for mutually exclusive options are shown here just because the Option Group Wizard allows you to select them as an option. This design is inconsistent and must be certainly avoided when building database interfaces.

SubForm/SubReport Control

The SubForm/SubReport control is used to show one-to-many relationships in a single interface. This control works like a window that you insert inside a form section (called the *master form*) to show another form (called the *subform* or *child form*). It has three special properties.

- *Source Object*: This allows you to select the form name (or report) that must be shown by the control.

- *Link Master Fields*: This indicates the field's names on the master form whose values will be used to synchronize records on the child form.

- *Link Child Fields*: This indicates the field's names on the child form whose values matches the value of the Link Master Field on the master form.

Note   If the Link Master Fields and Link Child Fields properties need to use more than one field to synchronize records on the master and child forms, separate the fields using semicolons on both properties. The fields don't need to exist as controls on the form or subform, but they need to be in the table or query used for the Record Source property.

Take as an example frmFD_GROUP created by the Form Wizard and shown in Figure 4-9. It is a master form with two levels of subforms that show the relationships between food category, food item, and common measures.

The master form shows the food category, the first subform shows food item records related to the selected food category, and the second-level subform shows all food item common measures records.

To synchronize the master record with the first-level subform, the Form Wizard defined these properties on the first-level subform control (Figure 4-64).

- Source Object = frmFOOD_DES Subform.

- Link Master Fields = FdGrp_CD (field from FD_GROUP table)

- Link Child Fields = FdGrp_Cd (field from FOOD_DES table)

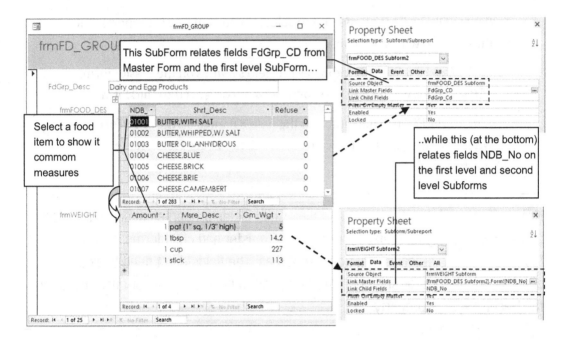

Figure 4-64. *The SubForm control requires that the Link Master Fields and Link Child Fields properties use a field that exists on each form's Record Source property and that has a relationship between the two tables*

To synchronize the master form and SubForm control records, set properties Link Master Fields and Link Child Fields to the FdGrp_CD field—the one that relates to both tables (check the Relationships window to verify how tables FD_GROUP and FOOD_DES relate).

By setting these properties, every time a new food category record is selected on the master form, Access applies a filter to the SubForm control using a SQL WHERE clause like this:

```
WHERE <SubForm Field> set to <FORM Field>
```

Considering that the master form shows FD_GROUP table records, that the SubForm control shows FOOD_DES records, and that both tables are related by their FdGrp_CD field, the WHERE clause must be as follows:

```
WHERE FOOD_DES!FdGrp_Cd =FD_GROUP!FdGrp_CD
```

But the second-level SubForm control creates a different scenario. In this case, the master form is indeed a SubForm/SubReport control that holds a form inside it (food item names), while the child form is another SubForm/SubReport control (common measures). Whenever a food item is selected on the first subform, the other subform must show its common measures.

To synchronize the first subform (now the master form) with the second-level subform (its child form), the Form Wizard defines these properties on the second-level SubForm control:

- Source Object = frmWEIGH Subform

- Link Master Fields = [frmFOOD_DES Subform].Form![NDB_No]

  (field NDB_No from FOOD_DES table of frmFOOD_DES Subform)

- Link Child Fields = NDB_No (field from WEIGHT table)

To select a field on a form that is inside a SubForm control, Access needs to use this syntax (after the control name it uses `.Form!` followed by the field name):

```
[SubForm control name].Form![Control Name]
```

The `[SubForm control name].Form!` part of the syntax selects the form inside the SubForm control, while `[Field Name]` indicates the SubForm control that holds the field information required to synchronize records.

For your knowledge, if you want to refer to a field on a master form from a subform, the correct syntax is as follows:

```
Form.Parent![Control Name]
```

Now the `Form.Parent!` part of the syntax sets a reference to the form where the SubForm control was inserted, while `[Control Name]` indicates the master form control that holds the field information required to synchronize records.

The result is quite good for records synchronization, but from my point of view, the form frmFD_GROUP appearance falls short regarding the user interface.

For a database production application—one that expects to receive user input of new records—the navigation buttons used on the master form and each subform can eventually help, but there is no doubt that this pollutes the screen with too much information. But considering the `sr28.accdb` database, the information it holds must continue "as is," with no record change or insertion. With this in mind, any form/

subform interface can be improved by manually creating the form/subform interface, using other approach to show related records.

Manually Creating a Form/Subform Interface

To manually create a form/subform interface, you must first create the master and child forms and then insert the subform on the master form using one of two approaches.

- By selecting the SubForm/SubReport control in the controls list, canceling the Form Wizard, and manually setting its Source Object, Link Master Fields, and Link Child Field properties

- By dragging the desired form that must be used as a subform directly from the Database window to the desired master form section

Using the second approach, Microsoft Access will automatically insert a SubForm/SubReport control and set its Source Object property to the name of the dragged form. Let's look at an example by following the next steps:

1. Open frmFOOD_DES_Continuous and note that it is a continuous form, showing many records at a time (Default View set to Continuous Form).

2. The frmFOOD_DES_Continuous form was created by the More Forms and Multiple Items tools and needs some changes to improve its appearance.

   a. Set the Form Header BackGround Color to White.

   b. The Form Header Label controls and Form Detail associated Text Box controls were resized to use the desired horizontal space.

   c. Form Footer had its Height property changed to allow it to receive a SubForm/SubReport control.

3. Select frmSubWeight in the Database window and drag it to the frmFOOD_DES_Continuous Form Footer section.

4. Access will insert the SubForm/SubReport control and set its Source Object property to frmSubWeight, defining it as a subform, and will show a warning message telling that it will set the form's Default View property to Single Form (Figure 4-65).

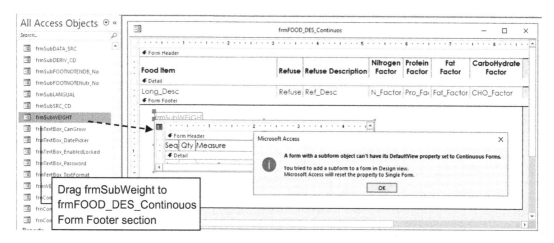

Figure 4-65. *Drag any form from the Database window to insert it as a subform on another form section. If the destination form has Default View set to Continuous Form, Access will issue a message indicating that it will change Default View to Single Form*

Attention   This message is acceptable whenever you try to insert the SubForm control in the Form Detail section, since Access can't show a SubForm control using a continuous record view. But it's clearly a (small) bug, because the Form Footer section doesn't interfere with this way of showing records.

---

5. Since the tables used for both forms are related by their NDB_No fields (check the Relationships window), Access will automatically set the SubForm control properties Link Master Fields and Link Child Fields to NDB_No field.

6. Select the master form (click in the form's top-left corner) and reset Default View to Continuous Form (Figure 4-66).

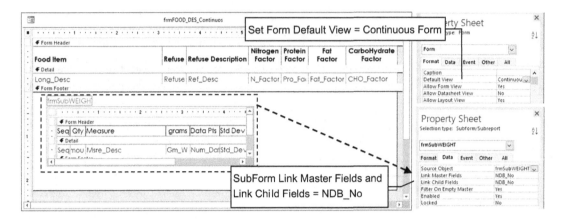

Figure 4-66. *Whenever you drag a form from the Database window to any form section of a continuous form, Access will set its Defaut View to Single Form. Change it again to Continuous Form and note that it inserts a SubForm control and automatically set its Link Master Fields and Link Child fields to the fields that relate both forms' Record Source properties*

7. Switch to Form view and note that frmFOOD_DES_Continuous is a continuous form with another continuous subform in its Form Footer section, automatically synchronizing its records (Figure 4-67).

Food Item	Refuse	Refuse Description	Nitrogen Factor	Protein Factor	Fat Factor	CarboHydrate Factor
Butter, salted	0		6.38	4.27	8.79	3.87
Butter, whipped, with salt	0		6.38			
Butter oil, anhydrous	0		6.38	4.27	8.79	3.87
Cheese, blue	0		6.38	4.27	8.79	3.87
Cheese, brick	0		6.38	4.27	8.79	3.87

frmSubWEIGH

Seq	Qty	Measure	grams	Data Pts	Std Dev
1	1	pat (1" sq, 1/3" high)	5		
2	1	tbsp	14.2		
3	1	cup	227		
4	1	stick	113		

frmSubWeight has no Navigation Buttons and is positioned on the Form Footer section

Record: ◄ ◄ 1 of 8790 ► ►► No Filter Search

Figure 4-67. *This figure shows that frmFOOD_DES_Continuous can have Default View set to Continuous Form and receive another continuous subform on its Form Footer section. Select any food item on the form to show its common measures on the subform*

By tweaking some SubForm control Format properties, you can insert another SubForm control on its Form Footer to also show LANG_DESC table records synchronized with the selected food item.

Figure 4-66 shows frmSubFOOD_DES in Design and Form views. It has two SubForm/SubReport controls on its Form Footer section: one for the frmSubWEIGHT and another to frmSubLANG_DESC, synchronizing two subforms as each food item is selected (one for the common measures and another for the Langual descriptors). Afterward, open frmSubFOOD_DES, press and hold the Page Down key to quickly select food items, and note how the two SubForm controls quickly synchronize its records (Figure 4-68)!

Note   Although frmSubWEIGHT and frmSubLANG_DES were not built in this chapter, it is supposed that at this point of this chapter you can fully understand how each subform works by just opening them in the form's Design view and investigating their properties.

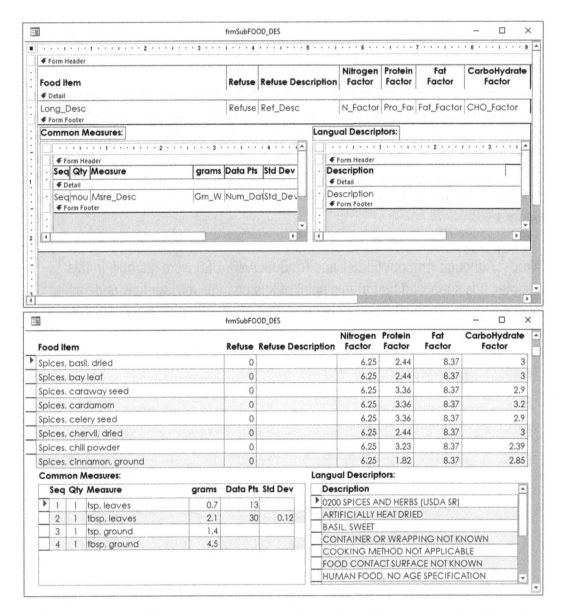

Figure 4-68. *frmSubFOOD_DES is a continuous form that uses two SubForm/ SubReport controls to show the "many" side records of two related tables. WEIGHT and LANGUAL (Record Source is set to qryLANGUAL and uses tables LANGUAL and LANG_DESC to show its records)*

And this is not all: open frmFD_GROUP_TwoSubFormLevels, and note that using the same approach, frmSubFOOD_DES was inserted into the form footer, improving considerably the interface proposed by the Form Wizard to frmFD_GROUP shown in Figure 4-64. It now can show more information using almost the same screen size (Figure 4-69).

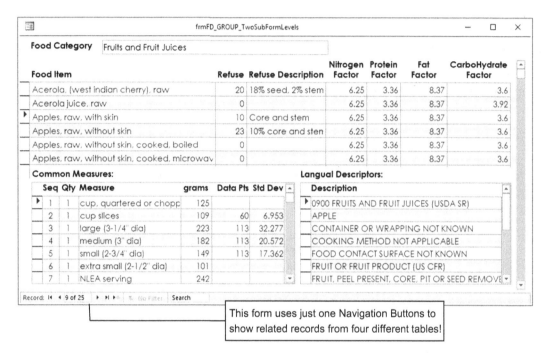

Figure 4-69. *Form frmFD_GROUP_TwoSubFormLevels has a SubForm/ SubReport control on its Form Footer section (frmSubFOOD_DES) that in turn has two SubForm/SubReport controls on its Form Footer section, creating two levels of subforms that easily synchronize records from four different database tables*

Using Aggregate Functions in Forms and Subforms

Looking at Figure 4-67, some may argue that by removing the navigation buttons from the forms used on the SubForm/SubReport controls, there is a loss of record information. How many food items are there in each food category? How many common measures and Langual descriptors?

These are reasonable questions that can be solved using the COUNT() aggregate function that can operate on all records shown by a form, which is especially useful when this form has Default View set to Continuous Form (see the section "Control Source for Expressions and Aggregate Functions" earlier in this chapter).

Use as an argument any field on the form's Record Source property that is guaranteed to be fulfilled for every record: the primary key field.

Form frmSubFOOD_DES_Aggregate uses this trick on all its SubForm/SubReport controls to count the records and show the result in its Form Footer section, using an unbound Text Box with Control Source set to Count([NDB_No]), and a specific Format property that adds a suffix to clearly indicate what is counted (Figure 4-70).

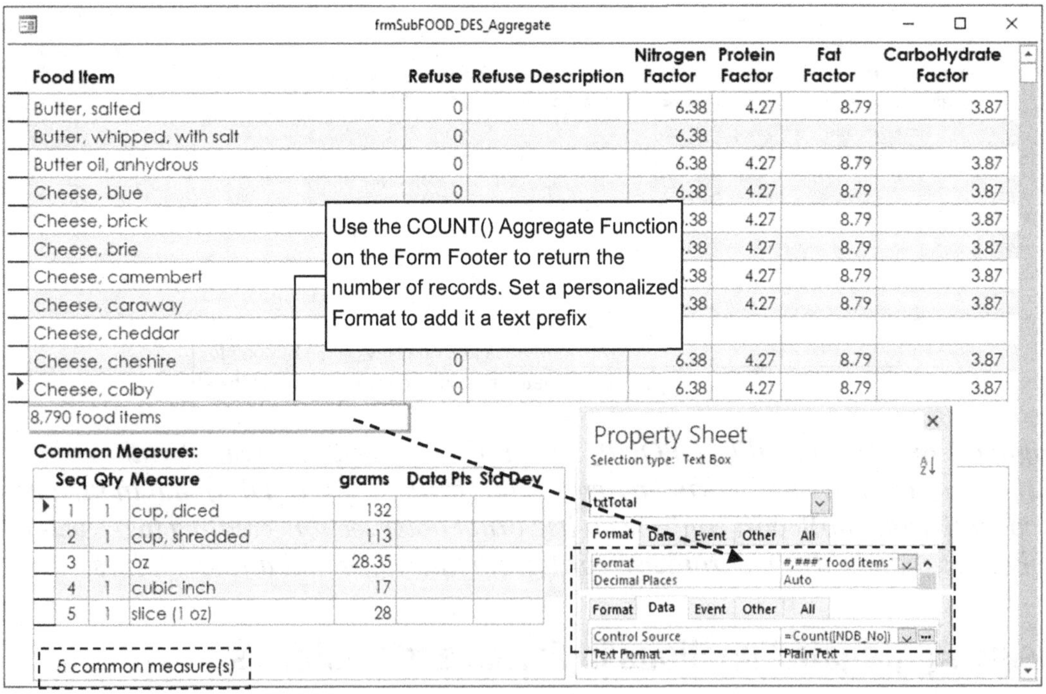

Figure 4-70. *Whenever you want to use subforms without the navigation buttons, place a Text Box control on its form footer and use the COUNT() aggregate function to return how many records it has (using the Format property, you can add a text prefix or suffix)*

Note   You are invited to open frmSubFOOD_DES_Aggregate in Design view, select each subform to check its name, and study how each one works.

You may note that frmSubFOOD_DES_Aggregate has the frmSub prefix, meaning that it will be used as a subform and that it also doesn't have navigation buttons. This is because it was inserted in frmFD_GROUP_Aggregate's Form Footer section as a subform, creating the desired effect of synchronizing records of four different tables and now showing how many records each subform has. Cool, isn't it? (See Figure 4-71.)

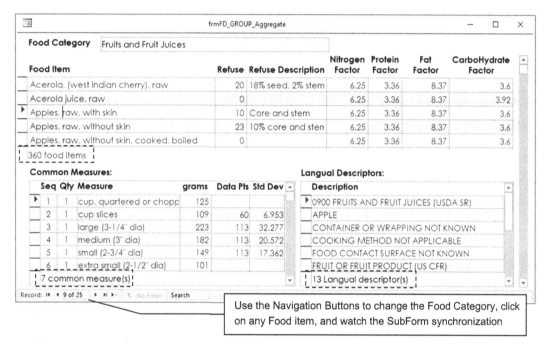

Figure 4-71. *The frmFD_GROUP_Aggregate single form allows you to navigate by each food category while showing how many food items and respective common measures and Langual descriptors exist using a single window. And with no code! Quite nice, huh?*

Chart Control and Chart Tool

The Chart control or the Insert Chart tool can be used to make a graphical presentation of a single record or query data. Both controls may need a single chapter—or a small book—to explore all its possibilities, but since there are lots of videos on the Internet about them, this section will focus on some issues that you need to know to produce the desired presentation on your forms and reports.

Microsoft Access 2019 allows you to create charts using two different applets.

- *Microsoft Graph*: Created with the Chart control, this is the traditional way of creating charts since Microsoft Access 2003.

- *Modern Charts*: Created with the Insert Chart tool, this uses a new chart engine that creates charts closely related to the ones that Excel 2019 offers.

The charts created with both tools have the same synchronization properties used by the SubForm/SubReport tool.

- *Link Master Fields*: This indicates the control or field names in the form (separated by commas if more than one is needed) whose values must be used to filter the records that the chart plots.

- *Link Child Fields*: This indicates field names in the chart query that must be used to synchronize with the form's Link Master Field property.

Note   As with the SubForm/SubReport tool, the names used by these properties don't need to be on the chart as a control but must be present in the query or table used by the form or chart to bring the desired records.

There is an enormous list of differences between both tools used to create charts. Here are some of them:

- The Chart control has an old and confusing wizard that may help you to create the chart, while the Insert Chart tool has none, so you must manually tweak many properties to produce the desired result.

- The Chart control produces charts with an appearance that may seem older than the modern charts created by the Insert Chart tool.

- The Chart control has many more customization options than the Insert Chart tool, which is still primitive in the way it allows the personalization of charts.

- For an unknown reason, both the Chart control and the Insert Chart tool expects that the records data came from a Total query (although you can change it later by a Select query).

- By default both chart types (and the Chart Wizard) expect to receive data on a row-by-row bases (series names are considered as field values). Only the Chart control allows the use of data on a column-by-column basis (series are considered as field names).

To guide you in creating a chart with Microsoft Access and the sr28.accdb database, this section will show how to produce two different graphics commonly used on a nutritional website for any food item:

- *Calories Breakdown*: A pie chart that shows the total percentage of calories that came from protein, fat, and carbohydrates on a food item (together they sum 100%).

- *%Daily Values*: A column chart that states the percentage of protein, fat, and carbohydrates a food item needs to provide to fulfill a person's daily ingestion need.

Creating a Pie Chart with the Chart Control

Every time you select the Chart tool and click a form section in Design view, Microsoft Access opens the Chart Wizard, no matter the state of the Use Control Wizards option. In other words, you can't get rid of it to create your first chart.

Since the Chart Wizard expects to receive data on a row-by-row basis, there is a need to create a query that returns the desired nutrients (protein, fat, and carbohydrate) and the calories each one gives, using different rows for each nutrient record.

To build such a query, you need to know some nutritional information regarding these three nutrients:

- As cited earlier in the section "Using the Expression Builder" in Chapter 3, protein and carbohydrate have 4 calories per gram, while fat has 9 calories per gram.

- Since DRIs[1] set adequate percent ranges for adults on the calorie intake from these nutrients, they can be used as a suffix to the nutrient names to give additional information on the chart.

  - *Protein*: 10%–35%

  - *Carbohydrate*: 45%–65%

  - *Fat*: 25%–35%

We can build such a query by inspecting the Relationships window and noting that we need to use the FOOD_DES table for nutrient codes (NDB_No) and names (Long_Des) and its related NUT_DATA table for nutrient amounts, using a criteria to return just the desired nutrient amounts by its Ntr_No code (Ntr_No).

Note   To use such Ntr_No criteria, inspect the NUTR_DES table to find that for nutrient names Protein, Total_Lipid (fat), and Carbohydrate, by Difference, the desired Nutr_No codes are, respectively, 203, 204, and 205 (they are between double quotes because the NDB_No field has the Short Text data type).

The IIF() Function

The IIF() function, also known as "immediate IF," is used to provide a logical test that can return one of two different values and can be used anywhere on an expression.

The IIF() function has this syntax:

```
IIF(Expression, True_value, False_value)
```

---

[1]Dietary Reference Intakes (DRIs): Acceptable Macronutrient Distribution Ranges, https://www.ncbi.nlm.nih.gov/books/NBK56068/table/summarytables.t5/?report=objectonly).

where:

- *Expression*: Required; is an expression or value that must be evaluated (0 is considered as False; any other value is considered as True)

- *True_value*: Required; is a value or expression that is returned when Expression is evaluated to True

- *False_value*: Required; is a value or expression that is returned when Expression is evaluated to False

Since the IIF() function is used on an expression, it always evaluates both True values and False values, although it returns just one of them. This may lead to unexpected errors, because if one of these arguments generates an error (like a zero division), IIF() will propagate such error.

Of course, you can nest another IIF() function inside the True_value or False_Value, something that can become difficult to follow according to the value that must be returned.

Note   You'll learn about the CHOOSE() function later in this book for a better alternative of nested IIF() functions.

Open the query qryFOOD_DES_ProtFatCHOCalories and verify how it was built to return the desired information.

- It relates FOOD_DES and NUTR_DATA by its NDB_No field.

- It uses In("203","204", "205") on the Criteria option of the Ntr_No field from the NUTR_DATA table to select just the desired nutrients.

- It uses the IIF() function on the Nutrient column expression to return each nutrient name suffixed by the respective nutrient range (click the Nutrient column and press Shift+F2 to better see it in the Zoom window).

  ```
  Nutrient: IIf([Nutr_No]="203","Protein 10-35%", IIf([Nutr_
  No]="204","Fat 20-35%","Carbohydrate 45-65%"))
  ```

Tip   This expression uses two nested IIF() functions (also known as an *immediate IF*) to check the record Ntr_No value and return the desired nutrient name. The IIF() function needs three arguments, separated by commas, and has this syntax:

```
IIF(<Test>, <value for Test=True >, <value for Test=False>)
```

The first IIF(<Test>,…) verifies whether Ntr_No is set to 203, and if it's True, it returns the argument when Test is set to True ("Protein 10-35%"), but if it's False, it uses another (nested) IIF() function on the argument when Test is set to False to verify whether Ntr_No is set to 204. If it's True, it returns Fat 20-35. If it's False, it returns Carbohydrate 45-65%.

Attention   It is important to note that whenever you need to nest IIF() function to test n conditions, you will need n-1 nested IIF() functions, which can turn your expression into a mess. As an alternative, you can use the CHOOSE() function, which will be explained later in the chapter.

- It also uses the IIF() function to build this expression for its Calories column (to multiply the nutrient's Ntr_Val field by the respective calories amount it has):

```
Calories: [Nutr_Val]*IIf([Nutr_No] In ("203","204"),4,9)
```

Show qryFood_DES_ProtFatCHOCalories in Datasheet view, and note how each food item has three records, each one using the desired nutrient name and adequate range, so the pie chart can be easily built (Figure 4-72).

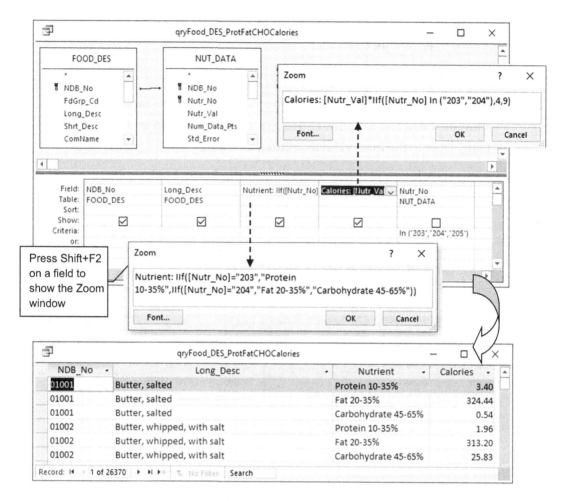

Figure 4-72. The query qryFood_DES_ProtFatCHOCalories uses the FOOD_DES and NUTR_DATA tables to return three records for each food item (one record for each nutrient listed as Protein, Fat, and Carbohydrate). It uses the IIF() function to build the Nutrient and Calories fields

Note   There is no need to calculate the percentage of calories that came from each of these three nutrients (by dividing each nutrient value by the sum of their values), because the Microsoft graph pie chart can automatically give this information by using data series values with the Percent option set.

Follow these steps to create a pie chart with the Chart Wizard using the qryFood_DES_ProtFatCHOCalories query:

1. Use the form's Design tool to create a new form.

2. Set the form's Record Source property to the FOOD_DES table, show the Field List window, and drag the fields NDB_No and Long_Desc to the form's Detail section.

3. Select the Chart tool in the controls list of the form's Design tab and click the Form Detail section to start the Chart Wizard.

4. On the first page of the Chart Wizard tool, select Queries in the View area, choose the qryFood_DES_ProtFatCHOCalories query in the list, and click Next to continue (Figure 4-73).

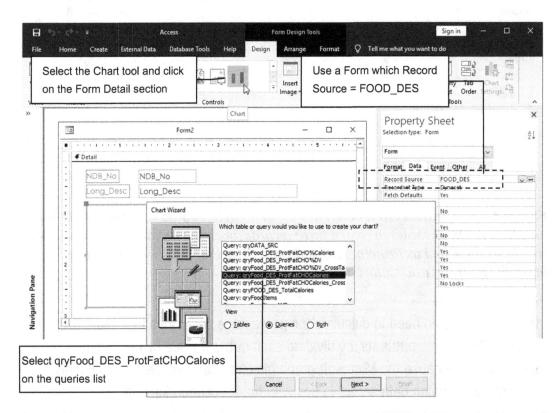

Figure 4-73. *On a new form, whose Row Source is set to FOOD_DES, select the Chart tool, click the form's detail section, and select qryFood_DES_ProtFatCHOCalories on the list*

5. The second Chart Wizard page asks which fields you want to use on the chart. Double-click the Nutrient and Calories fields (or select them and use the > button) to add them to the Fields to Chart list and click Next.

6. The third Chart Wizard page asks which type of chart you want to create. Click the pie chart and click Next.

7. The fourth Chart Wizard page asks how you want to use the selected fields, adequately proposing Nutrient as the series name (in the upper right of the chart preview) and SumOfCalories as the series values. Accept the default values and click Next.

Tip On this Chart Wizard page, you can drag the selected fields to the indicated positions of the chart preview. Double-click field SumOf Calories to change the aggregate function used to the Total field value (if any).

---

8. The fifth Chart Wizard page will detect the fields used on the form's Record Source property and in the query selected for the chart and, because they are related in the Relationships window, will propose them for the Chart control's Link Master Fields and Link Child Field properties (it adequately proposes the NDB_No field for both properties). Click Next (Figure 4-74).

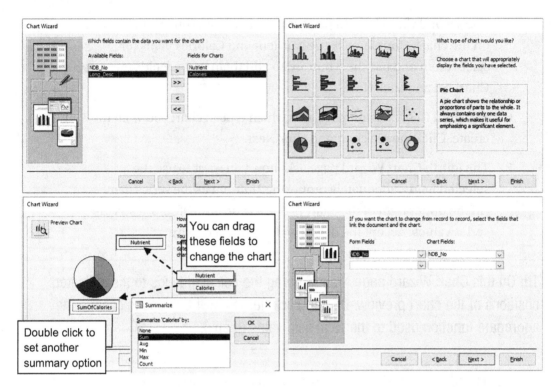

Figure 4-74. *The Chart Wizard asks to define the fields used by the chart, the type of chart, how the selected fields will be used on the chart, and which fields must be used on its Link Master Fields (Form Fields) and Link Child Fields (Chart Fields) properties*

9. The last Chart Wizard page asks for a title to be used on your chart and if a legend must be exhibited. Type **Calories Breakdown** as the chart title, keep "Yes, display a legend selected," and click Finish to close the wizard and insert the chart in the Detail section.

After the chart is created, select Form view, use the navigation buttons to change the form records, and note how the chart updates as each record is shown (Figure 4-75).

Tip   For the Chart control's Row Source property, the Chart Wizard sets by default a Total Query SQL instruction and may define the Link Master Field and Link Child Fields properties. To use all the query records on the chart, remove both control properties, click the ellipsis at the right of the Chart control's Row Source property to open the Query Design window, and change the Total query to a Select query.

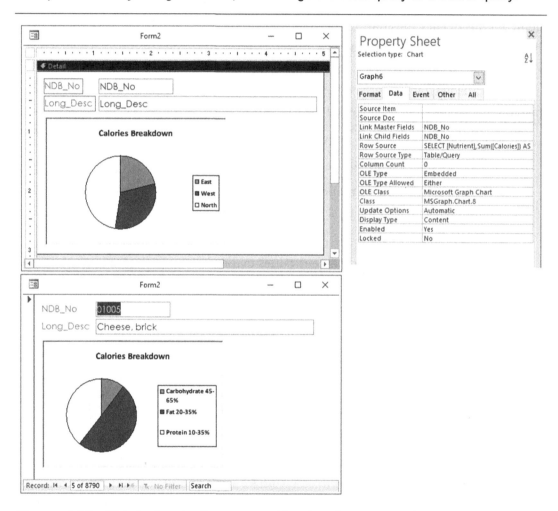

Figure 4-75. *This is the pie chart created by the Chart Wizard and inserted in the form's Detail section. Note that its Row Source property uses a Total query to show its data*

Note   This form is available as Form2 in the sr28_Forms_Overlapping. accdb file.

Customizing the Pie Chart

The Chart tool creates a Microsoft Graph OLE object in the form's Detail section that is fully customizable.

Double-click the chart in the form's design mode to use Object Linking and Embedding (OLE) to start the Microsoft Graph application and put the chart in Edit mode, where you can customize virtually any of its elements. Use the Microsoft Graph menu options or click the chart to select an option (such as legend, title, axis, series, pie slices, column bars, etc.). Double-click the selection to show the appropriate dialog box, where you can set it properties.

The Microsoft Graph interface has so many options that will be difficult to show them on this section, but to make the pie chart show percent values, follow these steps:

1. Double-click the chart in the form's Design view to start the Microsoft Graph applet.

2. Right-click the pie chart and choose Format Data Series in the context menu to open the Format Data Series dialog box.

3. Select the Data Labels tab, check the Percent check box, and click the Close button to add percent values to the chart.

Attention   After adding data labels to the pie chart, it may shrink the chart. Click near the border of the chart until a dashed border appears; click it and drag its handles to enlarge the chart.

---

4. Click any empty area of the form's Detail section to close the Microsoft Graph application and update the chart.

By using this procedure, you can change the chart slices background and border colors, data label fonts, chart title format, legend format size and position, and more. Feel free to try the options until you feel comfortable with this powerful (and sometimes confusing) tool.

Figure 7-76 shows the frmFOOD_DES_Pie_Chart tool form with the Calories Breakdown pie chart using the Data Series Percent option to automatically calculate percent values, new colors associated to each of its slices, and its legend reformatted.

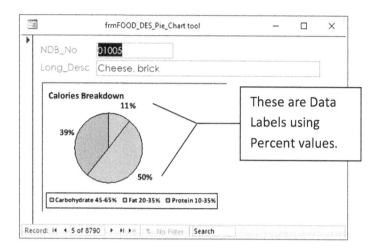

Figure 4-76. *Double-click the Chart control in Design mode to activate the Microsoft Graph applet and change any chart element. Right-click the pie chart, select Format Data Labels, and on the Data Labels tab, check the Percent option to change the calories values into % calories for Protein, Fat, and Carbohydrate*

Creating a Column Chart with the Chart Control

According to what is currently proposed by the FDA for the daily values required of a nutrient, an adult needs to consume at least 50g of protein, 78g of total fat, and 275g of total carbohydrates.[2]

Note   %Daily Value is the percent amount of a nutrient necessary to fulfill a daily diet. If 100g of food has 50g of protein, and the adult's daily value for protein is 50g, it indicates that 100g of this food meets the required amount.

So, the %Daily Values chart requires a query similar to the one used for Calories Breakdown that calculates the %DV for any food item, dividing its Nutr_Val field from the NUTR_DATA table by the proposed FDA Daily Value for each nutrient. But in this case, we can use another powerful function to better select what value must be returned: the CHOOSE() function.

---

[2]Daily Value on the New Nutrition and Supplement Facts Labels from U.S. FDA—Food and Drug Administration (https://www.fda.gov/food/new-nutrition-facts-label/ daily-value-new-nutrition-and-supplement-facts-labels#referenceguide).

The CHOOSE() FUNCTION

The CHOOSE() function allows you to select a single value from a list of up to 100 different arguments, constituting a far better alternative than nesting IIF() functions.

The CHOOSE() function has this syntax:

Choose(Item_index , Item_1, Item_2 ... Item_n)

where:

- *Item_index*: Required; this is an integer or expression that returns an integer value between 1 and the number of available items. If Item_Index is not an integer value, it will be rounded to the nearest integer.

- *Item_1, Item_2, Item_n*: These are values or expressions that indicate all possible returned valued.

The CHOOSE() function checks the Item_Index value and returns the associated value on its list of choices. For example, if Item_index is set to 2, CHOOSE() will return Item_2 value. It will return NULL if Item_Index is less than 1 or greater than the number of choices listed.

Like IIF(), the CHOOSE() function evaluates every possible item before returning the desired value. If any of these items returns an error, this error will be propagated by the CHOOSE() function.

Open the query qryFOOD_DES_ProtFatCHO%DV and note that it uses the same query strategy, with the difference that it now uses the CHOOSE() function for the expressions needed to generate the Nutrient and %DV fields (click each field and press Shift+F2 to show the Zoom window, as shown in Figure 4-77).

The Nutrient field records are suffixed with the recommended FDA Daily Value using this expression:

```
Nutrient: Choose(Val([Nutr_No])-202,"Protein 50g","Fat 78g","Carbohydrate 275g")
```

while the %DV field for each nutrient uses this expression:

```
%DV: [Nutr_Val]/Choose(Val([Nutr_No])-202,50,78,275)
```

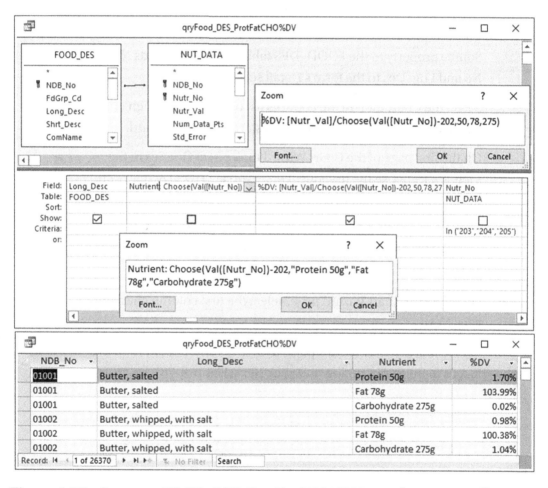

Figure 4-77. *Query qryFOOD_DES_ProtFatCHO%DV uses the CHOOSE() function to build the Nutrition and %DV field expressions*

Note   The Query expressions use the VAL() function that converts a numeric string into a numeric value (the Nutr_No field has the Short Text data type). Since Nutr_No returns three consecutive values (203, 204, and 205), Val([Nutr_Val]) - 202 returns 1, 2, or 3, which allows you to compose the desired nutrient name or to divide Nutr_Val by the adequate daily value.

Follow these steps to create a column chart with the Chart Wizard using the qryFood_DES_ProtFatCHO%DV query:

1. Use the Form Design tool to create a new form and set its Record Source property to the FOOD_DES table, adding the fields NDB_No and Lng_Des to the form's Detail section.

2. Select the Chart tool on the controls list of the Form Design tab and click the form's Detail section to start the Chart Wizard.

3. On the first page of the Chart Wizard tool, select Queries in the View area, choose the qryFood_DES_ProtFatCHO%DV query on the list, and click Next to continue.

4. On the second Chart Wizard page, double-click the fields Nutrient and %DV fields (or use the > button) to add them to the Fields for Chart list, and click Next.

5. On the Third Chart Wizard page, select the first column chart and click Next.

6. On the fourth Chart Wizard page, drag the Nutrient field from the X-Axis to the Series option and click Next (Figure 4-78).

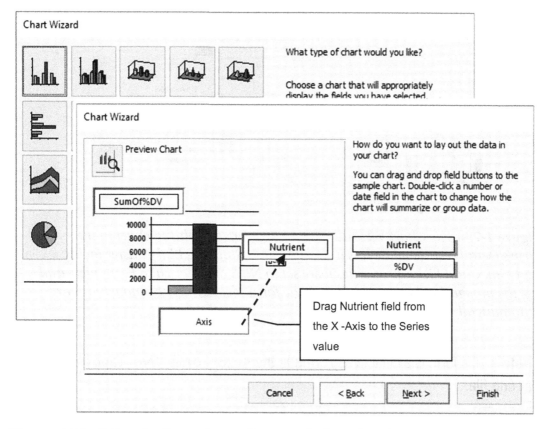

Figure 4-78. *Select the first column chart, and when the Chart Wizard asks how to use the data on the chart, drag field Nutrient from the X-Axis to the Series area*

7. On the fifth Chart Wizard page, accept NDB_No as the fields used on the Form Record Source property and click Next.

8. On the last Chart Wizard page, type **%Daily Values** for the chart title, keep the Yes, display a legend option selected, and click Finish to insert the chart on the Form Detail section (Figure 4-79).

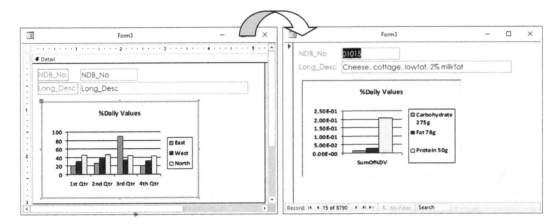

Figure 4-79. *The Chart Wizard will create a generic column chart in the form's Detail section while it is in Design view. Since the Link Master Fields and Link Child Fields properties were set to NDB_No, switch to Form view and use the navigation buttons to change the form record and note how the chart automatically updates*

Note   This form is available as Form3 in the `sr28_Forms_Overlapping.accdb` file.

Customizing the Column Chart

The Column chart created by the Chart Wizard has a standard appearance that can be improved by customizing many of its elements, which is made by double-clicking the Chart control in Design view to fire the Microsoft Graph applet and put the chart in Edit mode, where you can select the desired chart element and double-click it to change it as you like (almost the same way as when using Excel).

Figure 4-80 shows the frmFOOD_DES_Column_Chart tool form, where this chart receives a new appearance by changing these chart settings:

- The legend was dragged to the bottom of the chart.

- The Y-Axis Format was changed to Percent, with 0 decimals.

- The Series Data labels Values was shown using Format Percent with two decimals (double-click each data series and use the Format Data Series dialog box).

- The Series color was changed by clicking two times on the bar to select it and then double-clicking to change its border and background colors (this can also be done by double-clicking the associated small square on the chart legend).

- The X-Axis title was removed (double-click the X-Axis and use the Font tab to apply a white font color—the same as chart background).

- The default horizontal grid lines were removed (click them in the chart area and uncheck the Value Axis Grid line tool on the Chart toolbar or use the Chart ➤ Chart Options command to show the Chart Options dialog box).

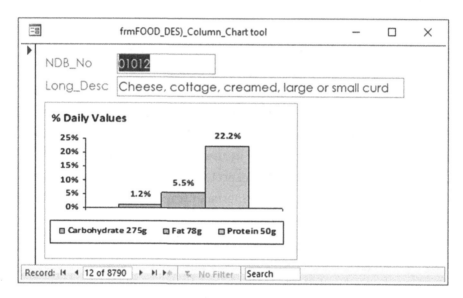

***Figure 4-80.** After creating a chart using the Chart Wizard, double-click the Chart control to show the Microsoft Graph applet and put the chart in Edit mode. Then select chart elements with the mouse and double-click them to change their settings (or use the menu commands available in the Microsoft Graph interface)*

Tip Whenever you use a Select query to create a column chart, which series values comes from different records grouped by a single record field (in this case the NDB_No field group different nutrients for the same food item), the Chart engine will not allow you to insert space between the bars chart because it considers them as a unit. To create a column chart that allows separate bars, use a Crosstab query (like qryFOOD_DES_ProtFatCHO%DV_Crosstab) where the field names define the chart series.

Creating a Modern Pie Chart with the Insert Chart Tool

The Insert Chart tool was designed by the Access Development team to somewhat approximate in the Microsoft Access interface what Excel has done since Microsoft Office 2007: a new interface to create and present charts.

"Modern charts" mainly use by default the Century Gothic font (instead of Arial used by the Chart control) and offer more color possibilities than the ones used by the Microsoft Graph applet. In other words, the Insert Chart tool creates a chart with a more modern appearance than the ones created by the Chart tool.

That said, the charts created with the Insert Chart tool are a totally different beast, with no Chart Wizard, using two different interfaces (the Chart Settings and Property Sheet windows). The Chart objects created are not intuitive (you can't select chart elements on the control using the mouse or double-clicking) and lack lots of common personalization settings.

The pie charts created with the Insert Chart tool accept only queries whose series values are presented on a row-by-row basis, and there is no option to transform the data values to a percent of its total, like the Chart control does. You have to calculate the desired percent values using a query.

Open qryFOOD_DESProtFatCHO%Calories on the Design tab and note that it does this job by using two queries:

- qryFOOD_DES_ProtFatCHOCalories to return nutrients and calories

- qryFOOD_DES_TotalCalories, which is a Total query also based on qryFOOD_DESProtFatCHOCalories to return the sum of calories each nutrient has

By relating both queries using the NDB_No field, qryFOOD_
DESProtFatCHO%Calories calculates the Calories Breakdown values each nutrient has,
allowing it to be used on a modern pie chart created with Insert Chart tool (Figure 4-81).

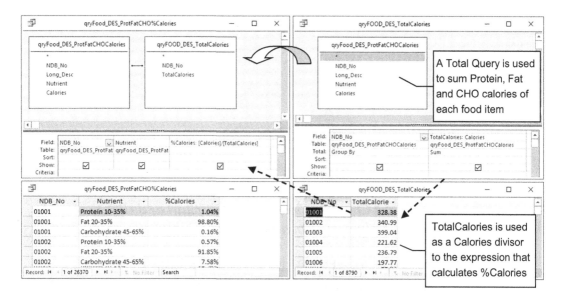

Figure 4-81. *To create a modern pie chart with the Inser Chart tool to show
Calories Breakdown vbalues, the query must return records on a row-by-row basis
and must calculate the %Calories each nutrient offers, since the Chart control
doesn't have this option*

The Insert Chart option has no wizard to guide you, although the process is
somewhat simplified after you are introduced to it.

Follow these steps:

1. Use the Form Design tool to create a new form and set its Record
    Source property to the FOOD_DES table, adding fields NDB_No
    and Long_Des to the form's Detail section.

2. Click the Insert Chart tool on the form's Design tab to expand it,
    select the pie chart, and click the form's Detail section to insert
    a new modern Chart object and show the Chart Setting window
    with the data area selected (Figure 4-82).

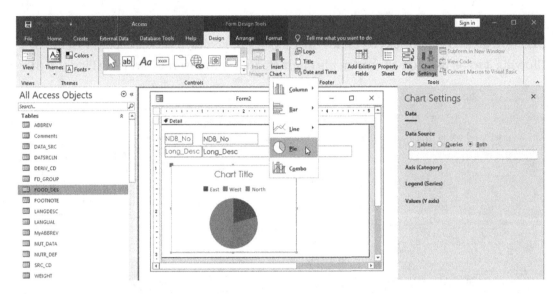

Figure 4-82. *Use the Insert Chart tool to select the pie chart and click the form's Detail section to insert the Chart control and show the Chart Settings window*

3. Select query qryFOOD_DESProtFatCHO%Calories in the Data Source box of the Chart Settings window to expand its Axis (Category), Legend (Series), and Value (Y axis) options showing all the selected query fields.

4. Check these field names in the Chart Settings window to define the pie chart:

    a. Axis (Category): Nutrient

    b. Value (Y axis): Calories

Note   The Chart Setting Legend (Series) option may be used whenever you want that the series name to come from a field different from the one selected on the Axis (Category) option.

---

5. Click the Format option at the top of the Chart Settings window and check the Display Data Labels option.

6. Show the Property Sheet window, select the Data tab, and click the ellipsis button to the right of the Link Master Fields (or Link Child Fields) property to show the Subform Filter Linker window where you will select the NDB_No field to allow a form record-by-record synchronization (Figure 4-83).

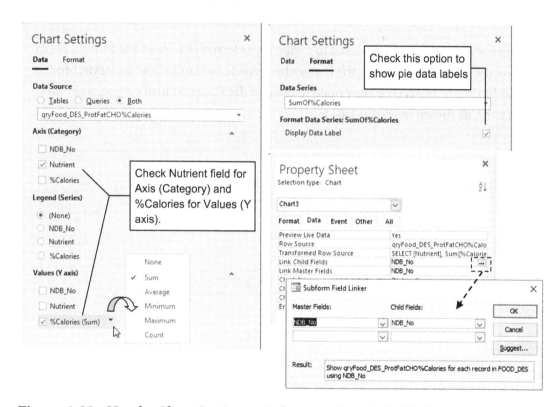

Figure 4-83. *Use the Chart Settings window to select the fields that must be used on the Axis (Category), Legend (Series), and Values (Y axis) options. Show the Property Sheet window and manually set the Link Master Fields and Link Child Fields properties (click the elipsis to right of one of these properties to show the Subform Field Linker window)*

Tip   The fields selected on the Values (Y axis) option will always be grouped by the SUM() function on a Total query created by the Chart Settings window (which is stored on the Transformed Row Source property in the Property Sheet window). To change the way the chart groups records (using all records with no grouping option), click the checked field arrow and select the desired group option.

After the Insert Chart tool is used to create a modern chart, show the form in Form view, use the navigation buttons to change the records, and note how they synchronize with the "modern" chart (you may need to change the Chart control's dimensions in Design view, as shown in Figure 4-84).

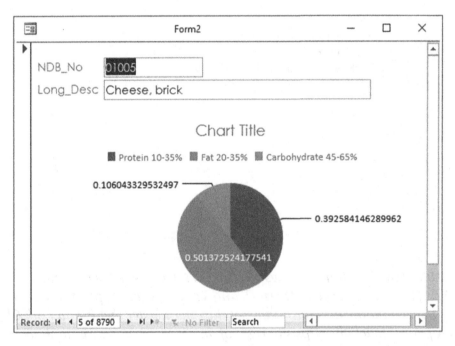

Figure 4-84. *This is the modern pie chart created by the Insert Chart tool to show Calories Breakdown, with no personalization settings*

Customizing the Modern Pie Chart

To customize the "modern" pie chart, you need to select the Chart control in Design view and use its Property Sheet to set some of its (many) properties to manually change the desired chart elements.

Figure 4-85 shows the chart reformatted after setting Properties Chart Title to Calories Breakdown and Primary Axis Format to Percent, which now exhibits the correct chart title and values using the adequate percent format (Figure 4-85).

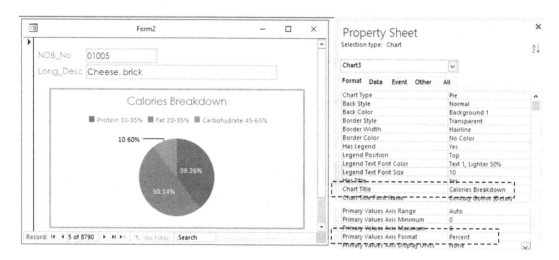

Figure 4-85. *Change the Chart Title and Primary Values Axis Format properties to make the chart show a more consistent interface for Calories Breakdown*

Note   Since the pie chart has no axes, it seems inadequate that both interfaces (Chart Setting and Property Sheet) offer such settings for a pie chart—among many other properties that should be shown for this type of chart.

Creating a Column Clustered Chart with the Insert Chart Tool

Use the Clustered Column option of the Insert Chart ➤ Column tool to create the %Daily Values column chart.

Contrary to the limitations of the "modern" pie chart, the Clustered Column chart created with the Insert Chart tool accepts data on a row-by-row basis (a Select query where different field record values name the series) or on a column-by-column basis (a Crosstab query that uses just one record and uses its Field names to name the series).

Follow these steps to make to create the %Daily Values column chart using the Insert Chart tool:

1. Create a new form, set Property Record Source to the FOOD_DES table, and add the fields NDB_No and Lng_Des to the form's Detail section.

2. Select Insert Chart ➤ Column ➤ Clustered Columns and click the Form Detail section to insert a new modern Chart object and show the Chart Settings window with the data area selected (Figure 4-86).

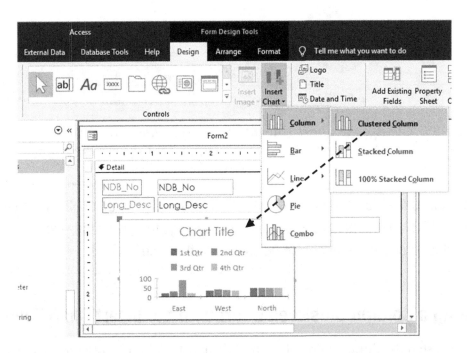

Figure 4-86. *To create a "modern" %Daily Values column chart, use the Insert Chart, Column, of Custered Column options and click the Detail section*

3. Set these options in the Chart Settings window's Data area:

   a. Set Data Source to qryFOOD_DES_ProtFatCHO%DV.

   b. Set Legend to Nutrient.

   c. Set Values (Y axis) to %DV (Sum).

4. Select the Chart Settings window format, use the Data Series box to select each nutrient name (Carbohydrate 275g, Fat 78g, and Protein 50g), and check its Display Data Label option.

5. Show the Property Sheet window, select the Data tab, and click the ellipsis button to the right of the Link Master Fields property to show the Subform Filter Linker window to automatically select the NDB_No field for record-by-record synchronization.

6. Select the Property Sheet Format tab and set these properties:

    a. Set Chart Title to %Daily Values.

    b. Set Primary Values Axis Format to Percent (Figure 4-87).

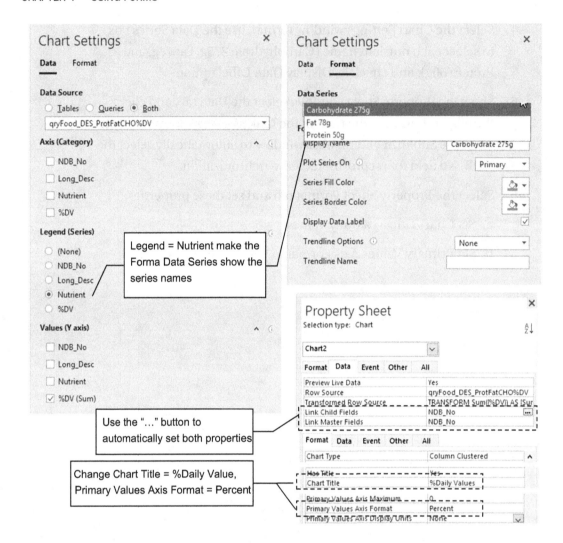

Figure 4-87. *Set Data Souce to qryFOOD_DES_ProtFatCHO%DV, set Legend to Nutrient (to show the nutrient names on the Format, Data Series box), set Values (Y axis) to %DV (Sum), and then use Format, Data Series box to select each series and check its Display Data Label option. Use the Property Sheet to change the Chart Title and Primary Values Axis Format properties*

After inserting the modern chart, select Form view and note how the modern column chart synchronizes the chart values as the records change (Figure 4-88).

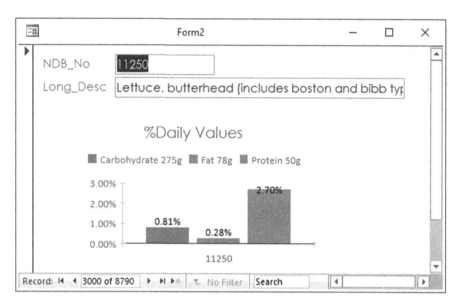

Figure 4-88. *This is a modern clustered column chart created with the Insert Chart tool that uses the Form and Chart NDB_No fields to synchronize chart values as the record changes*

Attention   Although the records show nutrient names in Protein, Fat, Carbohydrate order, there is no means to avoid alphabetically sorting the data series names on a modern clustered column chart legend.

Open frmFOOD_DES_Chart, and note that it has pie and column charts created with the Chart control and Insert Chart tool. The two left charts were created using the Chart Wizard and had many of its properties changed to make them more similar to the ones created with the Insert Chart tool (on the right). The most notable difference is the color palette that is limited on the Chart tool.

Also note that both column charts use a Crosstab query to separate its bars (both use qryFOOD_DES_ProtFatCHO%DV_Crosstab). Switch to the form's Design view, click (or double-click) each chart, and study their properties to better understand how each one works. See Figure 4-89.

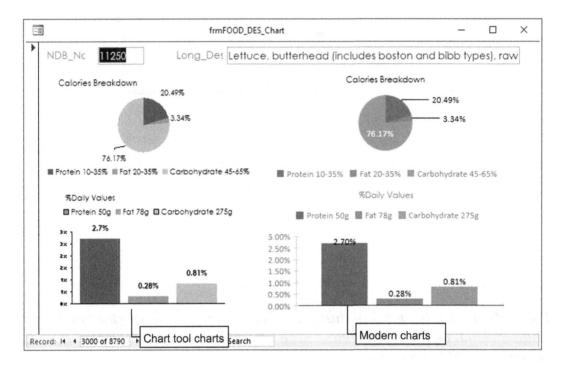

Figure 4-89. *Form frmFOO_DES_Chart shows that you can create charts with the Chart control that, after changing many of their properties, become similar to the ones with a "modern" appearance created with no effort with the Insert Chart tool*

A Database in a Form

Can we put an entire database in a single form? We certainly can, but in most cases it can be inadequate, generating a messy, too complex interface for the user.

But considering that nowadays most users have big screens, and maybe even widescreen monitors, you can use all this screen space to show a lot of data at the same time.

As an exercise, extract the sr28_Interface.accdb database from Chapter04.zip and open it. Microsoft Access will automatically show the frmSRDatabase form, which uses all controls, subforms, and chart tricks you learned in this chapter to show database tables relating its records on a single form. It also has a Combo Box in its Form Header section that allows quick searches to show any food item (Figure 4-90).

Note   frmSRDataBase is also available in the `sr28_Forms_Overlapping` database, along with all its subforms: frmSubDATA_SRC, frmSubDERIV_CD, frmSubFOOTNOTENDB_No, frmSubFOOTNOTENutr_No, frmSubLANGDESC_SubTotal, frmSubNUTR_DEF, frmSubSRC_CD, and frmSubWEIGHT_Subtotal.

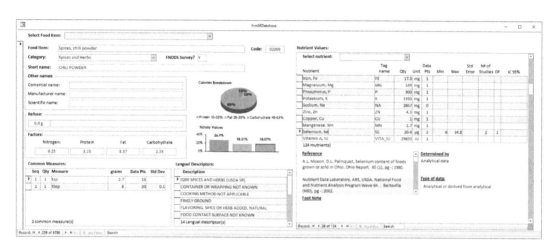

Figure 4-90. *This is frmSRDatabase that shows on a single screen all database tables, perfectly synchronized with the aid of the SubForm/SubReport controls and the Link Master Fields and Link Child Fields properties*

Attention   Figure 4-90 was captured on a widescreen monitor, running at 1920 x 1080 resolution. If your monitor doesn't have this resolution, you may see just part of the form but will be able to use its horizontal and vertical scrollbars to see all its content, which is also a learning process. You may plan ahead so your forms can appear as expected considering the resolution used by your users.It shows the "Spices, chili powder" food item (record 259) and has Selenium selected as nutrient—a combination of selected items that allow you to see that all subforms are correctly synchronizing the interface.

Form frmSRDatabase was built to show data—not to add new records. But with some small modifications and a better usage of the screen's horizontal space, it could easily be changed to a production application, ready to receive new data on all its fields—as long as the final user uses a widescreen monitor.

Besides the capacity of showing an entire database on a single screen, frmSRDatabase has two interesting things worth noting.

- It opens automatically whenever the database is opened, because its name was used to define the File, Options, Current Database, and Display Form options.

- It uses two Combo Box controls to make a food item (on the main form) or nutrient name (on the subform) record search. Both controls were created using the Control Wizard by dragging a Combo Box to the Form Header section. They execute a simple macro on its After Update event to show the desired record that will be discussed in the next chapter.

Note   How to use a Combo Box to make a database search will be explored in Chapter 5.

Summary

Microsoft Access has perhaps the best, easiest, and most capable form interface for creating graphic user interfaces.

It has a lot of functionality in its sections and ways of automatically showing records, an impressive set of useful properties, and a large set of controls you can use to create a modern, practical software interface for database applications.

In the next chapter, you will learn how to use macros to program Microsoft Access Forms and automate your database applications.

CHAPTER 5

Using Macros

The word *macro* (short for "macro instruction") became popular in the early 1980s with users of the Lotus 1-2-3 spreadsheet application. Macros were used to somewhat automate what was at the time the world's best-selling software for microcomputers.

In Lotus 1-2-3, macro code was stored in a spreadsheet's empty cells using a cryptic keystroke sequence that began with an apostrophe and a slash ('/) followed by a sequence of letters representing menu items to be executed. I will never forget the code because I expended a lot of time and effort creating a spreadsheet to control the milk producer's payroll of the dairy plant I worked at then, only to realize that when the 10th producer was inserted on the spreadsheet, the 640Kb memory limit of my PC-XT was reached, sending all my hard work to the trash in a second!

When Microsoft launched the Microsoft Office suite in 1988, using the new Microsoft Windows 3.0 graphical interface, it came with a word processor (Word), a spreadsheet program (Excel), and presentation software (PowerPoint) for the same price of a copy of Lotus 1-2-3. That's when the DOS software era ended, and the new macro code standard began.

Both Microsoft Word and Excel used a kind of macro code that was more textual and less cryptic than the one used by Lotus 1-2-3, but it still allowed the user to record and execute mouse or menu commands.

Microsoft Access was introduced in 1992, and unlike Word and Excel, used a special interface to create its macros that did not record menu commands. Instead, it offered a set of predefined actions that could be used to automate common database tasks, such as executing a query, opening a form, finding a record, etc., although it also offered the Access Basic programming language, which was a subset of the Basic language used just by Access.

The arrival of Visual Basic 4 in 1995 introduced Visual Basic for Applications (VBA) as a high-level programming language that replaced the old Word and Excel macros and also retired Access Basic. The Microsoft Access macros interface was retained, using almost the same interface as its first version.

© Flavio Morgado 2021
F. Morgado, *Introducing Microsoft Access Using Macro Programming Techniques*,
https://doi.org/10.1007/978-1-4842-6555-0_5

The Macro Actions list was kept the same up to Access 2016, when it received new actions, such as the ability to deal with errors and variable values (a *variable* is a name placed in computer memory to temporarily store values).

In this chapter, you will be introduced to Microsoft macros that execute simple tasks, with most of them coming from the Command Button control, and others from forms, reports, or control events, as a way to create a programmable interface to your database applications.

You can obtain all the database objects cited in this chapter by extracting file sr28_Macros.accdb from CHAPTER05.zip, which you can download from the following website:

- www.apress.com/9781484265543

Note   The sr28.accdb database, and all its variations used in this book, has smart record locks defined by referential integrity imposed between the FOOD_DES, ABBREV, and LANGUAL tables. This blocks users from inserting new records on FOOD_DES or deleting existing records from the FOOD_DES, FD_GROUP, and ABBREV tables (to name a few).

The Macro Window Interface

To understand how to build a macro, you first need to be acquainted with the Macro window, its actions, and its arguments, as well as how to create a new, stand-alone macro (one that appears in the Database window). Click the Macro command in the Macros & Code area of the Create tab to open the Macro window (Figure 5-1).

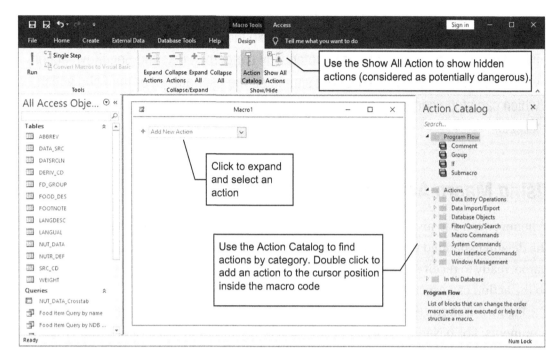

Figure 5-1. *The Macro window waiting to receive a new macro. Since this window was evoked from the Create tab's Macro command, it will allow you to save it as an stand-alone macro—one that appears on the Macros group of the Database window*

Note   To show macros in the Database window, click the down arrow in the top-right corner and select the All Access Objects option.

The Macro window shows all the actions that a macro must execute, from top to bottom. There are two ways to insert a macro action in the Macro window.

- Click the Add New Action box to expand its list of options and select an action from the list.

- Use the Action Catalog pane to select an action by category and double-click to insert it in the macro code (or drag and drop it to the desired position).

Note   Click the Show All Actions button to expand the list of available actions, including some actions considered potentially dangerous (like the SendKeys action, which can send a key sequence that simulates the user action, or the Echo action, which can stop windows from updating and may lead an application to seem to freeze).

Using Macro Actions

Whenever you add an action to the macro code, the action name is shown in bold using the default expanded view, where the action arguments are indented inside the action name, ready to receive a value. Some arguments are optional, and others are mandatory so the action can execute as expected.

Figure 5-2 shows the OpenForm action added to the macro code, with its six arguments: Form Name, View, Filter Name, Where Condition, Data Mode, and Window Mode. Since it is the only action in this macro code, it appears as the selected action in Edit mode, with a light gray background and controls that allow you to set its arguments. Click the small + button located in the action's top-left corner to collapse the code to a single line (with its arguments shown between parentheses).

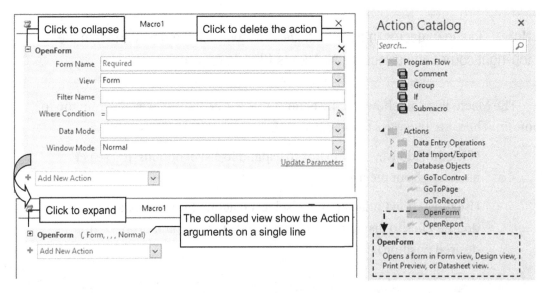

Figure 5-2.   *This is the OpenForm action selected with its six arguments. Use the + buitton in the top-left corner to collapse/expand its arguments list*

The OpenForm action is used to open a specific form window using the desired view mode (the default is Form view), with or without a filter or criteria to show the records; using a specific data mode (add, edit, or read-only records); and using a specific window mode: normal, hidden, icon (or minimized), and dialog (modal window).

You don't need to set all the action arguments, because many of them are optional; just the mandatory ones must be set. For the OpenForm action, the mandatory argument is the form name, which you can select from the Form Name argument box.

Figure 5-3 shows the same Macro window, now with the OpenForm action set to open the frmFood_Des form, which received the MaximizeWindow action (which has no arguments) to maximize the form window after it is opened (the green up arrow on the MaximizeWindow action row can be used to change the action order on the macro code flow). It was saved as a mcrOpenfrmFood_DesMaximized stand-alone macro.

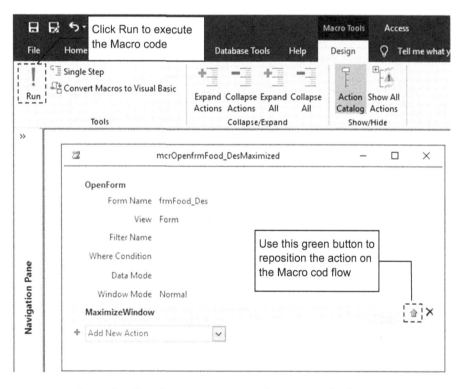

Figure 5-3.   *mcrOpenfrmFood_DesMaximized is a stand-alone macro in the sr28_Macros.accdb database that has two actions: an OpenForm action to open frmFood_Des and a MaximizeWindow action to maximize the form window*

You can execute the macro code in one of two ways.

- By clicking the Run command in the Tools To area of the Macro Design tab to execute all the macro actions at once and show frmFood_Des in a maximized state

- By clicking the Single Step command to put the macro into step-by-step execution and then click the Run command

When you click the Run command, frmFood_Des will open and be maximized in the blink of an eye. Although it will first open and then maximize, your computer is so fast that you won't perceive it as two steps.

By selecting the Single Step option and clicking the Run button, Access will show the Macro Single Step window, which allows you to execute one macro action at a time (Figure 5-4).

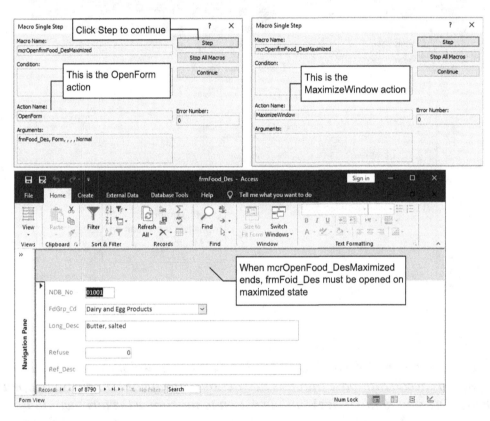

Figure 5-4. *Use the Single Step Macro execution option to execute macro actions on a step-by-step basis. This can help you find errors in your macro code*

Referring to Forms and Controls in Action Arguments

Sometimes you may need to refer to a form or control property in an action argument, such as to get the Control Value property or to find out which record a form is in (saved or new record) or if the record is being edited and needs to be saved or the edition discarded.

Depending on where the macro code is evoked, you may need to refer to a control value inside a subform or, on the contrary, refer from a subform to a control value that is on the main form.

For all these situations, you must rely on the Microsoft Access "full name" syntax to correctly refer to the desired objects and properties. Table 5-1 lists the most important collections, objects, and references you may need to use to apply the correct syntax to get the desired value.

Table 5-1. *Main Collections, Objects, and Property Used to Make Reference to Database Objects on Macro Action Arguments*

Name	Applies To
Forms, Reports	Collection that refers to all open forms (or reports)
Form, Report	Object that allows a form (or report) to refer to itself
Controls	Collection that refers to all controls on an open form or report
Parent	Property that allows an object to refer to the high-level object that contains it (a subform will refer to the main form that contains it)
Screen	Object that allows an object to refer to the form, report, or control that currently has the focus

Every time you open a new form (or report) in Form view, it is added to the Forms (or Reports) collection, with all the controls that it has inside its sections being added to the Controls collection. Also, you can refer to an object inserted on a collection using its order or its name.

Since a collection is a zero-based object, to refer to an object inside a collection by its order (the order that it was inserted on the collection), you can use the following syntax (where (0) refers to the first form opened in the Access interface):

```
Forms(0)
```

Note   Referring to objects inside a collection by their order is a powerful technique that can be used in VBA. VBA allows you to use a loop structure to interact with the collection elements. Since the macro code has no such programming structure, avoid trying to access a form by its collection order from a macro code.

Since there is no way to determine the order that each open form has inside the Forms collection, it is better to access it by its name, like this:

```
Forms("Form1")
```

Or you can use ! (an exclamation mark) to separate the collection name from the object name, which must be surrounded by brackets ([ ]) if the name includes a space. So, to refer to the forms called Form1 or frmMy Form (with the space on its name) when they are opened in Form view in the Microsoft Access interface, use this "full name" syntax:

```
Forms!Form1
```

Or use this form:

```
Forms![frmMy Form]
```

To access a form property for a form that is already open in the Microsoft Access interface, the correct syntax requires a dot (.) to separate the form name from the required property value.

To return the state of the opened frmForm1 Visible property, you must use the following "full name" syntax:

```
Forms!frmForm1.Visible
```

The same is true when referring to a control inside a form (or report). You can separate the form name and control name with ! (and to access a control property, separate the control and property names with a dot).

So, to return the Visible property of the txtName Text Box inside the frmForm1 form, use this "full name" syntax:

```
Forms!frmForm1!txtName.Visible
```

Note   By using the naming rule that Microsoft objects must not have space characters, you are discouraged from using brackets to surround the object name when referring to it in macro code.

If you want to access the frmSubAddresses subform that is inside the frmPersons form, you must use .Form (with a dot before the word Form) to separate the main form name from the subform name, followed by the subform control name, as follows:

```
Forms!frmFOOD_DES.Form!frmSubWEIGHT
```

Note   Since every control has a Name property, a subform control can use a name that is different from the form name it contains. Whenever this happens, use the control name instead. For example, if the subform Control Name property can be changed from frmSubWEIGHTto SubWEIGHT, the correct syntax to access this subform control must be changed to the following:Forms!frmFOOD_DES. Form!SubWEIGHT.

To access the txtAddress Text Box's Enabled property, inside the frmSubAddress subform that is inside the frmPersons form, use this "full name" syntax:

```
Forms!frmPersons.Form!frmSubAddresses!txtAddress.Enabled
```

Conversely, if you need to know any information regarding the main form from a subform perspective, use the Form object to refer to the subform (since a subform is not inserted in the Forms collection) and use .Parent (with a dot before the word *Parent*) to refer to the main form. The next "full name" syntax gets the main Form Name property for the form where a subform resides:

```
Form.Parent.Name
```

Tip   Whenever you want to make a form refer to itself in macro code, you can use both the Form object and the Forms collection using the syntax Forms!<FormName>.

To summarize, separate object names with !, separate object properties with ., and never forget that the Forms collection refers just to Form objects that are already opened in Form view in the Microsoft Access interface.

The Screen Object

The Microsoft Access Screen object has properties that allow dynamic references to different objects and their properties without knowing in advance which one has been selected by the user. Table 5-2 shows all Screen object properties and what they return.

Table 5-2. *Microsoft Access Screen Object Properties and Usage*

Property	Returns
ActiveControl	The active control value (if any)
ActiveDatasheet	The active datasheet reference
ActiveForm	The active form reference
ActiveReport	The active report reference
Application	The Microsoft Access window application
MousePointer	The mouse cursor
Parent	The main form (or report) where a subform (or subreport) is inserted
PreviousControl	The control value that has the focus before this control receives it

The Screen object needs a form or report open to return the desired property value or reference, which may require that the macro code first select the desired object by using the OpenForm or OpenReport action, or select an already opened form, report, or control using the SelectObject action.

The next syntax recovers the Visible property of the control that currently has the focus:

```
Screen.ActiveControl.Visible
```

Note   If you refer to the Screen object in an application where there is no active control (the form has no controls or all of them have their Visible or Enabled properties set to No) or no active form or report, the Screen object will return a runtime error, and the macro code will stop.

Tip   Since a lot of macro code runs from a Command Button (like a cmdSearch Command Button used to perform a search based on a value typed by the user on a Text Box control), whenever you click it to execute macro code, it receives the focus and becomes the object returned by the Screen.ActiveControl property. To allow the Command Button macro code to refer to the control that previously had the focus before receiving it, use the Screen.PreviousControl property.

Dealing with Macro Code Runtime Errors

When the macro code executes an action, it expects that the object referred to by its argument exists in the interface. If the object can't be found, the macro can't execute its code. It will generate a runtime error. Microsoft Access will show an error message and the macro will stop, showing the Macro Single Step window to indicate the action where the error occurred to the application user, creating what is popularly called an application *bug*.

To see how this happens, let's create a situation where a runtime error appears for testing purposes. Open mcrOpenfrmFOOD_DES_AddDeleteNewRecord in Design view and note that it has two actions (Figure 5-5).

- *OpenForm*: To open frmFoodDes with Data Mode set to Add, indicating that the form is open for inserting new records

- *RunCommand*: With Command set to DeleteRecord to delete the current record that the form shows

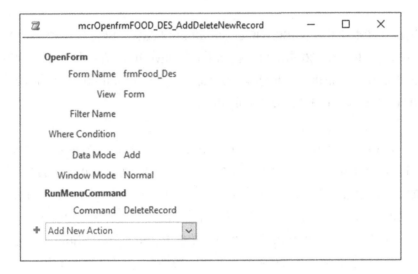

Figure 5-5. *The macro mcrOpenfrmFOOD_DES_AddDeleteNewRecord opens frmFOOD_DES on a new record, using the OpenForm action with the argument Data Mode set to Add. Then it tries to delete this new record using the RunMenuCommand action with the argument Command set to DeleteRecord*

The problem here is a classic one: there is no record to delete, because the form is positioned on a new record—one that does not exist yet.

Whenever you try to run this macro (by clicking the Run button of the Macro Design tab or by closing the Macro window and double-clicking the macro name in the Database window), when the code tries to executes the RunMenuCommand DeleteRecord action on a nonexisting record, it will generate a runtime error. Microsoft Access will issue an error message, and when the message is closed, it will show the Macro Single Step window stopping the code at this action (Figure 5-6).

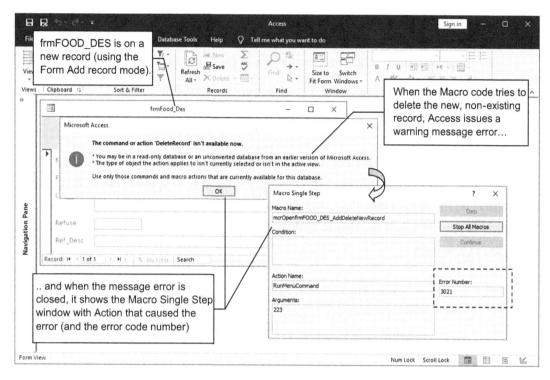

Figure 5-6. *When a macro code finds a runtime error, Microsoft Access issues a warning message, and after it has been closed, it stops the code and shows the Macro Single Step window with the action that caused the error, showing the error number*

The OnError Action

To avoid macro runtime errors from stopping the macro code, use an OnError action before the macro action that can generate the error. Since you cannot always anticipate which macro action will be the one that generates the error, it is better use the OnError action as the first macro code instruction.

The OnError action has these arguments:

- *Go to*: Specify the behavior that should occur when an error is encountered, using one of the following settings:

  - *Next*: Access will ignore the error and continue to the next action, recording the error details in the MacroError object.

- *Macro Name*: Access stops the current macro action and jumps to the submacro named on this argument, which must be created as the last macro code instruction using the Submacro action.

- *Fail*: Normal error behavior. This stops the current macro, displays the default error message, and shows the Macro Single Step window.

Open mcrOpenfrmFOOD_DES_AddOnErrorGotoNext in Design view, and note that it has as its first action the On Error Goto property set to the Next instruction. By using this technique, the error generated when there is an attempt to delete a nonexisting record will be ignored, and the macro code will execute normally, without giving any warnings (Figure 5-7).

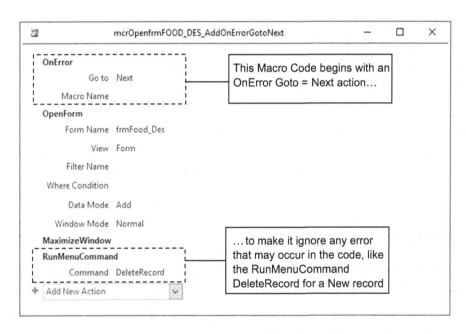

Figure 5-7. *To avoid errors in macro code, insert an OnError action with the argument Go to set to Next as the first macro action. All macro code errors will be ignored, and the code will run until it ends with no stops*

Try to execute the mcrOpenfrmFOOD_DES_AddOnErrorGotoNext macro code using the Single Step mode, and note that when the code tries to delete the nonexistent new record, it will do nothing, ending the macro silently.

Now you may ask, "Why not use an OnError Goto = Next action in all macro code?" Or better yet, "Why does macro code generate errors if we can silent them?"

The answer is simple: since you can't surely anticipate which macro action will generate an error, by silencing all possible errors, the macro code may not execute one or more actions without you even noticing that this happened! In other words, the macro code did not execute what was expected.

So, to guarantee that the macro code does not stop when a nonanticipated error occurs, use one of these two approaches:

- Set OnError Goto to Next to silence all errors, and if one or more runtime errors happens, use the If and MessageBox actions to access the MacroError object and show the last error occurred.

- Set OnError Goto to MacroName, and use a SubMacro action to create an "error trap" that stops to execute the code on the first runtime error and show it to the user.

Let's explore this object and actions in more detail.

The MacroError Object

The MacroError object holds information about the last error that occurred in the macro code, using these properties to describe the error:

- *ActionName*: This is the name of the action that generates the runtime error.

- *Arguments*: This is the specified action's argument values.

- *Condition*: This is the specific condition that generates the action runtime error.

- *Description*: This is the text description that represents the runtime error.

- *MacroName*: For a stand-alone macro object, this is the macro name as it appears in the Database window, or it is the event name that called the embedded macro code.

- *Number*: This is the default property; it returns the error number that generates the runtime error.

By default, whenever macro code begins to run, the MacroError object properties are reset (and MacroErrror.Number is set to 0), but whenever an error occurs, its properties will detail the error occurred.

Tip   Alternatively, use the ClearMacroError action (which has no argument) to reset the MacroError object properties.

Note   Since Number is the default MacroError object property, whenever you refer to the MacroError object alone (without choosing one of its properties), it will return its Number property, which contains the last runtime error code—or 0 if none.

Since some of these properties can return meaningless values in the context of the Access 2019 interface (like the Arguments property; see Figure 5-6), you can build a good warning message using just the MacroError Number and Description properties on a MessageBox action using a string expression like this:

```
="Error =" & MacroError.Number & ", Description:" & MacroError.Description
```

Attention   Every expression used in the macro code must begin with an equal (=) character so that it can be evaluated by the macro action argument.

The MessageBox Action

The MessageBox action shows a modal window message that has just the OK button, using a predetermined title, message, and icon. It has this syntax:

- *Message*: This is the message text that will appear to the application user.

- *Beep*: This sounds a beep when the message is shown.

- *Type*: This is the icon shown by the message, which can be set to None (default, no icon) or one of these icons:

- **X** Critical
- **?** Warning?
- **⚠** Warning!,
- **ⓘ** Information

- *Title*: This is the text displayed in the message box window's title bar. If this is left blank, "Microsoft Access" is displayed.

Since the MessageBox shows a modal window, the macro code stops until the window is closed and then continues to execute the next instruction (if any).

The IF Action

The If action is called a *multiconditional test* because it can make successive test conditions and execute different actions if one of them is true. It uses this structure:

```
If <Condition1 = True> Then
        <Execute this first Macro Action>
[ElseIf <Condition2> = True Then
        <Execute this second Macro Action>]
...
[Else
        <Execute this alternative Macro Action>]
```

The structure begins testing whether <Condition1 = True>, and if it is, <execute this first Macro Action> and then executes the next macro action. Items inside brackets are optional, meaning that you do not need to use one or more [ElseIf...] tests or the last alternative Else...] test.

Showing the Last Runtime Error

To show the last runtime error that may occur in macro code, set OnError Goto to Next as the first instruction, and use an If action as the last instruction to verify whether MacroError.Number is not 0. If it is, a runtime error will occur, and a MessageBox action is used to show a personalized error message. When the window closes, the macro code ends.

Tip   Since error codes can use negative and positive values, you must check whether MacroError.Number is different than zero to verify whether an error occurred. By convention, programming languages use <> (minor and major characters) as the different operators.

Open mcrOpenfrmFOOD_DES_AddShowLastError in Design view, and note that it begins with an OnError Goto = Next action and ends with an If MacroError.Number <> 0 action, and whenever this condition is True, it uses a MessageBox action to show a personalized message to the user (Figure 5-8).

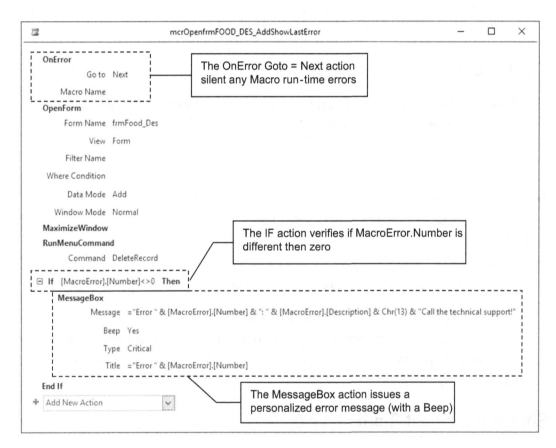

Figure 5-8. *mcrOpenfrmFOOD_DES_AddShowLastError has OnError Goto set to Next to silence any action error and uses an If action to verify whether MacroError.Number is different than 0. If it is, it uses a MessageBox action to show a personalized message to the application user*

This macro code window may seem scary for most people who look at it for the first time, mainly because it uses the Actions Expanded view, showing all possible Actions arguments, even when they are not used.

To understand the macro code logic, you can read the bold lines that define the macro action names. An alternative to get a better understanding of the macro code is to use the Collapse All command in the Macro Design tab to collapse all the macro actions to its names, hiding the arguments.

Figure 5-9 shows the mcrOpenfrmFOOD_DES_AddShowLastError macro window using the collapsed view, after the IF action is expanded by clicking the + sign located at its right. To check which arguments each action uses, just point the mouse to it to open a floating help window.

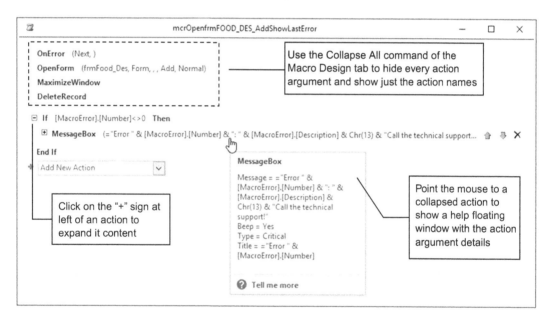

Figure 5-9. *To get a better undestanding of the logic behind a macro, use the Collapse All button on the Macro Design tab to collapse all actions to their names. Point the mouse to any action to show a floating help window with the action's argument details*

Click the Run (!) command on the Macro Design tab to execute the mcrOpenfrmFOOD_DES_AddShowLastError macro code, and note that when it tries to delete the inexistent new record, it uses a personalized message to show the error using the MessageBox action (Figure 5-10).

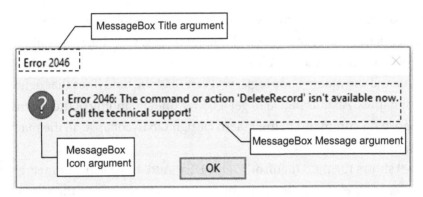

Figure 5-10. *The MessageBox action allows you to personalize the message window title and message, using string expressions that can gather information from other sources (like the MacroError object). It also allows you to choose an icon and play a beep*

Now pay attention to how the MessageBox action's Title argument expression was built.

```
="Error " & [MacroError].[Number]
```

It begins with = to indicate that it is an expression that needs to be evaluated and uses the & character to concatenate the "Error " (note the trailing space) string with the MacroError.Number value to compose a single string that will be used on the MessageBox Title argument.

Tip   When you type = to begin an expression on any action argument, whenever you type an object of a function name, Access will show all its properties and arguments in a list.

The MessageBox action's Message argument is a little bit more complex, as shown here:

```
="Error " & [MacroError].[Number] & ": " & [MacroError].[Description] &
Chr(13) & "Call the technical support!"
```

Besides the use of the & character to compose the Message argument, this time it also uses the Chr(13) function to concatenate a "line break" (carriage return character) on the string message. That is why the "Call the technical support!" expression appears on its own line of the MessageBox window (see Figure 5-10).

368

Note   CHR() is a VBA function that allows you to return the desired text character using its ASCII code as an argument. The Enter key (carriage return) has ASCII code 13. Many other characters not available on your keyboard can be used on string expressions using this technique. Google *ascii character codes* to find them!

Creating an Error Trap

The most common technique to deal with unexpected macro code runtime errors is to create what is called an *error trap*: a place that the error is directed to whenever it appears on the code.

To use this technique, the first macro action must have On Error GoTo set to Macro Name, and the last macro action must be a SubMacro, from where the code treats the error.

The SubMacro action works like a *subroutine*: a small code fragment that can be reused on the main code. It has these characteristics:

- It has just the Name argument to unique identify it on the same macro code (a single macro code can have many different named submacro actions).

- It must be the last macro code action.

- It is not sequentially executed by the macro code, unless it is called by an action that has the Macro Name argument (like the RunMacro or OnError action).

Note   A macro code's Submacro action can be called from outside by other macro code via the RunMacro action using as an argument the syntax MacroName. SubMacroName.

Open mcrOpenfrmFOOD_DES_AddErrorTrap in Design mode and take a look at its code (Figure 5-11 shows it using collapsed view to all its actions except the Submacro action and its arguments).

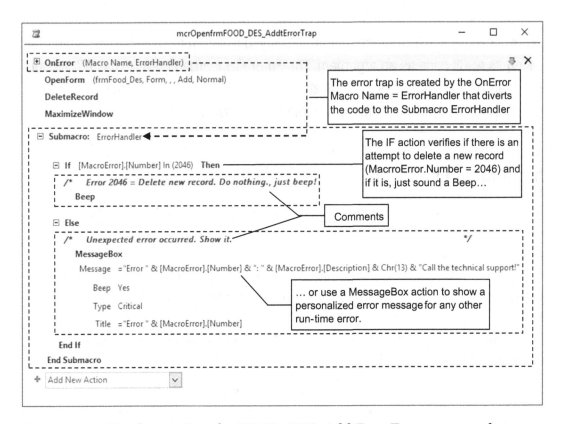

Figure 5-11. *Use the mcrOpenfrmFOOD_DES_AddtErrorTrap macro code to*
understand how to create an error trap to treat any macro code runtime errors. It
uses an OnError macro name, ErrorHandler as its first action, and a Submacro
ErrorHandler action as its last action to treat the error

The error trap strategy mcrOpenfrmFOOD_DES_AddtErrorTrap macro code has
some techniques that deserve a mention.

- The first action has OnError MacroName set to ErrorHandler to send
  the macro code to the submacro called ErrorHandler for any runtime
  error on the code.

Note   If the submacro name used by the OnError Macro Name argument does not
exist on the macro code, Access will generate an error when the code runs—this
time an unhandled error.

- The Submacro ErrorHandler first verifies the code If MacroError. Number = 2046 (this is the error code for an attempt to delete a new record, as shown in Figure 5-10). If it is true, it does nothing; it just makes a sound using a Beep action.

- It uses the two comment actions to insert comments on the code, so it becomes more understandable.

- If any other error occurs on the macro code, the IF...Else clause is executed, and the MessageBox action is used to show a personalized error message.

Click the Run (!) command to execute the macro code and note that now it just sounds a beep after the form is opened. Also note that the DeleteRecord and MaximizeWindow actions changed places. Since frmFOOD_DES is opened in Add mode (a new record), when the code tries to delete it, error code 2046 is raised, the macro code is diverted to the Submacro ErrorHandler, and a beep sounds, ending the code. The MaximizeWindow action is no longer executed (the Form window is opened in its default size and position in the Microsoft Access interface).

Note   Use Single Step mode to execute one action at a time and note the code flow. Note that the IF action does not appear in the Macro Single Step window— just the condition it tests.

Tips for Creating Good Macro Code

Now that you know that a macro is composed by predefined actions, some of them full of optional and mandatory arguments, follow these tips to create efficient macro code:

- *Select the correct form or control event*: By understanding when each event fires, the database interface will work as expected.

- *Use the correct macro action*: Study the macro actions to find the one that will do what you want to do, and avoid the use of a sequence of macro actions to do a task that could be done by the correct action.

- *Define the correct action arguments:* Provide the selected action with the arguments that will make it work as expected, not forgetting to use the appropriate syntax and that an expression begins with a = character.

- *Eventually use an error handling strategy:* Complex macros full of actions can generate runtime errors that will appear as "bugs" to your application users. By implementing a runtime error strategy, you will not avoid them but will be advised whenever they happen.

- *Keep the macro code simple and concise:* Use the minimum amount of actions to execute a task. The macro code will run faster and will be easier to will be easier to follow and fix.

- *Use comments to add meaning*: It is good programming practice to add comments to the macro code, because they can make it easier to understand what the code is trying to accomplish whenever there is a need to revisit it.

In the next section, you will learn about Microsoft form and control events, their fire order, and which ones must be used to correctly automate your database applications.

Microsoft Access Form and Control Events

To automate a graphical interface, where the user has a mouse and the ability to execute actions using a nonanticipated order, Microsoft Access (and any other graphic programming language) uses the concept of events.

An *event* is something that happens on the graphical interface whenever the user performs an action, such as open or close a form or report, insert or delete a record, select a control, click or double-click the control, leave the control (by clicking other controls or pressing the Tab key), update the control value, etc.

For an unknown reason, Microsoft Access has quite a different set of events from other Microsoft software development tools (like VB.NET and VBA), being richer in some ways while lacking some expected behavior, like the ability to automate drag-and-drop operations. Some of these events can be canceled using the CancelEvent macro action, which means that the expected Access action will not occur, such as opening a form or updating a record, for example.

Although tables, forms, reports, and controls have a different and extensive list of events, Table 5-3 shows the most important events you must use on Microsoft Access forms and controls, and it lists whether each can be canceled using the CancelEvent macro action.

Table 5-3. *Some Important Microsoft Access Form and Control Events You Can Use to Automate a Database Application*

Event	Use With	Cancellable?	Fires When
On Open	Form, Report	Yes	The object is about to be opened
On Load	Form, Report	No	The object was opened
On Activate	Form, Report	No	The object receives the focus
On Deactivate	Form, Report	No	The object loses the focus
On Current	Form	No	When a record is shown
Before Insert	Form	Yes	Before a new record is inserted
After Insert	Form	No	After a new record is inserted
On Timer	Form	No	After the Timer Interval property value has passed
On Unload	Form, Report	Yes	The object is about to be closed
On Close	Form, Report	No	The object had been closed
Before Update	Form, Control	Yes	Before a form record or control value changes
After Update	Form, Control	No	After a form record or control value changes
On Delete	Form	Yes	Before a record is deleted
After Del Confirm	Form	No	After a record is deleted
On Click	Control	No	When the user clicks the control
On Dbl Click	Control	No	When the user double-clicks the control

Understanding Form Events Sequence

To make a better use of form and control events, it is important that you understand the order in which they fire, so you can decide which event must receive some macro code to automate your database application.

To simplify this understanding, I separate the events into two classes.

- *Form events*: The ones that affect the Form window and its behavior.

- *Record events*: The ones that affect records and their values

Form Window Events

The easiest way to understand the firing order of the Form window events is to use an embedded macro on each event procedure, using a MessageBox action that shows the event name whenever it fires.

Open frmFD_GROUP_FormEvents in Design view, show the Property Sheet window's Event tab, and note that it has an embedded macro code on seven specific form events. Click any ... button located to the right of any event name that has embedded macro code to show its Macro window with the MessageBox action that indicates the event name that fires (Figure 5-12).

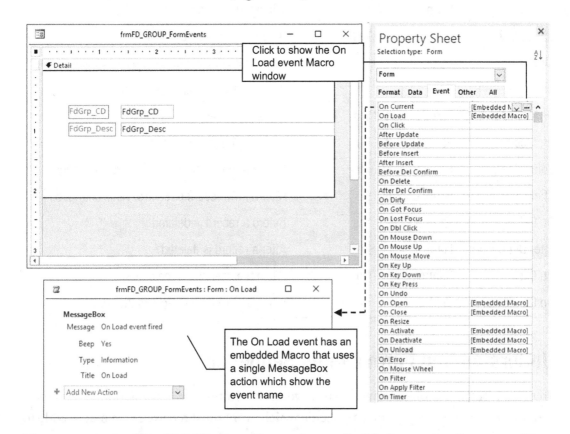

Figure 5-12. frmFD_GROUP_FormEvents has embedded macro code on specific events to allow you to view when each event fires

Show frmFD_GROUP_FormEvents in Form view and note that a MessageBox action will show each event name that fires whenever a form is opened and until the first form record is shown. Then close the form window and note the event names that fire whenever a form is closed (Figure 5-13).

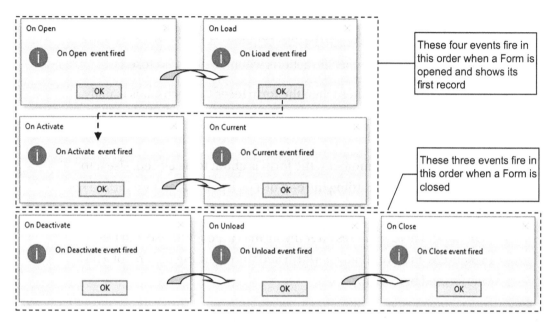

Figure 5-13. *This is the form events order whenever a form is opened (On Open, On Load, On Activate, and On Current) and closed (On Deactivate, On Unload, and On Close)*

Use these events to control specific actions on the form interface:

- *On Open*: Use this to prepare the form before it is shown. At this time, the form has not recovered its records from its Record Source property. This event can be canceled to prevent the form from opening.

- *On Load*: At this moment, the form already has records. Use this event to change the form appearance and eventually the control's Control Source property.

- *On Activate*: This fires when the form receives the focus. It is usually used to synchronize the form interface with the Ribbon commands (showing the Ribbon).

- *On Current*: This fires when a record is shown. Use it to synchronize the form interface record by record. (For example, you can hide controls on a new record and show them on an existing record.)

Use these events to control specific actions when the form is closed:

- *On Deactivate*: This fires when the form loses the focus. It is usually used to synchronize the form interface with the Ribbon commands (hiding the Ribbon).

- *On Unload*: At this moment, the form is about to be closed. Use it to perform actions regarding the end of a task performed by a form. This event can be canceled, preventing the form from being closed.

- *On Close*: This event fires after the form is unloaded. Use it to free resources and eventually perform actions regarding the end of a task performed by a form.

Form Record Events

Now open frmFD_GROUP_RecordEvents in Design view to realize how events affect form records. Show the Property Sheet window's Event tab and note that seven specific events received an embedded macro that uses just a MessageBox action to show the event name when fired.

Select the FdGrp_CD Text Box control, show the Property Sheet's Data tab, and note that this control, which is the table's primary key, received an expression on its Default Value property (Figure 5-14).

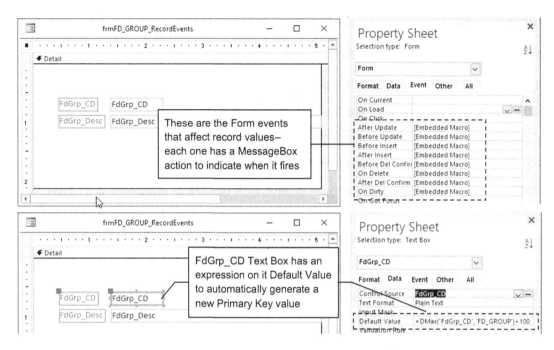

Figure 5-14. *Use frmFD_GROUP_RecordEvents form to learn when form record events fire and how to use a Text Box's Default Value property to generate a table's primary key*

Figure 5-14 shows that the FdGrp_CD Text Box uses an expression inserted in its Default Value property to calculate the new possible primary key value for a new record using the DMAX() domain aggregate function—another type of special Microsoft Access function worth mentioning!

Using Microsoft Access Domain Aggregate Functions

Besides the already covered aggregate functions, Access offers *domain aggregate functions* for use on expressions in places where a SQL instruction is not allowed (a macro, module, query expression, or calculated control of a form or report).

In this context, a domain is considered as any recordset returned by a table, query, or SQL instruction. Table 5-4 lists all the available domain aggregate functions and their usage.

Table 5-4. *Microsoft Access Domain Aggregate Functions*

Domain Aggregate Function	Usage
DLOOKUP()	Gets the value of a specified field on a domain
DCOUNT()	Counts the field or records on a domain
DFIRST(), DLAST()	Finds a field or expression value for the first or last record on a domain
DMIN(), DMAX()	Finds a field or expression maximum or minimum value on a domain
DAVG()	Calculates the average value of a field or expression on a domain
DSTDEV()	Calculates the sample standard deviation for a field or expression on a domain
DSUM()	Sums the field or expression values on a domain
DVAR()	Calculates the sample variance for any field or expression on a domain

Attention   The DFIRST() and DLAST() domain aggregate functions are affected by the domain sort order, while DMIN() and DMAX() are not!

All domain functions cited in Table 5-4 have the same syntax, as shown here:

DFunctionName("Expression", "Domain", "Criteria")

where:

- *DFunctionName*: This is one of the domain aggregate functions cited in Table 5-3.

- *Expression*: This is required; it is a string expression surrounded by quotes that returns a field name or expression against which the function will be applied.

- *Domain*: This is required; it is a string expression surrounded by quotes that returns a table, query, or SQL instruction whose records will be analyzed.

- *Criteria*: This is optional; it is a string expression surrounded by quotes that returns an expression similar to a Where clause of an SQL instruction (without the where keyword) that must be applied to the domain argument to filter its records.

The FdGrp_CD Default Value Property

As shown in Figure 5-14, the FdGrp_CD Text Box uses this expression on its DefaultValue property to automatically generate the next record's primary key value.

$$=DMAX("FdGrp\_CD","FD\_GROUP")+100$$

It finds the maximum value of the FdGrp_CD field on the FD_GROUP table (domain), without using criteria (all table records are used), and adds 100 to its value, creating a new, nonexistent primary key value whenever a new record is selected on the form.

And although the FdGrp_CD field has the Short Text data type, the expression automatically converted the DMAX()'s returned value to a number and summed it to 100, generating the next primary key code for a new Food Category record (a numeric string).

Note   The FdGrp_CD Text Box has the Locked property set to Yes to not allow it to be selected in Form view.

Inserting a New Record on the frmFD_GROUP_RecordEvents Form

Show the frmFD_GROUP_RecordEvents form in Form view and type any character in the Fd_Group Text Box. The form's Before Insert and On Dirty event fires, as soon as the new record receives any value in one of its fields (note that the FdGrp_CD Text Box automatically receives the next primary key value, as shown in Figure 5-15).

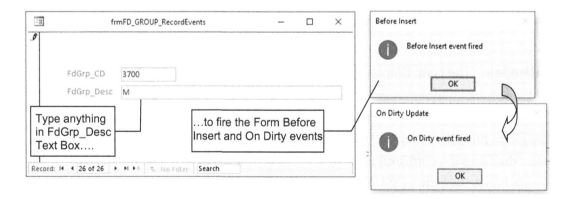

Figure 5-15. *When anything is typed in the FdGrp_Desc Text Box*

Continue typing the name of the new food category record, press Enter to update the control, and note how the FdGrp_Desc Text Box Before Update and After Update events fires.

Since this is the last control on the form tabulation order, after the FdGrp_Desc is updated, the form will try to leave the current record to select the next (another new record), which will successively fire the Form Before Update, After Update, and After Insert events (Figure 5-16).

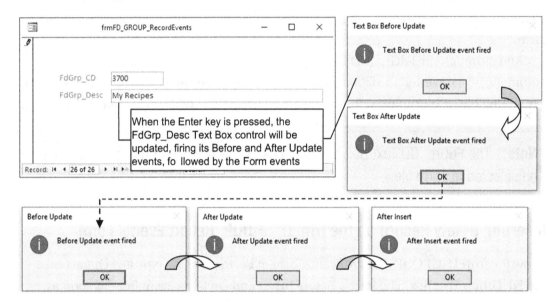

Figure 5-16. *Whenever the FdGrp_Desc Text Box is updated, the control's Before Update and After Update events will fire. Since the form property Cycle is All Records and it is the last control on the Form tabulation order, the form will try to leave the record, firing its Before Update, After Update, and After Insert events*

Attention   The Form Before Insert and After Insert events just fire for a new record.

Once the record has been saved and a new record has been selected, use the navigation buttons to return to the last inserted record, click the form record selector to select the current record, and press the Delete keyboard key to delete it.

This time, the form's On Delete and Before Del Confirm events fire, being followed by the Microsoft Access delete record confirmation, before the record is permanently deleted from the FD_GROUP table. After the record is deleted (becoming unrecoverable), the Form After Del Confirm event fires. See Figure 5-17.

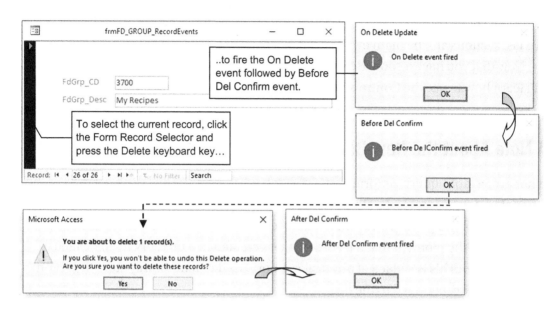

Figure 5-17. *Whenever a record is deleted, the Form fires the On Delete and Before Del Confirm events. Since record deletion can't be undone, Microsoft Access issues its own warning message. If the deletion is confirmed (by clicking Yes), the record is finally deleted, and the Form After Del Confirm event is fired*

Tip   To avoid receiving Microsoft Access confirmation for record deletions or action queries used to delete, insert, or update records, use the SetWarnings macro action, setting its argument Warnings On to No.

Caution   SetWarnings is a dangerous macro action that needs the Show All Actions option of the Macro Design tab to be checked before it appears in the Action list. It has the potential to disable all Microsoft Access messages until it is executed again using Warnings On set to Yes as the last macro action (which may require it to set OnError Goto to Next) or inside the error trap to guarantee that it will be executed before the macro code ends, so that Microsoft Access confirmations are turned on again.

There are many other control and form events to explore, but the ones cited in these two last sections are the main events used in a database application.

Now that you have a good idea about how form events fire, in the next section you will learn how to use the Controls Wizard to create macros that execute simple database tasks.

A Note About the New Record

Whenever a table, query, or form is at a new record, this record still does not exist in the associated database table. In other words, it was not yet saved to the disk.

As soon as you press any key on the new record field, the Form Before Insert event fires to signal the moment that a record image is created in a memory region called a *memory buffer*. This is a place of physical memory used to temporarily store the record structure before it is saved to the disk.

Note   Whenever a record enters Edit mode, Access shows a pencil icon on the Form Record Selector to indicate the existence of the memory buffer.

The same is true for any Form control: its Before Update event signals the moment that the control memory buffer is created on the physical memory—and that is why all Before events can be canceled. The memory buffer relates to a memory place that can be freed with no control or record changes!

The Control's After Update event fires after the control buffer is transferred to the record buffer, while the Form's After Update event fires after the record buffer was saved to the disk, and that is why no After Update event can be canceled (Figure 5-18).

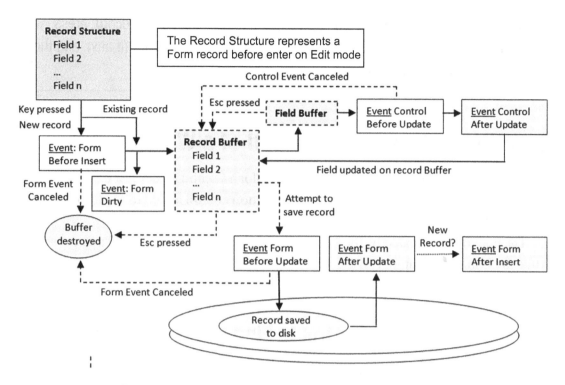

Figure 5-18. *Whenever a key is pressed on a Form record, it enters into Edit mode, creating Record and Field structures called memory buffers. Since these buffers are stored in physical memory, they can be destroyed by canceling any Before event. All After events fire after a field or record is updated and can't be undone*

Just so you know, you can discard any control changes while it is still in the control memory buffer by pressing the Esc key. The same is true for a form record that is in editing mode: by pressing Esc, its memory buffer is discarded.

Tip   To discard all record changes before they are saved to the disk, use the UndoRecord macro action, which discards the record memory buffer. Another approach is to use the SendKeys macro action to send an Esc key via code. It is considered a dangerous action because it has the potential to replicate the user keyboard keys (check the Show All Actions option on the Macro Design tab to make it appear in the Action list).

Note   Since changes to a record can be made to any field in the record, press the Esc key twice. The first Esc key discards the last control buffer (if any), and the second discards the record buffer.

Creating a Macro with the Aid of a Wizard

The Control Wizards can help create macro code for a Combo Box or List Box added to a Form Header or Detail section or a Command button control added to any form section whenever the form is in Design view.

The macro code created by the Combo Box Wizard can be used to find a form record, while the Command Button can execute many different tasks (such as open a query, form, or report; go to a record; etc.).

Using a Combo Box Control to Find a Form Record

Did you try frmSRDatabase (available in the `sr28_Interface.accdb` database that you can extract from `Chapter04.zip`), as shown in Figure 4-90?

It uses two Combo Box controls to allow you to find the desired information: one located in the Form Header section to allow you to search for a given food item and show all the database information related to it, and another located in the Nutrient SubForm Header section to allow you to select a nutrient by name.

You can easily create such functionality using the Controls Wizard on any form whose Record Source property was defined to a table, query, or SQL instruction and whose Form Header and Footer sections are visible in the form's Design view.

Follow these steps:

1. Open frmFOOD_DES from the `sr28_Macro.accdb` database in the form's Design view. Note that it has its Form Header section visible.

Note   To show a Form Header/Footer section in the form's Design view, right-click the Form Detail section and choose the Form Header/Footer option in the context menu.

2. Select the Combo Box control in the controls list of the Form Design tab, make sure that the Use Control Wizards option is selected in the controls list of the Form Design tab, and click the Form Header section to start the Control Wizards.

3. Select the third option: "Find a record on my form based on the value I selected on the combo box." Click Next (Figure 5-19).

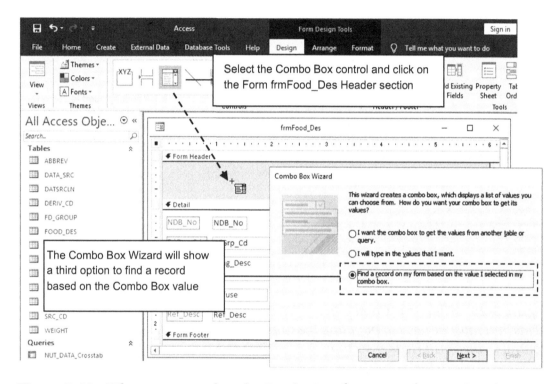

Figure 5-19. *Whenever you select the Combo Box (or List Box) control and click a Form Header (or Footer) section, the wizard will show a third option to allow you to find a record based on the control value*

4. Follow along with the Combo Box Wizard, using the same steps to create a Combo Box as used in previous examples.

   a. Select the table and fields that must be used to fill in the Combo Box list.

   b. Hide the table's primary key field (if needed).

   c. Give an expressive name to the Combo Box associated with the Label control (like "Select Food Item") and click Finish to insert the Combo Box in the Form Header section (Figure 5-20).

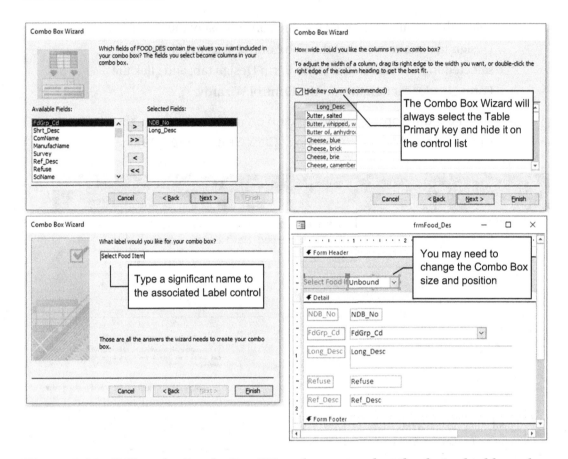

Figure 5-20. *Follow the Combo Box Wizard steps to select the desired table and fields that must be used to populate the Combo Box list and insert the search control in the Form Header section*

Note   Once the Combo Box had been inserted in the Form Header section, you may need to change its size and position to best show its Label Caption property and to give it more room to type the record information to be searched.

Change frmFOOD_DES to Form view, click the Select Food Item Combo Box control in its Form Header section, and type a shortened food name (like **straw** for "strawberries") to select the first food item that matches it, and press Enter to make the form jump to this record (Figure 5-21).

Tip   Press F4 to expand the List Box control and select any other food item that begins with the text typed on the Combo Box control.

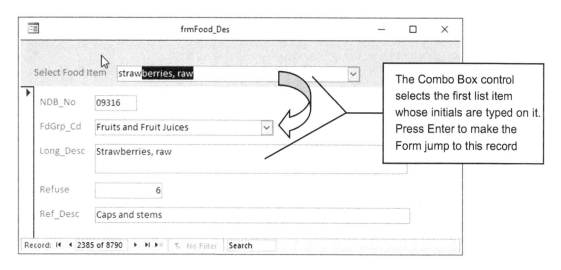

Figure 5-21. *Type a shortened form of any food item in the Select Food Item Combo Box located in the Form Header section to automatically select the first match (press F4 to expand the Combo Box list and select other food items that begin with the same text string)*

Note   You will find this form named frmFood_Des_SearchComboBox in the sr28_Macros.accdb database.

The wizard embedded the macro code in the Combo Box's After Update event because it immediately fires whenever the control changes its value.

Show the frmFood_Des_SearchComboBox form in Design view, select cboSelectFoodItem Combo Box After Update event on the Property Sheet's Event tab, and click the ellipsis button located to its right to show the macro code created by the wizard (see Figure 5-22).

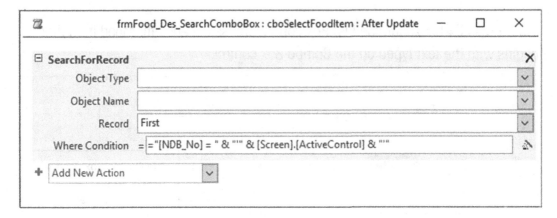

Figure 5-22. *The Combo Box Wizard used the SearchForRecord macro action with arguments for Record and Where Condition to allow you to select the first form record whose value matches the Combo Box value*

Figure 5-22 shows that the Combo Box Wizard used just the SearchForRecord action to find the first form record whose NDB_No value matches the value of the item selected on the Combo Box list.

The SearchForRecord Action

The SearchForRecord action has four different arguments.

- *Object Type*: This is optional; it is the object type on which it must act (it requires the Object Name argument with the selected object type names).

- *Object Name:* This is optional; it is the object name on which it must act.

- *Record*: This is mandatory; it is the record that it must return regarding the one selected by the action (which may vary according to the Where Condition argument).

  - *Previous*: This is the record that is before the found record.

  - *Next*: This is the record that is after the found record.

  - *First*: This is the first found record.

  - *Last*: This is the last found record (if any).

- *Where Condition*: This is optional; it is an expression that indicates the record to be found.

It sets the mandatory argument Record to First to allow you to select the first record that matches the item selected on the Combo Box control, and the optional Where Condition argument using the NDB_NO field to precisely select the desired form record.

The SearchForRecord Where Condition argument is the one responsible for matching the form record based on the selected Combo Box value using this expression:

```
="[NDB_No] = " & "'" & [Screen].[ActiveControl] & "'"
```

This expression compares the form's NDB_No field value with the value returned by the Screen.ActiveControl property, which is the form control that has the focus at the moment.

Since this macro code is executed from the cboSelectedFoodItem Combo Box After Update event, Screen.ActiveControl returns the selected control value, whichm according to Figure 5-20, is set by the Combo Box's hidden column that also contains the food item's NDB_No value.

Using the Command Button Control to Execute Actions

You can also use the Controls Wizard to define the macro actions that a Command Button executes whenever it is pressed by the user.

The Command Button control can be inserted anywhere in the form's Design view, being most commonly used in the Form Header section to execute actions related to the Form window or to its records. This makes tasks more obvious that are usually performed by the navigation buttons and allows you to run other macro code to automate your database application.

Attention   I sincerely recommend you insert obvious commands on your database forms that execute simple tasks, such as closing the window, going to a new record, deleting a record, printing something, etc. Although it sounds obvious to insert such buttons, you will never really know your application user's computer proficiency.

Follow these steps to insert a Close Command Button in form frmFoodDes_SearchComboBox's Header section:

1. Open form frmFoodDes_SearchComboBox in Design view.

2. Click the Command Button control in the controls list of the form's Design tab, point the mouse to where the top-left corner of the Command Button must be in the Form Header sectionm and click to start the Command Button Wizard.

3. In the Command Button Wizard, select Form Operations in the Categories list and Close Form in the Actions list (note that the wizard shows a picture that will be associated to the Command Button according to the selected action, as shown in Figure 5-23).

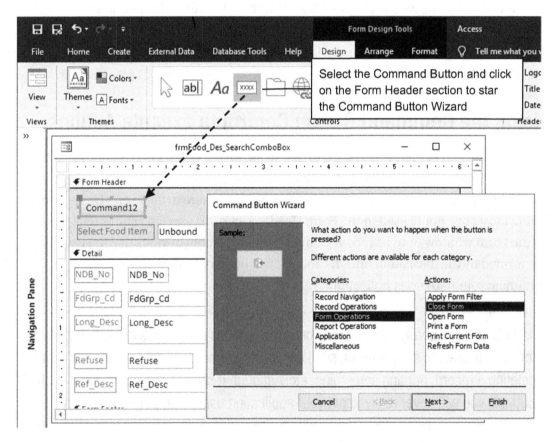

Figure 5-23. *To start the Command Button Wizard, select the Command Button control in the Controls list of the Form Design tab and click anywhere on the form's Design view. Most Command Buttons are added to the Form Header (or Footer) section, because this sections are static; they don't change as the form shows another record*

4. Click Next, and on the second wizard page, select the Command Button's appearance. This allows you to select a text or picture (although you can decide later if you want to show both). It offers two pictures (Exit Doorway and Stop). Check the "Show all pictures" option to see the list of internal icons available or use the Browse button to use a private icon collection.

Note   The default icons offered by Microsoft Access are very old-fashioned. To use modern icons, do a Google search for *Icons Freeware* and select an icon collection that best personalizes your application's appearance.

---

5. Keep the Picture option selected with the default Show Doorway picture and click Next to show the last wizard page.

6. On the last wizard page, type a significant name for this Command Button using the "cmd" prefix (cmdClose to a Close Form action) and click Finish to insert the control on the Form Header.

7. After the wizard closes, double-click the cmdClose Command Button inserted in the Form Header section to show the Property Sheet window and inspect its Format, Event, and Other tabs (Figure 5-24).

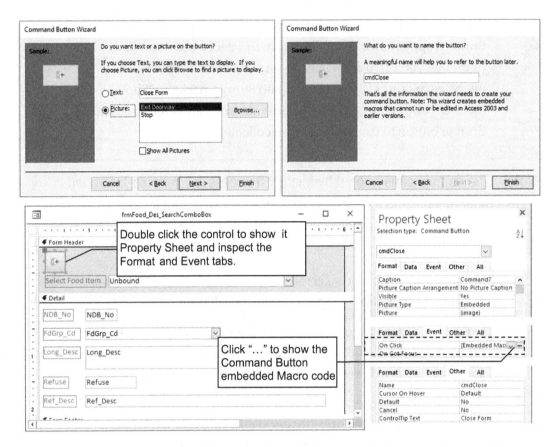

Figure 5-24. *Select the appropriate appearance for the Command Button (Text or Picture and a significant name). After the wizard closes, double-click the Command Button to show its Property Sheet*

The Command Button created by the wizard has only the Doorway icon, with no caption. By inspecting its Property Sheet Format tab, you will notice that it has Picture Type set to Embedded and Picture set to (image). Select the Event tab and notice that its On Click event was set to (Embedded Macro). Select the Other tab and note that Control Tip Text is set to Close Form.

Attention   Picture is the default wizard option for a Command Button action. It will select the best picture available according to the action you indicate that it must perform (for a Close Form action, it will select the "Open door" picture). Unless your application will be used by a multilingual audience, I sincerely recommend you use the Text option, typing a single word that succinctly describes what the button does (in this case, "Close" for the Close Form action).

To check the macro code embedded on the cmdClose On Click event, click the ... button right next to the event name to show the Macro window and note that it has just the CloseWindow action (Figure 5-25).

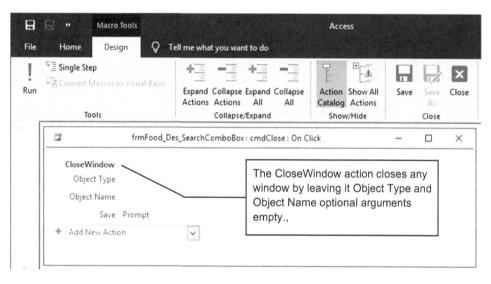

Figure 5-25. *This is the cmdClose On Click event macro code created by the Command Button Wizard. It has a single CloseWindow action that just uses the Save = Prompt mandatory argument*

The CloseWindow Action

The CloseWindow action allows you to close any window and has three arguments.

- *Object Type*: Select in the list the type of object to be closed (it requeries the Object Name argument with the selected object type names).

- *Object Name*: Type the name of an open object so it can be closed. If the object is not opened, the CloseWindow action will generate a runtime error, and the macro code will stop.

- *Save*: Control how the CloseWindow action deals with an object whose structure (not data) had been changed since it was opened.

  - *Yes*: Always save the object before closing it with no prompt.

  - *No*: Close the object without saving it with no prompt.

  - *Prompt*: This asks if the object must be saved before closing.

Switch to Form view and click the button to close the form. Since the CloseWindow Save argument was set to Prompt, if you have not saved frmFood_Des_ SearchComboBox, Microsoft Access will ask you to save it before closing it. Click Yes to save form before it closes and retain the Command Button control added to its Header section (Figure 5-26).

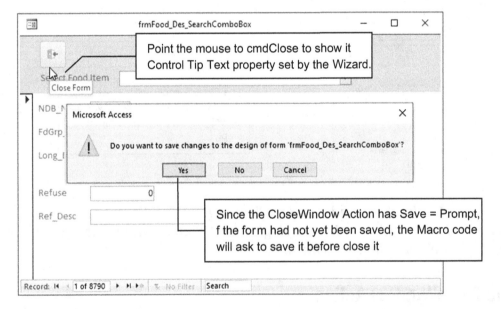

Figure 5-26. *Since cmdClose has macro code on its On Click event that uses the CloseWindow action with Save set to Prompt, it may ask you to save the form before closing it in case any changes were made since it was opened*

The Command Button Control

Since the Command Button control has specific properties purposely not covered in Chapter 4, it is a good idea to take a look at Table 5-5, which lists some of its specific properties and its usages, as well as the Property Sheet tab where you can find them.

Table 5-5. *Microsoft Access Command Button Control-Specific Properties*

Tab	Property	Usage
Format	Caption	Defines the control text.
	Picture Caption arrangement	Defines the Caption position if the control also has a picture.
	Picture type	Defines how the picture is stored in the control.
	Picture	Sets the control picture.
	Visible	Sets if the control is visible.
Data /Other tab	Enabled	Sets if the Command Button can be selected.
Event	On Click	Fires when the Command Button is pressed (use just this event).
Other	Default	Allows the Enter key to press the control and fires its On Click event. Only one Command Button can be set to Default on a form.
	Cancel	Allows the Esc key to press the control and fires its On Click event. Only one Command Button can be set to Cancel on a form.
	Auto Repeat	Allows you to successively fire the On Click event while the button is pressed.

Let's now see examples of how you can use some of these properties.

Inserting Other Command Buttons

You can insert other Command Button controls in the Form Header section to give to your database application users an easier way to add a new record and save and delete a record.

Using the Command Button Wizard, you can insert Command Button controls in any Form Header section to perform specific record actions by selecting the Record Operations option in the Category list on the first wizard page, such as Add New Record, Save Record, and Delete Record actions for each control, accepting the default image proposed by the wizard.

Figure 5-27 shows the frmFD_GROUP_ButtonImage form that received a Combo Box control that makes a record search and four command buttons added by the wizard to execute different record actions, using just images and the Control Tip Text property to identify what each one does.

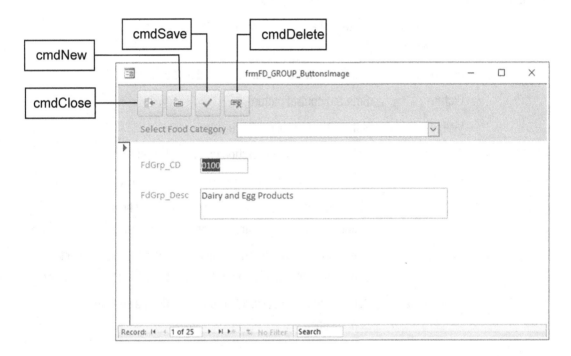

Figure 5-27. *The frmFD_GROUP_ButtonsImage form has a Combo Box for record search and four Command Button controls in its Header section created by the Command Button Wizard: cmdClose (to close the Form), cmdNew (to add a new record), cmdSave (to save a record), and cmdDelete (to delete the current record)*

Note   These buttons were inserted on a form where Record Source is set to the FD_GROUP table, because as cited in the first chapter, the sr28.accdb database has smart record locks imposed by referential integrity between the FOOD_DES, ABBREV, and LANGUAL tables that doesn't allow users to insert or delete records on the FOOD_DES table. This record lock also avoids the deletion of any existing food category record related to the FOOD_DES table records but allows inserting and deleting new categories.

Checking the cmdNew and cmdSave Macro Code

Show frmFD_GROUP_ButtonsImage in the form's Design view, and select the cmdNew Command Button control (located to the right of cmdClose; see Figure 5-27). Show the Property Sheet's Event tab and click the ellipsis button located to the right of its On Click event to show the Macro window with the code created by the wizard to add a new form record (or in other words, go to a new record).

Do the same with cmdSave, and analyze the code of both macros, which are shown side by side in Figure 5-28.

Atttention   Using a Save button is not really necessary but may be considered as a good programming practice, especially if more actions must be executed after a record is changed. After all, the data will be saved to the database whether or not the Save button is clicked when the user moves to another record, unless macros are added to prevent this from happening.

Based on the knowledge you gathered so far in this book, did you recognize these macro code techniques?

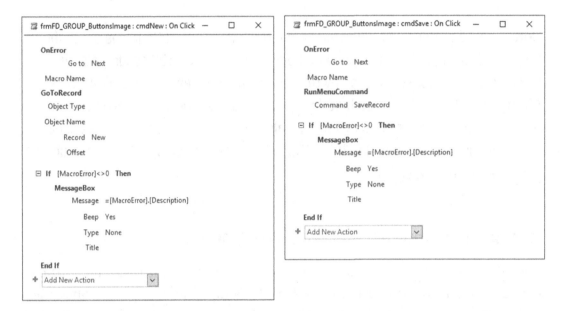

Figure 5-28. *Macro code created by the wizard and associated to the cmdNew and cmdSave Command Buttons to add a new record and to save the current record*

Sure you did! Both Command Buttons' macro code uses the "silent error" technique, with OnError Go to set to Next as the first macro action to disable any runtime errors, and IF as the last macro action to verify if MacroError.Number is different than 0. If it is, a MessageBox action will show the MacroError.Description property.

Considering the cmdNew macro code, note that the wizard used the GoToRecord action to move the form to a new record, while cmdSave used the SaveRecord action to save the current record (that appears as a RunMenuCommand with the SaveRecord argument).

The GoToRecord Action

The GoToRecord action used by the Command Button Wizard to show a new form record has four arguments.

- *Object Type:* Optional. This is the object type on which it must act (it will requery the Object Name argument with the selected object type names).

- *Object Name:* Optional. This is the object name on which it must act.

- *Record*: Mandatory. This is the record that it must return regarding the one selected by the action (which may vary according to the Where Condition argument).

  - *Previous*: The record that is before the found record.

  - *Next*: The record that is after the found record.

  - *First*: The first found record.

  - *Last*: The last found record (if any).

  - *Go to*: This allows you to use the Offset argument to jump a number of records.

- *Offset:* Optional. This is a positive integer value (or expression that evaluates to an integer) that specifies which record must become the current record. You can use Offset when:

  - *Record is set to Next or Previous*: Access offsets the current record forward or backward by the positive integer number of records specified by Offset.

  - *Record is set to Go To*: Access moves to the recordset record position (as shown by the form navigation buttons) that is equal to the Offset argument (if any).

Note   The GoToRecord action ignores the Offset argument when Record is set to First, Last, or New. It will generate a runtime error if the Offset argument is too large (using a value greater than the recordset records count) or if it receives a negative value.

Checking the cmdDelete Macro Code

Now take a look at Figure 5-29 that shows the macro code created by the wizard for the cmdDelete Command Button to delete any form record using both the Collapsed and Expanded views, side by side. Can you read and understand this macro code?

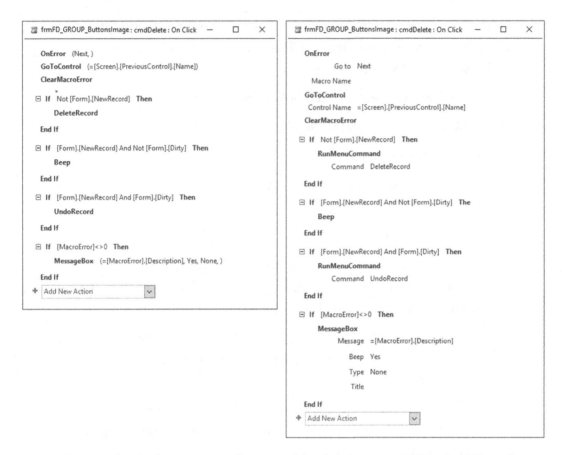

Figure 5-29. *This is the macro code created by the Command Button Wizard to delete any form record*

Congratulations!

The macro code use the "error silent" technique, already described for the cmdNew and cmdSave Command Buttons and moves the application focus from the cmdDelete Command Button (that received the focus when it was clicked) to the last Form control selected before using the GoToControl action with the aid of the Screen object's PreviousControl property, so it can delete the record.

Note that it uses an expression that begins with = so the previous control name can be evaluated.

```
GoTo Control
Control Name =[Screen].[PreviousControl].[Name]
```

The macro code then uses a ClearMacroError action to reset the MacroError object and uses three successive IF actions to make form record verifications.

The first IF action verifies if the form *is not* on a new record, using the Form object's NewRecord property. If it is not a new record, it executes a DeleteRecord action (which appears as a RunMenuCommand action using the argument Command set to DeleteRecord).

```
ClearMacroError
IF Not [Form].[NewRecord] Then
RunMenuCommand
Command DeleteRecord
End IF
```

Note   The NewRecord property is set to True whenever the form is at a new record and set to False for any existing record. By negating the NewRecord property, the expression Not Form.NewRecord returns True for any existing record.

The second IF action verifies whether this is a new record *that is not* in Edit mode, by negating the Form.Dirty property. If it is considered as True, a beep sound is emitted to call the user attention to the fact that the record does not exist and cannot be deleted.

```
IF [Form].[NewRecord] and Not [Form[.[Dirty] Then
  Beep
End IF
```

Note   The Dirty property is set to True whenever the record is in Edit mode, meaning that at least one of its fields had been changed and the record has not been saved yet. By negating the Dirty property using Not Form.Dirty, this expression returns True for any record that is not in editing mode.

The third IF action does the opposite. It verifies whether this is a new record that is in editing mode. If it is, undo the record using the UndoRecord action (which makes the new, unsaved record disappear from the memory buffer).

```
IF [Form].[NewRecord] and [Form[.[Dirty] Then
  RunMenuCommand
    Command UndoRecord
End IF
```

Note   The UndoRecord action has the same effect as pressing the Esc key whenever a new record is being edited.

Critics to the Delete Record Wizard Code

This is what can be considered as super-dimensioned macro code: it uses too many actions and strategies to execute a simple task such as deleting the current record.

I really don't know why the Command Button Wizard was programmed to do such a complex series of actions in order to perform such a simple task of discarding a record buffer (if any) and deleting the current record.

This next macro code fragment can easily do the same task using just three actions:

```
On Error
   Goto Next
RunMenuCommand
   Command UndoRecord
RunMenuCommand
   Command DeleteRecord
```

This code uses OnError Goto Next to disable runtime errors, executes a UndoRecord action to discard the record buffer (if any), and uses a DeleteRecord action to delete the record (if it exists; otherwise, nothing will happen).

Simple, isn't it?

Note   Because of the smart relationships record lock, you can only delete new food categories records created by this form that have no related FOOD_DES records.

Changing Command Button Appearance

To change the Button Control appearance and make it more understandable to the average user of your database applications, use the Command Button control's Caption property to define text that explains what the button does and use the Picture Caption Arrangement property to define the caption position if the control also has an image.

For your information, any control that has a Caption property (such as the Label control associated to any control type) can be used as a shortcut control selection by preceding one of its Caption property characters with the & (ampersand) character.

The & on a Caption property has these practical effects:

- It does not appear on the control text caption in Design view or Form view.

- It underlines the character that follows it, to clearly indicate the shortcut.

- The control can be accessed using the Alt+*underlined character* shortcut.

- Just one character will be effective as a form shortcut to the control. If more than one control uses the same shortcut character, just the first control on the form tabulation order will be selected.

- If more than one control has the same shortcut character repeated, focus will move to the next control with the same shortcut character.

- Most controls will be selected by using Alt+key shortcut, but the Command Button will execute its On Click event.

  For example, a Text Box control with the associated Label control of Caption = &Food Item can be easily selected by pressing Alt+F). Conversely, a Command Button with Caption = &Add can be clicked by pressing Alt+A.

  Forms frmFD_GROUP_ButtonsImageText and frmFD_GROUP_ButtonsText use these tricks to give a shortcut to the cmdClose, cmdNew, cmdNew cmdDelete, and cboSelect controls inserted in both Form Header sections. Each control has a unique underlined letter that allows you to execute it or access it using the Alt+*letter* combination (Figure 5-30).

403

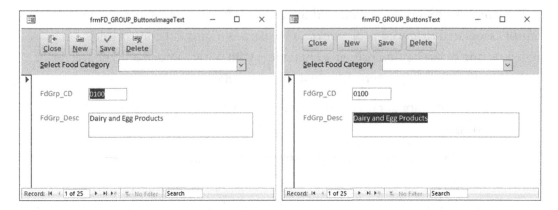

Figure 5-30. *Forms frmFD_GROUP_ButtonsImageText and frmFD_GROUP_ ButtonsText use the Caption and ControlTip properties to allow you to better identify what each control does. Each caption uses the & character to define the control shortcut (press Alt+S to put the focus on the Select Food Category Combo Box)*

Attention   Forms frmFD_GROUP_ButtonsImageText and frmFD_GROUP_ ButtonsText and the cmdDelete Command Button use this section's simplified version for the macro code record deletion. Verify this on your own.

The form frmFD_GROUP_ButtonsImageText uses the Caption, Picture, and Picture Caption Arrangement properties to allow you to show both a picture and a caption below the picture (Picture Caption Arrangement set to Bottom), while frmFD_GROUP_ButtonsText had its Picture property removed; click the Picture property on the Property Sheet Format tab, select the (image) text, and press Delete key to remove the associated button picture.

Attention   Using just images, image and text, or just text on Command Buttons to identify its actions is a interface layout decision that may impact the usage of your database applications. My experience shows that using caption text is effective, while the caption shortcut is unknown for most Windows users.

Creating Your Own Form and Control Events

Since you are now almost an expert on macro actions and form and control events, it is time to learn how to create your own macro actions to programmatically do interesting actions using selected form or control events.

This section will teach you to how you can use specific form and control events to create simple interface tricks that will radically improve the performance of your database applications.

Using the Form On Timer Event

Let's begin by learning how you can allow a form to automatically do an action after a certain amount of time elapses.

This can be done by using two form events.

- *Timer Interval*: While this does appear on the Property Sheet's Event tab, it is indeed a form property. It is an integer value that defines the amount of time in milliseconds that the On Timer event fires.

- *On Timer*: This is an event that fires whenever the Timer Interval amount has passed.

They work together in this way: whenever Timer Interval is set to a positive value, the Timer event will fire. For example, to make the On Timer event fire every one second, set Time Interval to 1000 (1,000 milliseconds = 1 second).

This is a useful trick that allows you to requery a control at specific intervals to indicate, for example, which new records were added to a database table (like a database restaurant application that runs on a network and updates restaurant orders after a specific amount of time).

The Requery Action

The Requery action is a powerful action that allows you to requery a control whenever some data changes in the user interface. By using it on some macro code, it will update different control type properties.

- A Text Box will have its Control Source property updated.

- Subform controls will have their Record Source properties updated.

- Combo Box and List Box controls will have their Row Source properties updated.

A single control name can be provided to the action, which requires this syntax:

- To update a control on current form, use just the control name.

- To update a control on another open form, use this syntax:

`Forms!FormName!ControlName`

Let's see this in action.

Creating a Floating Digital Clock

Let's suppose you want to create a floating digital clock—one that shows the time with a second of precision. It will need the following:

- A Text Box that uses the expression =TIME() to return the system time, with property Format set to the "hh:nn:ss" format

- Event Timer Interval set to 500, so the On Timer event fires at each half-second to allow a second of precision

- Runs macro code on the form's On Timer event that requeries the Text Box control

Open frmClock in Design view and note that its Detail section was set to a light blue background, with the txtTime Text Box, where the property Control Source is TIME() and the property Format is hh:nn:ss on the Format tab.

Note   "n" is the format character used for minutes because "m" is used for months.

Select Form in the Property Sheet list, and note that the form disables the Format, Event, and Other properties.

- Caption = Time (text of Form title bar)

- Border style = Dialog (fixed thin black border)

- Record Selector = No

- Navigation Buttons = No

- Scroll Bars = Neither

- Min Max Buttons = None

- On Timer = Embedded Macro

- Timer Interval = 500

- PopUp = Yes (Other tab, allow floating over the Access interface)

Click the ... button at the right of the Form On Timer event to show its macro code, and note that it has just a Requery action, with the argument Control Name set to txtTime.

Switch to Form view and observe the time being updated as each second passes (click the frmClock title bar and note that you can drag it outside the Access window, as shown in Figure 5-31).

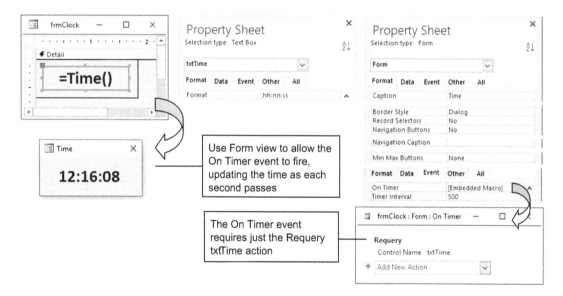

Figure 5-31. *The frmClock uses a PopUp window with a Text Box control that uses the TIME() function to show the system time within a second of precision. It uses Timer Interval set to 500 to fire the form's On Timer event every half-second*

Creating a Splash Screen Form

A splash screen is the window that appears when a professional application runs and automatically closes after two to three seconds, eventually opening another interface from where the user can begin using the application.

This is a typical scenario for the timer interval and On Timer event pair, using a form that has no title bar and shows the application name and version, before opening another form.

Open form frmSplash Screen in Design view, show the Property Sheet windows, and note that it has these Format, Event, and Other properties set (Figure 5-32):

- Auto Center = Yes

- Auto Resize = Yes

- Border style = None (to remove the title bar)

- Record Selector = No

- Navigation Buttons = No

- Scroll Bars = Neither

- Record Source = AppData

- Allow Additions = No

- Allow Deletions = No

- Allow Edits = No

- On Timer = Embedded Macro

- Timer Interval = 2000

- PopUp = Yes (Other tab, allow floating over the Access interface)

- Modal = Yes (stop interface actions until it is closed)

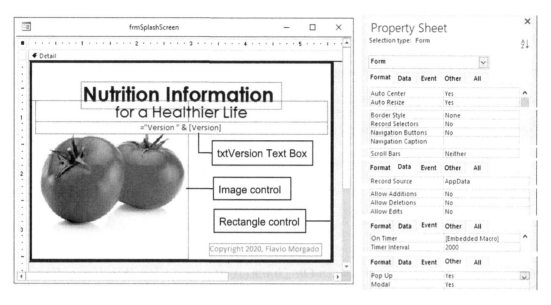

Figure 5-32. *frmSplashScreen has Timer Interval set to 3000, which makes the On Timer event fire after three seconds. Its On Timer event macro code closes the form window and opens frmFD_GROUP_ButtonsImageText*

Note the following:

- Property Border Style set to None removes the form's title bar and border so it receives a rectangle control to simulate the form border.

- Property Record Source set to AppData links the form to the AppData table that has just one record and field (Version), allowing you to centralize the application version information.

- The properties Allow Additions, Allow Deletions, and Allow Edits set to No mean record changes aren't allowed.

- The properties PopUp and Modal are set to Yes to allow a modal form to float over the Microsoft Access interface, not executing anything else until the form is closed.

Click the ... button at the right of the Form On Timer event and analyze its macro code (Figure 5-33).

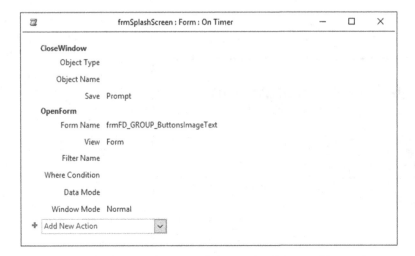

Figure 5-33. *The frmSplashScreen On Timer event uses a CloseWindow action to close its own window and an OpenForm action to show another form after it closes*

When the form is opened, it stays on the screen for about two seconds (2,000 milliseconds) due to Timer Interval being set to 2000, and when the On Timer event fires, the embedded macro code closes the form window and opens the frmFD_GROUP_ButtonsImageText form (Figure 5-34).

Attention   This is done only for demonstration purposes. In a professional application, typically some setup processing needs to be executed before the application can be used, so the splash screen will close when that setup processing has finished executing.

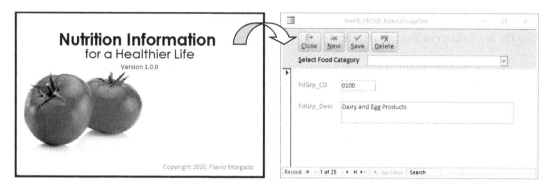

Figure 5-34. *Whenever frmSplashScreen opens, it stays on the screen for three seconds, automatically closes itself, and shows the frmFD_GROUP_ButtonsImageText form*

Tip   To make frmSplashScreen open when the database is opened, use the Display Form option in the Current Database area of the Options dialog box (File ➤ Options).

Synchronizing Interface Elements

The secret to having a successful, trustable database application is making sure it provides the desired information and synchronizes its interface elements quickly.

Speed comes from the correct use of tables and indexes and the efficient use of queries that can find the desired information quickly, while a perfectly synchronized interface needs experience and a good dose of observation of the form elements you offer to the user, that is supposed to facilitate its daily work.

This section will deal with interface synchronization regarding all the controls used to get database information and highlight how users expect your interface to work.

Synchronizing a Searching Combo Box

Considering frmFood_Des_SearchComboBox and all the other examples used by frmFD_GROUP_Button... forms cited in the previous sections, you probably noted that all of them lack synchronization between form records and the search Combo Box inserted in each Form Header section.

The search Combo Box control works well to search and show a form record, but it may create some confusion when:

- *A record changes the field value used in the list*: The new value will not be automatically propagated to the list.

- *A new record is inserted*: It will not be automatically shown in the search Combo Box list.

- *A record in the list is deleted*: It may appear in the Combo Box list as "Deleted" (new records added after the form is opened will not even appear in the list, as shown in Figure 5-35).

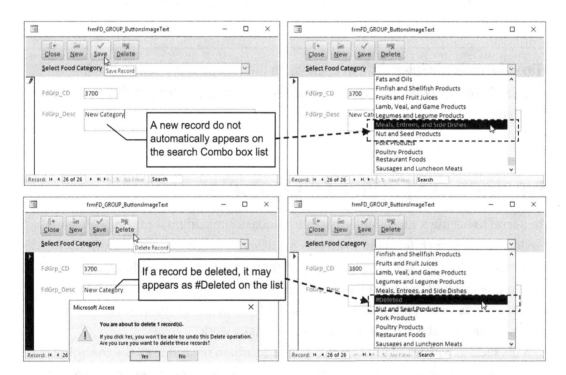

Figure 5-35. *When a new record is inserted, the search Combo Box does not automatically update to show in the list. And when a record that is already in the list is deleted, it appears as #Deleted in the control list*

- *Another record is selected after a record search*: The search Combo Box will continue to show the last record searched while the form shows different record data (Figure 5-36).

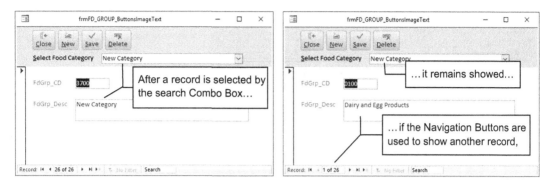

Figure 5-36. *The search Combo Box created by the Controls Wizard does a good job of finding the desired form record, but it is not synchronized with the form record operations (editing, inserting, deleting, and changing record operations)*

To synchronize the search Combo Box list with the same recordset currently shown by the form or to clear its value whenever the last searched record changes, use one of the following:

- *The Requery macro action*: To force an update of the search Combo Box's Row Source property whenever a new record is inserted or a current record is changed or deleted.

- *The SetProperty action*: To change control values whenever another record is selected on the form.

Open frmFD_GROUP_SearchSync in Design view, show the Property Sheet's Event tab, and note that it has embedded macro code on its On Current, After Update, After Insert, and After Del Confirm events (Figure 5-37).

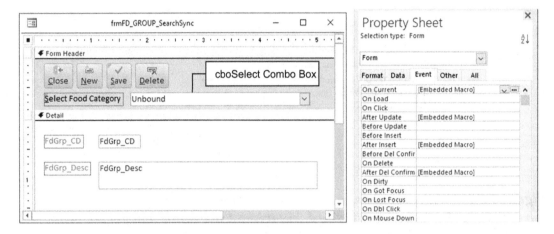

Figure 5-37. *frmFD_GROUP_SearchSync uses the On Current, After Update, After Insert, and After Del Confirm events to synchronize the search cboSelect Combo Box list and value whenever a record is inserted, updated, deleted, or changed by the user action*

Now let's see how these events' macros are coded to synchronize cboSelect with the form records.

Using Requery to Update a Combo Box List

Use the Requery action to update a Combo Box or List Box list of items so it keeps in sync with the form records.

Figure 5-38 shows the macro code for the frmFD_GROUP_SearchSync After Update event. It uses just the Requery action with the argument Control Name set to cboSelect.

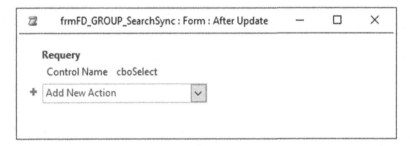

Figure 5-38. *frmFD_GROUP_SearchSync uses the Requery action in the After Update, After Insert, and After Del Confirm events to requery the cboSelect Combo Box list of items whenever a new record is inserted or an existing record is updated or deleted*

> **Note**   frmFD_GROUP_SearchSync's After Update, After Insert, and After Del Confirm events use the same macro code instructions.

Every time a record changes and is saved to disk (by clicking cmdSave or moving to another record), the After Update event fires and executes the Requery action, to force the cbpSelect Combo Box Row Source property to update its list of items.

The same will be true whenever a new record is inserted (the After Insert event) or deleted (the After Del Confirm event).

> **Attention**   To make different events share the same macro code, create a stand-alone macro (one that appears in the Database window) and select it on the Property Sheet's Event list. The advantage of this practice appears whenever the code is somewhat complex, allowing you to maintain one macro code for different objects. The disadvantage is that the form loses its integrity: part of its code now resides outside the Form object and may compromise the application stability if it is inadequately changed or even deleted.

Using the Set Property to Synchronize the Search Combo Box

To avoid having the cboSelect Combo Box keeps showing the last searched record when a different record is selected, use the form's On Current event, which fires for each selected record, to clear the cboSelect Combo Box.

This can be done using two different macro actions to change the control's Value property: SetProperty or SetValue.

The SetProperty Action

The SetProperty action has three arguments.

- *Control Name*: This is the name of the field or control whose property must be changed. Use just the control name (don't use the full syntax), or leave it blank to set a form property.

- *Property*: This is the property whose value must be set, whose name must be selected on the argument list: Enabled, Visible, Locked, Left, Top, Width, Height, Fore Color, Back Color, or Caption.

- *Value*: This is the property value to be set. Yes/No properties must use -1 for Yes and 0 for No.

Note   The SetProperty action does not allow you to set a property outside its property argument list. To set a different property, use the SetValue action.

The SetValue Action

Microsoft Access macros also have the SetValue action that allows changes to any property value. It was substituted by the SetProperty action because its Expression argument can be erroneously evaluated, leading to unexpected application results (see the following note). For that reason, it needs the Show All Actions option set on the Macro Design tab to appear in the Macro Action list.

It has two arguments.

- *Item*: This is the name of a control on the current form, or the full syntax for the object (control, form, or report) whose property must be changed.

- *Expression*: This is the value or expression that Access must use to set this item value. When it uses an expression, it requires the full syntax to refer to any objects used by the expression (like Forms!MyForm. Property or Forms!MyForm!MyControl.Property).

Note   If the SetValue Expression argument begins with a =, Access will first evaluate the expression before setting the property value. This evaluation process can lead to unexpected results if the expression is a string (and that is why it was substituted by the SetProperty action). For example, if the expression is set to =Reader, SetValue first evaluates it to the Reader object and will assume that it is representing a control or property named Reader on the form or report that called the macro.

The On Current Event

The On Current event fires whenever a record is selected, making it the event of choice to be used to synchronize the form interface for each shown record.

Inspect the On Current event macro code, and note how it clears the cboSelect Combo Box whenever another record is selected (Figure 5-39).

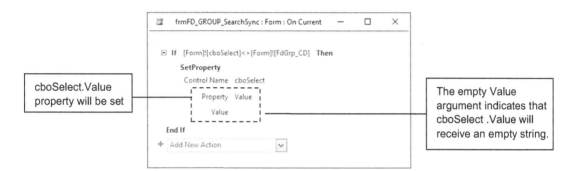

Figure 5-39. *The On Current event verifies whether the cboSelect value is different from the form's FdGrp_CD control. If it is, it uses the SetProperty action to clear cboSelect by changing its Value property to an empty string (the Value action argument is empty)*

The On Current event macro code uses an IF action to verify whether Form. cboSelect <> Form.FdGrp_CD. If it is, the cboSelect Combo Box shows a record different from the form's current record, and the code executes the SetProperty action to change the cboSelect.Value property to an empty string.

Note   The search cboSelect Combo Box hides the FdGrp_CD primary key in its first column, which is also the control value.

To test frmFD_GROUP_SearchSync form synchronization with the cboSelect Combo Box, do the following:

1. Add a new food category and click the cmdSave Command Button to save it. Expand the cboSelect list to verify that the new record now appears in the list.

2. Select again the last inserted food category record, change its name, and click cmdSave to save it. Expand the cboSelect list and verify that the list item was updated to reflect the edited food category.

3. Use cboSelect to search for any food category and use the navigation buttons to select another record: cboSelect will become empty.

4. Delete the new food category record. Expand the cboSelect list to verify that it has been removed from the list items.

Synchronizing a List Box Control

The List Box control is an excellent alternative to show one-to-many relationships on a form. It is a lightweight control that updates quickly, can have multiple columns, and can be easily updated by a Requery action executed by the form's On Current event.

It must be fulfilled with a query or SQL instruction, using the value that represents the "one" side of the relationship as criteria on the field that represents the "many" side of the relationship. This can be returned by the full name of a form control or a temporary variable.

Note   According to the Microsoft Access documentation, whenever you save a query, it is compiled and optimized, which makes it runs faster than a SQL instruction. It will be faster if its Criteria field is indexed.

Open frmFood_Des_Sync1 in Design view, and note that its Record Source is set to FOOD_DES (the food item table), with the NDB_No field (the table's primary key) and the unbound lstCommonMeasures List Box control to show related records from qryWEIGHTFullName (Figure 5-40).

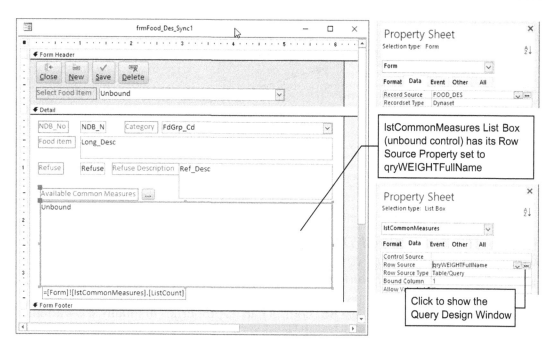

Figure 5-40. *This is frmFood_Des_Sync1 in Design view. It is bound to the FOOD_ DES table and uses the lstCommonMeasures List Box to show the WEIGHT table records, using qryWEIGHTFullName as its Row Source property*

Attention   Note the form control's design, that perfectly align then at left and right of lstCommonMeasures List Box borders (Labels to its left, other controls to its right), to give a more pleasant appearance to the record presentation.

Look at the form's On Current event macro code and note that it first uses the Requery lstCommonMeasures action to update the List Box's Row Source property and refills the list items. The next IF action is used to synchronize the search cboSelectFoodItem Combo Box, using the same technique explained in the previous section, as shown in Figure 5-41.

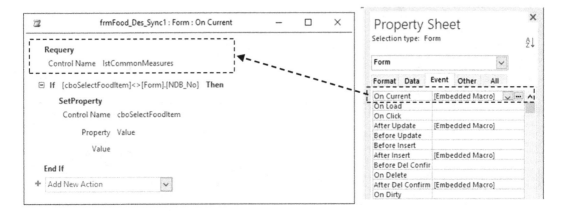

Figure 5-41. *Form frmFood_Des_Sync1's On Current event uses a Requery action to force lstCommonMeasure to update its list items for every record shown and to synchronize the cboSelectFoodItem that is positioned in its Header section*

The lstCommonMeasures List Box control had its properties manually set, without using the aid of the Controls Wizard. Select it in Form Design view, and note in the Property Sheet's Data tab that its Row Source Type property is set to Table/Query and Row Source is set to qryWEIGHTFullName.

Select the Row Source property on the Property Sheet and click the ... button located to its right to show the Query Builder for qryWEIGHTFullName (Figure 5-42).

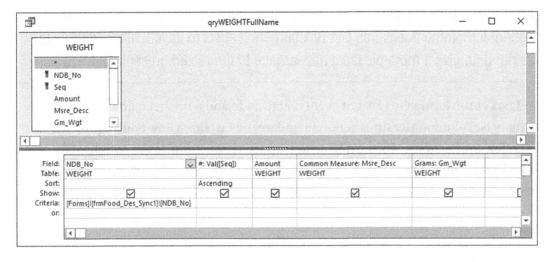

Figure 5-42. *This is qryWEIGHTFullName, used by frmFoodDes_Sync1's lstCommonMeagures List Box as the control's Row Source property. It uses the full name syntax on the NDB_No field criteria to filter its records, while aliasing some of its fields so they convey clearer information about their meanings*

The Query Builder shows that qry WEIGHT FullName returns five WEIGHT table fields, aliasing some of them so they can be better used on the lstCommon Measures Column Heads and so that it is linked to frmFood_Des_Sync1 by using the "full name" syntax on the NDB_No Criteria field. In other words, this form must be opened in Form view so that its current record can indicate which records must be returned using this expression:

`[Forms]![frmFood_Des_Sync1]![NDB_No]`

Also note that records are sorted ascending according to the Val(Seq) expression, in the # aliased query field. This is necessary because the Seq field (short for "sequence") is a Short Text field that identifies WEIGHT table common measures from most to less used measures. Since strings are classified by their ASCII code, 10 and 11 are considered to be smaller than 2, which may show a food item that has 11 (or more) common measures sorts as 1, 10, 11, 2, 3, 4, …. By using the VAL() function, the Seq string is converted to a number and sorts as expected.

Close the Query Builder, select the Property Sheet's Format tab, and note how lstCommonMeasures was defined to show the qryWEIGHTFullName records (Figure 5-43).

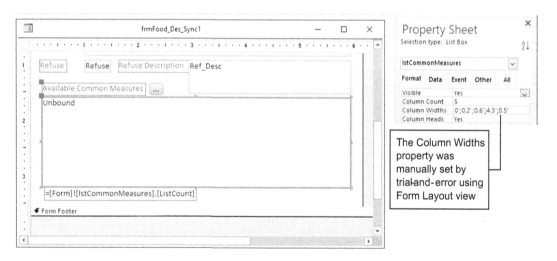

Figure 5-43. *The lstCommonMeasures List Box has Column Count, Column Widths, and Column Heads properties manually set to correctly show the records returned by its Row Source property*

Figures 5-40 and 5-43 show that lstCommonMeasures uses these Data and Format properties to format the List Box control columns:

- Bound Column = 1 (the query NDB_No field)

- Column Count = 5 (the query returns five fields)

- Column Widths = 0";0.2";0.6";4.3";0.5" (the first column is hidden, as indicated by the 0"; other columns were manually set by trial and error using the form's Layout view)

- Column Heads = Yes (to show Row Source field names as the List Box's first row)

Switch frmFood_Des_Sync1 to Form view and watch how lstCommonMeasures efficiently shows each food item's common measures. Click any form field (other than lstCommonMeasures), and keep the Page Down key pressed to successively change Form records and note how it quickly updates lstCommonMeasures to show the related WEIGHT table records (Figure 5-44)!

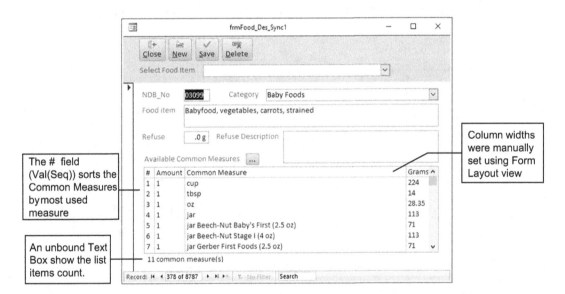

Figure 5-44. *The lstCommonMeasures List Box quickly updates all food item common measures stored as the "many" side of a relationship between the FOOD_DES and WEIGHT tables. The List Box Width and Column Width properties were defined using the Form Layout mode*

Showing How Many Items a List Box Has

To show how many common measures each food item has, frmFood_Des_Sync1 uses the txtCommonMeasures Text Box, positioned below the lstCommonMeasures List Box, which uses an expression and its Format property to show this information (Figure 5-45).

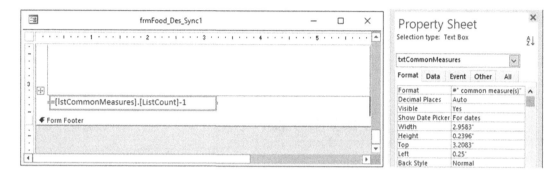

Figure 5-45. *The txtCommonMeasures Text Box positioned below the lstCommonMeasures List Box uses the expression =lstCommonMeasures ListCount -1 because when property Column Heads is Yes, the control adds one more item to its list*

The txtCommonMeasures Text Box uses this expression:

$$=lstCommonMeasures.ListCount\ -1$$

It uses the List Box control's ListCount property to return how many list items the control has. It needs to subtract 1 from this value because the property Column Heads set to Yes adds one more item to the control list.

Figure 5-44 also shows that the Text Box control adds the suffix "common measure(s)" using this Text Box's Format property (note that it has a space to separate the value from the text):

```
# " common measure(s)"
```

Using a Form to Edit Related Records

Since the List Box does not allow record changes, this approach needs to use a form that can be opened to allow you to change the "many" side of the relationship.

That is why lstCommonMeasures has the small cmdCommomMeasures Command Button right next to its associated Label caption (it uses a ellipsis on its Caption property to mimic the way Access does for calling its associated forms, like Query Builder.) The Command Button, when clicked, shows frmWeightFullName1 in a modal state (you can't use the Access interface until it is closed), showing just this food item's common measures (Figure 5-46).

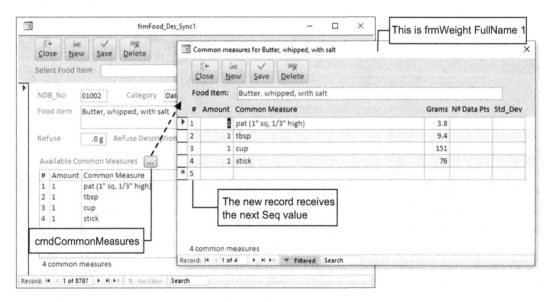

Figure 5-46. *Since the List Box control doesn't allow changing its content, use another form to show its records*

Note in Figure 5-46 that frmWeightFullName1 shows the current food item name on its title bar and on the txtFoodItem Text Box located in its Header section, besides having all the necessary Command Buttons to deal with form records. Also, note that the new record automatically receives the next common measure Seq value (5, for a fifth common measure).

Insert a new common measure for the selected food item, close the form by any means (click cmdClose on the Form Close button or press Alt+F4), and note that the new record automatically appears on lstCommonMeasures of frmFood_Des_Sync1 (Figure 5-47).

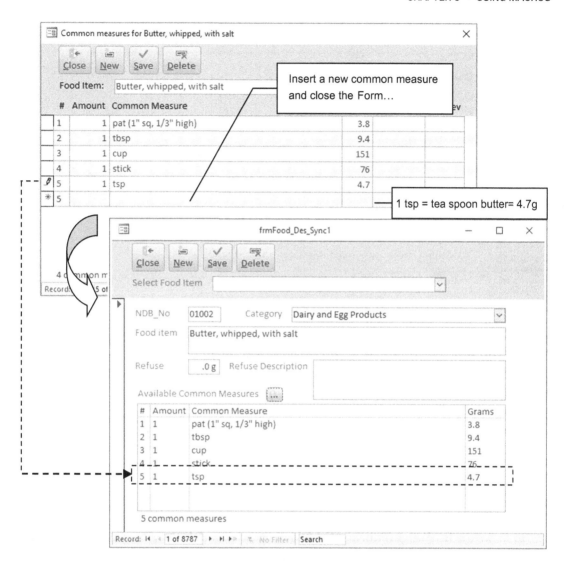

Figure 5-47. *After changing or inserting a record on frmWeightFullName1 for the current food item, after the form is closed, the lstCommonMeasures List Box from frmFood_Des_Sync1 will be updated to reflect the changes*

All these synchronous operations begin on cmdCommonMeasures' On Click event that executes the embedded macro code shown in Figure 5-48.

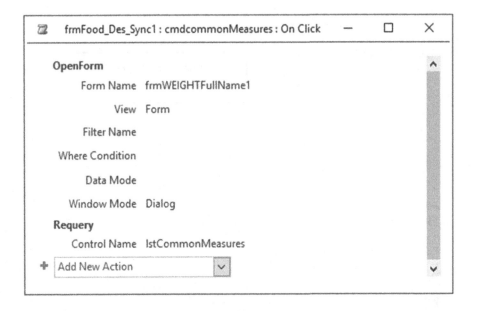

Figure 5-48. *The macro code embedded on cmdCommonMeasure opens frmWeightFullName1 on a modal state (using a OpenForm action with Window Mode = Dialog), which makes the code stop until the form is closed. When this happens, it executes the Requery action to update the lstCommonMeasures List Box*

Tip   You can also double-click lstCommonMeasures to show frmWeightFullName1 because it has the same macro code on its On Dbl Click event.

To make the frmWeightFullName1 form open in a modal state, it uses an OpenForm action with argument Window Mode set to Dialog, stopping the code at this point without allowing any Access interface interaction until the form is closed.

After the frnWeightFullName1 form is closed, it executes a Requery action with Control Name set to lstCommonMeasures, which forces the List Box to update its Row Source property and show any common measures changes.

The frmWeightFullName1 Form

To understand what happens in frmWeightFullName1, open it in Design mode and note its txtFoodItem Control Source property.

Then show the Property Sheet's Data tab and note that its Record Source is set to qryWeightFullName1. Click the ... at the right of the property name to show the Query Builder window and analyze how this query works (Figure 5-49).

> **Note**   Since the txtFoodItem Text Box has an expression on its Control Source property, it automatically avoids any changes on its value. In addition, it has its property Locked set to Yes to not allow it to be selected.

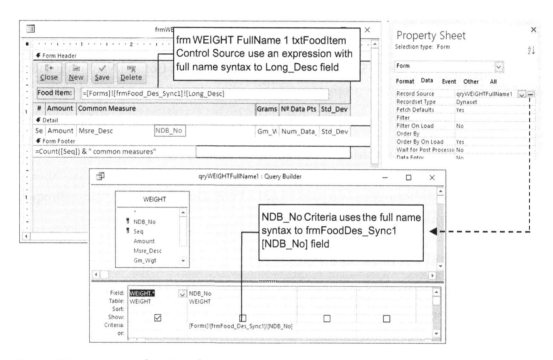

Figure 5-49. *Form frmWeightFullName1 uses the full syntax to frmFood_Des_ Sync1 on the txtFoodItem Text Box to show the current food item name and also uses it on the qryWeightFullName1 criteria, to show just the desired WEIGHT table records (without an alias on its name)*

To change frmWeightFullName1 title bar text, select the Property Sheet's Event tab and open its On Load embedded macro code (Figure 5-50).

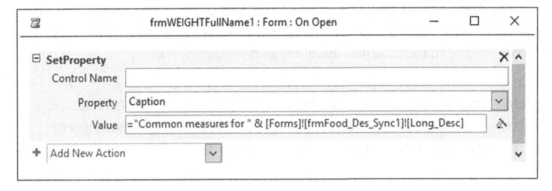

Figure 5-50. *frmwWEIGHTFullName1's On Open Event macro code uses a Set Property action to change the form's title bar text*

The On Load event uses a Set Property action that leaves its Control Name argument empty to set the Form Caption property, with this expression on its argument Value:

```
="Common measures for " & [Forms]![frmFood_Des_Sync1]![Long_Desc]
```

This expression creates a string that concatenates the "Common measures for " text with the full name syntax to the Long_Desc control that stores the food item name actually shown on the form frmFood_Des_Sync1's Long_Desc field (the same technique used to fill the form's txtFoodItem Text Box).

Inserting Related Records on a Form

To allow frmWeightFullName1 to insert new weight table records correctly related to the current record shown on its frmFood_Des_Sync1 field (the "one" side of the relationship), it uses a simple technique on the NDB_No Text Box by setting these properties (Figure 5-51):

- *Control Source = NDB_No*: This sets the field of the WEIGHT table that represents the "many" side of the relationship.

- *Visible = No*: This sets it to be hidden from the user; set this to Yes for every common measure record.

- *Fore Color = Border Color = #ED1C24*: This sets a red color on the border and text to allow you to identify it as a hidden control in Design view.

- *Default Value = Forms]![frmFood_Des_Sync1]![NDB_No]:* This
  receives the NDB_No value of the item shown on the frmFood_Des_
  Sync1 form.

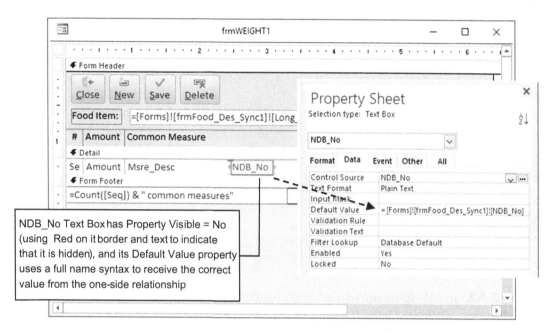

Figure 5-51. *To guarantee that each new common measure record inserted in the WEIGHT table receives the correct association, the hidden NDB_No Text Box Default Value property uses the full name syntax to the frmFood_Des_Sync1!NDB_No field*

Calculating the Next Sequence Number for a Common Measure

Since every common measure record for each food item has a sequence number (WEIGHT table's Seq field) to indicate its importance, whenever you need to insert a new record, it is a good idea to also calculate it automatically and not allow any user change on this sequence order.

That is why the frmFood_Des_Sync1 Seq Text Box (which uses the Label caption # to indicate a count) has Enabled set to No and Locked set to Yes, to not allow it to be selected, while its Default Value property uses an expression to allow you to return the next common measure sequence number (Figure 5-52).

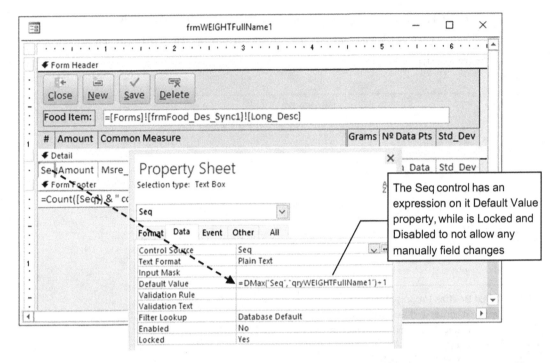

Figure 5-52. *frmWeightFullName1 Seq control is disabled and locked to not allow field changes, while its Default Value property has an expression that correctly calculates the next Seq field value*

The Seq Text Box's Default Value property uses this expression to calculate the correct sequence number for any new record:

$$=DMAX("Seq","qryWeightFullName1")+1$$

Once again, it uses the DMAX() domain function to retrieve the maximum value for the Seq field of the qryWeightFullName1 query (the form's Record Source) and adds 1 to the returned value, automatically sequence numbering each new record.

Using Temporary Variables

There is no doubt that frmFood_Des_Sync1 works well by using the full name syntax strategy to show each food item's common measures on its lstCommonMeasures List Box and manage them using the frmWeightFullName1 form.

But a problem arises whenever this full name syntax is used: frmWeightFullName1 can't be used if frmFood_Des_Sync1 is closed.

To circumvent this inconvenience, instead of using the full name syntax to a form control, use a *temporary variable*, which is a programming object that represents a place in the memory that can store a value to be reused by the code.

Access allows you to create two types of temporary variables on a macro code.

- *Local temporary variable*: A temporary variable that can be used just inside the macro code where it was defined

- *Global temporary variable*: A temporary variable that can be used anywhere in the database such as in another macro, an event procedure, or on a query, form, or report

To create a local or global temporary variable, use the SetLocalVar or SetTempVar macro action, which is the topic of the following sections.

The SetLocalVar Action

Use the SetLocaVar action to create a local temporary variable whose value can be used only in the macro in which it is defined.

The SetLocalVar action has two arguments.

- *Name*: The name of the temporary variable

- *Expression*: A reference to a control or an expression that will be used to set the variable value

---

Note   Do not precede the expression with the equal (=) sign because it can lead to unpredictable results when the expression returns a string that can be associated to a nonexisting object.

Tip   I suggest prefixing any local variable name with a *l* character (from "local") to easily differentiate it from any other object used in the code.

Once a local temporary variable is created with the SetLocalVar action, use the LocalVars collection to access its value on subsequent macro actions using this syntax:

`[LocalVars]![LocalVariableName]`

All local temporary variables will be removed from memory when the macro code ends.

The SetTempVar Action

Use the SetTempVar action to create up to 256 global temporary variables, whose values will be available as long as the database is opened on any condition or argument of a macro action or in an expression used on a query, form, report, module, or procedure where a value is required.

Note   Although Microsoft Access used the short expression "Temp" (from "Temporary") to name this action, it indeed creates global temporary variables, ones that can be accessed anywhere and will remain available until the database be closed (or by using the RemoveTempVar and RemoveAllTempVars macro actions).

The SetTempVar action has two arguments.

- *Name*: The name of the temporary variable

- *Expression*: A reference to a control or an expression that will be used to set the variable value

---

Tip   I suggest prefixing any global temporary variable name with a *g* character (from "global") to easily differentiate it from any local variables or objects.

Once a global temporary variable is created with the SetTempVar action, use the TempVars collection to access the desired global temporary variable value, using this syntax:

```
[TempVars]![GlobalVariableName]
```

The RemoveTempVar and RemoveTempVars Actions

Since all global variables will remain available while the database is opened, use the RemoveTempVar action to remove any global temporary variable from memory. It has a single argument.

- *Name*: The name of the global temporary variable to remove from memory

To remove all global temporary variables at once, use the RemoveAllTempVars action, which has no arguments.

Global Variable in Action

Select the Database window's Macros group, open the stand-alone mcrSetTempVars macro in Design mode, and note that it has two SetTempVar actions to define the gNDB_No and gLong_Desc global variables (Figure 5-53).

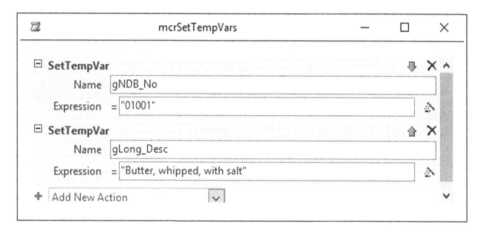

Figure 5-53. *The macro mcrSetTempVars uses the SetTempVar actions to set gNDB_No and gLong_Desc global variable values*

Attention   I couldn't set a temporary variable value whose name was prefixed with "gvar" characters (like gvarNDB_No). There is surely some bug that limits temporary variable names to a certain scope, and one of them is the "gvar" prefix.

It creates and sets the gNDB_No = "0100'1" and gLong_Desc = "Butter, whipped, with salt" global variables that represent the first FOOD_DES food item record's NDB_No and Long_Desc fields. Both are prefixed with the "g" character to identify them as global variables.

Execute mcrSetTempVars by clicking its Run (!) button on the Macro Design tab (or close the Macro window and double-click the stand-alone macro name in the Database window) to create the gNDB_No and gLong_Desc global variables and set their values.

Now open the qryWEIGHT_gNDB_No query in Design mode, and note that it uses the [TempVars]![gNDB_No] expression for the NDB_No field criteria to filter the records that must be returned. Run the query and note that it works, returning the desired WEIGHT table records (Figure 5-54).

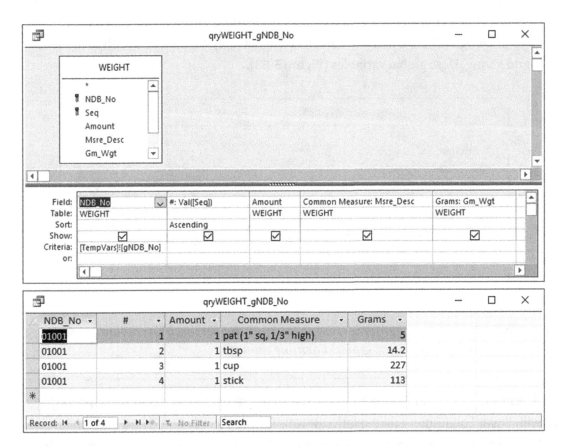

Figure 5-54. *The qryWEIGHT_gNDB_No query uses the TempVars collection to access the global variable gNDB_No as a criteria to filter its records*

Now open frmWEIGHT in Design view, show the Property Sheet's Data tab, and note that its property Record Source is set to WEIGHT, indicating that it accesses by default all WEIGHT table records.

Select the frmWEIGHT Property Sheet's Event tab and click the ... button right next to its On Load event to show the embedded macro code. Note that it uses two Set Property actions: the first sets the form's Caption property, and the second sets the txtFoodItem.Value property (both actions use the TempVars collection to access the gLong_Desc global variable, as shown in Figure 5-55).

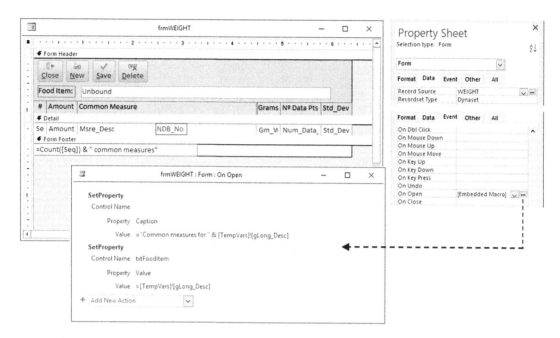

Figure 5-55. *frmWEIGHT returns all WEIGHT table records and uses embedded macro code on its On Load event to use the Set Property action to define its Caption property and txtFoodItem value using the TempVars!gLong_Desc global variable*

Open frmWEIGHT in Form view, and note that although it changed its title bar text (Form.Caption property) and txtFoodItem value, it returns all 15,439 WEIGHT table records (Figure 5-56).

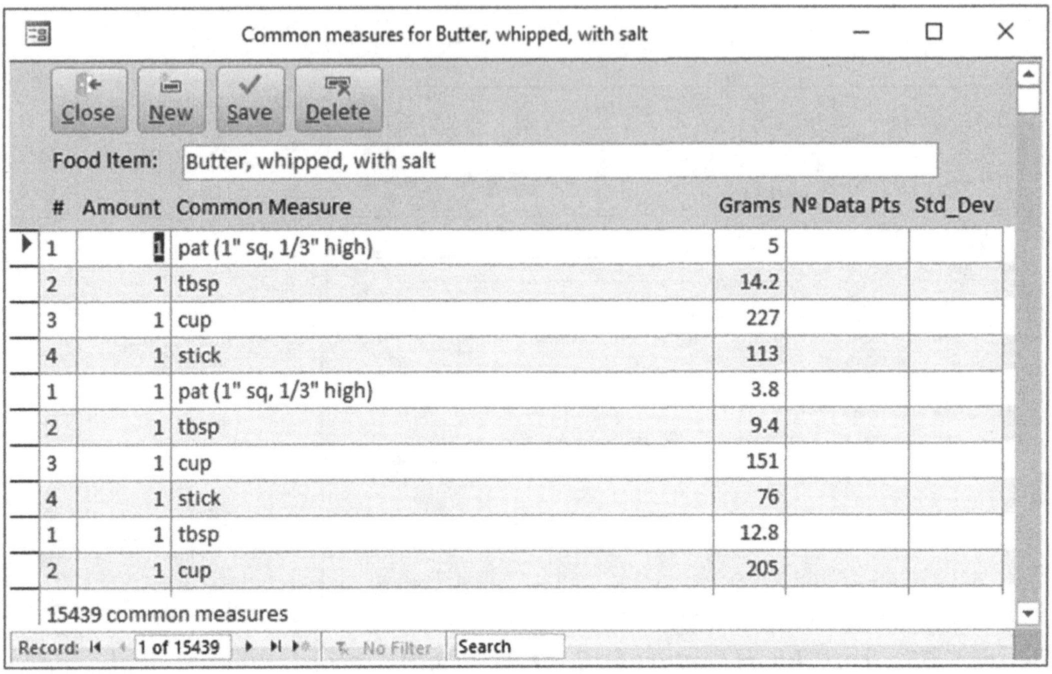

Figure 5-56. *Form frmWEIGHT returns all 15,439 WEIGHT table records, although its On Load event changes the Form.Caption and txtFoodItem.Values properties according to the value of the gLong_Desc global variable*

To see frmWEIGHT in action, open frmFood_Des_Sync2 in Design view, select the cmdCommonMeasures Command Button, show the Property Sheet window's Event tab, and click the ... button right next to its On Click event to show its embedded macro code (Figure 5-57).

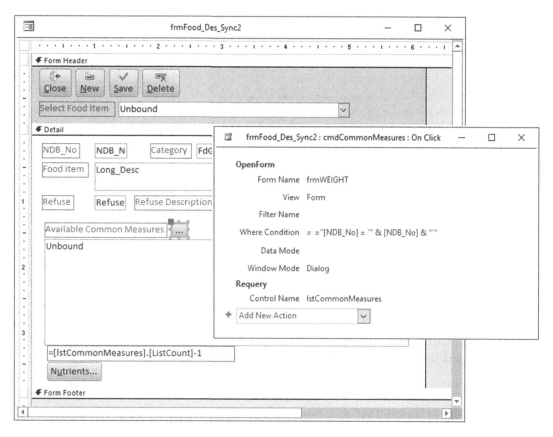

Figure 5-57. *The frmFood_Des_Sync2 cmdCommonMeasure On Click event uses an Open Form action whose Where Condition argument uses an expression that returns the desired form records*

This time, the macro code uses a new technique to show the desired frmWEIGHT records: it uses an expression on the Open Form action with argument Form Name=frmWEIGHT and its Where Condition argument to define which records must be returned (note that the expression begins with = to force its evaluation, embedding the Form [NDB_No] field between single quotes, because the value is a numeric string):

```
="NDB_No = '" & [NDB_No] & "'"
```

Knowing that the frmWEIGHT form's On Load event sets the form. Set the Caption and txtFoodItem.Value properties, show frmFood_Des_Sync2 in Form view, select any food item, and click cmdCommonMeasures to access its common measures records, as explained later (Figure 5-58).

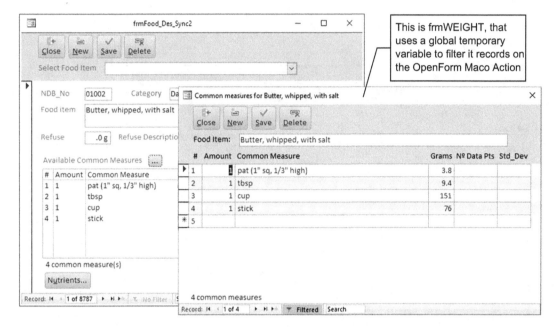

Figure 5-58. Although frmWEIGHT returns all WEIGHT records, by using a Open Form action's Where Condition argument, it can show the desired records

---

Note   By linking frmWEIGHT to a table instead of a query and using the Open Form action's Where Condition argument to select which records the form must show, it becomes an independent form that can be reused in other application scenarios without expecting that the base frmFood_Des_Sync2 form be open.

Synchronizing Independent Forms

Another technique that needs macro actions to work occurs when the developer decides to show the main side of the relationship using an independent, floating form, which has its property PopUp set to Yes. Whenever the record changes on the main base form, the forms must requery to show the desired records.

Form frmFood_Des_Sync2 uses this technique to show nutrient values for any food item, whenever the cmdNutrients Command Button, located below lstCommonMeasure, is clicked to show frmPopUpNutrients in its own window.

Tip   frmPopUpNutrients was previously positioned and saved in the form's Design view to appear slightly below and to the right of frmFood_Des_Sync2.

Figure 5-59 describes the frmPopUpNutrients control names and shows its Format, Event, and Other properties that were changed to make it function so you can get a better understanding of the explanations that follow.

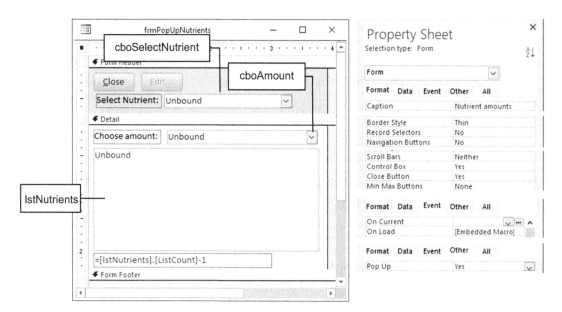

Figure 5-59. *frmPopUpNutrients control names*

Form frmPopUpNutrients has no Record Source property, meaning that it is an unbound form, not linked to any data source. Some of its properties were changed to make it behave as expected.

- *Caption = Nutrient Amounts*: Indicates the form's title bar text

Attention   There is no way to change a PopUp Form Caption property from an external source using a macro code.

- *Border Style = Thin*: Doesn't allow you to change the form size

- *Record Selector and Navigation Buttons = No*: Removes the record selector at the right and the navigation buttons at the bottom of window

- *Scroll Bars = Neither*: Doesn't allow any scroll bar

- *Control Box and Close Button = Yes*: Displays the icon in the window's top-left corner and the traditional "X" button to close it at the top-right corner.

- *Min Max Buttons = No*: Removes minimize, restore, and maximize buttons to not allow the form to change it size

- *PopUp = Yes*: Allows it to float over the screen as an independent form

---

Tip   Prefix every form whose PopUp property is set to Yes with the "frmPopUp" tag to easily distinguish its behavior from other form objects.

Updating frmPopUpNutrients Information

Use form frmFood_Des_Sync2's navigation buttons (or Page Down key) to show another record and note how frmPopUpNutrients requeries its controls to show nutrient information for the current food item (Figure 5-60).

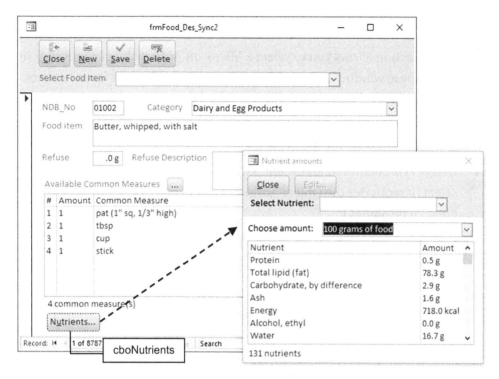

Figure 5-60. *Open frmFood_Des_Sync2 in Form view, and click its cboNutrients Command Button located below lstCommonMeasures to show current record nutrient values*

I think that by now you already know that frmFood_Des_Sync2 synchronizes frmPopUpNutrients using an embedded macro code on its On Current event. And since Microsoft Access macro actions do not allow requerying a control on another form, the macro code must execute this sequence of actions:

- Use the SetTempVar action to set the desired global variable values.

- Use the SelectObject action to select the frmPopUpNutrients window.

- Use the Requery action to update the desired controls.

- Use the SelectObject action to reselect the base form's frmFood_Des_Sync2 window.

The SelectObject Action

The SelectObject action allows you to select a Microsoft Access object window or its name in the Database window. It is useful to change the application focus between windows and execute macro actions that act on an object external to the one that executes the macro code.

The SelectObject action has three arguments.

- *Object Type*: Required argument. This indicates the object type to select (it requeries the Object Name argument with the selected object type names).

- *Object Name*: Required argument. This is the name of the object to select on the list, unless argument In Navigation Pane is set to Yes.

- *In Navigation Pane*: Optional. This allows you to select the object in the navigation pane if set to Yes (the default is No, to select the object window).

The Base Form's On Current Event

Click the frmFood_Des_Sync2 window, select the Layout view to show the Properties Sheet window's Event tab, and click the Form On Current event to show its macro code.

Figure 5-61 shows the frmFood_Des_Sync2 On Current event macro code actions sequence using a collapsed view so you can better understand its actions sequence.

Figure 5-61. *This is the frmFood_Des_Sync2 form's On Current event macro code using the collapsed view*

Note that frmFood_Des_Sync2's On Current event is full of Comment actions (bold, green actions) to indicate what each action does whenever another record is selected.

- The On Error Next action disables eventual runtime errors.

- An IF action synchronizes cboSelectFoodItem items located in the Form Header section (as explained earlier).

- Two SetTempVar actions are used to set gNDB_No and gLong_Desc global variables to the current record NDB_No and Long_Desc fields, respectively.

- A Requery action is used to update lstCommonMeasures.

- A SelectObject action tries to select the frmPopUpNutrients window. This action will raise an error if the form is not opened.

- An IF action verifies IF MacroError = 0, indicating that frmPopUpNutrients is opened and its window was selected. If it is opened, the application focus is set to frmPopUpNutrients and the following happens:

  - A Requery action is used to update the frmPopUpNutrients cboAmount Combo Box.

  - A SetValue action is used to set cboAmount to 100 (because NUTR_DATA nutrient values are expressed for each 100 grams of food).

  - A Requery action is used to update the frmPopUpNutrients cboSelectNutrients Combo Box.

  - A Requery action is used to update the frmPopUpNutrients lstNutrients List Box.

  - A SelectObject action selects frmFood_Des_Sync2 to return the application focus to the base form.

The final result you see on your computer screen is that the interface blinks for a second while updating the base form frmFood_Des_Sync2 lstCommonMeasures List Box. It then updates the frmPopUpNutrients controls, and the focus is returned to the base form.

Attention   By using VBA code, there is no need to change the application focus between opened forms, and the interface synchronization probably runs faster and smoother, without any interface blinks.

The frmPopUpNutrients Window

Although small, frmPopUpNutrients is full of advanced macro interface tricks that deserve to be mentioned, so you can measure the amount of knowledge you gathered so far on this book.

Using the frmPopUpNutrients interface controls, you can do the following:

- Requery the lstNutrient List Box control to recalculate nutrient values according to the common measure selected in the cboAmount Combo Box (Figure 5-62).

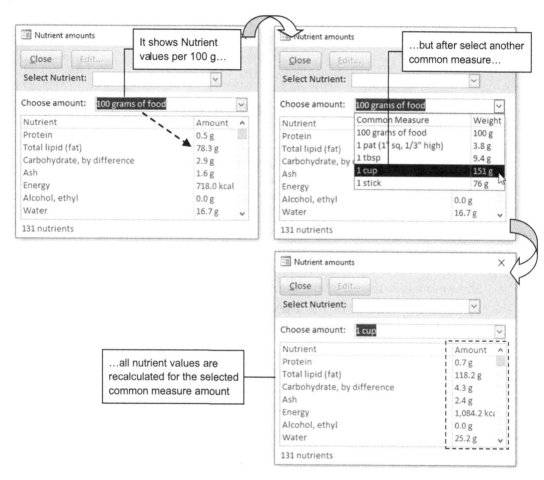

Figure 5-62. *frmPopUpNutrients shows nutrient values per 100 grams of food by default. But by selecting any other food item common measure, nutrient values are recalculated to this food item's portion size*

- Quickly select any nutrient in the lstNutrients List Box using the cboSelectNutrients Combo Box, located in the Form Header section (Figure 5-63).

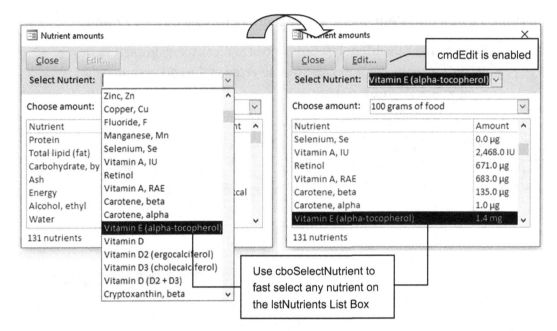

Figure 5-63. *Use cboSelectNutrient located in the Form Header section to quickly select any nutrient on the extensive lstNutrient List Box list of items*

- Show more information about the selected nutrient as a record automatically selected on the frmNutrients modal form (Figure 5-64).

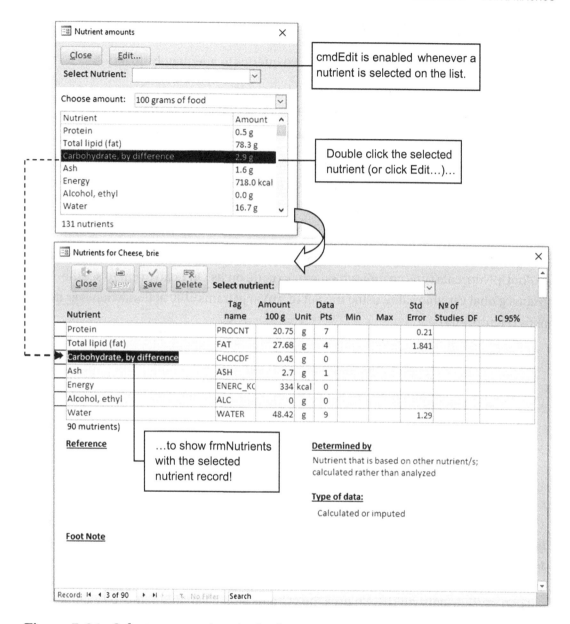

Figure 5-64. *Select any nutrient in the lstNutrients List Box to enable cmdEdit. Click cmdEdit (or double-click the desired nutrient) to open frmNutrients in a modal state, with the selected nutrient record*

Let's see how each of one of these tricks works!

Recalculating Nutrient Values

The frmPopUpNutrients form is based on two queries to adequately do its job.

- *qryNutrients_gNDB_No*: Used by cboSelectNutrient and lstNutrients is a Select query that uses the gNDB_No global variable to return just the selected food item nutrient names and amounts.

- *qryNutrients_gNDB_No_UNION_100g*: Used by the cboAmount Combo Box is a Union query based on qryNutrients_gNDB_No that also adds the "100 grams of food" text as its first record for every food item.

Since the NUTR_DATA table records show nutrient values for 100 grams of food, frmPopUpNutrients runs an embedded macro code on its On Load event to set the gGrams global variable value using the SetTempVar gGrams=100 action whenever it opens (Figure 5-65).

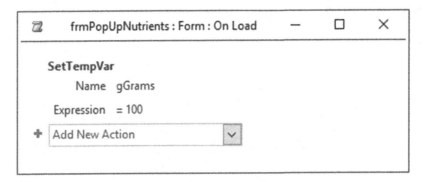

Figure 5-65. *This is the frmPopUpNutrients On Load event macro code, which uses the SetTempVar action to set gGrams to 100*

Then qryNutrients_gNDB_No uses the gGrams global variable value to calculate each nutrient value on its Amount field, while it uses the gNDB_No global variable value to return just current food item nutrients and their values (Figure 5-66).

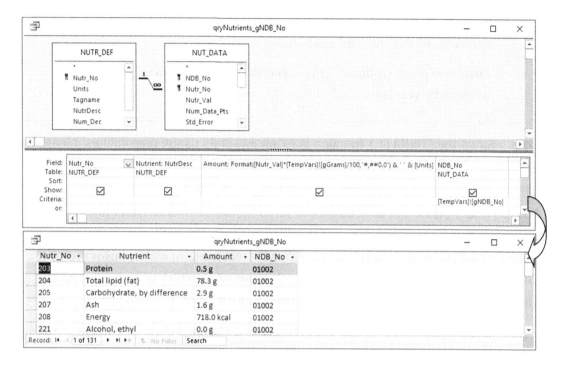

Figure 5-66. *qryNutrients_gNDB_No uses the TempVars!gNDB_No global variable to filter nutrient records for the selected food item, while using the gGrams variable on its Amount field to recalculate nutrient values*

To return the Amount column with nutrient values using a single decimal place of precision suffixed by its appropriate unit (like "g" or "kcal"), it uses the FORMAT() function.

The FORMAT() Function

The FORMAT() function works identically to the Format property already discussed in Chapter 2. It receives an expression and uses the same Format properties characters to return a formatted result.

The FORMAT() function has this syntax:

```
Format(Expr, [format], [firstdayofweek], [firstweekofyear])
```

where:

- *Expr*: Required. This is any valid expression or control name or field value.

- *Format*: Optional. This is a user-defined format expression between double quotes, using specific format characters.

449

- *Firstdayofweek*: Optional. This is used for days; define the first day of the week. By default, 1 means Sunday.

- *Firstweekofyear*: Optional. This is a constant that specifies the first week of the year (by default this is 1).

Note   Since the FORMAT() function is extensive in its usage possibilities, please refer to Chapter 2 for more information about special characters you can use to format a value or use the Microsoft Office site for more information about how you can use it to produce the desired format for text, numbers, dates, and hours.

Figure 5-66 shows that the qryNutrients_gNDB_No Amount column uses the TempVars.gGrams syntax to create a direct rule expression, which is further formatted with the FORMAT() function to allow you to recalculate records' nutrient values.

```
Amount: Format([Nutr_Val]*[TempVars]![gGrams]/100,"#,##0.0") & " " & [Units]
```

This expression first multiplies the NUTR_DATA Nutr_Val field value by the TempVars!gGrams global variable and divides it by 100 (grams). If gGrams = 100, it will multiply the Nutr_Val value by 1.

To show the result with one decimal place of precision, it uses the FORMAT() function with its Format argument set to #,##0.0, which means that it will always show 0.0 for zero values or use one decimal place of precision for other values, showing the thousand separator for values greater than 1,000.

The expression concatenates the FORMAT() function's returned value to the NUTR_ DATA [Units] field, creating expressions like "100.0 g" or "1,123,0 kcal."

The query qryNutrients_gNDB_No is then used to fill in both the cboSelectNutrient Combo Box and lstNutrients List Box controls list of items.

Formatting lstNutrients List Box

The lstNutrients List Box is an unbound control that uses these properties to show nutrient values for the selected food item (Figure 5-67).

- *Row Source = qryNutrients_gNDB_No*

- *Bound Column = 1*: This is the Nutr_No field that identifies the nutrient code.

- *Column Count = 3*: This specifies to use just the first three query columns.

- *Column Widths = 0,' 2.7'*: The bound column is hidden, the second column is 2.7 inches (manually set by trial and error), and the third column uses remaining List Box width.

- *Column Heads = Yes*: This shows "Nutrient" and "Amount" text on the first list item.

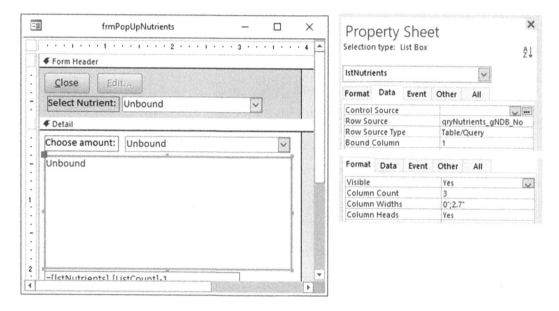

Figure 5-67. *To adequately show qryNutrients_gNDB_No records, the lstNutrients List Box sets some specific Format and Data properties. Note that the control returns the NUTR_DATA table's Nutr_No field whenever an item is selected on the list*

Whenever an item is selected on the lstNutrients List Box, this control's Value property is set to the Nutr_No value, indicating the nutrient code on the NUTR_DATA table.

Now let's see how cboAmount shows its list items and recalculates the lstNutrient values.

Formatting the cboAmount Combo Box

The cboAmount Combo Box uses a Union query to fulfill its list of items because it needs to add the fake "100 grams of food" record as the first list item for every food item.

Open qryWEIGHT_gNDB_No_UNION_100g in SQL mode to see how it uses the UNION instruction to group two Select SQL instructions. Execute the query to realize that it will return all the food item common measures plus the "100 grams of food" fake record as the first query record (Figure 5-68).

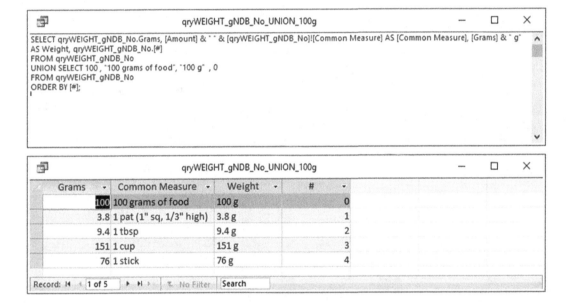

Figure 5-68. *This is qryWEIGHT_gNDB_No_UNION_100g in SQL view. It uses the UNION word to concatenate a query with a fake record that uses the "100 grams of food" expression on its Common Measure field's first record*

The qryWEIGHT_gNDB_No_UNION_100g has four columns: Grams, Common Measure, Weight, and # (to indicate the sort order). Just the first three are used to fulfill cboAmount Combo Box's list of items, which uses these properties (Figure 5-69):

- *Row Source = qryWEIGHT_gNDB_No_UNION_100g*

- *Bound Column = 1*: This is the grams field that indicates the nutrient amount in grams.

- *Column Count = 3*: This uses just the first three query fields.

- *Column Widths = 0', 1.9'*: The first column (Weight) is hidden, the second column is 1.9 inches (set by trial and error), and the third column uses the remaining control width.

- *Column Heads = Yes*: This shows "Common Measure" and "Amount" text on the first list item.

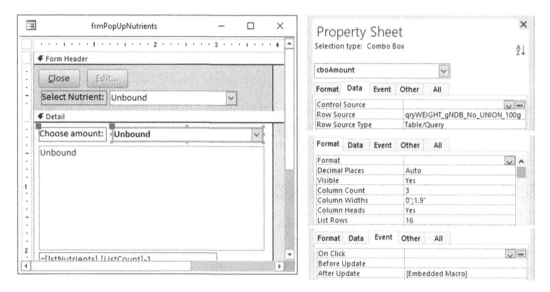

Figure 5-69. *To show the first three fields of the qryWEIGHT_gNDB_No_ UNION_100g query, the cboAmount Combo Box sets specific Format and Data properties. Since its Bound Column is set to 1, the control returns the Grams query field whenever a item is selected*

By setting these properties, whenever a common measure is selected on the cboAmount Combo Box, it returns the Grams field, which has the nutrient value in grams (Bound column = 1).

Based on Figure 5-68 and the knowledge you have gathered so far, you already know what happens: when an item is selected on the cboAmount Combo Box, its After Update event fires and executes the macro code that uses the gGrams global variable with the selected common measure Grams value and then uses a Requery action to force lstNutrients to requery and update its list items with the new nutrient values!

Figure 5-70 shows the cboAmount After Update macro code that executes these actions.

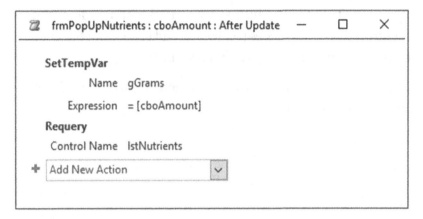

Figure 5-70. *This is cboAmount's After Update embedded macro code. It updates the gGrams global variable value and requeries lstNutrients to recalculate the nutrient amount for any available common measure weight*

Selecting an Item on a List Box Control

Since each food item can have an extensive amount of nutrient values and nutrients are not shown in alphabetical order, finding the desired nutrient by scrolling the lstNutrients list of items may be a painful task.

That is why frmPopUpNutrients offers the cboSelectNutrient Combo Box in its Form Header section: to allow you to quickly select any nutrient on the lstNutrients List Box by typing its initials and pressing Enter (as Figure 5-64 shows).

Note   Nutrient names are usually grouped by category so that a specific nutrient can be more easily found by anyone with a background in health sciences, who expects them to appear together on the list. For example, all macro nutrients (Water, Protein, CHO, Lipid, etc.), vitamins, amino acids, etc., should appear grouped. According to the `sr_doc.PDF` documentation, the NUT_DEF table offers the SR_Order field to allow you to group nutrients properly. That is why lstNutrients and cboSelectNutrient do not show nutrients in alphabetical order. Both controls use qryNutrients_gNDB_No in the Row Source property to show nutrient names grouped by SR_Order and then by NDB_No (nutrient code) fields.

To show the same nutrients of the lstNutrients List Box, the cboSelectNutrient Combo Box sets these Data and Format properties (Figure 5-71):

- *Row Source = qryNutrients_gNDB_No*

- *Bound Column =1*: This is the Nutr_No field that indicates the nutrient code.

- *Column Count = 2*: This uses just the first two query fields.

- *Column Widths = 0'*: The first column (Nutr_No) is hidden, and the second column uses the remaining control width.

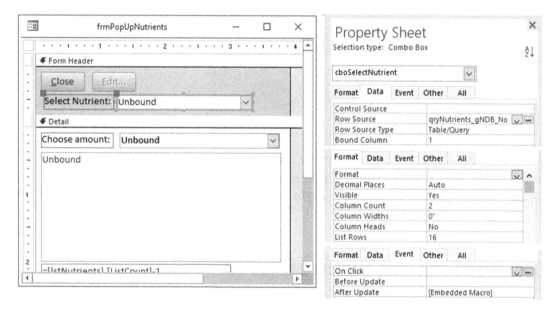

Figure 5-71. *cboSelectNutrient uses qryNutrients_gNDB_No to show the same nutrient names exibited by the lstNutrient List Box (grouped by nutrient category). Whenever a nutrient name is selected, it returns the associated Nutr_No nutrient code*

Since both the cboSelectNutrient Combo Box and lstNutrients List Box use the same base query, they return the same value (Nutr_No field), and the List Box control has the characteristic of selecting and showing the list item that has the control's Value property. To show the desired nutrient typed in the cboSelectNutrient Combo Box, just set lstNutrients to cboSelectNutrient to do the trick.

Of course, this is made on cboSelectNutrient's After Update embedded macro code, which uses a SetProperty action to equal both control values, and since the control is selected, it uses a second SetProperty action to change the cmdEdit Command Button's Enabled property to True (Figure 5-72).

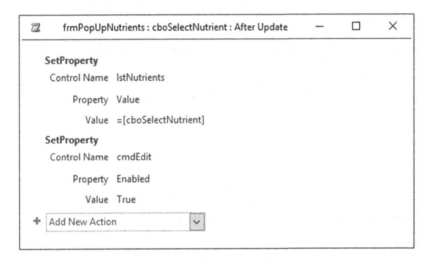

Figure 5-72. *This is cboSelectNutrient Combo Box's After Update embedded macro code. It uses a SetProperty action to set lstNutrients to cboSelectNutrient's value. As a bonus, it uses another SetProperty action to set cmdEdit.Enabled to True*

Opening a Form with a Record Selected

The last interface synchronization actions allowed by the frmPopUpNutrients form happen whenever the user selects an item on the lstNutrients List Box by clicking the control, and then enables cmdEdit on topo of the form, to allow edit the selected item on an independent window.

Whenever this happens, the lstNutrients List Box control will return the value of Nutr_No for the currently selected row, and its After Update event fires, executing an embedded macro code that changes cmdEdit Enabled to True, thus enabling the Command Button to allow you to edit the selected nutrient (Figure 5-73).

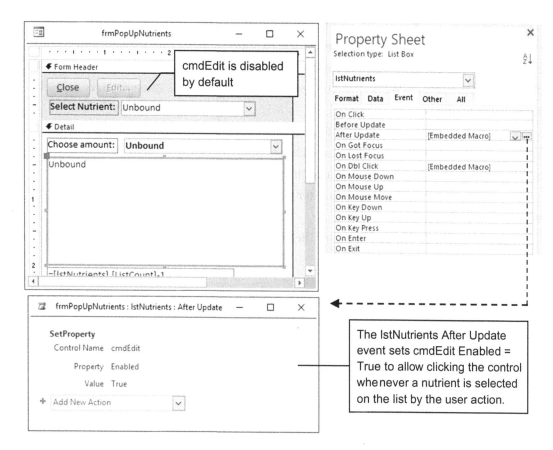

Figure 5-73. *To allow a perfect interface synchronization, whenever lstNutrients changes its value by the user action, its After Update event fire, executing a SetProperty action to set cmdEdit Enabled to True*

Note   For an unknown reason, the lstNutrients After Update event does not cascade fire when the List Box value is changed by an external event code. That is why the cboSelectNutrient After Update event needs to use a second SetProperty action to set cmdEdit.Enabled to True.

Now the form interface offers two options to edit the nutrient selected on lstNutrients List Box.

- By clicking the cmdEdit Command Button

- By double-clicking the lstNutrients Combo Box

Whenever one of these user actions takes place, it is expected that the frmNutrients form opens, uses the SearchForRecord action to automatically find the nutrient record selected on the lstNutrient List Box, and allows you to change its values (see Figure 5-64). After the edit process ends and frmNutrients closes, lstNutrients must requery to show any nutrient changes.

Since there is no macro action that allows the execution of another object's event macro code, the cmdEdit On Click and lstNutrients On Dbl Click events must duplicate the same macro code to show frmNutrients in a modal state and allow you to edit nutrients' record values (lstNutrients After Update event can't call the cmdEdit On Click event macro code and vice versa).

Figure 5-74 shows the cmdEdit On Click event (which is the same for the lstNutrients On DblClick event).

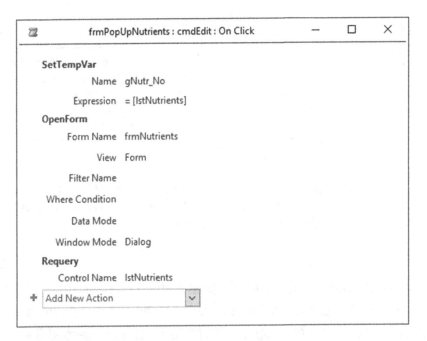

Figure 5-74. *This is cmdEdit's On Click event, used to allow editing of the selected nutrient on the lstNutrients List Box. It executes the same code used by the lstNutrients On Dbl Click event that also allows editing a nutrient by double-clicking it in the lstNutrients List Box*

The cmdEdit On Click macro code executes these actions:

- A SetTempVar action executes to set the global variable gNutr_No to the lstNutrients value.

- An OpenForm action opens frmNutrients using Window Mode set to Dialog, which will stop the code at this point until frmNutrients be closed.

- After frmNutrients closes, a Requery action updates the lstNutrients List Box so any record changes can be shown.

Attention   Whenever you have a PopUp form opened in the Access interface, the only way you can make another form open in front of it is by using the OpenForm action with the argument Window Mode set to Dialog.

When the OpenForm action opens frmNutrients, its On Load event will fire, executing the embedded macro code shown in Figure 5-75.

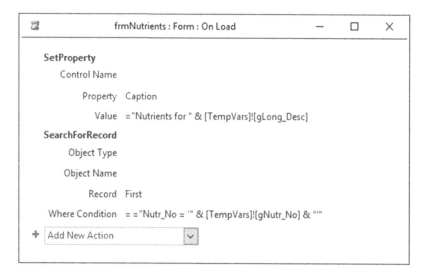

Figure 5-75. *This is frmNutrients' On Load event embedded macro code. It uses the gLong_Desc (nutrient name) and gNutr_No (nutrient code) global variable values to allow you to select the desired record*

The frmNutrients.Caption property changes the form's title bar text by using this expression:

```
'Nutrients for " & [TempVars]![gLong_Desc]
```

The SearchForRecord action uses this expression on its Where Condition argument (it encloses the gNDB_No value in single quotes because it is indeed a numeric string):

```
="Nutr_No = '" & [TempVars]![gNDB_No] & "'"
```

Figure 5-64 shows the result: the desired nutrient is selected on the modal form, which will stop all other interface operations until it is closed.

Summary

Microsoft Access macro codes are an excellent way to give you your first look at the world of programming database applications because it offers a high-level interface full of special actions that allow you to create sequential code without typing it. Just select the actions sequence and use the appropriate argument values to achieve the desired result.

In the next chapter, you will learn about reports and how to use them to create nice printouts with Microsoft Access.

CHAPTER 6

Using Reports

Microsoft Access reports are the way you can create a nice presentation of the database records. Like forms, they have a formal structure that, when understood, allows you to produce a great variety of high-quality printouts, from single resume records to complex corporation analysis.

In this chapter, you will learn how to create nice reports using Microsoft Access Report objects. You can obtain all the database objects cited in this chapter by extracting the file sr28_Reports.accdb from CHAPTER06.zip, which can be downloaded from the following website:

https://github.com/Apress/intro-microsoft-access-using-macro-prog-techniques

The Report Object Structure

The Report object in Microsoft Access has a structure similar to the Form object in terms of sections and their names, but they look different when they appear on a printed page.

Many people have complained about the way that Microsoft reports work, mainly because Access puts the different properties for different parts (such as the printed page, the report itself, its sections and group options, and the Text Box control behavior) in different places.

So, let's learn about the report structure with a hands-on example. To begin, use the Report Design command on the Create tab to open a new Report object window in Design mode. By default, it will show three basic sections: Page Header, Detail, and Page Footer.

Like a Form object, reports have Report Header/Footer and Page Header/Footer sections (although you can create other sections for grouping purposes). So, right-click any report section and choose the Report Header/Footer option in the context menu that appears to show these report sections in the report's Design view (Figure 6-1).

© Flavio Morgado 2021
F. Morgado, *Introducing Microsoft Access Using Macro Programming Techniques*, https://doi.org/10.1007/978-1-4842-6555-0_6

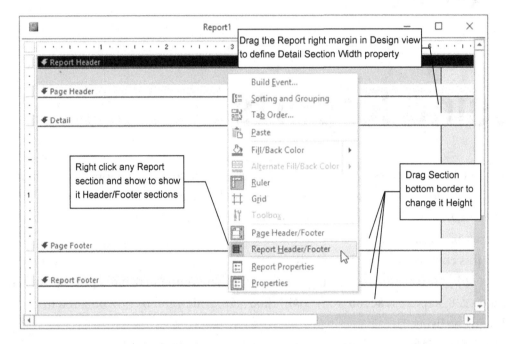

Figure 6-1. *A new Report object in Design mode, showing from top to bottom its Report Header, Page Header, Detail, Page Footer, and Report Footer sections*

Although these basic report sections mimic the same ones in a form, they behave differently and print in a specific order.

- *Report Header*: This is the first printed section, and it prints only once. This is supposed to be used as a first header that will appear only once before the Page Header section, although you can also use it on the first report pages to insert a report cover, introductory text, or explanations about what the report contains. In this case, this page will show a page header.

- *Page Header*: This prints a page header on every page (after the Report Header page). Use this section to insert report identifications, such as a logo, title, page number and count, date of print, credits, etc.

- *Detail*: This works like a form's Detail section whose Default View property is set to Continuous Form. It prints successively once for each record.

- *Page Footer*: This prints a page footer on every page (including first Report Header page). Use this section to insert report identifications, such as a logo, title, page number and count, date of print, credits, etc.

- *Report Footer*: This is the last printed page and prints only once. Use this section to make a final report and finish the document.

Setting a Report Section's Width and Height

The report width is set for all the report sections by dragging the report's Design view right margin to the desired size. In doing that, just the Detail section's Width property is changed, although this impacts all the other section widths.

The section height can be changed individually for each section. To change a section height, you must first select it by clicking in the section's name bar and then using one of these two methods:

- Show the Property Sheet window's Format tab and set the Section Height property to the desired vertical value, in inches.

- Drag the section's bottom border to the desired height, which for most sections is the next section's top border, or click the thin black line that separates the last white page from the report's gray area.

The Detail section, which prints for every report record, must have its height reduced to the minimum size required to print a record so it can convey enough information without generating unnecessary paper.

Tip   To hide any report section (including Detail), set its Height property to 0 inches (or drag its bottom border up until it has no height).

Maximum Allowed Pages on a Section

It is important to note that every report section (including Detail) has a maximum allowed height of 22 inches, which by default seems to allow print just two letter-sized pages (letter pages are 8½ × 11 inches).

Considering that a report section will print on independent pages, that it may also print the Page Header and Page Footer sections, and that the printed page also has top and bottom margins (defined in the Page Setup dialog box), all these heights can significantly reduce the effective vertical page space used by a section. This fact can automatically insert page breaks to extend it by up to four successive letter-sized pages.

This is important to know, because you can add a subreport to a section, and if it needs more than these three- or four-page limits, some of its data may not be printed due to the 22-inch section height limit having been achieved. Further, Access will not issue any complaints about this!

Report and Section Properties

You can set different properties for the report itself or for its sections to gain control over the printing process (and as you see later, there are also Group Section properties that can affect how records are grouped, sorted, and printed).

Some of them are equivalent to the form object properties that can be used to control the Report window appearance (such as Caption, Border Style, Control Button, Close Button, Restore, Min Max Buttons, PopUp, Modal, etc.) and will not be discussed in this chapter.

To facilitate the explanations in the upcoming sections, Table 6-1 describes specific Report object Format properties that deserve mention.

Table 6-1. *Report Object's Format Properties*

Tab	Report Property	Usage
Format	Default view	Defines the default view for a report when opened from the Database window. The default is Report view.
	Allow Report view	Indicates if the Report view can be used to show the report.
	Allow Layout view	Indicates if the Layout view can be used to show the report (this view allows you to change the report properties).
	Fit to Page	Allows you to set the report page width to automatically fit the page.
	Grp Keep Together	Specifies on a multicolumn report if group sections with the Keep Together property set to Whole Group or With First Detail will be kept together by page or by column.
	Picture Pages	Specifies which pages must show the Report Picture property.
	Page Header	Specifies whether the Page Header section must be printed on all pages or removed from Report Header, Report Footer, or both sections.
	Page Footer	Specifies whether the Page Footer section must be printed on all pages, or removed from Report Footer, Header Footer, or both sections.
Data	Record Source	Name of a table, query, or SQL instruction that returns the report records.
Other	Date Grouping	Defines how dates are grouped. The default is US System Settings; states that the first day of week is Sunday.

Table 6-2 specifies Format properties that can be used to control how each section will be printed. These properties relate to the Report Header section, the Report Footer section, and any other Group Header/Footer sections; they do not apply to the Page Header and Page Footer sections.

Table 6-2. *Section Format Properties*

Section Property	Usage
Height	Defines the section height used on a printed page
Auto Height	Allows the section height to adjust when controls are added to it
Can Grow	Allows the section height to extend to accommodate a Text Box or subreport content
Can Shrink	Allows the section height to reduce its size when it has no content
Keep Together	Keeps the section content on a single page
Force New Page	Allows you to insert a page break before or after the section content
New Row or Col	Allows you to insert a column break on a multicolumn report

In the next sections, you will learn how to use these properties on different Access reports.

Report Page Properties

The first step to create a report is to set the desired page properties, because they impact the way that many report and section properties will appear on a printed page.

Use the Page Setup command in the Page Layout area of the Page Setup tab of Report Design Tools to open the Page Setup dialog box. In this dialog box, you will find tabs to set the page size, margins, orientation, and column properties (Figure 6-2).

Note   The Page Setup tab of Report Design Tools has commands that work as shortcuts to the Page Setup dialog box tabs.

Page Size and Orientation

Use the Page Setup dialog box's Print Options and Page tabs to set the desired page size, print orientation, and margins that a report must use before starting the report creation.

Begin by using the Page tab to set the report's page orientation and size. Most Windows US printers use a letter-sized page as the default paper size and portrait orientation for it prints (Figure 6-2).

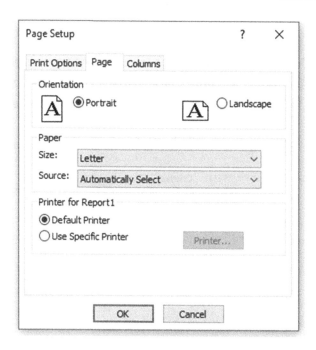

Figure 6-2. *In the Page Setup dialog box, define the paper orientation, size, and printer where to print the report before defining its section properties and content*

Tip   If your report demands a landscape orientation, set the report's Detail section's Width property accordingly, using the page's greatest dimension to allow a better distribution of controls inside using the report's Design view. For example, a Letter paper size setting can allow the Detail section to be set to 11 inches minus the page's left and right margins.

Note that Access allows you to set the report to print on the default system printer or on a specific printer (like a PDF printer, which common these days). Be aware that whenever you choose a specific printer, Access will expect that it is installed and available on the Windows system and will issue a warning message whenever you try to print a report on a unavailable printer.

Note   Different printers have different minimum margin size specifications. A PDF printer, for example, can use 0-inch margins, while most laser printers can't.

Margin Size

Use the Page Setup dialog box's Print Options tab to set the report's paper margins (in inches). By default, Access sets all paper margins to 0.25 inches, which limits a letter-sized page to ½ inch less in both its vertical and horizontal dimensions (Figure 6-3).

Figure 6-3. *This is the Page Setup dialog box's Print Options tab, where you can control the page margins*

Since a letter-sized page is 8½ × 11 inches, the effective size you can use to print a letter-sized page in portrait orientation is automatically reduced to 8 inches wide (maximum Width property of the Detail section) and to 10½ inches high, not considering the height of all report print sections summed but Detail section, which will print as many times as it can on each report page.

Caution   Access swaps the top and left, and bottom and right, margin sizes whenever you change orientations between portrait and landscape.

Considering that a report's Height properties for the Page Header and Footer sections are set by default to 0.25 inches, the effective vertical page area is reduced to other 0.5 inches, leaving 10 inches to print records in the form's Detail section.

Attention   If the form's Detail section's Width property is greater than the paper page width minus the page's left and right margins, Access will complain when it prints the report and may produce odd, half-filled print pages using the remaining information that could not fit on a single page.

Columns Properties

You can use the Page Setup dialog box's Columns tab to define a multiple-column report—one that can be used to lower the page count needed to print all the report records or to define a report that prints labels (Figure 6-4).

Figure 6-4. *Use the Page Setup's Columns tab to define a multicolumn report. This can be done by using the Details section's height and width or by ignoring the Details Width property and using a specific Column Size Width and Height values*

Note   As you will see later in this section, you can use the Labels command in the Reports area of the Create tab to show the Labels Wizard, which you can use to define a report that automatically prints different label sizes.

Using the Columns size, you can set the following:

- *Number of Columns*: Specify how many columns your report should have.

- *Row spacing*: Define the extra vertical space that must be added to the Detail section's Height property to separate each printed record (used by labels).

- *Column Spacing*: Define the space used to separate each report columns.

- *Column Size*: Manually set columns' width and height.

- *Same as Detail*: Define columns' width and height properties according to the Detail section's properties. Uncheck this option to manually set the column dimensions.

- *Column Layout*: Use one of the available options to define how Access will print the Detail section.

  - *Down, then Across*: Use this option to print normal, multicolumn reports that print information like a magazine or paper. It fills an entire column from the top down and then begins to fill the next column.

  - *Across, then Down*: Use this option when printing information that is expected to go from left to right, like labels or charts that convey report information, record by record.

Adding Date, Time, Page, and Credit

Database reports can convey more than just record data. They can be used to convey detailed data analysis about the last records inserted in the system.

So, take the time to add other important information such as the date and time of printing, page numbers, and the total page count, and give yourself credit for creating the report.

Such information should appear in the following places:

- In the Report Header section

- In the Page Header and Page Footer section

- In the Report Footer section (the last report page)

To add page, date, and time information to a report, use the tools in the Header/Footer section of the Design tab under Report Tools. This tab offers the Page Numbers and Date and Time tools; clicking them opens their respective dialog boxes, where you can select how the information will be formatted and eventually where it prints (Figure 6-5).

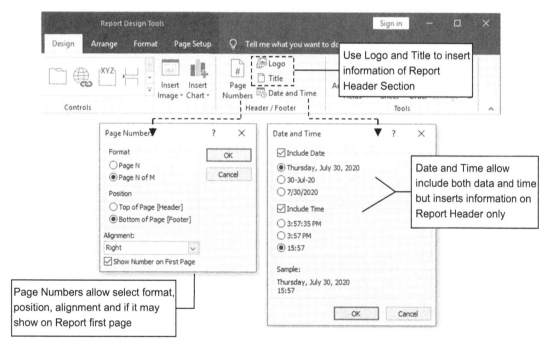

Figure 6-5. *Use the Report Tools Design tab's Header/Footer area to insert detailed information about page number and page count, the date and time of print, the report logo, and the title*

Figure 6-6 shows a new, unsaved Report window in Design and Print Preview mode that received all this information. Note the following:

- The Logo option uses the Apress trademark.

- The Title option received a special format using an 18-point Calibri Light font.

- The date and time by default are right-aligned in the report's Header section.

- To show the page number and number of total report pages, the Page Numbers dialog box inserted a Text Box that is right-aligned in the Page Footer section (as required). Its Control Source property received this expression and uses the [Page] and [Pages] Report properties. Note the whitespace used to correctly build the desired string, as shown here:

```
="Page " & [Page] & " of " & [Pages]
```

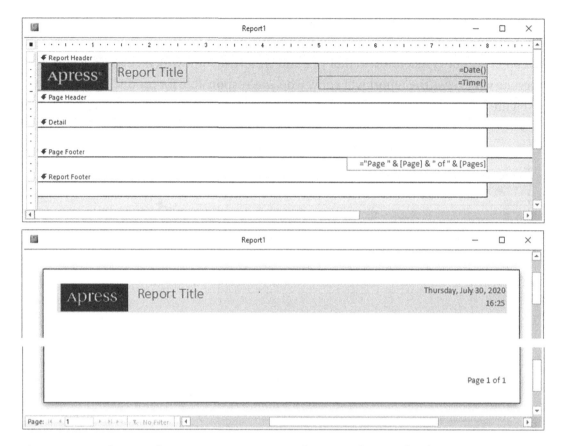

Figure 6-6. *This is a basic report structure showing the result of the Design tab's Header/Footer area tools used to add a logo, title, date, time, and page information to a report. Just the page number and page count information can be defined to print on the Page Header and Page Footer sections, and you can set their alignment*

Attention   The advantage of using such formatting options comes from the fact that you can use the Themes, Colors, and Fonts tools of the Themes area of the Design tab's Report Tools to easily change the report appearance.

Creating a Report Template

There is nothing wrong with the basic report structure shown in Figure 6-6, besides the fact that it is appears to be made by Access, not by you!

To add some design personalization to a basic report structure, you may show the date and time of printing on every page by moving its Text Box to the Page Header of the Footer section. I recommend that you add credit for your work on every page so everyone who views the report will know who was responsible for producing it.

Figure 6-7 shows rptApressTemplate in Design view and Print Preview mode.

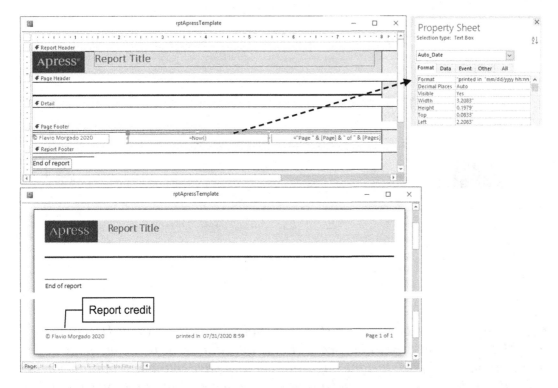

Figure 6-7. *This is the rptApressTemplate report in Design and Print Preview mode showing the beginning and end of the first page*

The report was changed in these subtle ways:

- The Report Header section lost the Date and Time Text Box controls.

- The Page Header section received just a 2-pt Line control. This will be used to show the required page information, such as field names that appear in the Detail section.

- All other report information (credits, date and time of print, page number, and page count) were transferred to the Page Footer section.

- The report uses the NOW() function to show the date and time of the print, using this personalized format:

  "printed in " mm/dd/yy hh:nn

- The Report Footer sections received Line and Label controls to define where the report ends.

Now, every other report that created in this chapter can be based on this basic report template, which will personalize my prints and save time, because I do not have to re-create this structure for every new report.

Since Access doesn't have a New Report From Template command, every time you need to reuse this report structure, you must do the following:

1. Select the report name you want to use as a template in the Database window.

2. Press Ctrl+C to copy it to the Clipboard.

3. Press Ctrl+V to show the Paste As dialog box, type a new name, and save it as new report.

That is why all reports that follow will have the same basic appearance.

Creating Simple Reports

In this section, you will learn how to create simple reports—ones that use just the Report Record Source records.

The examples provided will explore the Report, Section, and Group properties so you can get a better understanding of how they behave and how they can be used to produce nice, concise printouts.

Using a Table on the Report's Record Source Property

As with a form's Record Source property, this property defines the records and default sort order that a Report object will use to print, allowing the Add Existing Fields window to show all Record Source fields that can be dragged to any report section as a Text Box, Check Box (for Yes/No data types), or Combo Box (for fields that have a LookUp property defined).

Figure 6-8 shows the rptFoodItems report in Design view, which you can find in the sr28_Reports.accdb database. Its Record Source property was set to the FOOD_DES table, which has 8,789 records of food item names. This will make it print the Detail section 8,789 times.

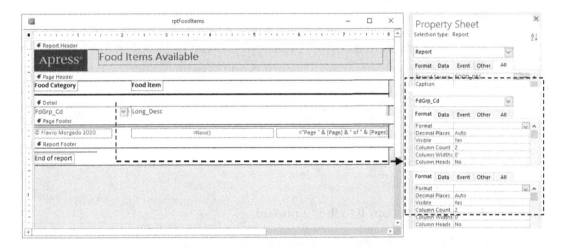

Figure 6-8. *This is rptFoodItems. With the property Record Source set to the FOOD_DES table, it will print its 8,789 records. It has fields FdGrp_Cd (Combo Box) and Long_Desc (Text Box) dragged to its Detail section. To show the food categories names instead of the code, the Combo Box had some properties changed the same way you changed them on a form*

Although it is quite simple, its structure allows a lot of interesting facts about how an Access report works.

- The report prints on a letter-sized page (8½ x 11 inches) using portrait orientation, with the Report Header/Footer and Page Header/Footer sections visible.

- The Height properties for the Page Header and Page Footer sections sum about 0.7 inches, which leaves a height of 9.8 inches for every page except the first and last pages (that also print the Report Header and Footer sections, respectively).

- The form's Detail section is 8 inches wide (the maximum width available for a letter-sized page, because it uses the default 0.25 inches for the Left and Right page margins).

- The FOOD_DES fields FdGrp_Cd and Long_Desc were dragged from the Add Existing Fields window to the form's Detail section as Text Box controls. Both controls have their Shape Outline color set to Transparent (no border).

- FdGrp_Cd was changed to a Combo Box control (by right-clicking it and selecting the "Change to" Combo Box) and had some properties manually set to allow it to show the food category names instead of the code.

  - Row Source = qryFD_GROUPAZ (which shows FD_GROUP records sorted by FdGrp_Desc field)

  - Bound Column = 1

  - Column Count = 2 (FD_GROUP table's FdGrp_Cd and FdGrp_Desc fields)

  - Column Widths = 0 (hide the FdGrp_Cd field)

- The Report Header section's Title Label Caption property was changed to Food Items Available.

- The Page Header section, which prints on every page, received two labels to identify each data column, above the Line control that separates the header from the page records.

- The Detail section's Height was decreased to its control's height to allow a maximum number of records per printed page.

Report View Properties

Microsoft Access has four different types of views, which you can select by clicking in the View option on the Design tab of the report's Design Tools ribbon.

- *Design view*: This allows you to define the report structure. It allows you to show sections, group options, insert controls, and define properties without showing how records will print.

- *Report view*: This is the default view, allowing you to view how records will print without the full report layout options (such as page margins, page breaks, columns, headers, and footers), although allow goes from first to last record printed.

- *Layout view*: This is the same as Form Layout view, which is similar to Report view but allows you to change the report, section, and control properties at runtime to fine-tune the printing appearance.

- *Print Preview*: This is the definitive view that shows a page-by-page printing style, allowing you to verify how the report will be printed with no user interaction.

Note   To change how a report is shown when opened from the Database window, change its Default View property. Use the Allow Report View and Allow Layout View properties to define whether these alternative views will be available to the application user.

Using Report View

Report view was created to allow the first report records to display without spending time to generate all the report pages. In previous Access versions, it printed the same way Print Preview does, but now it hides some formatting options.

In Access 2019, it allows you to identify the report sections by clicking them with the mouse, surrounding them by a red square, selecting report text and objects, and copying control values to the Clipboard.

To show rptFoodItems in Report view, click in the View option of the View area of the Report Tools Design tab. Figure 6-9 shows a partial view of its first and last records.

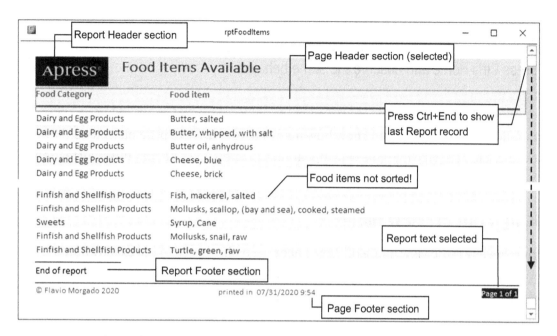

Figure 6-9. *This is rptFoodItems using Report view to show its records. It first prints the Report Header and Page Header sections. Then it successively prints the Detail section for each of its records. Using this view, at the end of report, it prints the Page Footer and Report Footer sections*

Note that it first prints the Report Header section, followed by the Page Header section and all records from its Record Source property, by successively printing the Detail section, which by default alternates the background color for each printed record, the same way a form does.

Report records are not sorted because it Record Source property is set to the FOOD_DES table. This means it receives the default record insertion table order, and the FdGrp_CD Combo Box control appears as a Text Box when the report shows how it will print its records.

Since Report view doesn't allow you to see the printed page, Page Footer sections print just at the end of the report, after the Report Footer section (press Ctrl+End to force all records to be printed and have the report engine show its last record).

Note   When you press Ctrl+End to force Report view to print all its records, you may notice that the Report window's vertical scroll bar moves somewhat slowly, taking some time to reach the end of the report. This happens because Record

Source is set to FOOD_DES, which has more than 8,000 records. This causes the Detail section to print more than 8,000 times. To return to the report's beginning, press Ctrl+Home and observe the same behavior.

Although the Report view gives a good idea of how printed pages will appear, its limitations don't allow you to know how many pages it takes to print all its records, nor how the selected page margins will appear on a printed page. To find this information, you need to use Print Preview mode.

Using Print Preview Mode

Print Preview is the view mode of choice because it allows you to see exactly how a report will look on a printed page, including the whitespace used by its page margins, page by page.

It prints fast because it shows one page at a time, offering navigation buttons that allow you to see the first, previous, next, and last pages (or type the page number desired). By navigating to the last printed page (using the navigation buttons or pressing Ctrl+End), it will show how many pages must be used to print all its records.

Tip   To make a report open by default using Print Preview mode, set its property Default View to Print Preview. To not allow the user to switch to Report or Layout view, set both Allow Report View and Allow Layout View to No.

Since the rptFoodItems report has its Default View property set to Report view, to show it using Print Preview mode, you must do the following:

1. From the report's Design view, click the View button arrow and select Print Preview.

2. Right-click its title bar and choose Print Preview.

3. Right-click it in the Database window and select Print Preview.

4. Use a macro with the OpenReport action where the argument View is set to Print Preview.

Note   When a report is shown in Print Preview, Access shows the Print Preview tab, full of tools that allow you to control page-related report options or export the desired report pages to other file formats (such as PDF, Excel, Text, etc.).

Figure 6-10 shows rptFoodItems in Print Preview mode using partial views of its first and last pages (reached after clicking the navigation buttons' last page arrow).

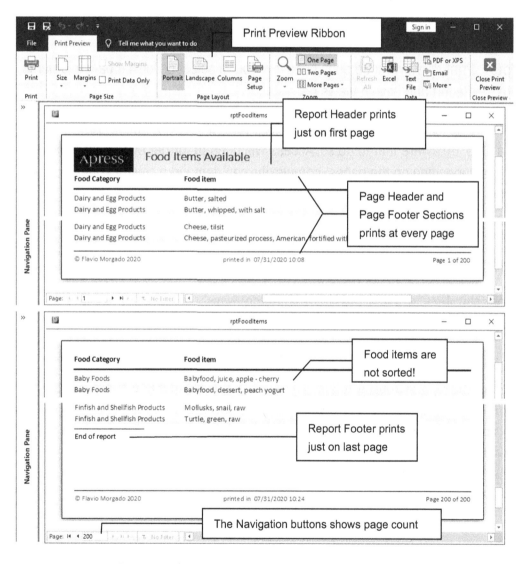

Figure 6-10.   *Use the report's Print Preview to show all the page details, including the Page Header/Footer sections on each page*

Now the report appears as it will print on paper with all its formatting options, including the following:

- The paper's whitespace will be defined by the default 0.25-inch page margins.

- The Page Header and Page Footer sections appear on every report page.

- It needs 200 letter-sized pages to print all 8,789 FOOD_DES table food categories and food item names, one per row.

Note   Print Preview mode does not allow you to select or format page elements, like the Report and Layout views do.

Tip   By using the Print Preview Zoom tool, you can show multiple report pages at a time. Be aware that to do so, Access will need to format every report page, which, depending on the pages' complexity, can demand a significant amount of time.

Sorting Report Records

Reports can show sorted records in two different ways.

- By using the query sort order to set its Record Source property

- By using the tools in the Group & Totals area of the Report Design tab

Since the report Group & Totals tools ignore any sort order that may be used by its Record Source property, for many years and versions, Microsoft Access reports did not obey any external sorting. Previous versions discarded the SQL Order By instruction and showed records using the table insertion order.

Let's see both in action.

Using a Query Sort Order

To change a report's sort order, employ a query as its Record Source property to sort the records in the order that they must appear on a printed page.

Open qryFOOD_DESbyCategoryAZ in Design view and note that it uses the FD_GROUP and FOOD_DES related tables to allow you to sort its records first by FdGrp_Desc (food category name) and then by Long_Desc (food item name). Figure 6-11 shows the FdGrp_Desc field used to sort the query.

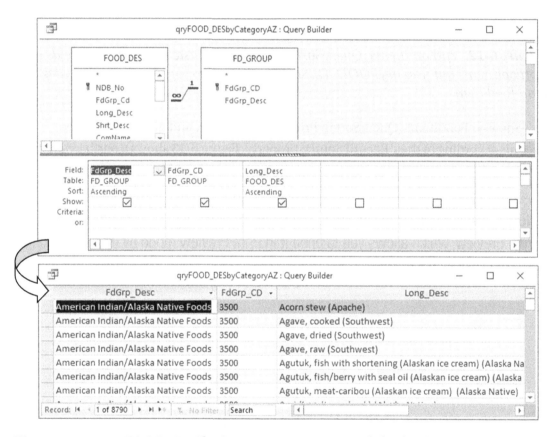

Figure 6-11. *qryFOOD_DESbyCategoryAZ sorts records by food category and then by food item name using ascending order on both fields*

Now open rptFoodItems_QuerySort in Design view, show the Property Sheet's Data tab, and note that its Record Source property is set to qryFOOD_DES_CategoryAZ, although it keeps using the FdGrp_Cd Combo Box bound to the food category code (while showing the food category name). In other words, this report doesn't have a food category name to use as a sort field (Figure 6-12).

483

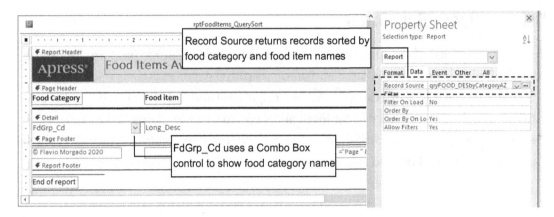

Figure 6-12. *rptFoodItems_QuerySort has the same basic structure and fields as rptFoodItems but uses qryFOOD_DESbyCategoryAZ to sort its records by category and food item*

Show rptFoodItems_QuerySort in Print Preview mode, and note that it shows records according to their Record Source property. Figure 6-13 shows a partial view of the report's first and last pages to allow you to appreciate its sort order.

Note   I changed the rptFoodItems_QuerySort report's Default View property to Print Preview, which allows you to open it in Print Preview mode by double-clicking it in the Database window.

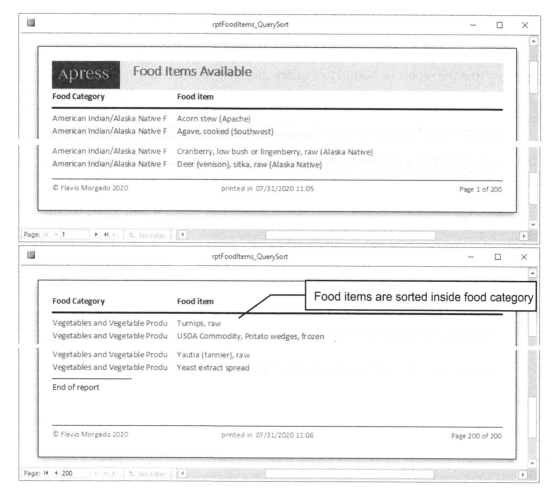

Figure 6-13. *This is the rptFoodItem_QuerySort report that uses a sorted query to show its records sorted by food category and then by food item*

Such an approach to sorting report records works well but adds excessive duplicate information by repeating the current food category name, page after page, until it changes to the next food category in the sorting order (which will be repeated again and again).

A better approach is to make the report ignore the Record Source sort order and use its own way of grouping and sorting records, which can be achieved by using a nonsorted query and applying the Group & Totals tools.

485

Grouping and Sorting Records

To make a report sort its records independently of its Record Source sort order, it is necessary that the report be bound to a query that returns field values, not its code. It must return categories and food item names, not sorted, so you can see the Report Design tab's Group & Total tools in action.

Figure 6-14 shows qryCategoryFoodItems in Design view, which also uses the related FD_GROUP and FOOD_DES tables to return two aliased textual sorted fields: FdGrp_Desc (alias for "Category" for the food category name) and Long_Desc (alias for "Food Item" for the food item name). Such an approach will allow the report to sort its own records in alphabetical order using just Text Box controls in the report's Detail section.

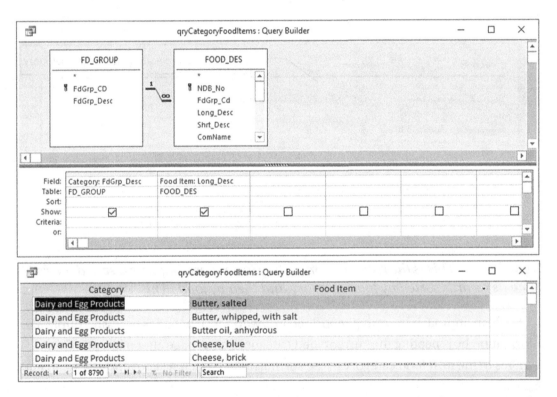

Figure 6-14. This is qryCategoryFoodItems, which returns the food category and food item names not sorted, to allow you to verify the Report Group & Total tools in action

Figure 6-15 shows rptFoodItems2 in Design view, whose Record Source property is set to qryCategoryFoodItems and uses just two Text Box controls bound to the Query Category and Food Item fields.

Note   Since qryCategoryFoodItems is not sorted, by opening rptFoodItem2 in Print Preview mode, its records will appear in the same order shown by Figures 6-9 and 6-10.

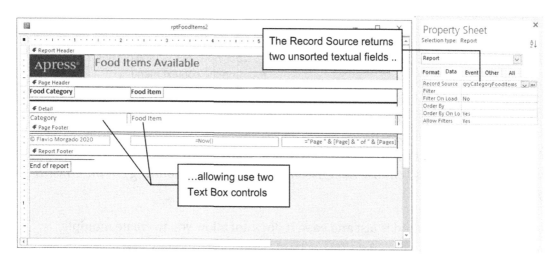

Figure 6-15. *rptFoodItem2 is bound to qryCategoryFoodItems, which returns two not-sorted textual fields (Category and Food Item) allowing the report to use two Text Box controls to show these field values*

To sort rptFoodItem2 using any of its controls, right-click the desired report control and select Sort Ascending (or Sort Descending) in the context menu that appears (Figure 6-16).

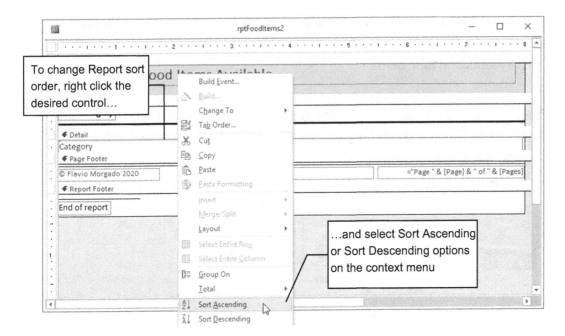

Figure 6-16. *To sort rptFoodItem2 on the Category field, right-click its control in the Detail section and choose Sort Ascending (or Sort Descending) in the context menu that appears*

Although this method is fast and easy, it does not allow you to create multiple, successive sorts like a query does (for example, sorting by category and then by food item inside the category).

To allow a report to use its own multiple, successive sorts, ignoring its Record Source's sorting option, use the Group & Sort tool in the Group & Totals area of the report's Design tab, which shows the Group, Sort, and Total window below the report's Design view. This is where you can select the records' sort order (Figure 6-17).

Figure 6-17. *To make a report use multiple sort on, use the Group & Sort tool of the Report Design tab to show the Group, Sort, and Total window below the report's Design view*

Note Whenever you right-click a report control and select Sort Ascending or Sort Descending, this field will be automatically added to the Group & Sort tool. If another control is selected and chosen as a sort field, it will replace the previously selected field in the Group & Sort tool.

Once the Group, Sort, and Total window appears below the rptFoodItem2 window in Design view, follow these steps to create a multiple sort order using its Category and Food Item fields:

1. To add the main report's sort order by category, follow these steps:

   a. Click the Add A Sort button to add a record sorting option. Access will show an orange bar with a sort option and will open a window with all fields returned by the report's Record Source property.

   b. Select Category to sort records by this field. Access will add the Sort by Category option followed by the "With A on top" option in the orange bar and will show the Add a Group and Add a Sort buttons below it.

Tip   Any Group Header section is sorted ascending by default and cannot avoid being sorted.

---

2. To add a secondary report sort order by food item, follow these steps:

   a. Click the "Add a sort" button again to insert another sort level.

   b. Select the "Food Item" field, keeping the "With A on top" option.

Access will insert the secondary sort option by "Food Item" in relation to the report's main sort order by "Category" (Figure 6-18).

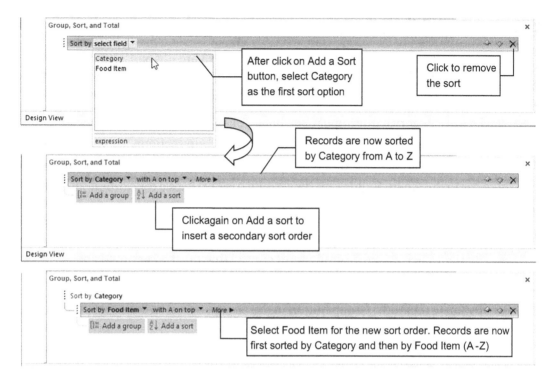

Figure 6-18. *Use the "Add a sort" button of the Group, Sort, and Total window to define how the report will sort its records, ignoring its Record Source sort order*

Note   To remove a Report Sort option, click in the "X" button located at the right of the orange sort bar.

To see the final result, right-click rptFoodItem2's title bar and select Print Preview to see that records are now sorted by the Report Group and Sort options using the Category and Food Item fields, producing the same result previously shown by Figure 6-13.

Note   rptFoodItems2_Sort, available in the sr28_Reports.accdb database, shows the qryCategoryFoodItems query's records sorted by the report's Sort options, by Category, and then by Food Item (and Default View is set to Print Preview to allow you to view its pages from the Database window), as proposed in this section.

Group and Sort Options

The printing results you saw in Figures 6-9, 6-10, and 6-13 are not bad, but they have in common the fact that the food category name is monotonously repeated for each printed record, row by row.

To make the category name appear just once, followed by all food items associated to it, the report needs to group records by adding new group sections. This is a strategy similar to a Total query, with the difference that a Total query groups records using a left-to-right order in the Query Builder window, while a report uses a top-to-bottom Group Section layout in the report's Design view.

Once again, this can be done in two different ways.

- By right-clicking the desired report control that must be grouped and selecting the Group On option in the context menu that appears

- By using the Add a Group button in the Group, Sort, and Total window, selecting the desired field

Both options will create another Group Header section between the Report Header and Detail sections, using the desired field (which will also change the report's sort order).

Note   By right-clicking any report control and selecting the Group On option, the field or expression used by the control will be used to define the new Group section, and Access will show the Group, Sort, and Total window below the report.

Figure 6-19 shows the result of using again rptFoodItems2, currently sorted by the Category and Food Item fields, and selecting its Category field (or control) to create a new Category Header Group section between its Report Header and Detail sections.

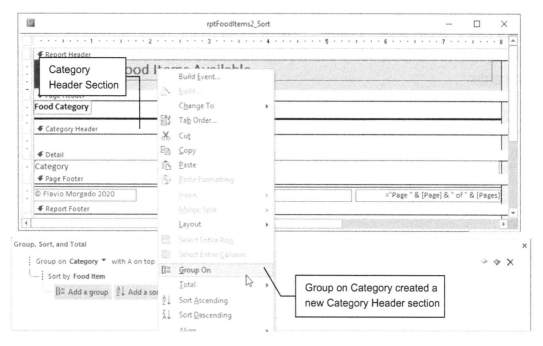

Figure 6-19. *Whenever a new group is created using the "Add a group" button and a <Field> is selected (or a control is right-clicked and Group On is selected in the context menu), Access creates by default a new <Field> Header section*

Note   By default, the Group & Sort tool does not show the <Field> Footer section.

Once a new group section is created in the rptFoodItem2 report, to make the Category field appear only once for every food item it has, reformat the Report layout by following these steps:

1. Click the Category Text Box control located in the Detail section and drag it to the Category Header section.

2. Increase the Category Text Box control width, keeping it left-aligned to the Category Header section's left border. Select the Format tab and check the Bold and Underline text formatting options.

3. Select Food Item Text Box in the Detail section and drag its left handle to the left, increasing its width, and leaving it slightly left indented in relation to the Category text box.

Attention   If rptFoodItems2 does not have a secondary sort order, use the "Add a sort" button of the Group, Sort, and Total window to specify a secondary food item sort order.

4. Remove the Category and Food Item labels located in the Page Header section (they will not be needed anymore), and reposition the horizontal Line control to the center of the Page Header section (Figure 6-20).

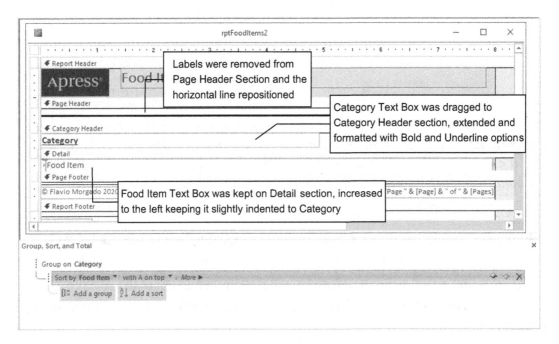

Figure 6-20. *Whenever the "Add a group" button is used, Access adds a new <field> Header section to the report to allow you to group its records*

Show rptFoodItem2 in Print Preview, and note that the report shows records sorted by category and food items, with the Category Text Box appearing just once for every food item record. Figure 6-21 shows partial views or the report's first and fourth pages, when the food category changes from "American Indian..." to "Baby Foods").

Note   rptFoodItems2_GroupSort, available in the `sr28_Reports.accdb` database, shows records grouped by category and sorted by food item as proposed in this section.

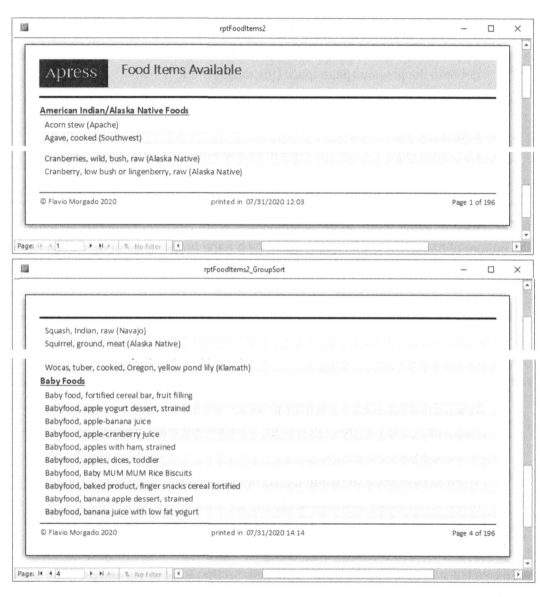

Figure 6-21. *The rptFoodItems2_GroupSort report is grouping records by category and sorting its Detail section by food item fields. Now the category name appears just once in the Category Header field for every food item record*

Now that you have a good idea about how to use the Group & Sort tool of the Report Tools Design tab, let's explore the other grouping options.

Keep Together, Repeat Section, and Force New Page Properties

To help control how the report text flows between printed pages, use the Keep Together, Repeat Section, and Force New Section properties, cited in Table 6-2.

- *Keep Together*: This forces a section to print on the next page if it does not fit in the previous page space (the default value is Yes).

- *Repeat Section*: This allows a Group Header section to repeat on every page or column (the default value is No).

- *Force New Page*: This allows a group to begin printing on its own page (and/or insert a page break after it) (the default value is None).

Note   Keep Together refers to the section itself. If the section height does not fit at the bottom of page, it will not be separated by a page break. The entire section will print on the next page.

Using a Category Header section on the rptFoodItems2_GroupSort report to print a food category name just once followed by all its food items improved substantially the layout, but there are still other things to note when records are spread across so many printed pages.

- Whenever a category needs to print its records using more than one page, the records on these new pages lose the reference to which category they belong.

- The next category to be printed can appear suddenly in the middle of the last page of the previous category.

Open the rptFoodItems2_SectionProperties report in Design view, select the Category Header section (named Group Header0) to show the Properties window, select the Format tab, and note that the property Repeat Section is set to Yes and property Force New Page is set to Before Section (Figure 6-22).

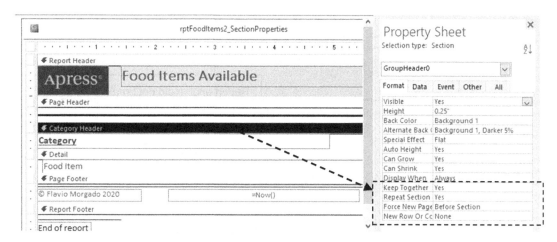

Figure 6-22. *rptFoodItems2_SectionProperties sets the Category Header section's Force New Page property to Before Section and the Repeat Section property to Yes, which makes each category begin on a new page and appear on every other page whose records belongs to it*

Show the report in Print Preview mode and note that now the category name appears on top of every page and each new category record begins on a new page. Figure 6-23 shows partial views of the report's page 1, where the "American Indian…" category begins and ends, and page 5, where the "Baby Foods" category begins.

Attention   Although the rptFoodItems2_SectionProperties report's Page Header property is set to All Pages and the Category Header property Force New Page is set to Before Section, Access did not separate the Report Header and Category Header sections in two different pages, since a Header (or Footer) section is not treated as a normal section, but one that must print on top of a page, right before the Page Header section.

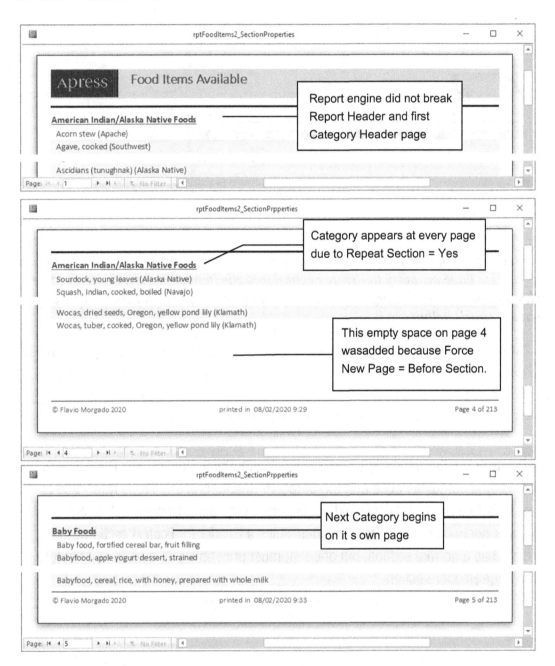

Figure 6-23. *These are pages 4 and 5 of rptFoodItem2_SectionProperties, whose Category Header section's Force New Page property is set to Before Section, and its Repeat Section property is set to Yes, to get control over how the report text flows across its pages*

To make the Report Header section print on an independent page, set the Report Header section's Force New Page property to After Section, creating a report page cover.

This is exactly what rptFoodItems2_SectionProperties2 does! Figure 6-24 shows it in Design view with the Report Header section selected (all the other properties remain the same). Note that the Report Header height was increased, it has a background color of White, and the Apress logo and Title Text Box were resized and dragged to another position.

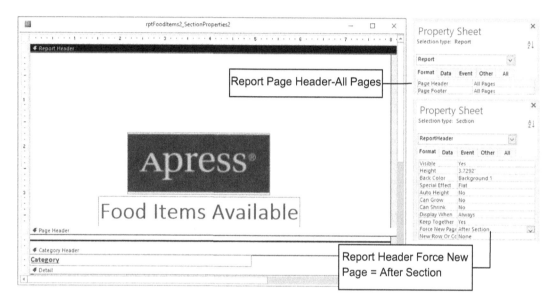

Figure 6-24. *Since the rptFoodItems2_SectionProperties2 report's Header property Force New Page is set to After Page, this report now has a cover page that is separated from first record pages. And since Report Page Header is set to All Pages, this page should also print the page header*

Show rptFoodItems2_SectionProperties2 in Print Preview mode, but now use the Two Pages option in the Zoom area of Print Preview's Design tab to view two report pages at a time (Figure 6-25).

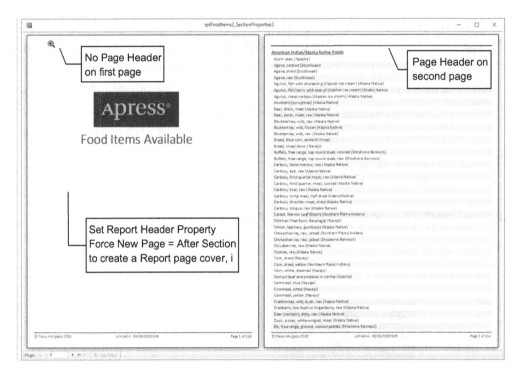

Figure 6-25. *This is rptFoodItem2_SectionProperties2 shown in Print Preview mode using the Two Pages option. Although the report's Page Header property is set to All Pages, the Page Header section refuses to appear in the Report Header section's first page*

Note   The report's Page Header property can be set to All Pages, Not with Rpt Hdr, Not with Rpt Ftr, or Not with Rpt Hdr/Ftr, as a clear indication that it can be printed on the report header, but it is not printing as it should.

Creating a Multicolumn Report

To create a different report layout and possibly reduce its page count, you can make the report's Detail section print using two or more columns by using the Page Setup's Columns tab options.

Figure 6-26 shows the rptFoodItem2_2ColSetWidth report in Design mode. It uses the following options on its Page Setup dialog box's Columns tab to allow it to print its Detail section in a two-column layout:

- Number of Columns = 2

- Columns Spacing = 0.25"

- Column Width = 3.75"

- Same as Detail = unchecked

- Column Layout: Down, then Across

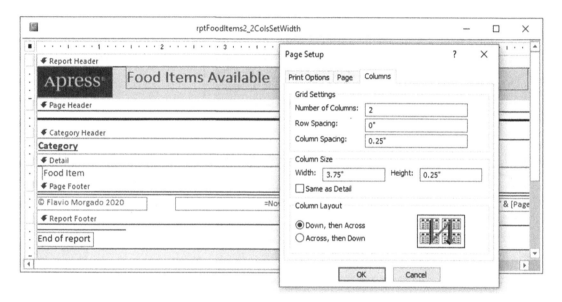

Figure 6-26. *To make a report print using two or more columns, use the Page Setup dialog box's Columns tab to define the Number of Columns, Column Width, and Column Spacing settings. To calculate the column width, consider the paper size width, the left and right page margins, and the number of columns and column spacing for each column (minus 1)*

Attention   Use this formula to correctly set a report's column width:Width=(PageWidth–(Left+Right margins))/N°Cols – (ColumnSpacing*(N°Cols-1) Since this report has Page Width set to 8.5 inches, has margins Left and Right set to 0.25 inches, uses two columns, has Column Spacing set to 0.25, it has a Column Width of 3.75 inches.

Figure 6-27 shows the rptFoodItem2_2ColSetWidth report in Print Preview mode. Since its Category Header property's Repeat Section is set to Yes and Force New Page is set to Before Section, the category name will appear at the top of each column (and if you move to the report's last page, you will note that it now uses just 115 pages to print the same 8,000 food item records).

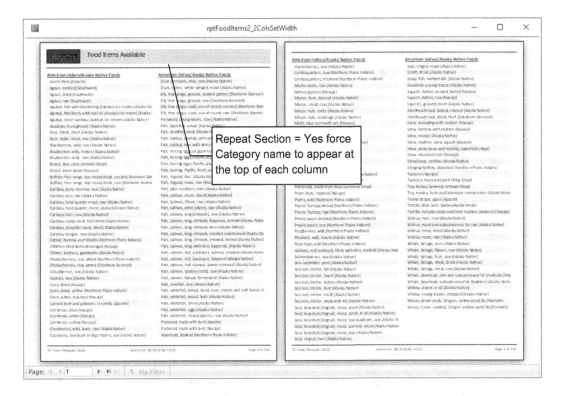

Figure 6-27. *This is the rptFoodItem2_2ColSetWidth report in Print Preview mode using the Two Pages format. It repeats the category name on each column header due to the Category Header property Repeat Section being set to Yes*

Attention   Microsoft Access is unable to show multicolumn designs in Report or Layout view. Column formatting is shown just in Print Preview mode.

There is a problem whenever you create a columnar report and do not take care of the Detail section controls widths. Their content may be truncated to the report column width showing a partial view of its content.

For the if the rptFoodItem2_2ColSetWidth report shown in Figure 6-27, since the Food Item Text Box's Width is set to 7.875" and the Page Setup's Column Width is set to 3,75 inches, every printed record shows just a partial view of its content.

Whenever you want to create a columnar report, assure that all control widths in the Detail section are not wider than the specified Page Setup's Column Size, and set their Can Grow property to Yes, making them increase a control's Height property so it uses as many lines of text as necessary to show its content.

Open the rptFoodItem2_2ColsDetail report in Design view, set the Food Item Text Box's Width property to 3,75' and Can Grow property to Yes. Show it in Print Preview mode, and note that now each food item value uses as many printed rows as needed to show its full content spread across the report column width (Figure 6-28).

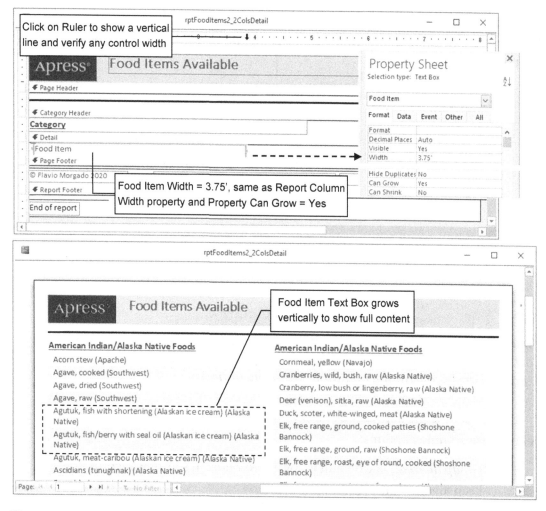

Figure 6-28. *To make a perfect columnar report, assure that the combined width of all controls in the Detail section is not wider than the Column Width property, and ensure the Can Grow property is set to Yes (as rptFoodItem2_2ColsDetail does)*

Attention   All report sections (except Report Header/Footer and Page Header/Footer) will obey the Page Setup Column Width setting.

Grouping Options

You may note in Figures 6-18 and 6-20 that whenever the rptFoodItem2 report receives a new group or sort option, a More ➤ option appears at the right of the orange grouping bar indicating that you can set other grouping options.

Open the rptFoodItem2_GroupSort report in Design view and click its Category More ➤ grouping option to expand it and show other possible grouping options for this field (Figure 6-29).

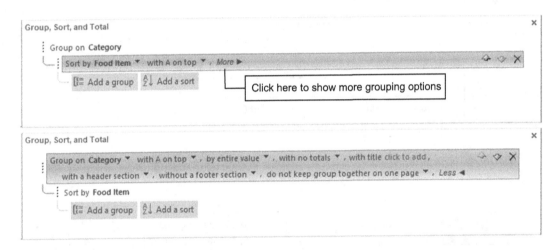

Figure 6-29. *Open the rptFoodItem2 report in Design view, check the Group & Sort option on the Design tab, and click Category Header's More ➤ option to expand it and show all the available grouping options*

Besides setting the field name and sort option (A-Z or Z-A), Access allows you to define these grouping options:

- *Group interval*: The default is "by entire value." It sets how records are keep together on a section:

  - *By entire value*: This uses the entire field as the sort key.

  - *By first character*: This uses just the first field character as the sort key.

- *By first two characters*: This uses the first two field characters as the sort key.

- *Custom*: This sets how many field characters to use as the sort key.

Note   A Date field data type can be grouped by day, week, month, quarter, or custom interval.

- *Totals*: The default value is "with no total." This allows you to use aggregate functions to summarize the desired Record Source field, using a small window (Figure 6-30).

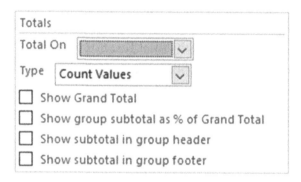

Figure 6-30.   *Use the Totals window that appears when clicking the "with no totals" option to select the field's aggregate function and where it will be inserted in the report (Grand Total is inserted on Report Footer and Subtotal can be inserted in Group Header, Footer, or both)*

Note   You can add totals on multiple fields, and you can do multiple types of totals in the same field.

- **Total on:** This allows you to select the field to be summarized (which can be different from the one used to group the current section).

- **Type:** This is the aggregate function to be used to summarize the total on the field: Sum, Average, Maximum, Minimum, Standard Deviation, Variance (for Numeric data types), Count values, and Count records (all data types).

Note   Use Count Values to count group records whose fields are not empty. In this case, Access will use the Count([Field]) function as the Text Box Control Source property; use Count Records to count all group records, empty or not. Access will use Count(*) instead.

- *Show Grand Total*: This adds a Text Box on the Report Footer section whose Control Source is set to an aggregate function that acts over all report records.

- *Show group totals as % of Grand Total*: This adds a Text Box on the Group Footer section that calculates the percentage of records it has relating to all report records.

- *Show in group header or Show in group footer*: This defines which group sections must display the total Text Box control. By selecting the "Show in group footer" option, Access will create and show the Group Footer Section below the Detail section to receive the Text Box control (and will set the With Footer Section option for the group).

Note   Once a field had been summarized, you can repeat the process using the "Total on" options to select and summarize another field. Access will stack all summarized Text Box controls in the desired header/footer.

- *Title*: This allows you to change the Caption property of the label associated to the control whose field is being summarized in the section header. It has no action if the Group control has no associated label.

- *With/Without a header section*: This allows you to add or remove the group's Header section. When a group's Header section contains controls, Access asks for confirmation before deleting it (this operation can't be undone).

- *With/Without a footer section*: This allows you to add or remove the group's Footer section. When a group's Footer section that contains controls is removed, Access asks for confirmation before deleting it.

- *Keep group together*: Use this last option to define how Access will print the group's Header section and its detail records:

  Do not keep group together on one page: This is the default option; use it when the group records can spread by different printed pages.

  Keep whole group together on one page: Access will keep together the group's Header section and all details records that fit on an entire printed page. This option may create a blank space of undetermined size in the page that precedes the group.

  Keep header and first record together on one page: Access will keep the group's Header section and first detail record in the same page (the group header will not print by itself at the bottom of a page).

Note   Microsoft Access allows you to create up to ten different group options, each one having its own Header and Footer sections.

Now that you have seen all the grouping options, let's look at how to use them in practical report applications.

Adding Group Totals

As explained earlier, a group total is a Text Box control added in the Group Header or Footer section that uses an aggregate function whose argument is one of the fields returned by the report's Record Source property.

To create a group total on a report, besides using the Total option in the group bar of the Group, Sort, and Total window, Microsoft Office allows you to select the desired control on the Report Design tab using one of these methods:

- Use the Totals tool in the Grouping & Totals area of the Report Design tab.

- Right-click the control and select Totals in the context menu.

Both options will show a list of available functions according to the field data type used by the selected control's Control Source property and will add a Text Box with the selected aggregate function in different report places considering the following:

- If the report doesn't have a group header, the Text Box with the aggregated function will be inserted in the Report Footer section (to create a grand total).

- If the report already have a group header (even for another field), Access will create the Group Footer section and will add the Text Box with the aggregate function in both the Group Footer (to create a group total) and Report Footer sections (to create a grand total).

To try the Access Report Total tools, let's return to rptFoodItems2_GroupSort that already has a Category group (which is sorted ascending by default) and a second ascending sort order by food item (see Figure 6-21). The aim is to count how many food items (records) exist in each food category (Group Total) and in the entire report (Grand Total).

Follow these steps to use the Totals option in the Group, Sort, and Total window to create a count of Category records:

1. Open rptFoodItems2_GroupSort in Design mode.

2. To create a total for the Category field, click the Group & Sort tool to show the Group, Sort, and Total window.

3. In the Group On Category bar, click the More option and select the "with no total" option to show the Total window and check all options (Show Grand Total, Show group subtotal as % of Grand Total, Show SubTotal on Group Footer, and Show SubTotal on Group Header).

Note   Since the Category field has the Short text data type, the only Total options available on Type options are Count Values and Count Records, which use the COUNT() aggregate function to respectively return the not null Category values or the record count for the selected scope.

Access will create the Category Footer sections and add Text Box controls to the Category Header and Category Footer sections to calculate the Category subtotal, and in the Report Footer section (named AccessTotalsCategory) to calculate the Report Grand Total using this expression on its Control Source property:

=Count([Category])

A second Text Box control is added above the category subtotal to calculate its percentage in relation to the report's grand total using this expression on its Control Source property (Figure 6-31):

=Count([Category])/[AccessTotalsCategory]

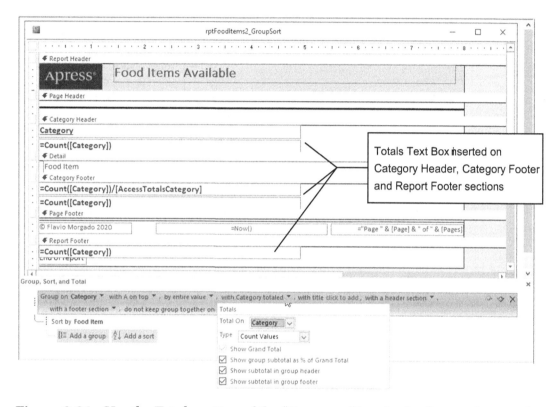

Figure 6-31. *Use the Totals option of the "Group on" bar in the Group, Sort, and Total window to insert a subtotal on both the Group Header and Group Footer sections and to insert a grand total in the Report Footer section*

Open the report in Print Preview mode and note that it now shows a record count below each category name, and after it prints its last food item record, this count seems to be positioned in the middle of the page (Figure 6-32).

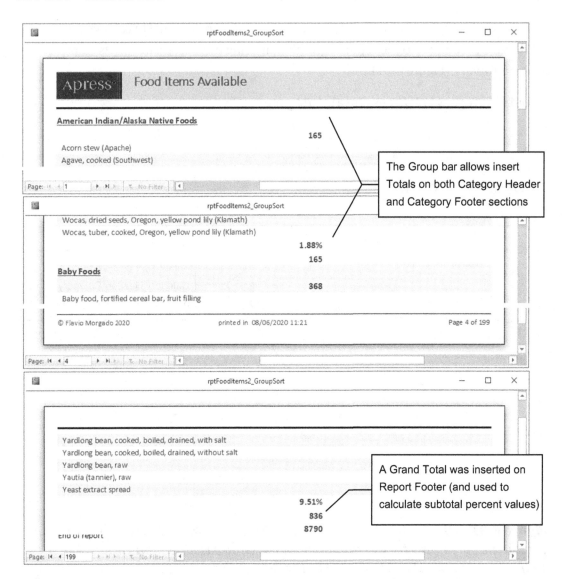

Figure 6-32. *Use the Group, Sort, and Totals window's Totals option to insert a Total Text Box in both the Group Header and Footer sections*

Note   This report was saved as rptFoodItems2_GroupSortTotal in the sr28_ Reports.accdb database.

Looking to the Total Text Box controls inserted in rptFoodItems2_GroupSortTotal, as shown in Figure 6-32, note the following:

- Since the Category Text Box inserted in the Category Header section doesn't have an associated label control, none of the Total Text Boxes inserted have one. If Category had it, Access will use its Caption property to name every inserted Total Text Box (and labels must be inserted to identify each total value).

- All Total fields received bold formatting.

- All of them seem to be centered in the page, but they are not. Since all aggregate functions return a number, all controls received the general format that right-align the number and left-align text (values appears on Total controls' right border).

- Access can count how many records any Group section has before printing them in the Group Header section.

- Access did a good job stacking the subtotal Text Box controls in the Category Header and Footer sections but did not replicate this behavior in the Report Footer section (the AccessTotalsCategory Text Box was positioned on top of other section controls).

Avoiding Group Totals Delays

What Access really does using its Totals tools is to add speed to help the user create Totals fields for any report control, by automatically creating the field Group Footer and Header sections and eventually showing the Report Footer section (if it is not still visible), which is excellent for those who don't want to learn how such boring things such as sections, groups, and aggregate functions work.

But what seems to be a sophisticated tool that works well in any situation can quickly degrade the Access performance if the report needs a more sophisticated Record Source property: one that uses a Total or Crosstab query or SQL instruction that use tables with a large number of records.

Open qryCategoryFoodItemsMacroNutrients in Design view, and note that it is a Crosstab query that uses the FD_GROUP, FOOD_DES, and NUT_DATA tables to return the food category, food item, and its main macro nutrients (Protein, Fat, Carbohydrate, and Energy). It uses expressions for its Nutrient field (Column Heading) and NutrVal field (Value), while it filters the NUT_DATA records by desired Nutr_No value, so it can return just the desired macronutrients (Figure 6-33).

Attention   The qryCategoryFoodItemsMacroNutrients fields Nutrient (Column Heading) and NutrVal (Value) use expressions to return the nutrient name and its values. Since NUT_DATA returns nutrient values by 100g of food, the NutrVal filed expression divides the Carbohydrate, Lipid, and Protein values by 100 to allow you to use the Percent format to show them as percent values. I will leave it to you to study these expressions.

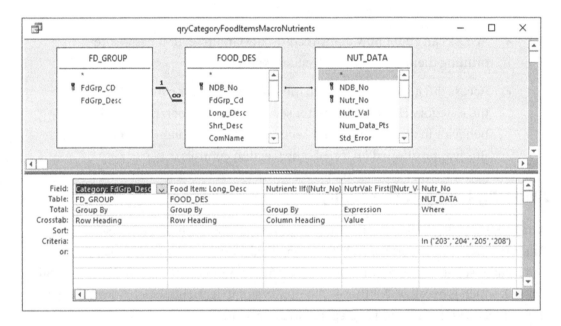

Figure 6-33.   *Query qryCategoryFoodItemsMacronNutrients is a Crosstab query that returns macronutrient values (Protein, Carbohydrate, Lipid, and Energy) for more than 8,000 food items*

Show qryCategoryFoodItemsMacroNutrients in query Design view mode, and note that it takes some time to generate the Crosstab query and show its results (Figure 6-34).

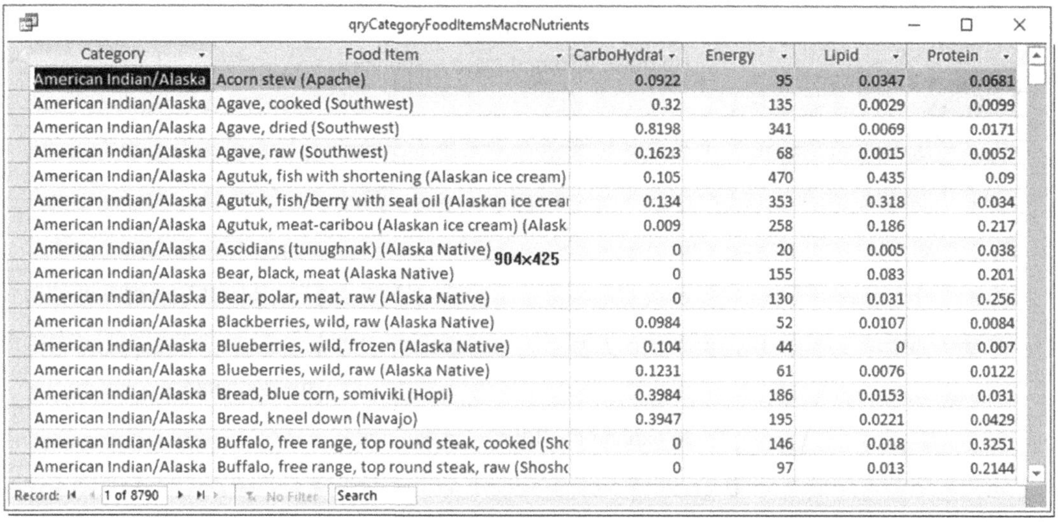

qryCategoryFoodItemsMacroNutrients

Category	Food Item	CarboHydrat	Energy	Lipid	Protein
American Indian/Alaska	Acorn stew (Apache)	0.0922	95	0.0347	0.0681
American Indian/Alaska	Agave, cooked (Southwest)	0.32	135	0.0029	0.0099
American Indian/Alaska	Agave, dried (Southwest)	0.8198	341	0.0069	0.0171
American Indian/Alaska	Agave, raw (Southwest)	0.1623	68	0.0015	0.0052
American Indian/Alaska	Agutuk, fish with shortening (Alaskan ice cream)	0.105	470	0.435	0.09
American Indian/Alaska	Agutuk, fish/berry with seal oil (Alaskan ice crea	0.134	353	0.318	0.034
American Indian/Alaska	Agutuk, meat-caribou (Alaskan ice cream) (Alask	0.009	258	0.186	0.217
American Indian/Alaska	Ascidians (tunughnak) (Alaska Native)	0	20	0.005	0.038
American Indian/Alaska	Bear, black, meat (Alaska Native)	0	155	0.083	0.201
American Indian/Alaska	Bear, polar, meat, raw (Alaska Native)	0	130	0.031	0.256
American Indian/Alaska	Blackberries, wild, raw (Alaska Native)	0.0984	52	0.0107	0.0084
American Indian/Alaska	Blueberries, wild, frozen (Alaska Native)	0.104	44	0	0.007
American Indian/Alaska	Blueberries, wild, raw (Alaska Native)	0.1231	61	0.0076	0.0122
American Indian/Alaska	Bread, blue corn, somiviki (Hopi)	0.3984	186	0.0153	0.031
American Indian/Alaska	Bread, kneel down (Navajo)	0.3947	195	0.0221	0.0429
American Indian/Alaska	Buffalo, free range, top round steak, cooked (Shc	0	146	0.018	0.3251
American Indian/Alaska	Buffalo, free range, top round steak, raw (Shoshc	0	97	0.013	0.2144

Record: 1 of 8790 No Filter Search

***Figure 6-34.** When qryCategoryFoodItemsMacroNutrients is shown in Query view, it takes a while to show all 8,790 food item records with the macronutrient information*

Now let's suppose you want to create a report that uses qryCategoryFoodItems MacroNutrients and the Report Totals tools to create statistics about each food category in the Category Footer section using the same section structure already explored in rptFoodItem2_GroupSort (that has a Category Header section, as shown in Figure 6-20).

Open rptFoodItems2_Statistics in Design mode and see that its Record Source property is set to qryCategoryFoodItemsMacroNutrients and that its Detail Section received Text Box controls to show Protein, Carbohydrate, Lipid, and Energy fields (with Label controls added to the Category Header section so they appear on top of each printed page, as shown in Figure 6-35).

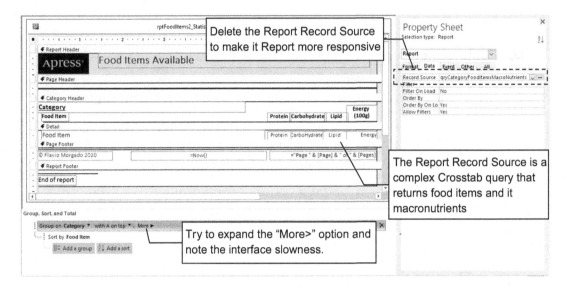

Figure 6-35. *Since the rptFoodItem2_Statistics report is bound to the complex Crosstab qryCategoryFoodItemMacronNutrients query, Access tries to continuously requery its Record Source property to synchronize its Group and Sort interface*

You may note that rptFoodItems2_Statistics takes some time to update the report's Design view (approximately the same amount of time that qryCategoryFoodItems MacroNutrients needs to show its records) and that the whole Access interface has become suddenly very slow.

Once rptFoodItems2_Statistics' Design view is updated, and since it has a Category Header Section created with the Group & Sorting tools, go ahead and click the "More ➤" option of Group on Category in the Group, Sort, and Totals window to show more grouping options (Access will get stuck again).

Select the Protein Text Box in the Detail section, and use the Group & Sorting area of the Report Design tab to select Totals, Average (or right-click the control and select Total, Average in the context menu). Access will get stuck once more to create the Category Footer field and insert a new Text Box using the =Average([Protein]) expression (Figure 6-36).

Note Since the Protein field has the Number data type, Access will show aggregate options such as Average, Standard Deviation, Max, Min, Variance, etc.).

514

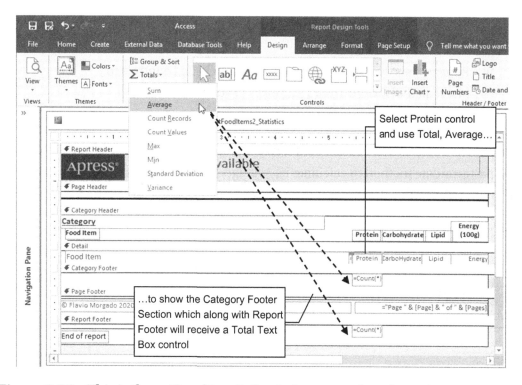

Figure 6-36. *This is the rptFoodItem2_Statistics report that shows Protein, Carbohydrate, Lipid, and Energy Text Box controls in its Detail section, where you can use the Totals, Average (or other aggregate function) to create a Protein subtotal average Text Box on Category Footer and a grand average on Report Footer*

The Access interface is being uncommonly slow, isn't it?

What is happening behind the scenes is Access is trying to synchronize the Report grouping interface by continuously requerying its Record Source property, in an attempt to show whether each possible grouping option has a footer, a total, using which aggregate function, on which field...

To set you free from this sort of updating nightmare, follow these steps:

1. Delete the report's Record Source property so Access doesn't have access to the query's complexity.

2. Copy and paste an existing Total Text Box that already uses an aggregate function using as an argument the desired field (like the Text Box that uses =Avg([Protein]) to return the Protein Average for a food category.

3. Change the aggregate function and/or its argument to calculate another statistic.

4. Repeat steps 2 and 3 to insert other Total Text Box controls to insert all the desired Total Text Boxes of your report.

5. When you finish, restore the report's Record Source property.

Figure 6-37 shows that Protein field received four different Total fields using the copy/paste/update method to calculate its Average, Standard Deviation, Minimum, and Maximum values while the report is unbound (has no Record Source property).

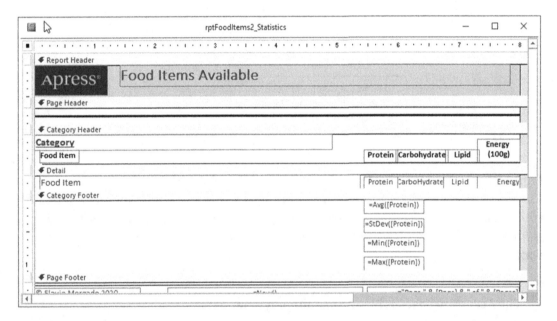

Figure 6-37. *To avoid the extreme delay shown by Access for some complex queries, remove the report's Record Source property and manually create the desired set of Total Text Boxes in the appropriate report section (use the Copy/Paste/Edit method to fasten your report design)*

To see the final result, open rptFoodItem2_StatitsticsTotal in Design mode and note that its Category Footer section has a single =Count([Food Item]) Text Box and different Text Box controls to calculate the Average, Standard Deviation, Minimum, and Maximum values for Protein, Carbohydrate, Lipid, and Energy.

It passed by the proposed strategy of removing the report's Record Source property and manually copying/pasting/updating the Total Text Box for all macronutrients (Figure 6-38).

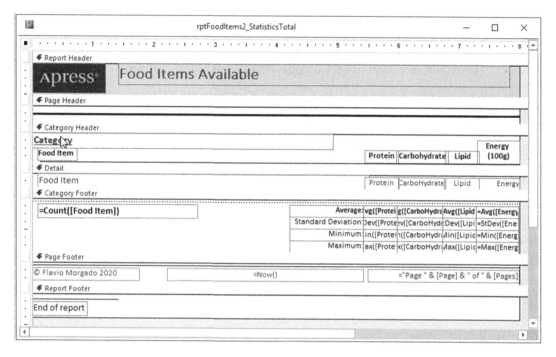

Figure 6-38. *This is rptFoodItem2_StatisticsTotal, which has Total Text Box controls in its Category Footer section to create a statistical list of each food category*

Explore rptFoodItems2_StatisticsTotal in Design view by showing the Property Sheet's Format tab and selecting each Category Footer's Text Box control, and note the following:

- To show the number of nutrients each category has, txtTotalNutrients uses bold text and receives this format to add the food items suffix (note the space before the suffix):

  #" food items"

- To show the Average, Minimum, and Maximum values for Protein, Carbohydrate, and Lipid, these Text Box controls received the Percent format with one decimal place (and all Average Text Boxes use bold text).

- To show the Average, Minimum, and Maximum values for Energy, these Text Box controls received this format to add the "kcal" suffix (note the space before the suffix):

  #" kcal"

517

- Standard deviation for all macronutrients received the Fixed format with three decimal places.

- The report is bound to qryCategoryFoodItemsMacroNutrients.

- A horizontal dotted line was positioned on top of the Category Footer section to separate the last printed record from the statistical data.

- Another smaller dotted line was inserted below the Average values, to separate it from Standard Deviation, Minimum, and Maximum values (since these statistical values indicate how the average is composed).

Show rptFoodItem2_StatisticsTotal in Print Preview mode, and note how it uses the aggregate functions to show statistics of each category after its last record is printed (Figure 6-39).

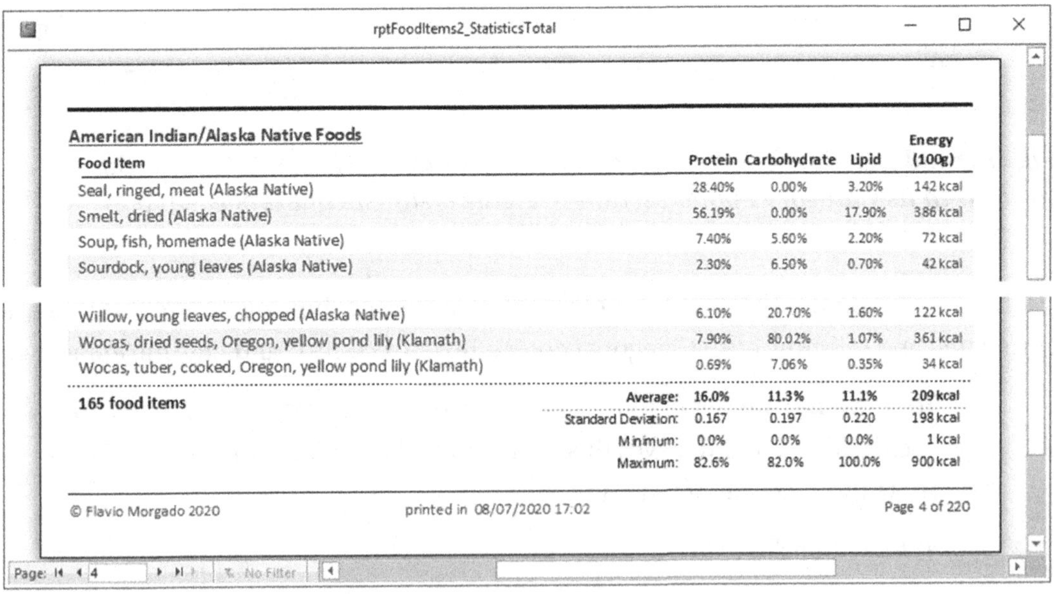

Figure 6-39. *This is rptFoodItem2_StatisticsTotal page 4 (begin and end) that uses aggregate functions in its Category Footer section to return statistical data of each food item category after its last record is printed*

Using Group Sorting Options

The Group Interval option found when you click the "More➤" option that appears at the right of the orange grouping bar of the Group, Sort, and Total window allows you to define how records are grouped and sorted on a report.

By default they are grouped alphabetically by the entire record value, but you can also choose to group them by one, two, or more of the first left characters (as explained in the "Group and Sorting Options" section), which can be useful to create printouts of a long list of records that can be easily found by first letter (or first two letters if they are many), like the old phonebooks for landlines did in the recent past.

To make a better use of such report functionality, you must do the following:

1. Create a new group for the field that will use the Group Interval grouping option.

2. Insert in this Group Header section a Text Box control and delete its associated label.

3. In this Text Box's Control Source property, use an expression with the LEFT() function to show the letter by which the records are grouped.

The LEFT() function has this syntax and arguments:

Left(String, Length)

where:

- *String*: Required. This is a field name or expression from which the leftmost characters are returned (if String contains Null, Null will be returned).

- *Length*: Required. This is a numeric expression that indicates how many characters to return. If Length = 0, LEFT() returns a zero-length string (""); if Length is greater than or equal to String number of characters, the entire String is returned. If Length is a negative number, an error will be returned.

To see how this can be done, open rptFoodItem2_Group1stChar in Design view and note the following:

- It has both a category header and a food item header.

- Select the Group & Sort option on the Design tab, click the "More➤" option in the Group On Food Item orange bar to expand it, and note that its Group Level is set to "by first character."

- Click the txtFirstChar Text Box inserted in the Food Item Header section and note that its Control Source property has this expression to return the first food item field character:

```
=Left([Food Item],1)
```

- The txtFirstChar Text Box is formatted as follows: Calibri, 14, Bold, Centered, Black background, white Foreground color.

- Show the Page Setup dialog box's Columns tab and note that it was formatted to print using a three-column format with a Column Width of 2.4 inches with a 0.1-inch spacing and using a "Down, then Across" layout (Figure 6-40).

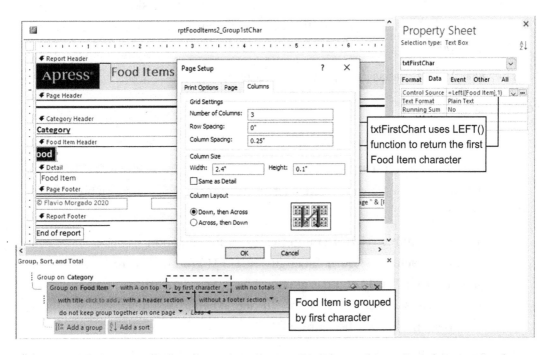

Figure 6-40. *The rptFoodItems2_Group1stChar report has a Food Item Header section that receives the txtFirstChar Text Box which has a Control Source of Left([Food Item],1) to return the first Food Item field's character, because its Group Level is set to "by first character." The report was also formatted to print in a three-column format, using a "Down, then Across" format*

Open rptFoodItems_Group1stChar in Print Preview mode, and note the final result, where each category groups its food items by their first letter (since Category Header has the property Repeat Section set to Yes, the category name appears on top of each column). Note that since the Category Text Box's property Can Grow is set to No, some food categories may not fit in a single-column width, like the "American Indian / Alaska Native Foods" food category.

Since the Food Item Text Box in the Detail section is wider than the column width and its property Can Grow is set to No, the food item name is truncated on each printed record (Figure 6-41).

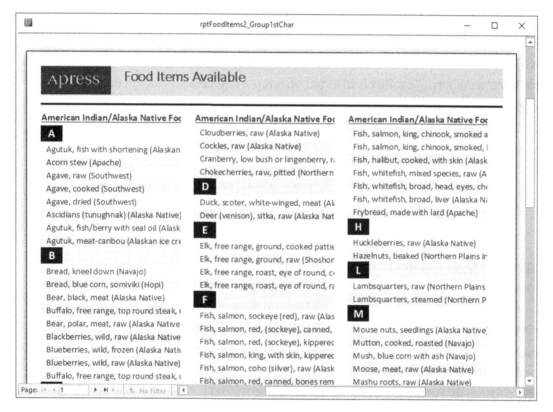

Figure 6-41. *This is rptFoodItems2_Group1stChar in Print Preview mode. Since its Food Item Header section has Group Level set to "by first character," its txtFirstChart Text Box inserted on Food Item Header uses the LEFT() function to show the report grouping*

Attention   As cited earlier, all report sections (but not Report Header/Footer and Page Header/Footer) obey the Page Setup Column Width setting, so whenever a report uses two or more columns, plan ahead for all other Group Header/Footer Control widths (and the Can Grow property) to guarantee that its content will fit into the desired column size.

Numbering Printed Records with the Running Sum Property

Besides using the aggregate COUNT() function to indicate how many records were printed in a section, Access also allows numbering each time a section prints using a Text Box control. When a Text Box is inserted on a report, Access shows the Running Sum property on the Property Sheet's Data tab.

The Running Sum property can be set to the following:

- *No*: This means it doesn't number prints.

- *Over Group*: The running sum restarts for each record in the group.

- *Over All*: The running sum accumulates for all report records.

To make a Text Box control have a running sum, set its Control Source property to an expression that indicates its first value (usually 1) to start and restart the running sum from 1.

Open rptFoodItems2_1stCharRunningSum in Design view, and note that now the Detail section has the txtNumbering Text Box whose Control Source was set to 1, with Running Sum set to Over Group, which means that it will count food items printed for each first letter group (Figure 6-42).

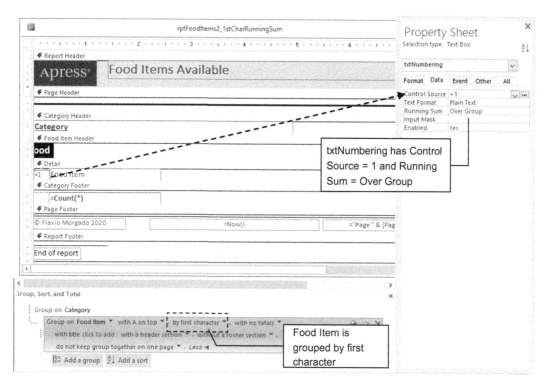

Figure 6-42. *The rptFoodItems2_1stCharRunningSum txtNumbering Text Box inserted in the Detail section has Control Source set to 1 and Running Sum set to Over Group. Since Food Item Header Group Level is set to "by first character," records will be numbered for each first letter (the =Count(*) expression inserted on Category Footer will count all category records)*

Open rptFoodItems2_1stCharRunningSum in Print Preview mode to observe how records are numbered under each first food item letter, while the Category Footer section shows how many food items were printed on each category (Figure 6-43).

Note the following:

- The Food Item Text Box in the Detail section has Column Width set to 2.3 inches.

- Since Food Item has Can Grow set to Yes, the entire food item is shown for each printed record.

- Both the Category Header and Food Item Header sections have Repeat Section set to Yes, which forces the Category and Food Item first letter to appear on top of each printed column.

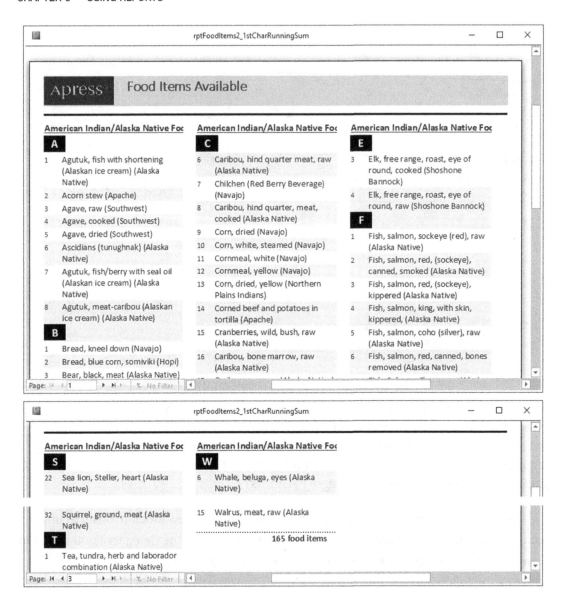

Figure 6-43. *rptFoodItem2_1stCharRunningSum numbers each food item according to its first letter using the Text Box's Running Sum property (numbering restarting at each new first letter group). The category footer shows how many food items a category has*

Using Subreports

A subreport is simply a report that will be inserted as a control on a main report using the same concept of a subform, which makes it perfect for showing the "many" side of a one-to-many relationship (although that can also be used to show other relevant data that does not need to be directly related to any main report field).

Whenever you create a subreport, keep in mind the following:

- Its page size and margins will be ignored.

- Its Page Header and Page Footer sections will not be shown in the main report.

- Columnar subreports may not appear as expected due to a consistent Access bug.

- You may use the subreport control's Link Master Fields and Link Child Fields properties to automatically synchronize it with some Main Report field.

- Since a subreport is simply a control, when it prints its pages, it must obey the Section Height limit of 22 inches (about three letter-sized pages), unless it is added to the Report Detail section.

To make it easier to understand how a subreport works and make better usage of the sr28 database structure, this section will be based on the creation of a Detailed Food Item report, so you can use it as a generic case of how to explore database table relationships on printed pages, using two main objects.

- *qryFOOD_DES_dynamic*: This is a dynamic criteria Select query that asks for a food item's NDB_No code so the report can render quickly for a single food item (Figure 6-44).

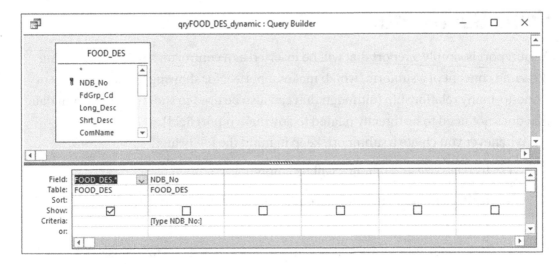

Figure 6-44. *This is qryFOOD_DES_dynamic, a Select query that returns a single FOOD_DES record using a dynamic criteria for its NDB_No field*

- *rptFoodItems3*: A main report specially prepared to allow you to insert subreports and understand how they behave (Figure 6-45).

Figure 6-45. *This is rptFoodItems3, grouped by NDB_No field, with Report Header/Footer, Detail, and Page Header/Footer sections*

There are some characteristics of rptFoodITems3 that deserve a mention:

- Record Source is set to qryFoodItems_dynamic (allows testing the report by typing the desired NDB_No to return a single food item).

- Its Report Header section has the property Force New Page set to the After section, which make it print as an independent report cover page.

- The Page Header section received the Apress logo with a light gray rectangle (that was sent to back) to simulate the default Report Header appearance, with two Labels to identify the NDB_No value and food item name.

- The NDB_No Header section has these properties:

    - Can Grow = Can Shrink = Yes (to allow the section grow and shrink automatically)

    - Keep Together = Repeat Section = Yes (to allow repeating it on every page, if necessary)

    - Force New Page = Before Section (to make each food item print on its own page)

- The txtRefuse Text Box inserted in the NDB_No Header section has these properties settings:

- Control Source: =IIf([Refuse]>0,"Refuse: " & [Refuse]

    & " g of " & [Ref_Desc])

    Supposing that Refuse is 60 and Ref_Desc is Bones and Skin, it creates a string like "Refuse: 60g of bones and skin."

- Can Grow = Can Shrink = Yes (allows txtRefuse to free up or use the vertical space it needs in the NDB_No Header section)

Since rptFoodItems3 Row Source is linked to qryFoodItems_dynamic, whenever this report is opened, it asks for the desired NDB_No string code to show its Long_Desc field and refuse information. Figure 6-46 shows how food items whose NDB_No property is set to 01001 and 13401 appear when the report is opened. (The former doesn't have a Refuse amount and shows nothing, while the latter has it and shows a refuse description right below the food item name.)

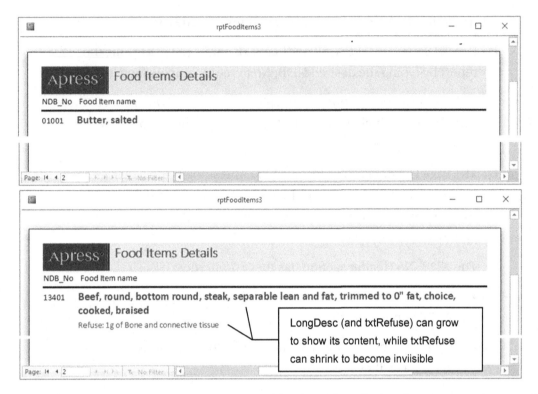

Figure 6-46. *The rptFoodItems3 report has a page header with an Apress logo and labels to identify the NDB_No and Food item name fields, while NDB_No Header has the NDB_No, Long Desc, and txtRefuse Text Box controls that will also appear on top of every page because the property Repeat Section is set to Yes*

Creating a Report from an Existing Form

A report can be manually created like any other report cited in this chapter or from an already existing form that can be saved as a report, which allows you to avoid unnecessary rework.

Instead of having to do the tedious task of re-creating a form (or subform) that already has a desired layout as new report, just open it in Design mode and ask Access to save it as a report.

But since the desired form might exist in an external Access database, first you may need to import the desired objects from an external database—something that can be easily done using Microsoft Access' External Data tab tools.

Importing Database Objects

Microsoft Access allows you to transfer different types of objects to the current database by using the Import & Link tools on the External Data tab, where you can select different sources of data.

By selecting the New Data Source tool in the Import & Link area of the External Data tab, you can choose among the different types of data sources to be imported as a table: From File, From Database, From Online Services, and From Other Sources.

When the data source is a Microsoft Access database, you can navigate through all its objects (such as tables, queries, forms, reports, and macros) and select the ones you want to import to the current database.

So, let's suppose you want to create a report that shows for each food item all its available common measures and LANGUAL descriptors (if any), using the same layout already defined in frmSubWeight_SubTotal and frmSubLANGDESC_SubTotal, as shown in Figure 4-71, knowing that both subforms are available in the sr28_Interface.accdb database (that you can extract from the Chapter04.zip file).

Follow these steps to import these subforms from the sr28_Interface.accdb database:

1. Use the External Data, New Data Source, or From Database, Access option to import objects in the Get External Data – Access Database dialog box using the title "Select the source and destination of data."

2. In the Get External Data – Access Database dialog box, click in the Browse button and locate the sr28_Interface.accdb database to open this database and show the Import Objects dialog box (Figure 6-47).

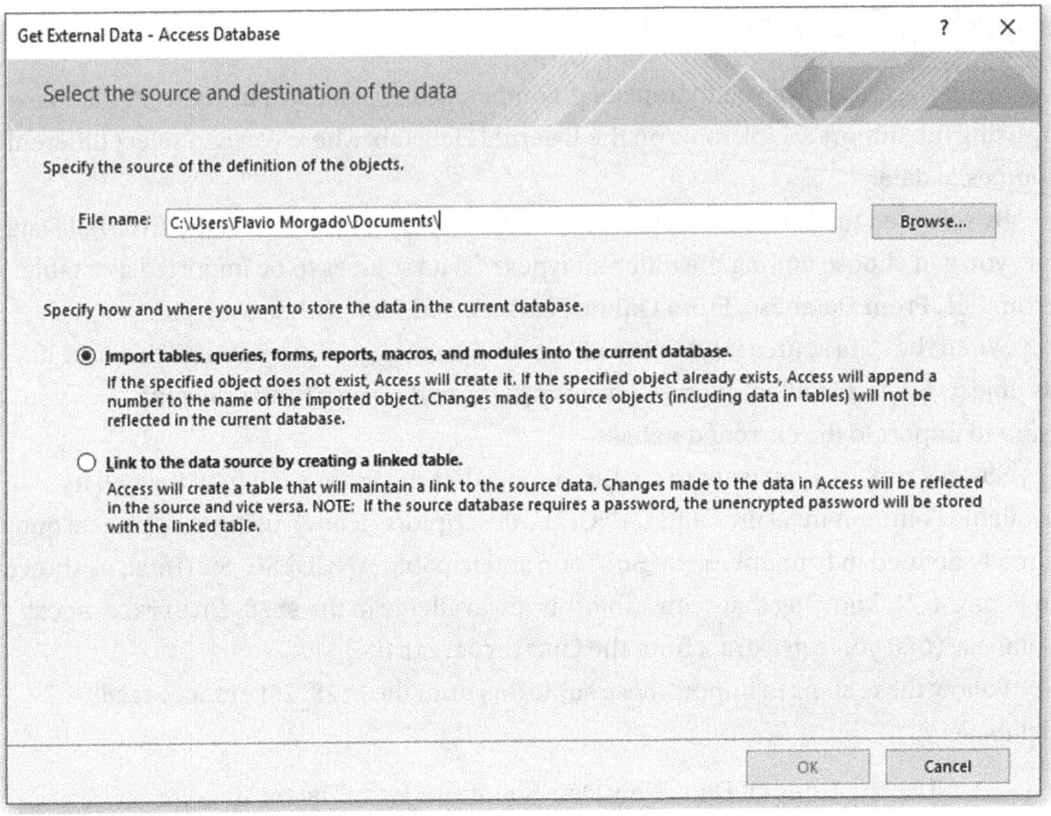

Figure 6-47. *Use the Get External Data box to import database objects from another Microsoft Access database to the current database*

Attention   A linked table is one that exists on another Access database—one that can reside in the same folder or another folder, within the same or another computer on a network. It may work like a local table regarding its records manipulation (add, edit, or delete records), but you can't change its structure (add, delete, or change Field properties or relate it to current database tables), and it keeps following any referential integrity that may be imposed on it in the database it resides in.

---

3.   Select the desired Microsoft Access database file, click OK to make Microsoft Access open the external database, and show the Import Objects window from where you can select which objects you want to import.

4. Having selected the `sr28_Interface.accdb` database, select the Import Objects Forms tabs to show all database Form objects.

5. Press and hold the Ctrl key to select frmSubWeight_SubTotal and frmSubLANGDESC_SubTotal (Figure 6-48).

Tip   Whenever you import a form or report from an external database, be aware that you may need to also import its dependent objects, like queries and macros used by the object and like the controls' properties or events. The Import Objects window's tabs allow you to select different objects and import them all in a single operation.

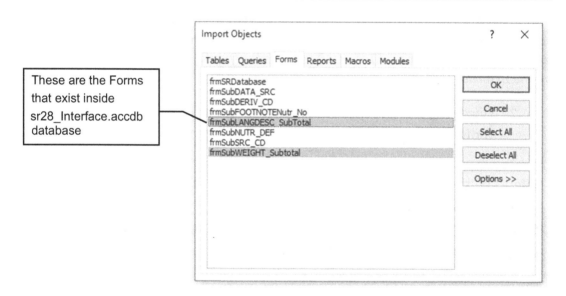

Figure 6-48. *Use the Import Objects dialog box to select all the desired objects that you want to import from the external Microsoft Access database*

6. After selecting the desired objects to import, click OK to import them and close the external database. Access will show the Save Import Steps dialog box, where you can save these steps to import the same objects again (Figure 6-49).

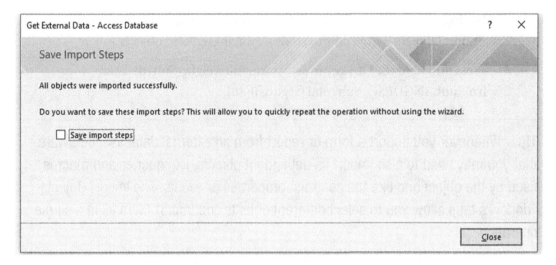

Figure 6-49. *Check the "Save import steps" option if you want to reimport the same objects in the future. When you click Close, Access will ask for a name to be associated to these steps, which can be selected using the Saved Imports command on the External Data tab*

7.   Once the import operation ends, check the Database window to verify that all desired database objects are already there.

Note   The sr28_Reports.accdb database used by this chapter already has a copy of the frmSubWeight_SubTotal and frmSubLANGDESC_SubTotal subforms imported from the sr28_Interface database. If you import other copies, the new ones will receive the same name with a consecutive count suffix.

Converting a Form into a Report

To save any form as a report, you must do the following:

1.   Open the form (using Form or Design view).

2.   Execute the File ➤ Save As ➤ Save Object As command.

3.   In the Save As dialog Box, select the As Report option.

Although it is quite easy to convert a form to a report, Microsoft Access 2019 created a somewhat confusing way of using the File ➤ Save As option because whenever you select File ➤ Save As, it offers by default the "Save Database as" option, which can make you close the current database or oblige you to use up to four mouse clicks to change a single form to a report (Figure 6-50).

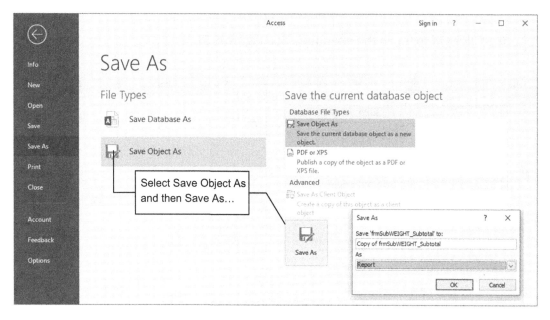

Figure 6-50. *To convert a form to a report, use the File ➤ Save As option, which shows the Save As window. You need to select Save Object As and then click the Save As button to show the Save As dialog box*

Since this is such a common operation, it is recommended that you add the Save Object As option to the Quick Access toolbar (the small buttons located in the Access window's top-left corner) so you can execute this task using a single mouse click operation, by following these steps:

1. Right-click the Quick Access toolbar and choose "Customize Quick Access toolbar" to show the Access Options dialog box, with the Quick Access toolbar selected.

2. The Access Options dialog box for the Customize Quick Access toolbar has two list boxes: to the left is the list of commands and to the right is the list of selected commands.

3. For the "Choose commands from" option, select the File tab to show all the File commands.

4. Scroll the list of commands to select the Save Object As option and click the Add >> button to add it to the list of selected commands.

5. If desired, use the arrows buttons to the right of the list of selected commands to reposition the Save Object As option.

6. Click OK to finish the operation. See Figure 6-51.

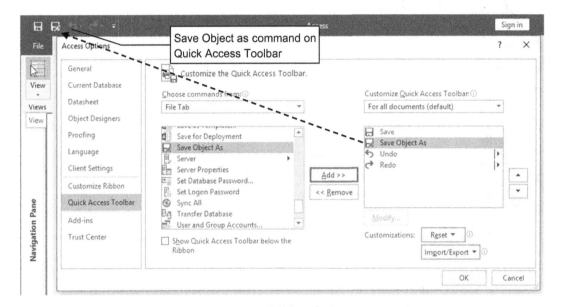

Figure 6-51. *Use the Access Options dialog box's Quick Access Toolbar option to personalize the Quick Access toolbar by adding a Save Object As command to it*

You are now able to use the Save As Object command by using a single mouse click to save any object with another name or eventually with another object type (if available).

To convert frmSubWeight_SubTotal to a report, follow these steps:

1. Open frmSubWeight_SubTotal using Form or Design view.

2. Click the Save As Object command on the Access Quick Access toolbar.

3. Change the object name (Access always prefixes the current object name with "Copy of ") to rptSubWeight_SubTotal (or whatever you like).

4. Change the object type to As Report and click OK to create the desired report (Figure 6-52).

Note   Repeat the previous steps to also convert the frmSubLANGDESC_SubTotal form to the rptSubLANGDESC_SubTotal report.

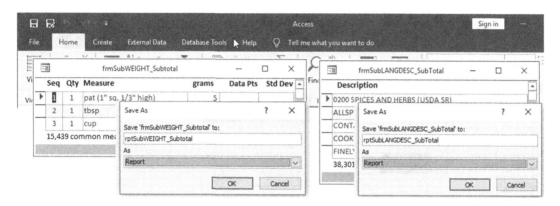

Figure 6-52.   *Open frmSubWEIGHT_Subtotal (and frmSubLANGDESC_SubTotal) and use the Save Object As command to save it as a report called rptSubWEIGHT_ Subtotal (and rptSubLANGDESC_SubTotal)*

Inserting a Subreport on a Main Report

To insert a subreport on a main report, follow the same strategy used to insert a subform on a main form: open the main report in Design view, select the subreport in the Database window, and drag it to the desired main report section.

Access will add it as a subreport control in the main report, and since it cannot be used to insert data, there is no need to take care of its Height property in the Main Form section. Its Can Grow property is automatically set to Yes, allowing the subreport to grow down the page as much as necessary to show all its records.

Note   Do not forget that all subreport records must fit in the 22-inch height limit of any report section.

To create a report that shows food items and their common measures, follow these steps:

1. Open rptFoodItems3 in Design view.

2. Select rptSubWEIGHT_Subtotal in the Database window and drag it to the rptFoodItems3 Detail section.

3. Show the Properties Sheet's Data tab for the rptSubWEIGHT_
    Subtotal control, select its Link Master child property, and click
    the ... button to show the Subreport Field Linker that will propose
    the NDB_No field to link both reports (Figure 6-53).

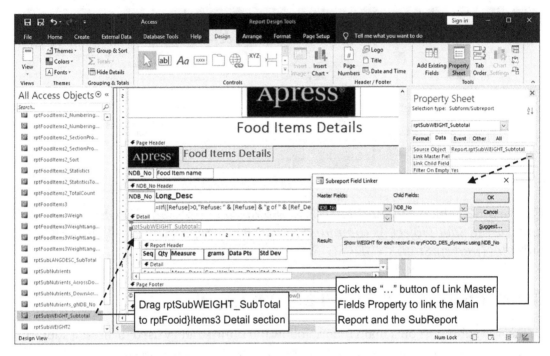

Figure 6-53. *Drag the desired report to a section of a main report in Design vew to add it as a subreport control. Use the Link Master Fields' ... button to show the Subreport Field Linker and easily set its Link Master Fields and Link Child Fields properties*

4. Since the subreport control has a border, use the Format tab's
    Shape Outline tool to give it a transparent outline.

5. Repeat steps 2 to 4 to add rptSubLANGDESC_Subtotal to
    the right of rptSubWEIGHT_Subtotal and link it to the main
    rptFoodITems3.

Note   You may need to manually reposition and align both subreports by its Top on Detail section so the main form's Width property is not greater than 8 inches, as shown in Figure 6-54.

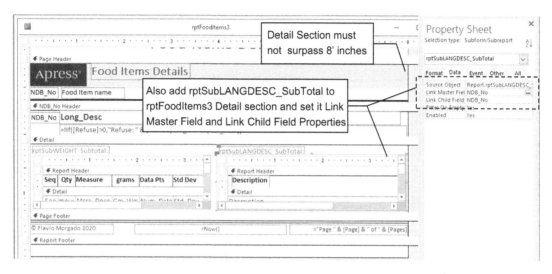

Figure 6-54. *This is rptFoodItems3 after receiving rptSubWEIGHT_Subtotal and rptSubLANGDESC_SubTotal on its Detail section, taking care to keep the main report's Detail section to less than 8 inches*

6. Open rptFoodItems3 in Print Preview mode and type a valid NDB_No code (one that you can copy from the FOOD_DES table for a given food item) and navigate to its second page to see how the subreports will behave (Figure 6-55 proposes using NDB_No = 13401).

Note   Although both subreport controls are the same size in the main report's Detail section, they use different vertical spaces to print all their records according to the food item selected.

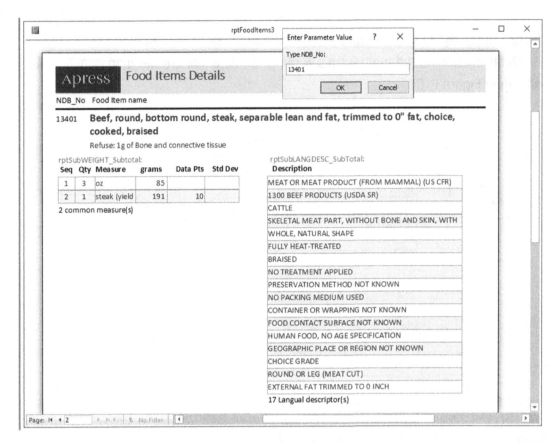

Figure 6-55. *This is rptFoodItems3's second page for food item NDB_No set to 13401. Although the subreports have the same vertical size in the main report's Detail section, they may grow or shrink to show their records (if any) because their properties Can Grow and Can Shrink were set to Yes*

Note This report was saved as rptFoodItems3_WgtLang in the `sr28_Reports.` `accdb` database.

Setting the Subreport's Height Property

Whenever a subreport whose Can Grow property is set to Yes is observed in the report's Design view and it has controls below its lower border in the same section in which it resides, when it grows vertically, it will push all the controls under its last printed section.

Let's suppose for a moment that you want to add Calories Breakdown and %Daily Values information to the food item report shown in Figure 6-55, using the same charts employed by frmSRDatabase found in the sr28_Interface.accdb database (shown in Figure 4-90).

Open rptFoodItems3_WgtLang_Chart in Design mode, and note that it received those charts right below the rptSubWEIGH_SubTotal subreport. Both charts are linked to the report's NDB_No field by their Link Master Field and Link Child Field properties (Figure 6-56).

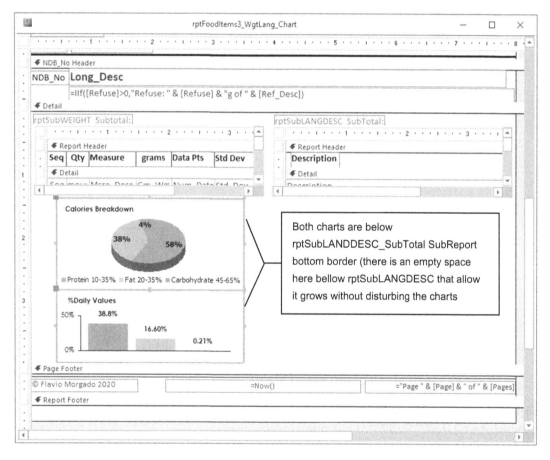

Figure 6-56. *This is the rptFoodItems3_WgtLang_Chart report, which received the Calories Breakdown and %Daily Values charts used previously in another section of this book and were positioned below the rptSubLANGDESC_SubTotal subreport's bottom border*

Although one can expect that rptSubLANGDESC_SubTotal can grow without disturbing the chart's position (since neither of them are on its growth pathway), this is not what happens when the subreport grows to show its records: since both charts are below its bottom border, the report engine will push them down, forcing them to print below the last subreport printed section (Figure 6-57).

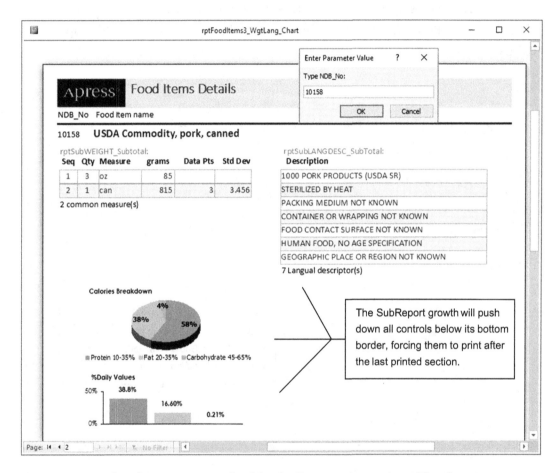

Figure 6-57. *The charts were pushed in the last section printed by the rptSubLANGDESC_SubTotal subreport*

To make a subreport grow vertically without disturbing what is below its bottom border—even though not on its growth pathway—assure that the subreport height in Design view goes at least a little down from the last object's top border whose position should not be disturbed when it grows to show its records.

Figure 6-58 shows how you can fix it. Using the report's Design view, drag the rptSubLANGDESC_Subtotal subreport bottom border so it passes a little bit below the %Daily Values chart's Top Border.

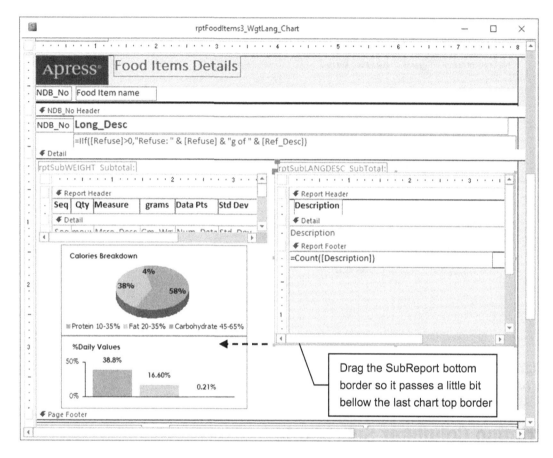

Figure 6-58. *To make a subreport grow without disturbing the controls that are below it, drag its bottom border so it reaches a position that passes a litle bit below the top border of the last control in the same section it resides*

Now, when the report is opened to show whatever number of Langual records a food item has, the Calories Breakdown and %Daily Value charts' vertical position will not be disturbed by the subreport's growth (Figure 6-59).

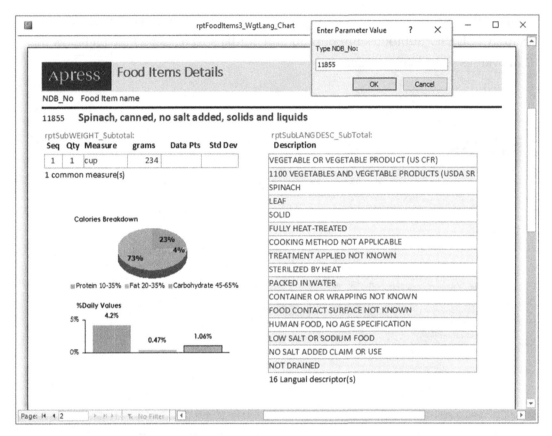

Figure 6-59. *Now the subreport can grow without disturbing the vertical position of other controls in the same section*

Printing Columnar Subreports

The food item report can be improved by showing all nutrient amounts it may have using a columnar presentation, with nutrients grouped by classes (macronutrients, elements, vitamins, amino acids, fatty acids, etc.).

Nutrient codes and names are stored on the NUTR_DEF table, and by observing their Nutr_No codes, a trained person can note that they are grouped into up to eight different classes according to its Nutr_No code ranges. Table 6-3 shows these nutrient class orders, the class names, and the Nutr_No code ranges as defined by the sr28.accdb database.

Table 6-3. *Nutrient Classes Order and Names*

Class Order	Class Name	Nutr_No Range
1	Macronutrients	<=1200
2	Carbohydrates	<=2200
3	Elements	<=6240
4	Vitamins	<=8950
5	Fatty Acids	<=15600
6	Sterols	<=16200
7	Amino Acids	<=18100
8	Other	>18100

Since nutrient values are stored on NUT_DATA (which has about 600,000 records), the first step is to create a query that returns nutrients grouped by classes for a single food item, which is exactly what qryNutrients_gNDB_No does, using the gNDB_No global temporary variable set by mcrSet_gNDB_No Macro (that uses a SetTempVar action to set gNDB_No = "01001"), whose Query Design view is shown in Figure 6-60.

Note   Since qryNutrients_gNDB_No uses the [TempVars]![gNDB_No] as criteria to its records, run mcrSet_gNDB_No before showing the query using Datasheet view.

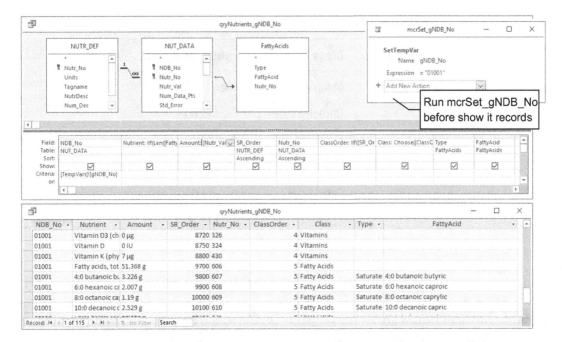

Figure 6-60. *This is qryNutrients_gNDB_No, which returns nutrient names and values grouped by classes for a single food item whose NDB_No code is stored on the gNDB_No global variable (scroll the records down to see the FattyAcid names)*

There are some characteristics of qryNutrients_gNDB_No that deserve to be mentioned.

- Records are first sorted by SR_Order (according to the sr28doc.pdf documentation, this is a common sort order for nutritional reports) and then by Nutr_No, using ascending order.

- It uses the FattyAcids table, which I created based on Table 2 of the sr28doc.pdf documentation (page 30) that shows "Systematic and Common Names for Fatty Acids, to return the Type and FattyAcid columns, so this nutrient names has a more legible, understandable meaning.

- Since the FattyAcids table relates to just specific nutrient Nutr_No codes, it has a Join property that "Includes all records from NUT_DATA and only those records of FattyAcids where the joined fields are equal."

- The Nutrient column uses an expression with the IIF() function to switch the nutrient name between the FattyAcid and NutrDesc fields according to the length of the FattyAcid column.

```
Nutrient: IIf(Len([FattyAcid])>0,[FattyAcid],[NutrDesc])
```

- The Amount column uses an expression that concatenates nutrient values and their units.

```
Amount: [Nutr_Val] & " " & [Units]
```

- The ClassOrder column uses a complex expression with many nested IIF() functions to return the desired nutrient class order of appearance in the report, according to it Nutr_No range (as cited in Table 6-3).

```
ClassOrder: IIf([SR_Order]<=1200,1,IIf([SR_ORDER]<=2200,2,
IIf([SR_ORDER]<=6240,3,IIf([SR_Order]<=8950,4,
IIf([SR_Order]<=15600,5,IIf([SR_ORDER]<=16200,6,
IIf([SR_Order]<=18100,7,8)))))))
```

- The Class column uses an expression based on the ClassOrder column value and a CHOOSE() function to return the desired nutrient class name:

```
Class: Choose([ClassOrder],"Macro Nutrients",
"Carbohydrates", "Elements","Vitamins",
"Fatty Acids","Sterols","Amino Acids","Other")
```

Now open the rptSubNutrients_DownAcross report in Design view, showing its Property Sheet window (Figure 6-61).

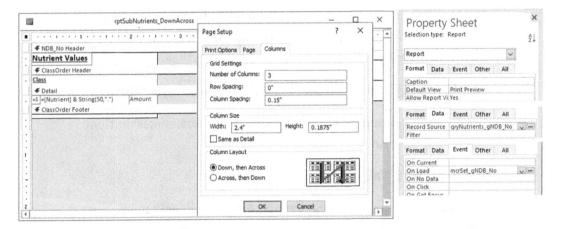

Figure 6-61. *This is rptSubNutrients_DownAcross, which is set to print on three columns using Column Layout set to "Down, then Across"*

Using rptSubNutrients_DownThenAcross in Design view, open the Property Sheet window and note the following:

- On the Format tab, its Default View property is set to Print Preview (to see its columns).

- On the Data tab, its Record Source property is set to qryNutrients_gNDB_No.

- On the Event tab, On Load is set to mcrSet_gNDB_No (to set the gNDB_No whenever the report is opened).

- On its Page Setup Column tab, it uses the following:

  - Number of Columns = 3

  - Column Spacing = 0.15 inches

  - Column Width = 2.4 inches

  - Column Layout = Down, then Across

- It has two Group Header sections.

  - *NDB_No Header*: With a Label control whose Caption is "Nutrient values" formatted as Calibri 12pt, Bold, Underline

  - *ClassOrder Header*: To sort its records first by ClassOrder field, with the property Repeat Section set to Yes and with a Class field's Text Box formatted as Calibri 10pt, Bold, Underline

- Its Detail section has a Text Box with an expression that concatenates the [Nutrient] field with the STRING() function to fill the gap between the nutrient name and its amount with a succession of dots:

```
=[Nutrient] & String(50,".")
```

The STRING() function generates a string that repeats a character a specified number of times and has this syntax:

```
String(Number, Character)
```

where:

Number: Required. This is the length of the returned string.

Character: Required. This is an expression that indicates the character used to build the returned string. If it has more than one character, the leftmost will be repeated.

Switch the rptSubNutrients_DownAcross report to Print Preview, and note that it prints nicely as a main report. It uses a three-column layout that has the expected way to read columns (reading "down, then across" like in a newspaper). It has a "trailing effect" created by the STRING() function that fills the space between the nutrient name and its amount with dots to improve readability (Figure 6-62).

Note   Since the report uses a Text Box with the expression =[Nutrient] & String(50, ".") to add 50 dot characters as a suffix for each nutrient name, you cannot set this Text Box's Can Grow property to Yes because it will make almost every nutrient name use two or more lines to print. Try it for yourself!

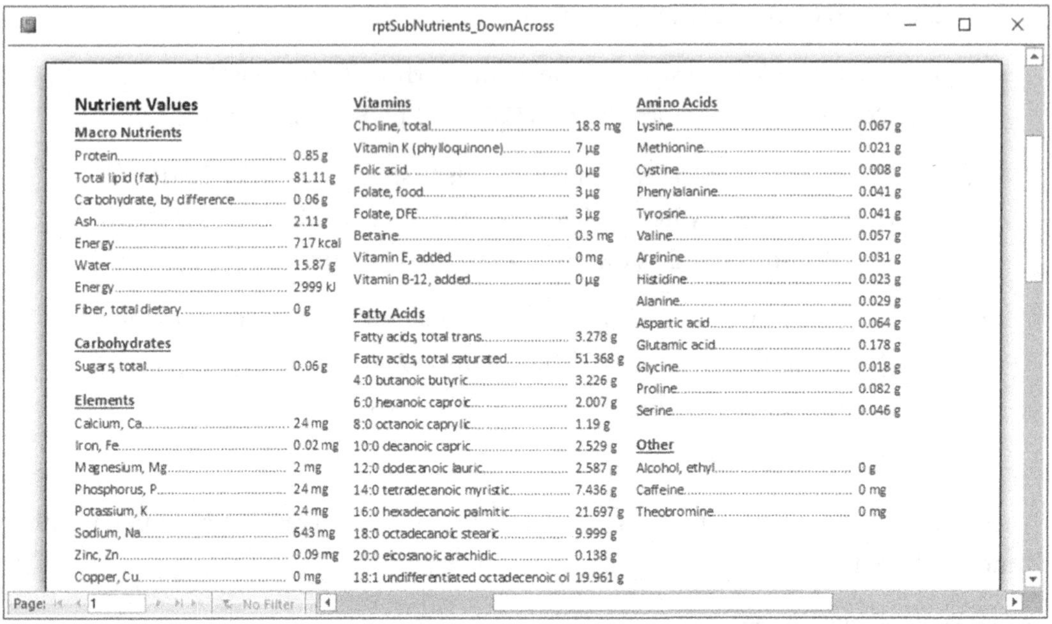

Figure 6-62. *This is rptSubNutrients_DownAcross that shows all the nutrient values for a food item whose NDB_NO value is 01001 (set by mcrSet_gNDB_No Macro), using a three-column layout reading down and then across*

Now that you know that rptSubNutrients_DownAcross prints nicely when it is opened from the Database window as a main report, it is interesting to note that when it is used as a subreport inside a main report, Access fails to print its columns.

This happens because Access had a persistent bug up to Access 2003 that allowed you to print a columnar subreport using the "down, then across" layout if it was inserted in the main report's Detail section—a condition that worsened since Access 2007 that doesn't allow print columns to be read "down, then across" in subreports, regardless of the section they are placed in on a main report.

To see an example of this, let's open rptMain_SubDownAcross_Detail in Design view. Note that it has rptSubNutrients_DownAcross inserted as a subreport in its Detail section (Figure 6-63).

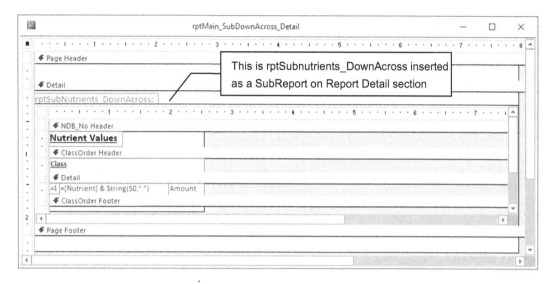

Figure 6-63. *The rptMain_SubDownAcross_Detail report received rptSubnutrients_DownAcross as a subreport in its Detail section with the expectation that it prints using its three columns with the Column Layout property set to to "Down, then Across"*

Note that although the subreport's Detail section is just about 2.5 inches wide, the subreport control uses all the main report's Detail section's width of 8 inches, so it can try to print its three columns.

Switch rptMain_SubDownAcross_Detail to Print Preview and note that Access will fail to print the rptSubnutrients_DownAcross subreport using its three-column "Down, then across" layout (note the subreport control's black border). It prints it using a one-column layout keeping the default column width defined by the original subreport's Page Setup dialog box. See Figure 6-64.

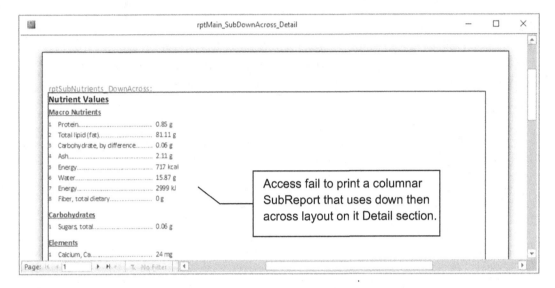

Figure 6-64. Access fails to print a columnar subreport that uses the "Down, then Across" layout; it uses a one-column layout although it keeps using the original Column Width property

---

Note   Open the rptMain_SubDownAcross_Group and rptMain_SubDownAcross_ RptFooter reports in Design view, and note that they received the rptSubNutrients_ DownAcross subreport in their NDB_No Header section and Report Footer section. Switch them to Print Preview mode, and note that Access can't print a column "Down, then Across" subreport.

Now open rptSubNutrients_AcrossDown in Design view, and note that it has the same basic structure with subtle differences.

- Its Column Layout property is set to "Across, then Down."

- It ClassOrder Header section has the Repeat Section property set to No.

- It has a Running Sum property set to Over Group on a Text Box to the left of the nutrient name to restart the nutrients count for each nutrient class.

- To make it more pleasant to view, the ClassOrder Footer section has the New Row Or Col property set to After Section (which guarantees that each nutrient class begins on a new row). See Figure 6-65.

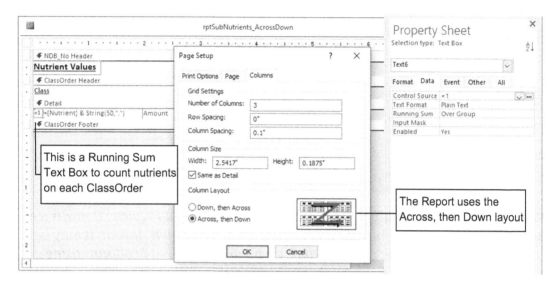

Figure 6-65. *This is rptSubNutrients_AcrossDown that prints using the "Across, then Down" layout. It has a Running Sum Text Box to count the nutrients on each nutrient class*

Open rptSubNutrients_AcrossDown in Print Preview mode, and note that it also prints nicely—but may be considered inadequate to read because our eyes are trained to read columns from top to bottom—although the report counts the nutrients on each class to indicate the reading order (Figure 6-66).

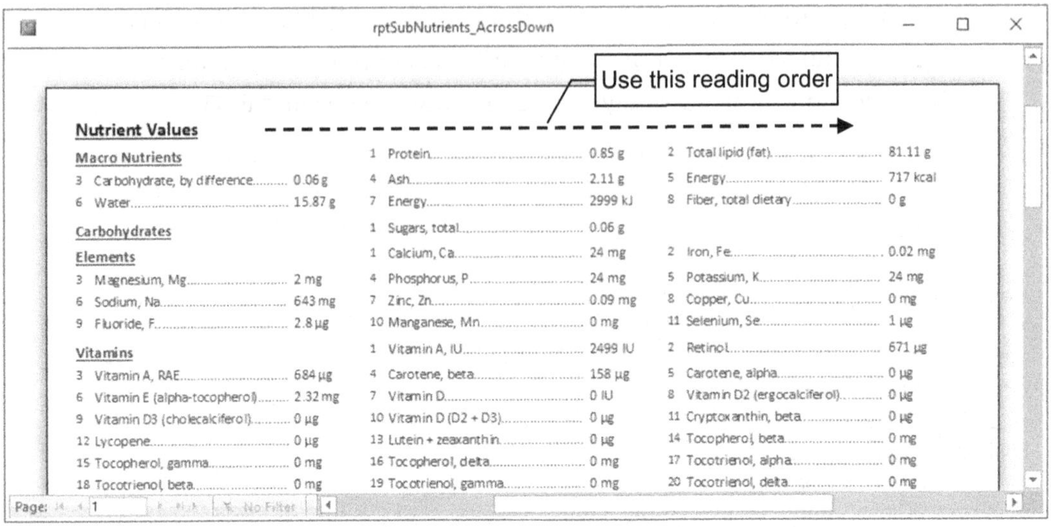

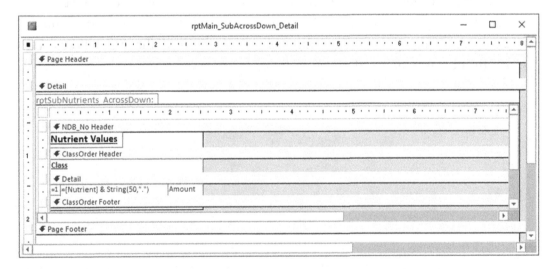

Figure 6-66. *This is rptSubNutrients_AcrossDown on Print Preview; it prints well using a three-column layout, but due to its "Across, then down" layout, it may be considered inadequate for reading, since we are trained to read columns using a top-to-bottom layout. To help the reader, nutrients are numbered on each nutrient class, which always begins on a new row*

Now open rptMain_SubAcrossDown_Detail in Design view and note that it had rptSubNutrients_AcrossDown inserted as a subreport in its Detail section (Figure 6-67).

Figure 6-67. *This is rptMain_SubAcrossDown_Detail, which received on its Detail section the rptSubNutrients_AcrossDown subreport*

Switch rptMain_SubAcrossDown_Detail to Print Preview mode, and note that now, the subreport is printed correctly, using its native three-column layout, just because its Column Layout is "Across, then Down." It shows each nutrient category beginning on a new row because the ClassOrder Footer section has the property New Row or Col set to After section, to improve the report's legibility (Figure 6-68).

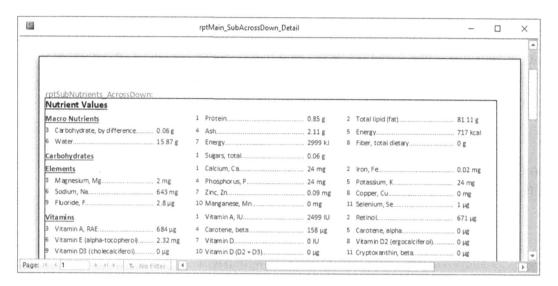

Figure 6-68. *To make a columnar subreport print as expected, Column Layout needs to be set to the "Across, then Down" option*

Note   Open the rptMain_SubAcrossDown_Group and rptMain_SubAcrossDown_RptFooter reports in Design view, and note that they received the rptSubNutrients_AcrossDown subreport on their NDB_No Header section and Report Footer section, respectively. Switch them to Print Preview mode and note now Access prints a columnar subreport no matter which section it resides in just because they use the "Down, then across" layout.

The lesson here is quite simple: to print a multicolumn subreport, you need to set Column Layout to "Across, then Down"—until a service pack fixes this Access bug!

To finish this section, note that the `sr28_Reports.accdb` database also has rptSubNutrients, which is a copy of rptSubNutrients_AcrossDown with the difference that it is bound to qryNutrients. That is also a copy of qryNutrients_gNDB_No but does not filter its records, showing nutrients for all possible food items.

Attention   By opening qryNutrients in Datasheet view, it will return all nutrients for the more than 8,000 food items of the FOOD_DES table, meaning that it is a complex query that may take some time to run. Your computer can appear to freeze, but it is not actual frozen—it is just trying to recover more than 600,000 nutrient values from the NUT_DATA table.

To see the final result, open rptFoodItems3_WgtLang_Nutrients in Design view and note that it is similar to rptFoodItems3_WgtLang_Chart (see Figure 6-58) with subtle differences.

- It has a first NDB_NO Header section that prints the Food Item name (and refuse part, if any). Its Repeat Section property is set to Yes (to allow it to print it on top of each food item page).

- It received a second NDB_No Header section, to where its subreports and charts were moved, and the property Repeat Section is set to No.

- It received the rptSubNutrients subreport on its Detail section (whose the Outline was set to Transparent, and Link Master Fields and Link Child Fields were set to NDB_No, as shown in Figure 6-69).

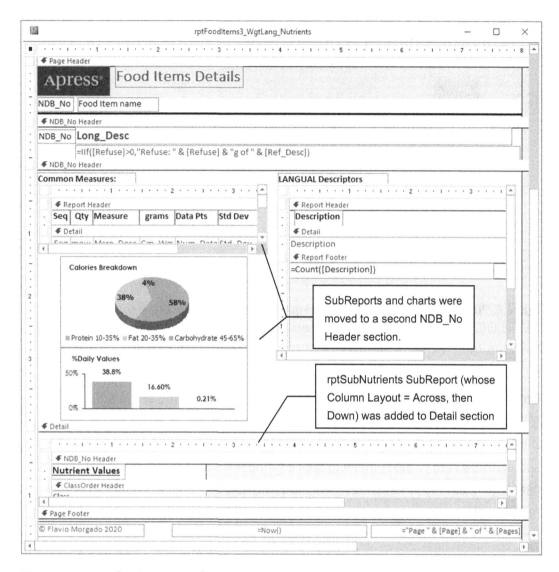

Figure 6-69. *This is rptFoodItems3_WgtLang_Nutrients, which received a second NDB_No Header section to where its subreports and charts were moved*

Open rptFoodItems3_WgtLang_Nutrients in Print Preview mode, and since it is bound to the qryFOOD_DES_dynamic query, it will ask for a NDB_No code (try 13401) that when typed will make the report return all the desired food item information, including a last page that prints a multicolumn subreport (using the awkward "Across, then Down" layout, as shown in Figure 6-70).

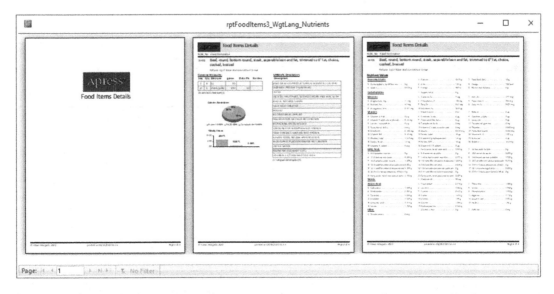

Figure 6-70. *This is rptFoodItems3_WgtLang_Nutrients using a multiple-page view, so you can see all its subreport and chart controls. By setting Column Layout to "Across, then Down," a multicolumn subreport can print as expected*

Note Figure 6-70 shows rptFoodItems3_WgtLang_Nutrients printing the rptSubNutrients subreport on its own page because it was inserted on the Report Detail section with the property Keep Together set to Yes. This means if the entire subreport can't fit in the remaining space of the second page, it will print on the next page (some food items have less nutrient data and may fit on the second report page).

Microsoft Access Report Events

As previously explained for the Form object, a report also fires events, and you can use some macro code to allow the user to control how a report will print. As explained in Table 5-3, some of these events can be canceled by using a CancelEvent macro action (notably the Report Open and Unload events).

A Report object has window events (that fire a single time when a report is opened or closed) and report section events (that fire when a section is formatted, reformatted if necessary, and finally printed).

They are somewhat difficult to follow because report window events fire differently depending on the way a report is shown (Report view, Layout view, or Print Preview), and the section events may fire multiple times while a page is formatted and then fire again when the page is finally sent to the printer.

Attention   Double-click the rptFoodItems2_Events report in the `sr28_Reports` database window to see how it fires its window and section events. It has a macro that uses the MessageBox action associated to the Report On Open, On Load, On Unload, and On Close events, and also to the Report Header/Footer, Page Header/ Footer, and Detail Section Format and Print events.

To create user interaction with a report, use these events:

- *On Load*: This shows a form in modal state where the user can cancel the report opening or set a filter on its records (since this event can be canceled).

- *On Load or On Open*: This shows a pop-up form that continuously floats over the report window, allowing you to change the report's Record Source property.

- *On Unload or On Close*: This closes any form opened by the On Load or On Open event.

Let's see some examples of how we can use such strategies.

Using Macros to Set the Report Records Scope

You can give the user a chance to change a report's recordset scope by employing a strategy that uses a form, macro code, and temporary global variables. You select a criteria and print options to be used to print a single report or several.

This is simple to do by using a macro that at the end uses the OpenReport action.

The OpenReport Action

Use the OpenReport action in a macro to open a report using a specific view or send it directly to the printer, with or without restricting the records it prints.

The OpenReport action has these arguments:

- *Report Name*: Required. This is the report name to be opened.

- *View*: This is the view mode in which the report will open. It can be set to one of the following:

  - *Print*: Prints the report immediately

  - *Design*: Opens the report in Design view

  - *Print Preview*: Opens the report in Print Preview mode

- *Filter Name*: This is the name of a query that includes all the fields needed by the report.

- *Where Condition*: This is a valid SQL WHERE clause used to select records. If you select the Filter Name argument, this condition will be applied to the filter query.

- *Window Mode*: This is the mode that the Report window will appear in (it may require the use of "overlapping windows").

  - *Normal*: This is default mode; the report will show regularly on its window.

  - *Hidden*: This report will open and format its records but will be hidden (its Visible property is set to No).

  - *Icon*: This report will open minimized in the Access window.

  - *Dialog*: This report will open in a modal state; all Access interaction will stop until the report is closed.

To use the OpenReport action and give the database application users greater control over what records must be printed by one or more reports, use a form with controls that allow you to define the criteria that will filter their records using one of these strategies:

- A print form, where the user can select the desired report and use its controls to set common criteria that affect their recordsets

- A dedicated form that is used by the report itself before or after it is opened, to change its recordset

Let's see how these two approaches work.

Using a Print Form

A print form must be a clear, concise, simple interface that allows you to select the desired report, to set options to limit the record scope, and to easily select to preview it or send it directly to the printer.

Double-click frmPrintReports in the Database window to open it in Form view and realize that it was conceived to do exactly this (Figure 6-71).

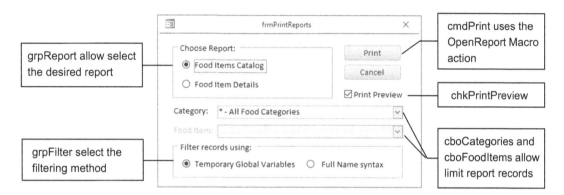

Figure 6-71. *This is rptPrintReports that allows you to select a report, a print method, and different ways of filtering its records using the OpenReport Macro action*

The form frmPrintReports is a didactic form created to demonstrate two different ways to filter report records (grpFilter), using two different print methods (chkPrintPreview) for two different reports ("Food Items Catalog" or "Food Item Detail"), which makes its cmdPrint On Click event macro code very extensive, using a set of IF macro actions to deal with all those options.

Let's see how cmdPrint's On Click event macro code groups its instructions by first checking the grpFilter option.

Using Temporary Global Variables

Whenever the Temporary Global Variables option is selected in the grpFilter Option Group, the OpenReport action doesn't need to use its Where Condition argument. Report records are filtered according to the gFdGrp_CD and gNDB_No Temporary global variables values, because they are used as criteria for both reports' Record Source properties, and the OpenReport action just needs to set the desired View argument.

Figure 6-72 shows that the macro code associated to cmdPrint's On Click Event begins by checking whether If [grpFilter]=1 (whether the Temporary Global Variables option is selected). Then it checks If [grpReports]=1 (whether the Food Items Catalog report option is selected). Finally, it checks If [chkPrintPreview]=True to set the OpenReport action's View argument to Print Preview or Print to print the rptFoodItems_Catalog report.

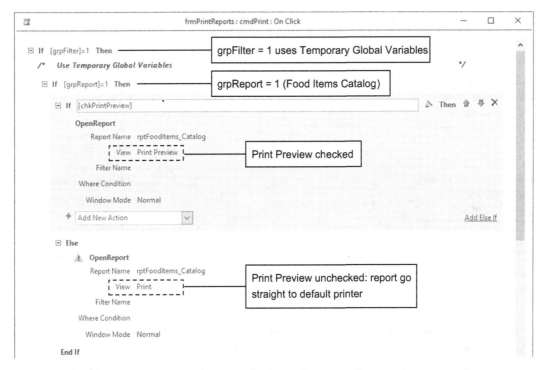

Figure 6-72. *This is cmdPrint's On Click event macro code, which begins by checking grpFilter to set the filter method, then checks grpReport to verify the selected report, and finally checks chkPrintPreview to decide how to use the View argument of the OpenReport method*

Note   The macro code fragment shown in Figure 6-72 is repeated to print rptFoodItems_Detail using the Temporary Global Variables method.

Whenever the Temporary Global Variables method is selected, cboCategory and cboFoodItem are responsible for setting the gFdGrp_CD and gNDB_No global variable values using their After Update events. These events fire whenever a food category or food item is selected (whenever frmPrintReports is open or cboFoodITem is empty, gNDB_No = "*").

Using Full Name Syntax

The alternative "full name syntax" method uses the control's full name syntax (Forms!FormName!ControlName) to allow you to use the Where Condition argument of the OpenReport action to filter report records according to the values selected in the cboCategory or cboFoodItem Combo Box control.

So, whenever this option is selected, the grpFilter After Update event fires, and the gFdGrp_CD and gNDB_No global variables are set to "*" so the Report Record Sources that use those variables can return all their records.

Figure 6-73 shows the code fragment of cmdPrint's On Click event that runs whenever grpFilter=2 (when the "Full Name syntax" option is selected) to print either rptFoodItems_Catalog or rptFoodItems_Detail in Print Preview. Each OpenReport method uses different Where Condition arguments.

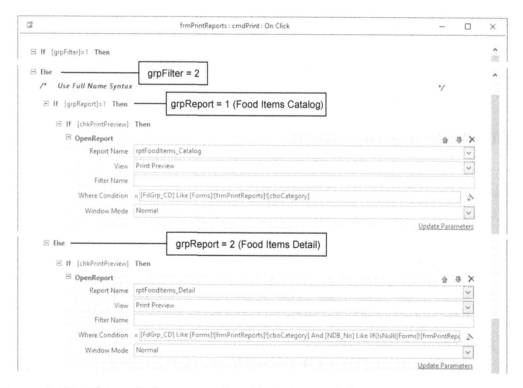

Figure 6-73. *This code fragment of cmdPrint's On Click event macro code shows what happens when grpFilter = 2 (the "Full Name syntax" option selected). Now the OpenReport action uses its Where Condition argument to filter report records*

Whenever grpReport = 1 (the "Food Items Catalog" option selected), cboFoodItem is disabled and set to Null (see Figure 6-71 above), so to print rptFoodItems_Catalog using Print Preview mode, the OpenReport action needs to set its Where Condition argument to an expression that uses the Like operator to compare the [FdGrp_CD] field with whatever is selected on the cboCategory Combo Box.

```
[FdGrp_CD] Like [Forms]![frmPrintReports]![cboCategory]
```

But since rptFoodItem_Details uses values selected in the cboCategory or cboFoodItem Combo Box controls, its OpenReport Where Condition argument needs to use a more complex expression (note that it uses "AND" to also test the [NDB_No] field using the Like operator).

```
[FdGrp_CD] Like [Forms]![frmPrintReports]![cboCategory] And [NDB_No]
Like IIf(IsNull([Forms]![frmPrintReports]![cboFoodItem]),"*",
[Forms]![frmPrintReports]![cboFoodItem])
```

This time the expression uses the IIF() function to verify whether cboFoodItem is Null, in which case it returns *. Otherwise, it uses the full name syntax to return the control value (in bold).

A Note About frmPrintReports

The frmPrintReports form is didactic in the way that it synchronizes its elements to give the user a good experience. I will leave it to you to select its options and print both reports to see how they behave. Please, check the following:

- Its controls are perfectly aligned to the right and left, adujstong Combo Box widths to allow such alignment.

- cmdPrint's Default property is set to Yes, so by pressing Enter, cmdPrint's On Click event fires, and the selected report is printed.

- cmdCancel's Cancel property is set to Yes, so by pressing Esc, cmdCancel's On Click event fires, and frmPrintReports closes.

- cboCategory uses a Union query to show its options ("* - All Food Categories" plus all available food categories sorted ascending, returning * or the FdGrp_CD field value).

- If you delete cboCategory's value making it Null, cmdPrint will be disabled.

- cboFoodItem is enabled whenever the Food Item Details option is selected (and is disabled and empty if the opposite).

- Whenever cboFoodCategory is set to * - All Food Categories, cboFoodItem is filled with all 8,500 food items sorted ascending, but when a category is selected, cboFoodItem shows just this category of food items.

- The rptFoodItems_Catalog and rptFoodItems_Details reports used by rptPrintReports are versions of rptFoodItem2_1stCharRunningSum (see Figure 6-43) and rptFoodItems3_WgtLang_Nutrients Reports, respectively (see Figure 6-70).

- By selecting FoodItem Detail, choosing an item from cboFoodCategory, and leaving cboFoodItem empty, rptFoodItem_ Detail, rptFoodItems_Detail will print all the available food items.

Attention   I will leave it to you to check all frmPrintReports controls' macro code to understand how it works to perfectly synchronize its interface.

Tip   By selecting FoodItem Detail, setting cboFoodCategory to * - All Food Categories, and leaving cboFoodItem empty, rptFoodItems_Detail will print about 20,000 pages (one or two pages for each food item), which will require great effort from your computer that may seem to freeze. Press Ctrl+Break to stop the operation or wait (several minutes) to finish the operation. If you are using a laptop computer that does not show a Break keyboard key, use one of these tips (excepted from Wikipedia): Ctrl + Fn + F11 or Fn + B or Fn + Ctrl + B on certain Lenovo laptops Ctrl + Fn + B or Fn + B on certain Dell laptops Fn + Esc on Samsung.Ctrl + Fn + ⇧ Shift on certain laptops.

Using a Dedicated Form

The expression *dedicated form* refers to a form that is used exclusively by one or more reports. The report shows the form using the report's On Open event, and the form can be as follows:

- A modal form that is opened in a modal state allowing you to set filter criteria before the report is shown

- A PopUp form that is opened with the report and keeps floating over its window, allowing you to continue filtering its records

To demonstrate how to use both dedicated form options to limit the scope of the report records, we'll be using versions of rptFoodItems_Catalog because of its fast printing method that needs to use three new macro actions: CancelEvent, Echo, and DisplayHourGalssPointer.

The CancelEvent Action

The CancelEvent macro action allows you to cancel all "Before" form and control events (BeforeDelConfirm, BeforeInsert and BeforeUpdate), as well as some events fired by the Form or Report window (ApplyFilter, Delete, Dirty, Filter, Format, On Open, On UnLoad, Print) or by controls (DblClick, Exit, KeyPress, MouseDown, NoData).

It is useful to allow the macro code to cancel a form or report's open or close operation, or to cancel, change, or add data to the database if it fails the macro code validation conditions.

The CancelEvent action has no arguments.

The Echo Action

The Echo action allows you to enable or disable the screen updating while the macro code is running and/or set a small text message to be displayed in the Microsoft Access status bar (the one that appears at the bottom left of the Access window).

The Echo macro action uses these arguments:

- *Echo On*: Turns Echo on/off to enable/disable the screen updating

- *Status Bar Text*: Sets the text to display in the status bar when Echo On is set to No

Note   The Echo On = No action can be used more than once in a macro to allow successive changes to the status bar text while the macro runs.

When the macro finishes, Access automatically sets Echo On to Yes and repaints the window.

Tip   For macro code that executes long, complex operations (such as running a lengthy query), you should use the DisplayHourGlassPointer action to change the mouse pointer to an hourglass icon while the macro is running and return it to a normal state when the macro ends.

The DisplayHourGlassPointer Action

The DisplayHourGlassPointer action allows you to change the mouse pointer to an hourglass image to provide a visual indication that the macro is running.

The DisplayHourGlassPointer action has one argument.

- *Hourglass On*: Yes (display the hourglass icon), No (display the normal mouse pointer)

Access automatically resets Hourglass On to No when the macro code ends.

Using a Dedicated Modal Form

A dedicated modal form opens using the OpenForm macro action's Window Mode = Dialog argument and is called from the form's On Open event. It has controls to set every desired filter condition and usually has two command buttons: OK to show the report, and Cancel to cancel the operation and avoid the report opening.

To make this mechanism work, the modal form needs to set at least two temporary global variables.

- gCancel is a global variable that works as a flag to signal if the modal form's Cancel button was selected, so the Report On Load event can be canceled using a CancelEvent macro action.

- One or more global variables to define the filter condition offered by the modal form that are used as criteria to the OpenForm's Where Condition argument or to its Record Source property.

The Dedicated Form frmDialogSelectCategory

Open frmDialogSelectCategory in Design view to note that it obeys the conditions defined for a dedicated form, with one Combo Box to set the report filter criteria and two Command Button controls.

- *cboCategory*: This is a Combo Box control whose Record Source is set to qryCategoriesUnionAll and whose Default Value is set to *.

- *cmdOK*: This is a Command Button control whose Default property is set to Yes (clicked when Enter key is pressed); use it on the On Click event's two SetTempVar actions to set gFdGrp to [cboCategories] and gCancel to False and then use a CloseWindow action to close itself.

- *cmdCancel*: This is a Command Button control whose Cancel property is set to Yes (click when the Esc key is pressed); it uses a CloseWindow action on its On Click event to close itself (Figure 6-74).

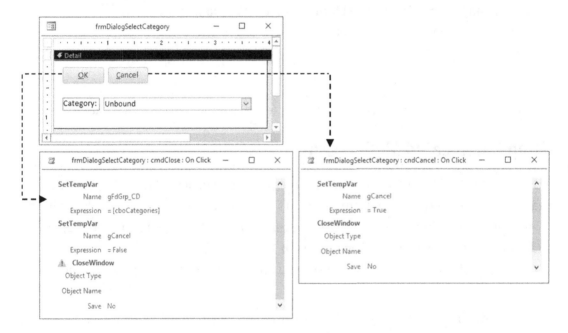

Figure 6-74. *The frmDialogSelectCategory uses cboCategory to set the desired food category, and it uses cmdOK to set gFdGrp_CD to [cboCategory] and gCancel to False to signal that the modal form was not canceled. It uses cmdCancel to set gCancel to True to signal that the operation must be canceled*

Close frmDialogSelectCategory, open rptFoodItems_Catalog_Dialog in Design view, show the Property Sheet window's Event tab for the Form object, and check its On Open event (one that can be canceled by the CancelEvent macro action), as shown in Figure 6-75).

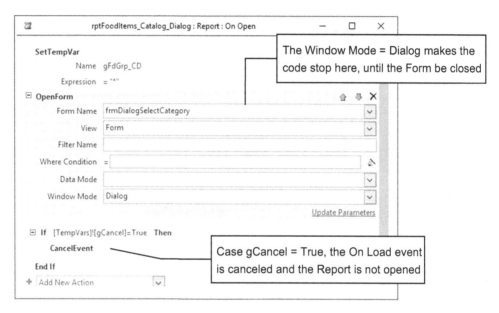

Figure 6-75. *This is the rptFoodItems_Catalog_Dialog report's On Open event, which uses an OpenForm action to open the frmDialogSelectCategory form in a modal state. After the form is closed, it checks the TempVars!gCancel global variable value to verify whether the event must be canceled*

The rptFoodItems_Catalog_Dialog's On Open event executes these sequential actions:

1. It uses SetTempVar to set gFdGrp_CD to *.

2. It uses OpenForm to open frmDialogSelectCategory using Window Mode set to Dialog, which will stop the code on this instruction until the form is closed.

3. IF [TempVars]![gCancel] is True, it indicates that frmDialogSelectCategory cmdCancel was clicked.

4. If the IF condition is True, it uses a CancelEvent action to cancel the Report On Load event, and the report is not opened.

To see the dedicated form in action, close the report and double-click it in the Database window. Access will try to open the report that, when firing its On Load event, shows frmDialogSelectCategory in a modal state that will stop its macro code, waiting for a user action (Figure 6-76).

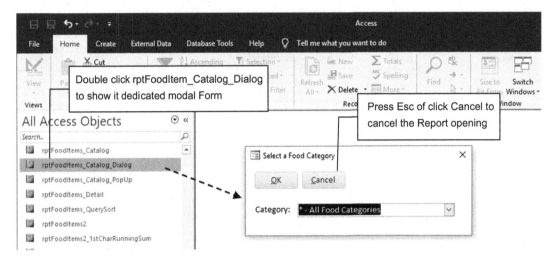

Figure 6-76. *Double-click rptFoodItem_Catalog_Dialog in the Database window to show the frmDialogSelectCategory form on a modal state, where you can select a category scope or click Cancel to avoid opening the report*

By selecting Cancel on frmDialogSelectCategory, gCancel=True, the form will close, and the CancelEvent action will cancel the report's On Load event, keeping it from opening. Alternatively, by clicking OK (with or without selecting a category), frmDialogSelectCategory will close, and the report will open showing the desired records (Figure 6-77).

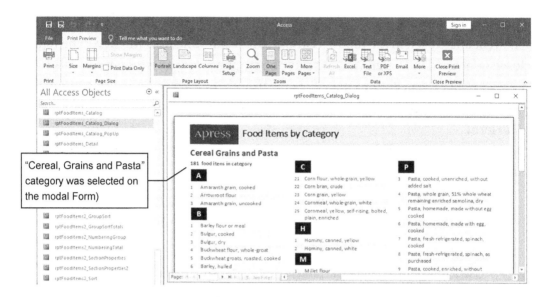

Figure 6-77. *By selecting a food category, the gFdGrp_CD temporary global variable is set to the desired food category scope, which is then used by the report*

Note This is a great way to create reports that can use a more complex dedicated form, full of controls so you can select all the possible filter conditions, without disturbing the basic database user interface whenever a new report is developed. Its disadvantage is that to apply another filter criteria, the report needs to be closed and opened again.

Using a Dedicated Pop-Up Form

A dedicated pop-up form has controls to allow you to set criteria conditions to be applied to the report record set (or by the OpenReport action's Where Condition argument) and has its property PopUp set to Yes to keep it floating over the Report window while it is open.

Since a report doesn't have a Requery method, a dedicated pop-up form needs to close it and open it again so its Record Source or Filter condition is updated. This is a situation that happens whenever a report is successively shown in Design view and then in Print Preview—simple tasks that can be done with macro code that uses the OpenReport action.

Considering that the dedicated pop-up form must be shown by the report's On Open event and closed in the report's On Unload event—that fires whenever the report is closed or opened in Design view—it must be stripped from all window controls (Control Box and Close Button) that allow the user to inadvertently close it. Otherwise, the user will be obliged to close and open the report to regain access to the dedicated pop-up form.

So, to correctly use a dedicated pop-up form to continually filter report records, it must do the following:

- The form should have no OK or Cancel Command Button and should have the properties Control Box and Close Button set to No, to not allow the form to be closed by a user action.

- Use a temporary global variable (gRptUpdating) that acts as a flag to signal to the Report On Unload event not to close the dedicated pop-up form when it is fired by the process of being successively changed to Design view and Print Preview to update its records.

All these open and close report operations makes the Access windows blink and update, so to make the macro code work better without disturbing the application interface so much, it must be inside a pair of Echo No, Echo True actions.

The Dedicated Form frmPopUpSelectCategory

To use a dedicated pop-up form, a report needs to show it from its On Open event and close it using its On UnLoad event when the user closes the Report window (but not when the report is open in Design view, a condition that also fires its On Unload event).

Open the rptFoodItems_Catalog_PopUp report in Design view, show its Property Sheet window's Event tab, and inspect its On Open and On Unload events (Figure 6-78).

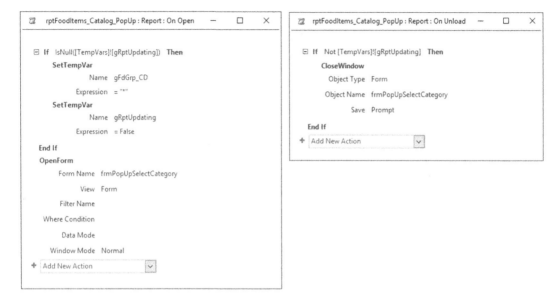

Figure 6-78. *This is the macro code for the rptFoodItems_Catalog_PopUp report's On Open and On Unload events*

Figure 6-78's left side shows that when the rptFoodItems_Catalog_PopUp report opens, its On Open event first uses the IF Isnull(gRptUpdating) macro action to verify whether the global variable gRptUpdating was already set. If it is null, it uses two SetTempVar actions to set gRptUpdating to False and gFdGrp_CD to *. Then it uses an OpenForm action to open frmPopUpSelectCategory using Window Mode = Normal, so it can float normally over the Report window.

On the right side of Figure 6-78, note that rptFoodItems_Catalog_PopUp's On Unload event, which executes when the report is closed, uses the If Not gRptUpdating action to verify whether gRptUpdating is False (since Not False is True), and if it is, it uses a CloseWindow action to close the Report window.

Now open the frmPopUpSelectCategory form in Design view, click cboCategory, and use the Property Sheet window to show its After Update event macro code (Figure 6-79).

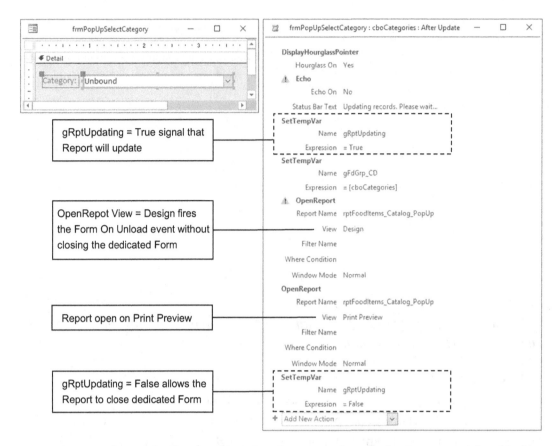

Figure 6-79. *This is the frmPopUpSelectCategory form's cboCategory After Update event, which uses DisplayHourGlassPointer, Echo, and the gRptUpdating variable to avoid the form being closed when the Report UnLoad event fires. It uses two OpenReport actions to open rptFoodItems_Catalog_Pop in Design view and then in Print Preview to make it update its records*

The code begins by using a DisplayHourGlassPointer action with its Hourglass On property set to Yes to change the Windows mouse pointer to indicate that the system is busy. Then screen updating is disabled using an Echo action with Echo On set to No.

To signal to the form's UnLoad event that the report is updating, a SetTempVar action is used to set gRptUpdating to True, and a second SetTempVar action sets gFdGrp_CD to [cboCategory] to allow the Report Record Source query to update its records.

Two OpenReport actions are executed in sequence over rptFoodItems_Catalog_PopUp. The first sets View to Design argument (which makes the Report Unload event fire), and the second sets View to Print Preview, which reopens the report and therefore updates its records (making its Report Load event fire).

Note   If you are wondering why I did not close and open the report again, I did this for instructional reasons: some report properties (such as Record Source) can be set only in the report's Design view. The same is true for the Report Grouping options, which although not covered in this chapter can be changed on the fly using this approach.

The macro code ends using another SetTempVar option with gRptUpdating set to False, to allow that frmPopUpSelectCategory to be closed by the report's On Unload event whenever the user decides to close its window.

Figure 6-80 shows rptFoodItems_Catalog_PopUp open after selecting "Cereal, Grains and Pasta" in the dedicated pop-up form to update its records.

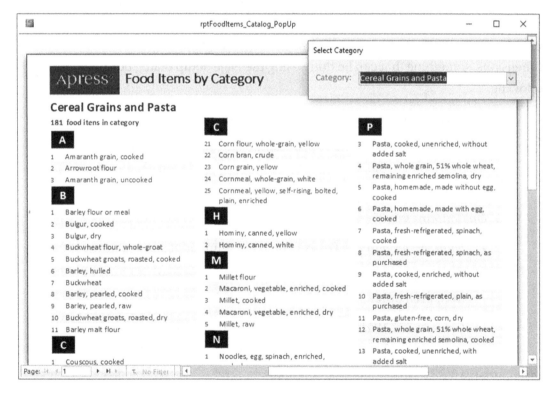

Figure 6-80.   *This is rptFoodItems_Catalog_PopUp with its Record Source updated by the frmPopUpSelectCategory dedicated form (which sequentially opens it in Design view and Print Preview)*

Attention   The Echo action doesn't work as expected in Access 2019, since it doesn't correctly freeze screen updates. Change the food category on frmPopUpSelectCategory and note that the Ribbon switches to show the tools offered by the report's Design view and Print Preview. To get a better experience with the report updating process, keep the Property Sheet, Add Existing Tabs, and Tab Order windows closed (because Access tends to update them when the report is opened in Design mode using the macro code).

Printing Labels

Printing labels using Access reports is an easy thing. Using the knowledge that you have gathered so far in this book, you can anticipate that to print labels using an Access report, you just need to mimic each individual label size on the report's Detail section dimensions, something that can be done using the Page Setup dialog box to define the following:

- *On Page tab*: The label's page size and orientation.

- *On Print Options tab*: The Top, Bottom, Left, and Right margins used to separate the top, bottom, left, and right labels from the page margin.

- *On Columns tab:* These label dimensions:

  - *Number of Columns*: Equivalent to the number of labels per row

  - *Row Spacing and Column Spacing*: To set how labels separate from each other

  - *Column Size Width and Height*: To define the width and height of the report's Detail section so it becomes identical to the label size

Since label pages are bought from different manufacturers, Microsoft Access (like Microsoft Word) offers a Label Wizard that does all the hard work for you. Click the Labels command in the Reports area of the Create tab.

Tip   To enable the Label command on the Create tab, Access requires that a table, query, form, or report that has a Record Source property selected in the Database window to use it as the Label report's Record Source property.

After you select the FOOD_DES table in the Database window and clicking the Create tab's Label command, Access shows the Label Wizard window, where you can use the "Filter by manufacturer" Combo Box to select the label brand and use the List Box above it to select the specific label size (which already defines all Page Setup dialog box options and the Detail Section dimensions, as shown in Figure 6-81).

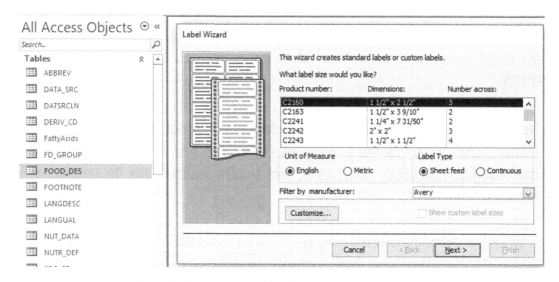

Figure 6-81. *Use the Labels command in the Report area of the Create tab to start the Label Wizard, which will quickly configure a report to print labels of a specific size*

If the manufacturer name is not available and you cannot find a similar label size, use the Customize button to show the New Label Size window. Click the New button to open the New Label dialog box where you can define the new label name, its page dimensions, the number of labels per row, and all the available label spaces (Figure 6-82).

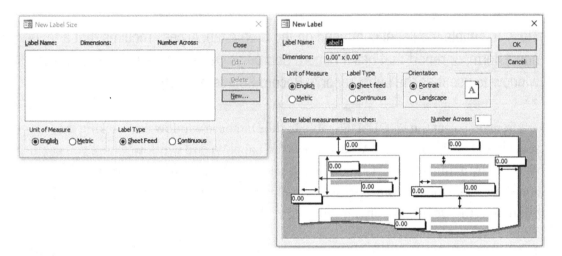

Figure 6-82. *Use the Customize button of the Label Wizard window to show the New Label Size window, where you can click New to create a new label page from scratch*

Note   Unfortunately, Microsoft Access traditionally does not allow the Customize button to show details for the selected label brand and size, as Microsoft Word does using its Mailing tab. Click Labels, click Option, and then click the Detail command.

When you finish, the new label will appear in the Label Wizard List Box window whenever "Show custom label sizes" is checked (which will be enabled after the first customized label is created).

After selecting the desired label page size and type, click Next to show the second Label Wizard page, where you can select font attributes to be used on each label. Click Next to show the third Label Wizard page, where you can select the fields available in the report's Record Source, which must be printed on each labels. Double-click the desired field, or select it and click the > button to add it to the Label list, as shown in Figure 6-83.

Tip   Use the keyboard to insert a space, comma, or hyphen, or press the Enter key to insert a line break before inserting the next desired field, composing each label row.

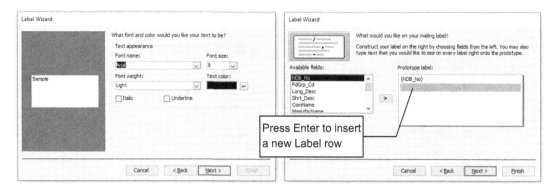

Figure 6-83. Use the second and third Labels Wizard pages to define the font attributes used on each label and the fields that the label must print. Use the keyboard to build textual expressions and add punctuation or a new label line

Add all the desired fields in the position and order that they must appear on each label and click Next to show the fourth Label Wizard page, where you can choose a field to sort the labels (Figure 6-84).

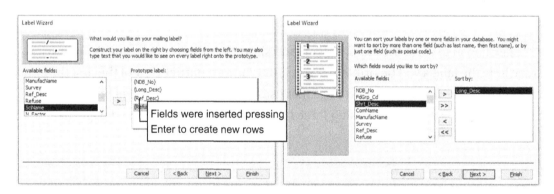

Figure 6-84. After adding all the desired fields in the position and order that they must appear on each printed label, click Next to set the label sort order

Click Next one more time and choose a name for the label report (Access will propose "Label" followed by the report's Record Source). See Figure 6-85.

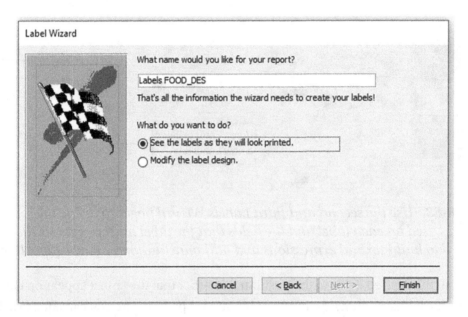

Figure 6-85. *The last Label Wizard page will create and save the report, proposing to name it as "Label" followed by the report's Record Source. Click Finish to show the label report in Print Preview mode*

Click Finish to close the Label Wizard and show the label report using Print Preview to see how the labels will be printed. Figure 6-86 shows a partial view of the first three label rows for the first label report page that uses an "Avery, C2160" label brand, whose label size is 1 ½' × 2 ½' inches, using three labels per row on a letter-sized page (as defined by Figure 6-81).

Tip   To avoid losing label pages because of an incorrect selection (or the use of a poorly defined brand and size) of a label, before printing the label pages, print the first page of the report using conventional paper of the same page size as the label. Then place this print on an empty label page and look at it against the light to see whether the print fits correctly.

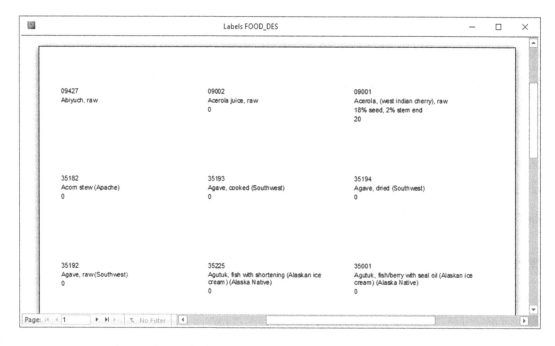

Figure 6-86. *This is the Labels FOOD_DES report, created by the Label Wizard to print Avery, C2160 labels using the FOOD_DES table, sorted by its Long_Desc field*

Attention   Label printing requires that the Column Layout option on the Page Setup dialog's Columns tab be set to "Across, then Down"—the expected way to print a multicolumnar report for labels.

Report Section Runtime Properties

Microsoft Access uses the Section runtime properties that can be accessed by event macro code to allow changes to the way it prints any of its sections. Table 6-4 shows these properties and their usage.

579

Table 6-4. *Report Runtime Section Properties*

Property	Usage
MoveLayout	Indicates whether Access must move to next printing location (True/False)
NextRecord	Indicates whether Access must advance to the next record (True/False)
PrintSection	Indicates whether Access should print the current section (True/False)
FormatCount	Read-only; stores the number of times the Section Format event fires
PrintCount	Read-only; stores the number of times the Section Print event fires
HasContinued	Read-only; is available only on the Section Format event to indicate whether the current Section has been continued from the previous page
WillContinue	Read-only; is available only on the Section Print event to indicate whether the current section will continue on the next page

Note   To check the value of any of these runtime Section properties in the macro code, enclose its name in square brackets (like [NextRecord]). To set the value of the MoveLayout, NextRecord, and PrintSection properties, use the hidden SetValue macro action (check the Show All Actions option to make it available in the Actions list).

MoveLayout, NextRecord, and PrintSection Properties

In the next sections, we'll cover the MoveLayout, NextRecord, and PrintSection properties; feel free to study how to use the other runtime properties on your own.

These three runtime Section properties are defined as True by default before any Section Format or Print event fires, but whenever you combine their values between True/False, you can control exactly how Access will move the printing head from row to row, printing the current section or not and skipping the current record or not.

Since they are always True, create some macro code in the Section Format event that uses a SetTempVar action to set a global temporary variable that counts how many times the Section Format event fires and keep any of these properties as False.

Let's see how to use them with some practical examples.

Skip the First *n* Printing Positions

Leave MoveLayout set to True while setting PrintSection and NextRecord to False to make Access skip the next print position, leaving it blank. If the Report section should print an entire row, it will be skipped, leaving a blank row on the report page. For a multicolumnar report, the next column position will be skipped. In the case of a label report, the next label will be skipped.

This is especially useful whenever you want to use partially printed label pages that still have a lot of empty labels,and you want to start printing at the first unused label in the page.

Double-click the Labels FOOD_DES_Skip_5_Labels report in the sr28_Reports Database window and note that it skips the first five labels, beginning with printing the first record in the sixth label position (Figure 6-87).

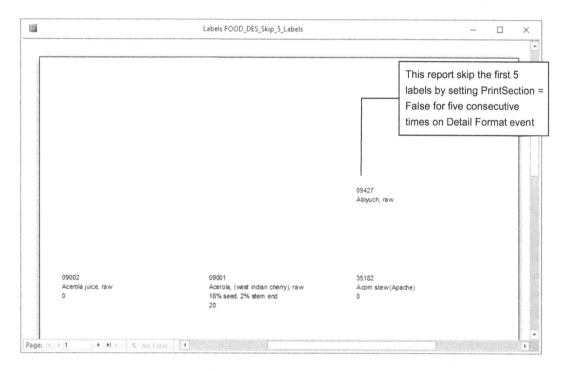

Figure 6-87. *This is the Labels FOOD_DES_Skip_5_Labels report, which sets PrintSection to False and NextRecord to False in the Detail Format Event to begin printing an the sixth label position without losing any records*

Open the label FOOD_DES_Skip_5_Labels in Design mode and check that its On Load Event macro code uses a SetTempVar action to set the global variable gLabelsSkipped to 0. Then select its Detail section's On Format Event macro code and check that it uses an IF action to verify whether gLabelsSkipped < 5.

If it is, it uses a SetTempVar action to increment the gLabelsSkipped variable to count the times that the Detail Format section fired using an expression that makes the variable refers to itself:

```
=[TempVars]![gLabelsSkipped] + 1
```

Two other consecutive SetValue actions set [NextRecord] to False (to not move the record pointer) and PrintSection to False (to not print the current record, as shown in Figure 6-88).

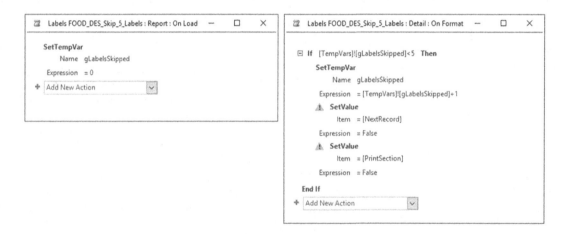

Figure 6-88. *The Labels FOOD_DES_Skip_5_Labels report uses the global variable gLabelsSkipped to control how many times the Detail section event fires. While its value is lower than 5, it keeps setting NextRecord to False and PrintSection to False, allowing Access just to move the printing location (since MoveLayout is True by default)*

Tip   Whenever you set the PrintSection property to False, do not forget to also set NextRecord to False or Access will skip the record that should be printed at this position.

Create Copies of Each Printed Label

Set NextRecord to False while leaving MoveLayout and PrintSection with its default True value to make sure Access keeps printing the current section for the desired number of times without moving to the next record, literally making copies of it (which is especially useful when creating label copies).

Double-click the Labels FOOD_DES Make_3_Times report in the sr28_Reports Database window to show it in Print Preview and note that each label is printed three times (since it has three labels per row, each rows uses a single record value, as shown in Figure 6-89).

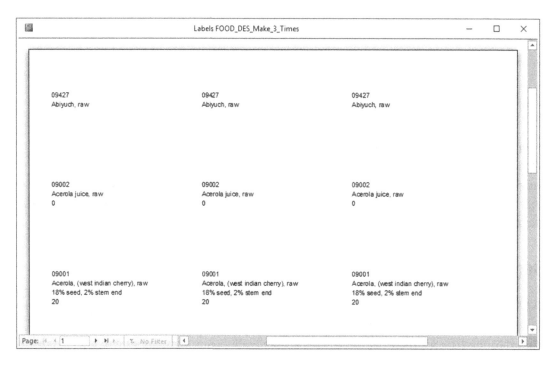

Figure 6-89. *This is the Labels FOOD_DES_Make_3_Times report, which sets NextRecord to False in the Detail Format Event to copy each food label twice*

Open Labels FOOD_DES_ Make_2_Copies in Design mode and check that its On Load and Detail Format events use the same strategy employed before to skip the first *n* labels. The Report On Load event uses a SetTempVar action to set the global variable gRecordsCopied to 0, while its Detail On Format event uses an IF action to verifies if gRecordsCopied is less than 2. If it is, a SetTempVar action increments the gRecordsCopied variable, counting the times that the Detail Format section fired, while a SetValue action sets [NextRecord] to False to not move the record pointer, copying it twice.

Since these copy operation must be repeated to the next record, the IF...ELSE clause uses another SetTempVar action to set gRecordsCopied to 0 again, allowing the next record that is printed to also be copied (Figure 6-90).

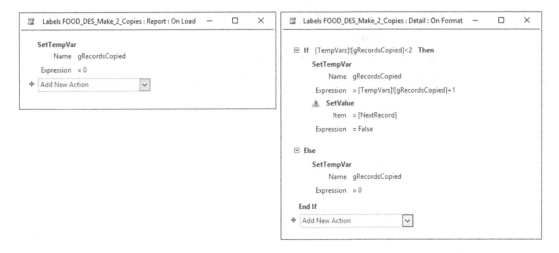

Figure 6-90. *The Labels FOOD_DES_ Make_2_Copies report uses the global variable gRecordsCopied to control how many times the Detail section's Format event fires, setting NextRecord to False while gRecordsCopy is less than 2. When this condition is False, the Else clause sets gRecordsCopied to 0 to allow copying the next record*

Begin Printing on a Specific Record

Set PrintSection and MoveLayout to False while leaving NextRecord with its default True value to be able to avoid printing the current record, while still advancing to the next record in the report's record source. This is especially useful whenever you want to print labels beginning on a specific record.

Double-click Labels FOOD_DES Skip_5 Records report in the sr28_Reports Database window to show it in Print Preview, and note that it skips the first 5 records shown in Labels FOOD_DES report (Figure 6-86) and begins printing its labels using the sixth record of its record source ("Agave dried (Southwest)"), as shown in Figure 6-91.

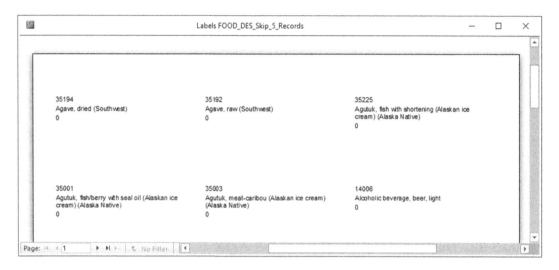

Figure 6-91. *This is the Labels FOOD_DES_Skip_5_Records report, which sets MoveLayout and PrintSection to False five times on the Detail Format Event to begin printing the report on its sixth record*

Open Labels FOOD_DES_ Skip_5_Records in Design mode and check that its On Load and Detail Format events keep using the same strategy: the Report On Load event uses SetTempVar gRecordSkipped = 0, while its Detail On Format Event uses IF gRecordSkipped < 5. If this condition is True, a SetTempVar action increments the gRecordSkipped variable, counting the times that the Detail Format section fired, while two consecutive SetValue actions set [MoveLayout] to False (to not move the printing head) and PrintSection to False (to not print the current record), avoiding printing the first five records. See Figure 6-92.

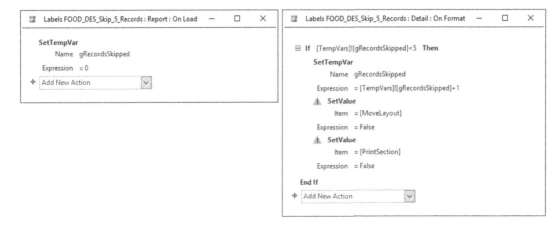

Figure 6-92. *The Labels FOOD_DES_ Skip_5_Records report uses the global variable gRecordsSkipped to control how many times the Detail section event fires, setting MoveLayout and PrintSection to False while gRecordsSkipped is less than 5*

Putting It All Together

To see how you can use all these techniques together to gain better control over a label report, double-click the Labels FOOD_DES_Dialog report in the sr28_Reports Database window to force it to open frmDialogSetLabels in a modal state, where you can decide how the labels should be printed (Figure 6-93).

Figure 6-93. *This is frmDialogSetLabels, which is automatically opened by the Labels_FOOD_DES_Dialog report's On Open event to allow control over how the labels will be printed*

The techniques used by this form and report were discussed previously in this chapter, and I will leave it to you to study both objects' macro code to understand how they work. Note the following:

- frmDialogSetLabels' cmdOK On Click event sets variables that define the position of the first record to be shown (gSkipRecords) and how many labels must be skipped, copied, or left unused using a set of temporary global variables (gCopyLabelsValue, gBlankLabesValue, and gSkipLabelsValue), as shown in Figure 6-94.

Figure 6-94. *This is frmDialogSetLabels cmdOK's On Click event, which sets temporary global variables to allow you to determine how many records must skipped and/or how many labels must be skipped, copied, or left unnused*

- The cboFirstRecord Combo Box control uses a Row Source property that shows records in the same order used by the Labels FOOD_DES_Dialog report.

- To define how many records must be skipped, the cmdOK On Click uses this expression:

```
=NZ([cboFirstRecord].[ListIndex],0)
```

It uses cboFirstRecord.ListIndex, a zero-based property that defines the selected item position in the list. Since by default cboFirstRecord is Null, the expression uses the NZ() function to convert Null to Zero (in case nothing is selected in the list).

- frmDialogSetLabels synchronizes its interface using the After Update event of each of its Check Box controls (check this for yourself).

When frmDialogSetLabels closes, the Labels FOOD_DES_Dialog report ends its On Open event and begins formatting the label report using somewhat extended code in its Detail section's On Format event (Figure 6-95 shows the macro code using the Collapse All Actions option).

```
Labels FOOD_DES_Dialog : Detail : On Format                                    —    □    ×

/*    Check if records must start be skipped                                        */
⊟ If  [TempVars]![gRecordsSkiped]<[TempVars]![gSkipRecords]   Then
        SetTempVar  (gRecordsSkiped, [TempVars]![gRecordsSkiped]+1)
      ⚠  SetValue  ([MoveLayout], False)
      ⚠  SetValue  ([PrintSection], False)

⊟ Else
      /*    Check if there must be blank labels                                      */
      ⊟ If  [TempVars]![gLabelPrinted] And [TempVars]![gLabelsBlanked]<[TempVars]![gBlankLabelsValue]   Then
              SetTempVar  (gLabelsBlanked, [TempVars]![gLabelsBlanked]+1)
            ⚠  SetValue  ([PrintSection], False)
            ⚠  SetValue  ([NextRecord], False)

      ⊟ Else
              SetTempVar  (gLabelsBlanked, 0)
              SetTempVar  (gLabelPrinted, False)
            /*    Check if initial labels must be skiped                             */
            ⊟ If  [TempVars]![gLabelsSkiped]<[TempVars]![gSkipLabelsValue]   Then
                    SetTempVar  (gLabelsSkiped, [TempVars]![gLabelsSkiped]+1)
                  ⚠  SetValue  ([NextRecord], False)
                  ⚠  SetValue  ([PrintSection], False)

            ⊟ Else
                    /*    Check if labels must be copied                             */
                    ⊟ If  [TempVars]![gLabelsCopied]<[TempVars]![gCopyLabelsValue]   Then
                            SetTempVar  (gLabelsCopied, [TempVars]![gLabelsCopied]+1)
                          ⚠  SetValue  ([NextRecord], False)

                    ⊟ Else
                            SetTempVar  (gLabelsCopied, 0)
                            SetTempVar  (gLabelPrinted, True)
                      End If
                  End If
              End If
          End If
```

Figure 6-95. *This is the Label FOOD_DES_Dialog report's On Open Macro code event. It uses all the techniques already described in the previous sections to allow you to skip records and skip, copy, or leave blank labels in the report*

All the techniques described in the previous sections are used in the report's On Open event, and I will leave it to the reader to study how it works, noting the following:

- It took me some time to produce this macro code, because it executes its actions in a predefined order, since macros only have the If... Then...Else action to make program flow decisions.

- It needs to nest several IF actions, one for each available frmDialogSetLabels option.

- Comments were inserted to allow easy identification of what each IF function does.

- The technique that was used to begin printing labels on a predefined record position selected by the cboFirstRecord Combo Box was shown here for pure didactic reasons. Since FOOD_DES is a somewhat extended table (with about 8,500 records), the report's On Open event will eventually execute the Detail section's On Format Event thousands of times with NextRecord set to False to begin printing in the desired record—a specific query can do this almost instantly with no computation effort.

Summary

The Microsoft Access Report object is a capable, powerful software tool, full of options, properties, and events that allow you to produce any kind of printout using the records returned by its tables or queries.

It does have some problems that can be addressed in future service packs or new Access versions, such as the following:

- The Group & Sort window must be improved, becoming a more reactive interface especially when the report uses a complex query (such as a Crosstab query that uses extent tables).

- The subreport printing must be fixed to allow you to print a multicolumn subreport on any report section using the Page Setup, Columns, Column Layout, and Down, then Across options.

These are just small issues that can be easily fixed to improve Microsoft Access.

Index

A

Access table *vs.* excel spreadsheets, 2
Action query, 198
    append query, 205
    delete query, 203
    MyABBREV table, 198
    update query, 208

B

Bound controls, 251

C

Cascade delete records, 103
Combo Box Wizard, 384
    Form Header and Footer sections, 384
    frmFood_Des_SearchComboBox, 387
    SearchForRecord action, 388
Command Button control, 389
    change appearance, 402
    Close command, 389
    CloseWindow action, 393
    cmdSave macro codes, 397
    to delete, 399
        IF action, 401
        OnError Goto Next, 402
    form's design view, 389
    GoToRecord action, 398

    insert command, 396
    specific properties, 395
Crosstab query, 183
    ABBREV table, 185
    Heading field order, 188
        copy/paste errors, 191
        NutrDesc field values, 189
        Open qryNutrients, 193
        PIVOT statement, 190
        transposed values in notepad, 196
    NUTR_DEF table, 185
    TRANSFORM FIRST statements, 187

D, E

Database creation, 4
Datasheet view
    add fields, 43
    AutoNumber data type, 43
    Click to Add option, 46
    Field Validation area, 45
    Fields tab, 41
    Indexed Validation Field options, 43
    Name & Caption tool, 44
Dedicated form, 564
    CancelEvent action, 564
    dedicated modal form, 565
    dedicated pop-up form, 569
    DisplayHourGlassPointer action, 565

M

N, O

S

Printed in the United States
By Bookmasters